Builders and Dreamers

Builders and Dreamers

Habonim Labor Zionist Youth in North America

EDITED BY

J. J. Goldberg

AND

Elliot King

Herzl Press
NEW YORK

Cornwall Books
NEW YORK • LONDON • TORONTO

Cornwall Books
440 Forsgate Drive
Cranbury, NJ 08512

Cornwall Books
25 Sicilian Avenue
London WC1A 2QH, England

Cornwall Books
P.O. Box 338, Port Credit
Mississauga, Ontario
Canada L5G 4L8

Herzl Press
110 East 59th Street
New York, NY 10022

The paper used in this publication meets the requirements
of the American National Standard for Permanence of Paper
for Printed Library Materials Z39.48-1984.

Library of Congress Cataloging-in-Publication Data

Builders and dreamers : Habonim labor Zionist youth in North America
/ edited by J.J. Goldberg and Elliot King.
    p.   cm.
  ISBN 0-8453-4839-6. — ISBN 0-8453-4841-8 (pbk.)
  1. World Habonim (Organization) 2. Labor Zionism—United States.
3. Labor Zionism—Canada.   4. Jewish youth—United States.
5. Jewish youth—Canada.   6. Labor Zionists—United States—
Biography.   7. Labor Zionists—Canada—Biography.   8. United
States—Ethnic relations.   9. Canada—Ethnic relations.
I. Goldberg, J. J. (Jonathan Jeremy) II. King, Elliot.
DS150.L47B85   1993
320.5′4′09569409041—dc20   √ 91-58244
                                               CIP

שִׁיר הָעֲבוֹדָה וְהַמְּלָאכָה

מִי יַצִּילֵנוּ מֵרָעָב?
מִי יַאֲכִילֵנוּ לֶחֶם רָב?
וּמִי יַשְׁקֵנוּ כּוֹס חָלָב?
לְמִי תּוֹדָה, לְמִי בְּרָכָה? –
לָעֲבוֹדָה וְלַמְּלָאכָה!

ח.נ.בְּיַאלִיק

Oh, who can save us hunger's dread?
Who always gave us ample bread,
And milk to drink when we are fed?

Whom shall we praise, whom shall we bless?
To work and toil our thankfulness.

—Chaim Nachman Bialik, "The Song of Work and
Toil," sung before meals at Habonim gatherings.
(Hebrew translation by Jesse Sampter. Reprinted by
permission of Histadruth Ivrith of America.)

Contents

Articles and Contributors

Foreword

From Chicago to Buffalo, 1935:
"We Were Not Wrong."

Ben Cohen

New York 1985

Back in Chicago when I was growing up during the early years of the Great Depression, it was still fashionable to hope and fight for a better world. There were two great visions then that captured the popular imagination on the Jewish street—socialism and Zionism. We belonged to the party that combined the best of both, the Labor Zionist movement called Poale Zion.

Those were heady, historic days, the eve of perhaps the most momentous period in Jewish history. Our Labor Zionist movement was just coming into its own as the leader of the Jewish people's national renaissance. We, the members of the party's youth wing, were well aware of our role in history.

During the latter part of 1934 and 1935, however, our attention was diverted by a heretical plan emanating from that bastion of heresy, New York City. It seems that the New York leadership of our Young Poale Zion Alliance had decided to create a new American children's organization to promote the ideals of Zionist labor. It was to incorporate such infantile activities as scouting (with woodcraft, yet!), camping, and other such programs, far removed from the purview of a serious Socialist Zionist Theoretical and Intellectual Movement, such as we thought we were.

And so, in the wisdom of our years—some of us were nearly fifteen when it began—four members of the Chicago Young Poale Zion, Ruthie Greenberg, Jack Ginsburg, Harry Sosewitz (later to be known as Yehiel Sasson), and Benny Cohen set off in October for the city of Buffalo as a delegation to the national YPZA convention. We were instructed by the Chicago movement to fight the creation of Habonim to the death. We were fortunate that Harry's father was driving from Chicago to New York City on business, so we got a ride to the convention. Between the four of us, I doubt we had bus fare for one.

At the convention, we fought valiantly for our cause and were sure that we had convinced many that our view was correct. But when the vote was taken, we found to our chagrin that we were a small minority. We returned to Chicago crestfallen, convinced our movement was doomed.

We were wrong. Over the years, Habonim was able to build summer camps across North America, build kibbutzim across Israel, and build character in its members. Thousands and thousands of young Jews have grown up in Habonim. Wherever you look in Israel or in the American Jewish community, you will find us playing a leading role.

Each of us has had that singular experience of meeting a former Habonim member, even one we never knew, and feeling instantly that common bond, that instinctive recognition, as if we were old friends.

But did we really create the scouting and camping movement proposed in 1935? No. We hardly did any scouting as such, but in our efforts to "scout," we created a network of summer camps with an atmosphere of Jewish and Hebrew living, a program of self-help and shared work and *chavershaft*— camaraderie—that have become models for every other Jewish camping movement.

Did we become a pioneering movement? Yes and no. While we sent many people to Israel, *aliyah* was never the one and only goal in life for us. We have six kibbutzim to our credit: Kfar Blum, Ma'ayan Baruch, Gesher Haziv, Urim, Gezer, Grofit. Yet those who opted not to go to kibbutz or Israel were not looked down upon as second-class people.

Did Hebrew become our spoken language? No. But it did salt our daily lives, and hundreds of words became part of our common vocabulary.

Did we ever become a mass movement? Obviously not. Our program never became the simplified, minimalist credo that some of Habonim's founders had in mind. Somehow, those of us who remain from the Chicago delegation think we got our way anyway.

In the past half-century, the world and the Jews have gone through one of the most convulsive eras in human history: World War II, the Nazi Holocaust, the nuclear bomb, the creation of the State of Israel, the Vietnam war, the collapse of Lebanon. It has been an era of wars, pestilence, tragedy, horror—and some glory, too.

Habonim has responded to all these events. No one member of Habonim can describe it all, for no one remains in a youth movement that long. The story of each decade must be told by its youth.

The miracle of Habonim is the miracle of the continuity of a vision and an ideal, of one generation passing that vision to another.

Each generation makes that vision its own, in its own way, with its own character and panache. That indeed is a miracle.

Preface

This is the story of a unique North American subculture which has persisted for more than a half-century on the landscape of Jewish community life. It often numbered no more than two thousand youngsters. At times it was invisible to anyone but its own members and their families, yet it has been one of the most independent and politically sophisticated forces in American Jewish life. As the North American standard bearer of this century's most important Jewish message, it helped lead the way in the struggle for the Jewish state. Later, with its mixture of social idealism and Jewish commitment, it stood as a challenge to the quiescent America of the 1950s, a rebuke to the youthful excesses of the 1960s and an antidote to the conservatism of more recent decades.

It is the Labor Zionist youth movement: Habonim ("The Builders").

Habonim has never been a massive force in a society that worships the mega-phenomenon. It has never appeared in *Time* or *Newsweek*. And yet, whenever young American and Canadian Jews have been called upon to take history's center stage, on campus and in the synagogue, in the fields of Israel and the office-towers of New York, Habonim members have been at the forefront.

Perhaps more important, Habonim has been a decisive influence—often *the* decisive influence—in the lives of those who have passed through its ranks. Graduates of Habonim have gone on to become leading actors in the modern Jewish drama, and are to be found today at the helms of so many fields of endeavor in North America and Israel—in politics and the rabbinate, in communal work, education and labor—that Habonim sometimes seems to be nothing less than an officers' training corps for the Jewish people of the late twentieth century.

For the veterans of American Labor Zionism, and for those who have followed its highest calling and settled in the land of Israel, 1935 is remembered as the year of Habonim's founding.

The date is correct, although other years are equally significant. One might date the movement's birth to 1920, the year that the Young Poale Zion Alliance was founded as the youth wing of the socialist Zionist party Poale Zion. Or one might point to the planting on these shores of Gordonia, the Labor Zionist pioneering youth movement that began in Baltimore in 1925 and later merged into Habonim.

In fact, the emergence of Habonim as an independent youth movement, born of the political party Poale Zion but independent of it, came in stages:

the formation of Young Poale Zion children's clubs in the late 1920s; the creation in 1935 of a national children's division named Habonim; the 1938 merger with Gordonia; and the first national convention of Habonim, in 1940, where the movement's principles were adopted and the Young Poale Zion Alliance was transformed into the senior division of Habonim.

Then, too, one cannot understand the birth of Habonim without understanding its lineage as a child of two other movements: socialism and Zionism.

* * *

Socialism, the worldwide crusade for economic democracy and the dignity of working people, arose as a political force in Europe less than a century before the Buffalo convention of the Young Poale Zion that created Habonim. Organized socialism in America was less than a half-century old.

Zionism, the political movement for Jewish national renewal in the land of Israel, arose in its modern form with the convening of the first Zionist Congress in 1897 by the visionary Budapest-born journalist, Theodor Herzl.

It was a year later, in 1898, that these two world shaking ideas were combined by Dr. Nachman Syrkin into one explosive mixture that would one day lead the Jewish people into its new era of nationhood. Within months of the appearance of Syrkin's revolutionary pamphlet, "The Jewish Question and the Socialist Jewish State," clubs were forming throughout Central and Eastern Europe called Poale Zion ("the Workers of Zion"). The first Poale Zion clubs appeared on these shores just after the turn of the century.

However one chooses to mark history, it is appropriate to look back from the current moment—ninety years after Herzl and Syrkin, fifty years after the creation of Habonim, forty years after the rebirth of Israel—and attempt to evaluate the impact of the Labor Zionist idea on those who tried to live by it.

This volume is an attempt to look at the Labor Zionist youth movement in North America from the viewpoint of its members and graduates. We have endeavored to follow the history of the movement, from its earliest years to the present day, on three planes: the development of the organization and its ideas; the experience of the young members in the movement; and the mark they left on Jewish history in Israel and North America.

In assembling the material presented in this book, the editors sought a balance between the needs of the casual reader who may never have encountered Habonim, and the desire of Habonim graduates to find a token of remembrance in this volume.

Readers unfamiliar with Habonim may find some of the terminology unclear, particularly the use of Hebrew words. Here we ask the reader's forbearance. The experience of Habonim is the experience of a hardy subculture, which has survived and thrived in the midst of—and yet been largely invisible to—the larger American culture.

The movement's special language, a strange amalgam of English, Hebrew, and "Habonim Hebrew," used to describe key values in movement life, is an essential part of that experience—both for the graduates and, we trust, for those with the patience to explore these pages. Our use of Hebrew terms is kept to an essential minimum. A glossary is appended at the end. Those who persist past the first few pages will find the words quickly becoming familiar. Simply remember, where the word is unfamiliar, to pronounce "ch" as the Hebrew sound familiar in "Chanukah," and you will find yourself rewarded by the sense of *chalutziut* (pioneering) which is the mark of a new *chaver* (member) of Habonim.

This book is a tribute to all the *chaverim* of North American Habonim and of Young Poale Zion, Gordonia and Dror, whose continuing story through more than a half-century of building and dreaming is told in these pages.

J. J. GOLDBERG
New York, 1992

Acknowledgments

Volunteers, contributors, and professionals—without those three, very little would be accomplished in today's Jewish community. But sometimes there is a transcendent factor uniting all three—a reason, a motive, a cause, as it were, that inspires the dedicated efforts of everyone involved in a project. Surely that can be said about the endeavor to record and evaluate a half-century and more of the Habonim experience both in North America and in Israel—a labor of love culminating in the publication of this book.

The work on this volume began several years ago, in connection with the celebration in 1985 of the fiftieth anniversary of Habonim's founding. Many devoted colleagues and friends—true *chaverim,* to use Habonim terminology—have participated since then. We are particularly grateful to the following volunteers in this effort:

David Breslau and Shirley Lashner Shpira, for compiling and preparing most of the material originating in Israel and for reviewing several drafts of the entire text;

Nahum Guttman, for likewise reviewing the manuscript and for providing crucial assistance in several stages of this project;

Ruby Vogelfanger, for serving as treasurer and New York coordinator of the sponsoring committee;

Gene Burger, Ben Cohen, Fradle Freidenreich, Chava Reich, Peter Reich, Rubin Salz, Marc Sussman, Sidney Troy, and the late Sarah Lederman, for their active participation in the committee;

The leadership of Habonim-Dror for their assistance and cooperation throughout the process.

In 1985 the late Susan Brecher and her family provided major funding without which this project could not have been initiated or implemented.

Since then scores of Habonim alumni, parents, and friends have added to the fund, which has been used not only to publish and promote this book but also to provide seed money for a long-term endowment fund for Habonim. This reflects the purpose of this entire effort: preserving the past while providing for the future of the Labor Zionist youth movement in North America. We are grateful to all those who have contributed in so many different ways to this endeavor.

Elliot King did the initial work of compiling material for the book and preparing an early draft. J. J. Goldberg undertook the major responsibility of editing several versions of the text and producing it in its final published form, as well as writing most of the unsigned introductions to various sections of the book. The committee is especially grateful to J. J. Goldberg for his central role in this effort. We also acknowledge our partnership with our publishers, Kalman Sultanik and Sam Bloch of Herzl Press and Julien Yoseloff and Michael Koy of Cornwall Books.

Finally, a word of appreciation to—and a note of explanation about—the authors of the articles comprising this volume. They range in age from young adults to active retirees, spanning the generations of Habonim. Wherever possible, they have been identified by the city and year in which they wrote their respective pieces. Some of the names will be recognized as those of pre-eminent leaders in various areas of public, communal, or professional life in Israel and in North America. Others may be less well known, but their contributions to Habonim both in the years of their membership in the movement and through their articles in this book are no less significant. Accordingly, in the best Habonim tradition of cooperation and equality, no further identification of any author has been provided, although we are of course honored and privileged to conclude this work with the message of the president of Israel, Chaim Herzog.

It should also be noted that a number of the authors have passed away since they wrote the articles that appear in this book—some of them in recent years. The committee determined that it would be impossible to prepare a complete and accurate listing of all those who played key roles in Habonim and are now no longer with us, but we continue to feel the loss of each and every one of our departed *chaverim*.

The reader will see that many of the articles were written in recent years specifically for this book. Others were published in earlier periods of time, going back to the 1930s. Among the important sources of material were two other books, both edited by David Breslau in connection with the twenty-fifth anniversaries of Habonim and its camps: *Adventure in Pioneering* (1957) and *Arise and Build* (1960). While both volumes are now out of print, they still shed much light on the movement's early years, and some material from them appears in this book. Understandably, special emphasis has been given here to the three challenging decades that have elapsed since the publication of the two earlier books. Additional sources for all three texts have been the publications of Habonim: *Furrows, Haboneh,* and various internal newsletters for members and leaders.

It is our hope that this book will serve to enhance understanding of a significant movement in Jewish life while generating renewed dedication to the programs and purposes of Habonim.

Daniel Mann
Chairman
Habonim Publications
and Endowment Fund
Bethesda, Maryland 1992

Builders and Dreamers

Part I

1
The Early Years

The Birth of Labor Zionism: From Bilu to Poale Zion

In the summer of 1882, a group of sixteen young Russian Jews—fifteen men and one woman—sailed into Jaffa port in Turkish-ruled Palestine, intent on reestablishing the ancient Jewish state.

The sixteen were the first wave of a tiny group—it never numbered more than 525 at its height—that called itself Bilu, after the initials of the Hebrew phrase, *Beit Ya'akov, lechu v'nelcha*—"house of Jacob, come, let us go up." The phrase, taken from the prophet Isaiah, was adopted as a motto by an organization founded that spring by students in Kharkov, in the Ukraine. Their aim was to rebuild the ancient Jewish homeland on principles of social justice and self-labor.

"Hopeless is your condition in the West," the Biluim declared in a manifesto written in Constantinople, en route to Palestine. "The star of your future is in the East. Deeply conscious of this, and inspired by the true teaching of our great master Hillel, 'If I am not for myself, who will be for me?' we propose to form a society for national ends."

The word "hopeless" had very immediate meaning for the Jews of Russia in 1882. The five million Jews of the tsar's empire, the largest Jewish community in the world, had been subjected for a century to cruel restrictions, designed to force their assimilation into Russian Christendom *or* to keep them separate, impoverished and powerless. There had been a brief period of emancipation during the 1860s and 1870s, under the relatively enlightened Tsar Alexander II, but that enlightenment came to a sudden end in the spring of 1881, with his assassination.

In April and May 1881, the Jews of Russia were subjected to a sudden wave of horrors: riots and pogroms, restrictive legislation and economic sanctions. Over the next two decades, the imperial Russian government pursued a policy that seemed deliberately aimed at the destruction of Russian Jewry.

As outrage followed outrage, Jews began to seek radical answers to their living hell. Political reform under the tsar now seemed all but impossible.

Most Jews looked to three solutions: social revolution, emigration to America, or return to their ancient homeland.

The first organized attempts at a return to Zion were tentative and sporadic. A network of clubs sprang up in the towns and villages of the Pale of Settlement, collectively known as Chovevei Zion or Lovers of Zion. For the most part they were little more than discussion groups. A few thousand Jews actually emigrated to Palestine, where they founded the first modern Jewish colonies outside the ancient cities. Within a decade, most of these colonies were economically stagnant, dependent on hired Arab laborers and handouts from the French philanthropist Baron Edmond de Rothschild. Of the hardy band of Bilu, committed to self-liberation through their own labor, little survived but a memory.

*   *   *

Returning to Zion was not the only response to the outrages of 1881 and 1882. The death of Tsar Alexander II, which snuffed out any hope of reform in imperial Russia, drove thousands of Jews—especially the young—into the arms of the fledgling socialist movement.

Socialism, as a concrete plan for societal change, was little more than thirty years old in 1881. The Socialist International, the first world gathering of parties devoted to workers' emancipation and economic democracy, had convened less than two decades earlier. In most of Europe, the idea of socialism was still a far-off and vaguely suspicious notion. For the desperate Jews of Russia, however, the notion of total social revolution had a powerful appeal. Socialist groups began springing up in Yiddish-speaking towns and shtetls from Lithuania to the Ukraine; within two decades they were a mass movement. (Shortly after, a totalitarian mutation would arise called communism.)

In the intellectual ferment of the Russian Pale, socialists and Zionists were deeply hostile to each other's ideals. In the eyes of the socialists, Zionism was seen as escapism. It meant turning one's back on the problems of Russian society and moving off to a foreign land to recapture some romantic dream of a lost kingdom. Perhaps most importantly, the socialists objected to Zionism's social character as a mostly middle-class movement that appeared intent on transplanting European capitalism to the Middle East.

For Zionists, on the other hand, socialism represented a rejection of many of the irreducible values of Jewish communal life. Most socialists rejected the value of separate nations and cultures, especially of Jews. Indeed, by the 1890s, it seemed that many of the most prominent of the young radicals working to organize Russia's downtrodden peasants and workers happened to be young Jews who had abandoned their heritage to follow the secular god of revolution.

It remained for one eccentric, Russian-born graduate student in Berlin to come forward in 1898 and argue that Zionism and socialism need not be sworn enemies, that the two philosophies could be compatible, even complementary. The booklet, "The Jewish Question and the Socialist Jewish State," written in German by Nachman Syrkin, revolutionized Zionism and set the stamp for the future Jewish state.

"Without the working people, Zionism is lost," Syrkin wrote. "The wheels of the Jewish republic will not turn without the strong arms of the Jewish worker. Zionism must take into account the socialist tendencies of the Jewish working class and the desire of the middle class and the intelligentsia to preserve its economic independence. Zionism in the end must necessarily mingle with socialism. The Jewish state must necessarily be socialist."

Syrkin's pamphlet struck a deep chord among the radical youth of Central and Eastern Europe, and within a year dozens of groups had been organized that called themselves Poale Zion—the Workers of Zion. In 1901, Syrkin published his "Call to Jewish Youth," this time in Russian, urging young Jews to battle against both the anti-Zionist assimilationism of the socialists and the antisocialist conservatism of the Zionist movement.

In 1907, in Cracow, the first world conference of Poale Zion parties and clubs was convened. Delegates gathered from Russia and Poland, America, Britain, and Austria-Hungary. There were representatives, too, of the Second Aliyah, the new wave of radical immigration that had begun to set down roots in Palestine. Poale Zion's leading ideologist was no longer Syrkin, however, but a brilliant twenty-three-year-old organizer from the Ukraine named Ber Borochov.

Borochov had established his brand of Poale Zionism a year earlier, at the founding conference of Russian Poale Zion, in a document called "Our Platform." It was a careful Marxist analysis of Jewish history, and it argued in Marxian "scientific-socialist" terms that Zionism and socialism were necessary partners.

Unlike Syrkin, Borochov rejected the idea that the new Jewish state was to be founded on a socialist basis. Borochov, the Marxist Zionist revolutionary, insisted that the Jewish state must be founded by private enterprise and capitalist initiative. In time, he claimed, the Jewish workers in the new Jewish commonwealth must rise up in revolutionary class struggle and impose socialism.

Borochov, Syrkin, and their followers battled out the details of the future socialist Jewish commonwealth for decades. In the fields and villages of Palestine, though, the young Jewish *chalutzim*—the pioneers who were working to build the commonwealth brick by brick—were frequently left cold by the debate. The concrete experience of transforming a young Jewish intellectual from Minsk, Vienna, or Pittsburgh into a Middle Eastern farmer had little to do with the theory of class warfare. It was a daily struggle against fear, exhaustion, and disease.

One of the earliest American Poale Zionists, Pinchas Cruso, who moved from Russia to Palestine before settling in America on the eve of World War I, participated in one of the early Zionist workers' communes at Petach Tikvah. The commune, or *kvutza,* was a band of only a few dozen men and women—boys and girls, really—who lived together in the village of Petach Tikvah, seeking day labor and pooling their incomes.

Years later, in America, Cruso recalled an incident that summed up the foibles of the ideological debate raging among the early chalutzim. The kvutza had proposed opening a communal laundry to lift one daily burden from the exhausted young workers. The ideological hard-liners in the group, led by a young David Ben-Gurion, were adamantly opposed to the "bourgeois" luxury of exploiting a "servant" to wash the workers' underthings.

In the end the liberals won out, and the laundry was established. Cruso was assigned the role of accepting the dirty linens at the end of the day, and he recalled with glee how he opened up for "business" on the first day, as a sheepish-looking Ben-Gurion appeared with a bundle of dirty clothes.

Not surprisingly, the idea that ideology had its limits soon grew into an ideology all its own.

Where the Poale Zion argued—endlessly, in the minds of some chalutzim—over the nature and tasks of the future Jewish working class, other groups arose to emphasize the internal, emotional revolution required to create the new Jewish working man and woman. These groups had various names, including Ze'ire Zion (the Youth of Zion), Hapoel Hatza'ir (the Young Worker), and even the "nonparty group." What they shared was an aversion to doctrinaire socialism and a distaste for the politics of the Socialist International.

For many of them Labor Zionism included a deeply spiritual element that expressed itself in love of the land, reverence for nature, and a belief in the transforming value of physical labor. These nonsocialist socialists found their ideological leader at the end of the first decade of this century in a forty-eight-year-old Russian Jew who came to Palestine to preach the values of self-redemption through labor and renewed links between the Jew and the land. His name was Aaron David Gordon.

In 1909, a group of young Jewish agricultural laborers received a patch of farmland on the edge of the Sea of Galilee, at a place called Umm Juni. There they founded the first permanent farming commune, Degania. Unlike the Petach Tikvah commune and similar groups around the country, Degania did not seek day labor and pool its members' incomes; instead, they farmed their own land, collectively. In socialist terms, they had graduated from collective consumption to collective production.

Degania became the model for all future collective Jewish farming in Israel, and Gordon, with his love of land, labor, and nature, was their spiritual father. Within five years there were a dozen such communes, called kvutzot or kibbutzim, dotting the Galilee. By 1920 the kibbutz, together with its less collectivist cousin the moshav, were the dominant form of farming society in the burgeoning Zionist community of Palestine. In the years to come these socialist colonies invited young Jews to spend summers with them and learn their values. They sent out *shlichim*—emissaries—to establish clubs in the diaspora, encouraging other young Jews to join them.

By the mid 1920s, the creations of Labor Zionism—kvutzot and moshavim, parties, self-defense units, and the Histadrut labor federation that united them all—formed a powerful network of institutions working in Palestine to make a reality out of the dreams of Nachman Syrkin, Ber Borochov, and A. D. Gordon.

Pioneering Zionism Comes to America: The First Hechalutz

The first stirrings of a Labor Zionist youth movement in America were in 1904–5, with the founding of the nonpolitical pioneering circle Hechalutz. Its single goal was to bring young Jews to Palestine to join in the practical work of redeeming the land. This first Hechalutz organization had only a handful of members, and its ideas were vague. The organization's first by-laws, adopted in the summer of 1905, show both its idealism and political innocence:

> Our name, Hechalutz, expresses the essence of our ideology. We are the vanguard of our people in its struggle for regeneration in its homeland. Our outlook and our convictions require no sanction of theory. We are children of the Jewish nation. Our close ties with it are natural as those of a family. Only abnormal people lack national consciousness or find expression for it in chauvinism.

By 1908, Hechalutz was putting out a newsletter and even enrolled a few of its members in an agricultural college. That year the organization joined together with a few youngsters from other early Zionist groups to form Ha'ikar Hatza'ir, "the Young Farmer." The organization reached its heyday in 1912, when it sent four members to settle in Palestine. The four joined what would become Kibbutz Kinneret, where they were known as "the American Kvutza." The aliyah of 1912 depleted the energy of Hechalutz, and it faded.

Hechalutz was renewed in 1915 by two leaders of the Second Aliyah who had fled Palestine to escape a Turkish crackdown and who were living in New York. The two, the future Israeli president Yitzhak Ben-Zvi and the future prime minister David Ben-Gurion, worked closely with the central committee of the American Poale Zion party to recruit potential pioneers. They traveled throughout the nation to enlist candidates willing to go to Palestine, once World War I ended, to begin the peaceful work of building the new Jewish homeland. About one hundred fifty people joined Hechalutz and began learning Hebrew and studying agriculture; negotiations were conducted for the acquisition of a training farm on Long Island.

In November 1917, much of the careful groundwork came to a halt as a result of a statement released by the government of Great Britain. In a letter dated November 2 and addressed to Lord Rothschild, a leading British Zionist, Foreign Secretary Arthur James Balfour announced that "His Majesty's Government view with favour the establishment of a national home for the Jewish people" and would work to help achieve that goal.

The Balfour Declaration, the first formal recognition of Zionist goals by a major power, touched off a mood of millennial hopefulness among Jews everywhere. At last it seemed that Jewish statehood was a realistic goal, perhaps even close at hand. In response, a large group of American Hechalutz, including Ben-Gurion himself, enlisted in the British army's Jewish Legion and went off to fight for Palestine and the Crown.

More than a decade would pass before there would be a third, more lasting attempt to build an American Hechalutz organization. This time, however, it was organized along entirely different lines, serving primarily as a training network for those who had come to the aliyah decision through a process of Zionist education. That education, in turn, was provided by youth movements arising among the American Jewish youth themselves, explicitly committed to the ideology and theory of Labor Zionism. The first of those movements was Young Poale Zion.

An American Labor Zionist Youth Movement: Yunge Poale Zion, the "Young Workers of Zion"

Moshe Cohen
Los Angeles 1950

The Labor Zionist youth movement appeared in the arena of American life at a time when no organized socialist youth movement existed. Socialism was still an imported product; its application to American realities found little response.

Zionism was somewhat more popular. Zionist youth clubs existed in the various centers of American Jewish life, although most were not Zionist in the activist sense that the term is applied today. Nor were these youth groups banded together in any sort of organization bearing a distinct ideological, political, or educational character.

The period from 1911 to 1920 was a "prehistoric" period, in which the Labor Zionist party Poale Zion first began forming youth divisions in the eighteen- to twenty-one-year-old age group, known in Yiddish as *Yunge Poale Zion*. These groups were organized spontaneously, made up primarily of immigrant youths who were familiar with the Zionist and labor movements from the old country. Coming to America, they naturally sought out a familiar social and political environment. As such, the youth groups founded in those days were Yiddish-speaking.

The Poale Zion party occasionally recognized these young elements and formed special committees for organizing them. A senior *chaver,* as the members were known, would devote an hour or two a day to correspondence, issuing programs, and similar routine activities on a local scale. The Committees on Youth did not have the finances for any extensive activity. The national youth budget for the year 1917–18 was less than four hundred dollars. This sum included the secretary's salary, literature, postage, traveling expenses, and a dozen other items. National income from dues that year was less than seven hundred dollars.

In spite of the lack of leadership, literature, and central organization, the movement's achievements during that period were considerable. The year 1917–18 was probably the peak year, numbering some twenty-five clubs with a membership of about seven hundred. The strongest centers were New England and New York. Chicago consisted of three clubs, but our members controlled and led the local Maccabee Children's Clubs with a membership of over five hundred. An attempt was made at that time to organize English-speaking clubs: the principle was that English was to be a transitional language only, and that within a short time the club was to conduct its educational work in Yiddish.

The cultural level of the movement in that period was very high. Yiddish and Hebrew literature, Jewish history, Jewish folk and labor songs were popular and well established. Study circles were formed, the most popular subjects being political economy, socialism, and trade unionism. The popularity of those subjects is an indication of the fact that our youth were primarily workers. Their orientation was toward socialism and diaspora work; Zionism as a personal ambition was weak.

A key role in the movement of that era was played by the Yiddish language publication, *Yunger Yiddisher Kemfer,* a youth offshoot of the weekly Poale Zion magazine *Yiddisher Kemfer.*

In the early 1920s, at one of the party's youth conferences, a resolution was proposed to include an English section in the publication. The resolution was sharply debated, and had to be submitted to a general referendum of the movement. The referendum recognized the "rights of English," at the same time stipulating that the English section must occupy not more than one-third of the publication.

This period also marked the beginning of a "youth library" of movement publications. Three pamphlets were published: one on socialism, in Yiddish, and a pamphlet on Poale Zionism and a call to Jewish youth, both in English.

In fund-raising, our movement made valuable contributions—the favorite campaign was the Palestine Workers Fund (now the Israel Histadrut Campaign). In many cities it was actually inaugurated at the initiative of the youth. In the two collections of 1917–18, our youth raised three thousand dollars. The movement also participated in activities for the Jewish National Fund, in the sale of the *shekel* for the World Zionist Congress, in American Jewry's nationwide election campaign in 1918 to the postwar American Jewish Congress, and in promoting the Poale Zion daily newspaper, *Die Zeit.*

During the war years, from 1915 to 1918, some of the leading lights of world Poale Zionism gathered in America and added an atmosphere of dynamism to the American movement. These included the ideological leaders of the European movement, Nachman Syrkin and Ber Borochov, along with David Ben-Gurion and Yitzhak Ben-Zvi, two of the key leaders of the chalutzim, the young Zionist pioneers who were actually building a homeland in Palestine. Ben-Gurion and Ben-Zvi were particularly active in reorganizing the Hechalutz pioneering organization in this country, building on the leadership of our movement.

In 1919, led by Ben-Gurion and Ben-Zvi, some of our most active chaverim enlisted in the Jewish Legion and left for Palestine to fight for the Jewish homeland. Our youth movement suddenly found itself thrown into disarray.

The movement was still very much a European transplant in this era. The chaverim who came from abroad knew little of American conditions. The very name of the organization, Junior Poale Zion, is indicative of the fact that the groups were simply the youthful counterpart of the Poale Zion Party. The separate youth organization filled a social need rather than an educational one.

* * *

The second cycle in the development of our youth was the period of 1920–29. During those years an attempt was made to penetrate American youth. The leadership of that time called the first convention in August 1920 in Pittsburgh, where assembled delegates represented some two or three hundred members. At that convention the delegates decided to forge the Junior Poale Zion clubs into an organization called Young Poale Zion, which was then declared an autonomous organization working in close cooperation with the party. A constitution was written and a leadership elected. The principles of the new organization were as follows:

> The aim of the Young Poale Zion movement is to educate and prepare the Jewish youth for the struggle for the liberation of the Jewish nation, for the upbuilding of the National Homeland in Eretz Israel and for the emancipation of the Jewish working class together with the workers of all nations.
> The Young Poale Zion movement is a section of the Poale Zion Party of America. The specific purpose of the youth movement is to prepare and to educate the American Jewish youth to aid and to become active partners in the struggle of the Party.
> The Young Poale Zion movement dedicates itself to the fight against assimilation and to the education of Jewish youth in the spirit of progressive Jewish nationalism.
> The work of our members will consist of two parts: First, practical Poale Zionist and national Jewish activity; second, education and self-education along the lines of secular and Jewish culture.
> The language of the movement is Yiddish.
> The youth movement is autonomous. The Central Committee will consist of nine people, five from the ranks of the youth, and four senior chaverim; one of the seniors will serve as secretary. The nine chaverim must be elected by the

Convention. The four seniors must be approved by the Central Committee [of the Party]. Changes in personnel are subject to a movement referendum.

Decisions and action opposed to party policy can be vetoed by the Central Committee.

The decision to found an autonomous movement left the delegates feeling charged with responsibility. Nevertheless, postwar recovery was slow. At the second convention in Hartford, in September 1922, it was reported that the organization was composed of thirteen clubs: six in New England, three in New York City, two in Montreal, and one each in Rochester and Toronto. No publication appeared, and practical activities were meager. Total membership was two hundred, rising to only four hundred the following year.

A monthly Yiddish-English publication called *Yugnt* was launched. The Yiddish section was rich in content, its tone militant and socialistic; the English section was limited in size, socialism was treated with kid gloves, and the revolutionary tone was absent. *Yugnt* was not merely a publication in two sections, Yiddish and English; it was, in reality, two organs—the Yiddish written for a working, class-conscious, and revolutionary element; the English for liberal American youth, who knew little of Jewish national problems and still less of social problems.

It must be remembered that the third decade of this century was one of the most critical periods in the social history of the United States—the Jazz Age. American Jewish youth, very much a part of its generation, was drawn into the whirling life of the country and contributed largely to the "spiritual activities" of that period.

Small wonder, then, that our leadership was at a loss for an approach to American Jewish youth. As a result, activities were again restricted to the Yiddish-speaking elements. The 1923 report tells of great fund-raising activity on behalf of Palestine—the movement raised two thousand dollars for the Palestine Workers Fund—and of participation in trade union activities, strikes, picketing, and so forth.

Considerable advances were made in 1923–24: *Yugnt* began appearing regularly; Labor Zionist schools were formed in New York and in Chicago for leadership training; ten thousand dollars was raised for the Jewish National Fund, the Palestine Workers Fund, and the Labor Sanitarium Fund, the latter sponsored by the Farband Labor Zionist fraternal order. Libraries, dramatic circles, and choirs were established in many cities.

Labor activities were intensified that year. In Paterson, New Jersey, leading chaverim of our movement played a prominent role in the silk workers' strike; the secretariat of the bakers' strike in New York was headed by one of our members; and the St. Louis club contributed greatly to the furriers' strike in that city.

That year seven new clubs were formed consisting of American-born elements. With them a new problem arose. At last we had begun to penetrate the American youth, but what was the educational program for these groups? Were they capable of understanding the essence of socialist Zionism?

By the mid-1920s, one-fourth of our movement consisted of American born youth. The monthly publication was enlarged, the English section enriched. Simultaneously, a special activity was conducted on behalf of the institutions of secular, Yiddishist education which were flourishing in those years, such as the Jewish Teachers Seminary in New York, and the elementary level Labor Zionist afternoon schools, or folk-shuln, around the country.

*   *   *

In 1928, for the first time, children's clubs were formed. There were two or three, composed of children between the ages of thirteen and sixteen. The clubs were Junior Young Poale Zion, and their permanent status was confirmed in a convention resolution.

Again, we were at a loss as to what to do with the children. Many chaverim questioned the organization of children's groups at all: How, they asked, can one teach Poale Zionism to children of that age? Very few foresaw that in just a few years these children's groups would constitute the major part of our organization.

That year, 1928, witnessed a growing interest in the Palestinian youth movement Hanoar Ha'oved. A Palestinian delegation toured the country and devoted much of its time to our youth clubs. Ties were formed with the Histadrut labor federation in general and Hanoar Haoved in particular.

Unfortunately, growth of activity was not always accompanied by growth in numbers. The American elements drawn into the movement were between the ages of seventeen and twenty-one; Labor Zionism was strange to them, and it was difficult to retain membership. Little was found to attract them in the movement's Yiddish-speaking social life. In 1929, when a new secretariat was elected, many of the groups were sadly disorganized.

From the viewpoint of ideological development, 1929 was a most important year. A few of our chaverim began to talk about *chalutziut,* or pioneering in Palestine. At first the term was merely an abstraction, but when we published the pamphlet "Tel Chai and Trumpeldor," some chaverim began to grasp the real meaning of Labor Zionism. An article in the pamphlet by the kibbutz movement leader Yitzhak Tabenkin, on the twenty-fifth anniversary of the Second Aliyah, taught our chaverim the meaning of such concepts as chalutziut, *kibbush avodah* (A. D. Gordon's concept of personal conquest of labor), and *hagshama* (self-realization). In Detroit, a group was formed under the name of "Kvutza"; its aim was to prepare to leave for Palestine within two years. Some of its chaverim were sent to agricultural colleges, and plans were drawn up for a *hachshara,* or training farm. Several Young Poale Zion members joined the "Kvutza" from its inception.

In the last days of August 1929 we were assembled at our Washington convention when news came that Arab riots had broken out in Palestine. It was like an electric shock, turning the session on chalutziut from a theoretical discussion into an immediate, burning question. And the answer was clear: "Young Poale Zion must strengthen the position of the chalutzim in Palestine."

A few members immediately announced their readiness to leave for Palestine. In 1929 our youth saw in the events in Palestine an attack on our people's national honor. Chalutziut became synonymous with self-defense.

The Rise of the Yishuv: Zionist Pioneering Comes of Age

The 1929 Arab riots in Palestine were no isolated incident. As Zionism marched steadily toward its goal of building a functioning, modern Jewish society in Palestine, the Arabs who lived there began to realize that the country was being transformed beyond recognition. Thirty years after Herzl's first Zionist Congress and twenty years after the founding of the first kibbutz, the Jewish community in Palestine was well on its way to becoming a self-confident, self-supporting nation-in-the-making.

The *Yishuv*—"the Settlement," as the Zionist community of Palestine was called—had grown by 1929 from a few score Russian dreamers into a thriving society of nearly two hundred thousand souls. The Second Aliyah, that rag-tag band of Russian youths last seen seeking day labor at the turn of the century, were now men and women in their forties, living in kibbutz and moshav cooperative farming villages or in cities like Petach Tikvah and Tel Aviv, working in factories and offices.

In the meantime, more waves of aliyah had followed. The Third Aliyah, which came to Palestine between 1919 and 1923, consisted of thousands of young East European Jews fleeing World War I, many of them greatly influenced by the Bolshevik Revolution. As for so many young Jews around the world, the Communist takeover in Russia represented the possibility of a new socialist era to them. Their fire helped fuel a new militance in Palestinian Zionist labor.

Along with the mass immigration from Eastern Europe came a small trickle of pioneers from North America, some of them members of the Young Poale Zion who were determined to put the movement's ideas into action. One of these was Goldie Mabovitch Meyerson, who would go on to become Golda Meir, Israel's fourth prime minister. Born in Russia and raised in Milwaukee, Golda first joined Poale Zion as a teenager in Denver, where she was living with a sister. Returning to Milwaukee during World War I, she became a schoolteacher and married Morris Meyerson. Together they decided to settle in Palestine in 1921, choosing Kibbutz Merhavia in the legendary Jezreel Valley.

From Milwaukee to Merhavia, 1921: "They Couldn't Imagine an American Girl Would Do the Work"

Golda Meir
Kibbutz Revivim 1971

When, while still in America, I decided to settle in Palestine, I knew that I would go to a collective settlement. I chose Merhavia because a friend from Milwaukee was already there. To my astonishment, Meyerson and I were not immediately accepted. As we had arrived in July, we were told that no applications could be considered in the middle of the summer. We would have to wait until Rosh Hashanah, when the kvutza knew who was staying and who was going, so that new members could be accepted in place of those who were leaving.

Meanwhile, we went to Tel Aviv, then being built. Our group from the United States made a tremendous impression on the Tel Aviv of the time. One day I met a Tel Aviv woman who, upon learning that I had come from the United States, clapped her hands in astonishment: "Thank God, now the redemption is near—at last Jews have come from America (the millionaires). Now it will be all right!"

Shortly before Rosh Hashanah, we applied to Merhavia to be accepted as members and again received a negative reply. Only two members supported us; one of them was my friend. One reason for the rejection was that this community of unmarried men and women did not at that time want families. Babies were a luxury the young kibbutz could not afford. The greatest opposition came from the "veteran" women, who had been in the country all of eight years; they could not imagine that an American girl would do the hard physical work required.

Despite the rejection, we were invited to come to Merhavia for two or three days so that the members could look us over. I well remember my first day's work. It was the threshing season, and they told me to "sit" on the board of the threshing machine that revolved in the barn and threshed the grain. My efforts at work did not make as great an impression on the young men as the phonograph and records we brought with us. It was the first time anyone had arrived with a hornless phonograph, which aroused general admiration. Of course, they would have been happy to accept the phonograph as a dowry without the bride who owned it, but we would not agree to that. They finally accepted us after a third meeting of the whole kvutza. After that, I had to be careful not to make any slip expected of an American girl.

---

*Reprinted from *Pioneers from America* (Tel Aviv, 1981).

I forced myself to eat every kind of food or dish, even if it was hard to look at, let alone swallow. The food generally had a most unpleasant taste because of the oil we bought from the Arabs: it was not refined, kept in leather bags and bitter as gall, but it was the base for all our dishes.

Every month a different member took her turn in the kitchen. Conditions were so grueling that two weeks before her turn came around, the girl in question would generally become depressed. With plain common sense I decided to take things as they came, including kitchen duty. I never considered work in the kitchen demeaning.

In those days we drank from enamel mugs, which looked fine and shiny so long as they were new, but after a little while began to chip and rust and became repulsive. I decided to stop buying these mugs, although we sometimes reached a state when we were left with two or three glasses, from which we drank in turn. For the whole kvutza I bought nothing but glass.

Another "bourgeois" feature I introduced into our kvutza was a white sheet spread as a tablecloth on Friday night, with a vase of wild flowers— that adornment gave us a bad name throughout the Emek. I also insisted on ironing my dress or blouse carefully. This was also viewed as a "bourgeois" weakness.

The farm was not particularly well developed, and we lived mainly on work for the Jewish National Fund, digging holes for planting trees. The holes naturally had to be dug in a rocky hill and be dug deep enough to hold their shape. After a day's work of this kind, I used to long to wash and have a rest. But I overcame such desires and went to help in the kitchen, though I was so tired that an ordinary fork seemed to weigh a ton. But you get used even to such hard work.

The Struggle for Palestine— and for the Diaspora

Even as the pioneers of the Third Aliyah were struggling to adapt to the life of a new Jewish working class, the Yishuv greeted a new wave of aliyah. The Fourth Aliyah brought with it a new phenomenon: a Zionist urban middle class.

Fleeing Poland, where the collapse of the economy in 1924 was followed by a wave of political reaction, the immigrants of the Fourth Aliyah had no dream of forging a revolutionary new society. They wanted nothing more than to recreate the middle-class life they had known in Warsaw and Lodz. They were not recruits for the labor movement, but more often were its enemies. They settled in Tel Aviv and Jerusalem, opened stores and businesses, and began pouring into the Palestine sections of diaspora-based, probusiness General Zionist parties.

Slowly but surely, the Jewish state was taking shape—not the shape the first visionaries had dreamed of, to be sure. It had gone beyond dreams and was becoming a reality.

On the world scene, too, Zionism was gaining stature and recognition. In 1917, thanks to the efforts of the World Zionist Organization and especially of the young Polish-British chemist, Chaim Weizmann, Great Britain had become the first world power to recognize formally, in the Balfour Declaration, the Zionist goal of a Jewish homeland in Palestine. A year later, with the collapse of Turkey during World War I, Palestine came under British control. The land of Israel now had a government sympathetic to the Jewish national rebirth. Five years after that, the League of Nations granted a mandate to Britain to govern Palestine. The goals of Zionism were formally enshrined in international law.

Under the terms of the mandate, the World Zionist Organization and its offshoot, the Jewish Agency, were given legal standing to represent the Jews of Palestine and Zionists worldwide in their dealings with Britain and other powers.

Now began the battle for the soul of Zionism, for the Labor Zionists were not the only force in Jewish life with a vision of the Jewish state. There were the General Zionists, who aspired to a state built by private capital and ruled by the middle class, and there were religious Zionists as well, whose notion of a Jewish state was a state governed by traditional Judaism. The Jewish Agency and the World Zionist Organization became the battleground where the future shape of Israel was to be decided.

During the course of the 1920s, David Ben-Gurion and others worked hard to unite the various Labor Zionist parties, once led by the likes of Syrkin and Borochov, into a single, powerful labor party. In 1920, they created the Histadrut, a unified organization of working men and women that was to transcend the political parties, serving as union, employer, teacher, and more. In 1929, the labor parties themselves merged to form Mapai—the Eretz Israel Workers Party. Together, the Histadrut and Mapai spread their influence throughout the Yishuv. Their leader, secretary of the Histadrut and *de facto* leader of the Yishuv, was Ben-Gurion.

As the struggle within Zionism grew more intense, the diaspora also became a battleground. Every few years there were Zionist elections to choose the delegates to the World Zionist Congress, which, in turn, elected the Jewish Agency Executive that governed the Yishuv.

To Ben-Gurion and many of his colleagues, Zionist organizing in the diaspora was less important for its political fruits than for its human ones. To them, Zionism was a very personal message. Harking back to Syrkin's "Call to Jewish Youth," and to the personal example of A. D. Gordon, they were determined to bring Jewish youth bodily to Palestine as chalutzim. The machinery through which they worked was the chalutzic Zionist youth movement, and the vision they held was that of *Am Oved*—a nation of workers.

*   *   *

The youth movement was a new phenomenon, but it was not a Zionist invention. Rather, it was a new form of adolescent education that was spreading through Central and Eastern Europe on the eve of World War I: youth leading youth in an idealized "youth society," aspiring to live the pure, non-bourgeois life here and now.

Such adolescent societies were an outgrowth of a new romanticism of youth that swept industrial Europe at the end of the nineteenth century. The Boy Scouts, born in England in 1909, were its best-known creation; J. M. Barrie's "Peter Pan" may be its most enduring cultural statement.

Zionism adopted the youth movement concept in Austria in 1913, with the birth of Hashomer Hatza'ir ("The Young Guard"). Formed as a free-spirited, almost mystical band of youth-leading-youth, Hashomer Hatza'ir was to become a staunchly Marxist group by the late 1920s. To many minds it was a narrowly sectarian one (though to others a vanguard pioneering force). And so it remained for years.

The experience was an instructive one for Zionist labor, however. In the youth movement Zionism found a model that could be adopted throughout the diaspora, shaped to the needs of the kibbutz movement and wedded to Labor Zionism. As the 1920s proceeded, Palestine's labor leadership encouraged the formation of Zionist youth movements throughout the countries of the diaspora. *Shlichim,* emissaries from the Palestine labor movement, were dispatched abroad to encourage the formation of these youth groups, inculcating the goal of living a life of physical labor on the kibbutz.

By 1930 a network of such youth groups existed throughout Europe and America, with names like Blau-Weiss (Blue-White), Hechalutz Hatza'ir (Young Pioneer), Dror (Freedom), Netzach, Hanoar Hatzioni, Gordonia, and—beginning in 1928 in England and South Africa—"The Builders," or *Habonim.*

Uniting all the youth movements was the young adults' organization that trained the would-be kibbutzniks in farming and communal life—Hechalutz.

*   *   *

The purpose of the Hechalutz organization was to facilitate the aliyah of well-trained groups of pioneers prepared for the difficult task of settling on the soil. The hardships of the first waves of chalutzim had taught the Zionist leadership the necessity of teaching their children well.

During the 1920s a trickle of North Americans moved to kibbutz, many of them members of the Young Poale Zion, Hashomer Hatza'ir and Gordonia. Efforts were made in 1924 to acquire a training farm in New Jersey to prepare the would-be pioneers, but without lasting success. Some, like the so-called "Detroit Kvutza"—twelve graduates of that city's United Hebrew Schools who decided to become chalutzim under the influence of Poale Zion—sought out their own training in agriculture schools. The Detroit Kvutza moved to Palestine in 1930, where they helped to found Kibbutz

Ramat Yochanan. Another group, Kvutzat Gordonia, moved from Philadelphia to northern California in 1927 and rented a chicken farm which they operated for five years. They eventually broke up and settled in Palestine individually.

Finally, in 1932, the Committee for the Pioneer—Va'ad Lema'an Hechalutz—was established by a coalition of American Zionist organizations, including the Young Poale Zion Alliance, Gordonia, Young Judaea, Junior Hadassah, and the Avukah college Zionist organization. The new Hechalutz organization held its first national convention in 1933. A second convention, in 1935, included members of the left-wing Hashomer Hatza'ir for the first time.

Under the leadership of a shaliach from the Histadrut, Hillel Giladi of Kibbutz Degania Bet, the new Hechalutz sprang to life. A group of twenty-eight chalutzim sailed for Palestine in 1932 and settled at Degania. Later that year, the new organization received its own full-time shaliach, Lasya Galili of Kibbutz Afikim. In 1934, a second group of Americans sailed for Palestine, settling first at Kinneret and later at Afikim.

With organizational backing and full-time staff in the persons of its shlichim, Hechalutz finally began to establish training farms that were able to endure past the first drought or winter. Farms were leased near Baltimore and Minneapolis, and then two permanent sites in New Jersey were purchased—Hightstown (1934) and Creamridge (1936).

The need for two separate farms, less than twenty miles apart, reflected the most delicate problem facing Hechalutz through much of its existence: the partisan bickering between its two main components, Habonim and Hashomer Hatza'ir. Hashomer Hatza'ir in fact resisted joining the new organization for the first two years. When it agreed, after the personal intervention of David Ben-Gurion, it was only with the guarantee that it could train its chalutzim separately from those of the other chalutz movements. It was given control of the farm at Hightstown, and the other movements—principally Habonim—moved to the new farm at Creamridge.

The Anoka Farm, Minnesota, 1933: "Together We Switched to Agriculture"

Nahum Guttman

New York 1989

It was a derelict eighty-acre spread, abandoned by an unfortunate farmer in the early 1930s when the depression hit the tillers of the soil especially hard. But in the spring of 1933, it started a new life. A group of inexperienced, city-bred young men and women took possession of the rundown farmstead some twenty miles north of Minneapolis and transformed it into a *hachshara,* a training farm for would-be Zionist pioneers.

As an outpost of the Hechalutz organization on the Minnesota plains, the Anoka farm stood out from its neighbors. The newcomers knew next to nothing about farming when they came, and the fallow land would take time to stir under their plows. More importantly, though, the young pioneers planned to make their future not in the Midwest, but in the distant Middle East.

A quartet of Minneapolis Young Poale Zionists launched the enterprise after a year or two of planning. The prime mover was Yehuda Strimling, whose limited academic background was more than balanced by his strong sense of devotion and remarkable mechanical ability. Yehuda went on aliyah before the farm began its actual operations. A full-fledged chalutz, he settled for a while on kibbutz, then spent the major part of his life in Moshav Bet Herut with his Minneapolis-born wife Aliza. He died in 1978.

Then there was his cousin, Samuel Labovitz, and me. We were classmates in high school and at the Minneapolis Talmud Torah. Together we entered the University of Minnesota as engineering candidates, and together we switched to agriculture as our farm venture ripened.

Perhaps most important, there was my brother, Zvi, who led the actual settlement on the farm and single-handedly held the fort until reinforcements began to arrive from all parts of North America. For months, Zvi lived on the Anoka farm alone, with weekend help from Young Poale Zionists who came down from the Twin Cities.

Then came the steady flow of trainees: the trio who motorcycled from Toronto, Shlomo Stern, Sol Barkofsky, and David Weiss; the attractive newlyweds, Mucie and Kip Kaplansky, also from Toronto; red-headed Herman the German, the first refugee from Nazi Germany to join our ranks; Jack from Chicago, the genius at fixing any machine that needed it; Miriam German, also from Chicago, who was to become my sister-in-law.

It was a mixed colony of young people, all united by the common dream of aliyah. And some actually made it. Zvi and Miriam Guttman settled at Kibbutz Afikim and lived there a half-century, where they are buried together in a cemetery overlooking the Jordan River. Shlomo Stern also lived out his days in the Jordan Valley. Sol Barkofsky, now Barkai, still lives at Kibbutz Degania Bet. The Kaplanskys, after a stint at Afikim, returned to Canada and opened a thriving bakery business.

Our mentor was a world-famous wheat-rust expert at the University of Minnesota, Dr. Moses N. Levine. A devoted Labor Zionist, he was fond of quoting the teachings of the nineteenth-century Zionist philosopher Moses Hess, who said we Jews were a "ghostly people" destined to wander the face of the earth.

It was Dr. Levine who found our farm its manager-instructor, in the person of Joe Ball, an elderly, stocky, white-maned Scandinavian. Without Joe Ball, the farm would have remained derelict. When Joe came to us, it was already late in the season, and there was no time to break in the neophytes for the most essential task: plowing the fields and planting a crop. Joe moved quickly, hiring a neighboring farmer and a tractor to break the sod and put down some seeds of flax. We all crossed our fingers and hoped we had not planted too late.

Once the flax sprouts were knee-high, I was sent with a handful of plants to show to the agronomists at the agricultural experiment station on campus. They got excited and hurried out to the farm to see if it was really true that we had raised this crop. They were impressed—we had the best flax in the state of Minnesota that year. There had been a late frost that destroyed the crops of other farmers, but because we were late, we skipped the frost and came out ahead.

Joe Ball was a sort of Aaron David Gordon type, all for manual labor, short of small talk. He had an uphill battle getting his young chalutzim to dispense with their interminable debates in the fields—debates that he believed impaired our value as workers. On the other hand, we felt the ideological fine-points needed to be tuned before the job could be done right. In the long run, Joe was right: the biggest talkers were the first to come back from Israel.

Even though we were city kids, there were times when we were able to call up the most unexpected skills. Once, when the first calf was born, Mr. Ball tried to teach us how to wean the youngster from mother cow to milk pail. He had some trouble getting the idea across to some of the chaverim, but I volunteered to take over and deftly held the calf to its new source of nourishment, putting two fingers into its mouth and drawing it toward the pail, while Ball and the others looked on in wonderment. It was a trick I had picked up during my last summer job, working at a little truck farm near Lake Minnetonka.

One of the outstanding events of our year was the annual picnic held on the premises during the summer. The entire Labor Zionist movement and the members of the general Jewish community were invited for a Sunday of fun and inspiration. One year, my bearded Orthodox grandfather came out with a friend of similar background, and the Minneapolis daily paper interviewed them, running a story and picture of the patriarchs the next day: Jews return to the land.

Our contacts with the media were quite good. Joe Ball's son, Joe Junior, was a newspaperman in St. Paul, and he visited us on occasion. About a decade later, during a visit to Washington, I looked him up—he was now Senator Joseph Ball of Minnesota—and found he had turned out to be the spitting image of his old man. We had to cut our chat short when he was called to a Senate meeting chaired by a man who would later play an even more crucial role in the birth of Israel: Senator Harry S Truman of Missouri.

Another group in the city that was helpful to us was a circle of Jewish businessmen led by a laundry tycoon, A. M. Gross. He had lived on a farm in the Dakotas, and was enthusiastic about getting Jewish youngsters back to the farm during the depression era. He suggested that we open our hachshara to those who were interested in becoming American farmers, but we turned him down. As it turned out, even his own son Leo, a Talmud Torah classmate of mine who inherited the laundry, ended up spending most of his years in Israel.

Most Young Poale Zionists in Minneapolis never went to live on the farm for more than a few weeks at a time, or, like myself, only went to the farm on weekends, spending weekdays in studies. Still, the hachshara was always the focus of our thoughts and activities.

Some of the other hachshara farms of American Hechalutz, like the ones in Creamridge, New Jersey, Smithville, Ontario, and Colton, California, continued even after the birth of Israel in 1948 as important way stations for movement members en route to kibbutz. Our hachshara on the Minnesota plains only lasted a few years, and is scarcely remembered by the current generation of Minneapolitans, even those who went on to settle in Israel without the benefit of its agricultural training. But its spiritual impact persists. It turned part of Minneapolis into an unusual Zionist enclave on the broad expanse of the American Midwest. When Hillel Giladi of Degania Bet came to visit us once, he called it an oasis in the American wilderness, and so it was.

From Chicago to Afikim, 1934: "I Knew I Was Headed for Palestine"

Zvi Brenner
Kibbutz Afikim 1985

My story actually starts in Poland, passes through America, and reaches Palestine—all before Habonim even existed.

When I was eleven years old and living in Poland, I used to accompany my father to lectures of the Jewish Socialist Bund. My father was a real Jewish proletarian, and quite devoted to the message of the Bund: Zionism is a diversion from the battle for justice here at home. Even then, though, I knew I was headed for Palestine. Not long after, I joined Hechalutz Hatza'ir.

When I was fifteen, my family emigrated to the New World. America, in the early 1930s, was trapped in the deepest depression, and I took whatever jobs came along to pay my night school tuition for college courses.

Somehow, still, there was always time for other things, and when it came time to look for a congenial Zionist organization, I found the Young Poale Zion Alliance. Most of the members of YPZ were immigrants like me, and they subscribed to a concept of socialist Zionism that was straight out of the old country.

We were active in the general socialist movement, but we decided to devote our primary efforts to reviving Hechalutz, the settlement organization that had existed sporadically in America since the turn of the century. Together with members of Hashomer Hatza'ir, we set up a Hechalutz communal house in Chicago. Eventually, we were able to buy some land, and we established training farms outside Minneapolis and Baltimore.

I went to live on the Hechalutz farm near Baltimore. It wasn't much. We had some land, a house, two cows, a few chickens, and absolutely no money. We subsisted on a starvation diet. Although we made a small income from the sale of our produce, it was woefully inadequate. I remember collecting stale bread and cake in town, ostensibly to feed the livestock, but actually to feed ourselves. Each of us had to find a job away from the farm to raise money for aliyah.

In 1933, our Hechalutz organization held a national convention. At this time the British government, which ruled Palestine under a League of Nations mandate, was giving out a limited number of entry certificates to Jews who wanted to settle in the Holy Land. Whenever certificates came in, the Hechalutz leadership would see to it that they were distributed to active members of Young Poale Zion and Hashomer Hatza'ir who were ready to go to Palestine.

Most of the certificates were for couples, but there were a few for individuals. In order to send as many people as possible, several shotgun weddings were performed. I was lucky enough to receive a certificate for only one person.

When our group arrived in Palestine, the members of Hashomer Hatza'ir went to Kibbutz Ein Hashofet, and we, the young Poale Zionists, went to Kibbutz Afikim. In 1934, the Afikim group was still living in temporary quarters at Hatzer Kinneret. I worked at all kinds of jobs but primarily at preparing the permanent site of the kibbutz.

Like so many others, I received some rudimentary military training and saw my first action in 1936. We were informed that Kibbutz Ramat Hakovesh, to our south, was severely threatened by marauders from the surrounding Arab villages. The British were doing nothing to help the kibbutz; I volunteered to join the reinforcements sent by the Haganah, the Yishuv's underground defense force.

There were attacks almost every night, but one night the onslaught was more murderous than usual. Finally, the British arrived with an armored force. I climbed on one of their tanks to brief them on our situation, and from that moment on it was my job to serve as liaison between the kibbutz defenders and the British.

After things calmed down, I returned to Afikim, but the Haganah had its eye on me. I was sent to a military training course headed by one of the Haganah's top commanders, Yitzhak Sadeh. For most of the courses, our instructors were British officers.

In early 1938, in response to the two-year-old Arab uprising, the British government began restricting Jewish land acquisition. The Jewish Agency responded with its "Tower and Stockade" policy: in a single night, a group of settlers would stake a claim to a plot of land and erect structures to defend it. When the sun rose there would be a new Jewish settlement in Palestine. It was a forceful way to express our rejection of British restrictions.

I was working as a house painter at Afikim when I heard that the Haganah was assembling a unit to establish a Tower and Stockade settlement at Hanita, on the Lebanese border in the Western Galilee. I remember going from room to room on the kibbutz, offering to paint whatever bits and pieces of furniture the owners had, hoping that they in turn would support me as one of the two members Afikim would send to Hanita. To this day I do not know if the vote went in my favor out of respect for my defense skills or in gratitude for my paint jobs.

The very night that we reached the new site, we were attacked by armed Arab bands. We managed to hold them off and get the tower and stockade up. From then until the end of Passover 1938, we were constantly on the defense against attack.

During Passover of that year, Orde Wingate, a captain in the British army, arrived with a letter of introduction from Haganah commander Eliyahu Golomb instructing us to take him into our confidence. Although he was not Jewish, Wingate was a staunch believer in our cause. I was chosen to be his guide and to initiate him into our work. From then until he left the country, I was always with him.

Wingate was convinced we needed to use more aggressive tactics. He mobilized the Special Night Squads, a unit with 180 soldiers—120 Jews from all ranks of the Haganah and 60 British volunteers. We trained at northern kibbutzim, at Ein Harod, Geva, and Afikim. We were expected to be not only in top fighting form but in perfect physical condition as well.

Wingate's strategy was to search out and attack Arab bands before they could attack us. This often required long marches beyond the borders of Palestine. Eventually, Wingate was expelled from the country by his superiors who disapproved of his actions.

When the night squads were disbanded, I returned to Afikim. A short while later, I attended a Haganah officers course, but my new role was short-lived. Within several months the participants were rounded up and sent to the jail in Acre. We were tried by a British court and sentenced to ten years in jail for participating in underground military activity. After eighteen months we were freed, due to the efforts of several quasi-official Jewish organizations.

By then, World War II had begun. Soon after getting out of jail, I volunteered for the British army. It was not until 1944 that the Jewish volunteers were recognized as our own brigade, the Jewish Brigade, and allowed to fight under our own blue-and-white flag. I was wounded during the fighting on the Italian front and spent my last three months of the war in hospitals in Italy, Egypt, and finally back home, in Palestine.

2

The Founding of Habonim

Into the Whirlwind of History

Saadia Gelb
Kibbutz Kfar Blum 1985

The problems of the world were not a popular topic in America of the early 1930s. The flapper era and the Jazz Age had come to abrupt halt due to the stock market crash of October 1929, and with each passing day, people were more and more concerned with the day-to-day problems of personal survival. Isolationism, always a strong streak in the American character, was growing. Those who were aware of social problems were flocking to the parties of the revolutionary left. The Communist Party was enjoying its heyday.

As a result of prohibition, crime flourished and gangsters openly ruled the streets. Some had names like Capone and Anastasia; others were named Lansky, Siegel, and Buchalter. There were Jewish names on the FBI's "Ten Most Wanted" lists. Even Orthodox rabbis occasionally found their way into the criminal world, issuing ritual permits on wine that eventually found its way to smugglers.

The violent anti-Semitism in Europe encouraged an American counterpart, social anti-Semitism. Jews were excluded from the upper levels of society; Jews could not join certain clubs. Jews rarely became university professors, and when they did win tenure, it was almost always on science faculties, not in the humanities and social sciences.

In America of 1930, no one cried "Black is Beautiful." America demanded submersion into the "melting pot"; minorities were expected to assimilate and disappear. For those who struggled with the unresolved dilemma of Emancipation—living in modern society while retaining a Jewish group identity—there were few role models. Some of us were attracted to ideas like cultural pluralism, but the notion of pluralism continued to grate on the nerves of America's ruling class, viewing it as a Jewish invention. For them, the message of "Abie's Irish Rose" was the greatest concession possible.

In an age that discouraged flaunting one's ethnic identity, the Jewish community had little room for Zionism. The Orthodox, with the exception of the religious Zionist party Mizrachi, opposed it outright. Reform Judaism, still led by affluent Jews of German origin who were well-rooted in American soil, opposed Jewish nationalism in principle. The Conservative movement, though supportive of Zionism, had not yet rooted itself firmly and was preoccupied with internal organizing.

As for the Jewish philanthropies, their organizational structures were openly and frankly assimilationist: Jewish philanthropic leaders viewed the social services they supported as a way of bringing their benighted Russian Jewish brethren into the American mainstream. The professional staff, particularly social workers in Jewish community centers and family organizations, was strongly influenced by communists who sought to use the institutions for their own agenda.

There was a Zionism among American Jews, but it was not the personal Zionism of the chalutzic youth movement. Zionism in America, from the aristocratic Supreme Court Justice Louis D. Brandeis to the Reform Rabbi Stephen S. Wise, was a way of supporting the work of others. It was said that American Zionism was a Jew giving money to a second Jew to save a third Jew from the anti-Semites across the ocean.

It was against this background that the founders of Habonim dove into the whirlwind of history. Any Zionist act was significant. We were very few; our task was to survive, to endure, to retain our identity. We had few pretensions, and we knew the limits of our strength. But we worked in the ancient tradition that even a few can make a difference, and we acted in the fervor and freshness of youth. And we did achieve something.

Education, Politics and Pioneering: The Debate Over Habonim

Jacob Katzman
New York 1985

The Young Poale Zion Alliance underwent a sudden transformation in August 1929. From a socialist organization with a theoretical commitment to the goals of Zionism, YPZA became a chalutzic organization with a clear focus on aliyah.

In some ways, the movement had been in transition for nearly a decade. Originally an organization of Yiddish-speaking immigrant youth in their late teens and early twenties, we were becoming—gradually—a movement with an appeal to American-born, English-speaking high school students.

But the transition from political Zionism to chalutzic, personal Zionism happened virtually overnight. The impetus was the Arab rioting that broke out in Palestine in August 1929. We were assembled at our national convention in Washington, D.C., when the news broke. Under the stars at the Washington Jewish Community Center, the delegates spontaneously gathered, and member after member rose to pledge himself to seek the earliest possible means of getting to Palestine. Most never did go on aliyah, but aliyah had now become the central objective of the youth movement. No one ever forgot the emotional intensity of that night.

Soon, aliyah groups were organized in Detroit and other cities. A committee was formed to foster pioneering aliyah on a national scale. In 1932, the first group left. Before long others followed: to Ramat Yochanan, Na'an, Ramat David, Afikim, and Degania Bet. In order to foster and facilitate aliyah, Young Poale Zion joined with two other youth movements, Hashomer Hatza'ir and Gordonia, to form the American Hechalutz settlement organization.

Perhaps the most fertile seed leading to the formation of Habonim was the opening of a summer camp, YPZA Camp Kvutza, in Accord, New York, in 1932.

The camp's name, *kvutza,* was a term used synonymously with kibbutz in those days. We were purposely recalling the communal farming movement in Palestine, and the name resonated in the life of the camp. Campers did all the upkeep work themselves, coping with extremely primitive conditions. They were profoundly affected by living, working, and learning together in a setting that simulated communal life. At that point, too, scouting was introduced into the educational program.

After that summer's experience, the YPZA national executive talked long and hard about whether to introduce scouting into the general program for younger groups which were made up of children between the ages of ten and sixteen. First called "Juniors," then *Knospen* ("Buds" in Yiddish), these children came mainly from the Labor Zionist afternoon "folk-school" network and from Labor Zionist households. The members of the national executive recognized that these new groups needed an organizational structure and an educational approach distinct from that of YPZA itself.

At the 1932 YPZA convention in Philadelphia, over the Labor Day weekend, we decided to introduce elements of scouting into the Buds' program. In the summer of 1934, a week-long meeting was held at Camp Kvutza in Accord, where the youth movement's ideology and structure were hotly debated. Over the next year, the actual basis for Habonim was developed, to be ratified at the coming convention in Buffalo, New York.

For those of us involved, it was a stimulating and exciting period. Throughout the American Jewish community, ideological debate was hot and heavy between communists and socialists, nationalists and assimilationists, Zionists and anti-Zionists. Socialist Zionism, which sought to ride several horses simultaneously, had a hard time defining itself in the ideational maelstrom. And the debates spilled over into our discussion about Habonim.

Some chaverim put the primary stress on Zionism. To give the children a clear-cut objective, they argued, the emphasis must be chalutziut, or pioneering aliyah. Others held that to strive for a socialist society in the land of Israel was not enough; we must address ourselves to the social ills of the United States, Canada, and the world. After all, they said, America and the world were in the throes of the Great Depression, and communism and fascism were racing across Europe. In Germany, Hitler was building Nazi power. And totalitarianism had its ardent sympathizers here, too.

In any event, many of the YPZers were themselves working youth. Most, certainly, had come from working-class homes where they imbibed the passion of the trade union struggle and an ideological commitment to socialism and against fascism.

But those who insisted that the primary focus should be on building the Jewish homeland countered that it was precisely during strife-riven times that Jewish youth must concentrate on Jewish national needs. No one else would.

After days of heated debate, those at the meeting at Accord hammered out a compromise. Chalutziut in Eretz Israel was recognized as "an end in itself in the realization of Socialist Zionist ideology." At the same time, the delegates reaffirmed that "the struggle of the working class against capitalism, fascism and oppression and for the establishment of socialism, are integral parts of our Socialist Zionist ideology." The struggle for the rebirth of the Jewish homeland could not be isolated from the struggle for socialism—or vice versa. The final resolution decreed that every member of Poale Zion must dedicate himself to the twofold struggle. Essentially, this debate and its resolution became the ideological basis of Habonim, setting it apart from other youth organizations on the Jewish scene.

At that same meeting at Accord in 1934, close scrutiny was given to the nature of the scouting program that was to be introduced for the younger groups aged ten to eighteen. The English word "scouting" did not sit well with many members. It raised the image of the American Boy Scouts, whom many of us saw as a jingoistic, strutting band of not-so-innocent youth. In the labor movement, there had been allegations that the Boy Scouts had been scabs in some places.

Along the same lines, some delegates opposed the introduction of a Habonim shirt or uniform. Worse than the Boy Scouts, a shirt would be reminiscent of the odious brown and black shirts in Europe.

In the end, the Hebrew word tzofiut was accepted. Somehow it seemed less strident than "scouting," and more in keeping with A. D. Gordon's notions of man's relationship to nature. Shortly after Habonim was officially formed, the blue shirt with its insignia was introduced.

Next on the agenda at that pivotal meeting in Accord was a debate about training for aliyah. What was the proper path for members who, upon graduation, do not choose to go on aliyah? Was there any room for them in Labor Zionism? Should they be expected to join the senior movement?

The more extreme view was that self-fulfillment through aliyah must be the sole objective of Habonim. Members who did not make aliyah betrayed the movement's principles. They could not be sincere Labor Zionists and should not be accepted for membership in the party—although they might perhaps find a place in the movement's fraternal order, the Farband, or in the Pioneer Women.

The moderates argued that although self-fulfillment through aliyah was Habonim's central aim, it would be folly—given the human tendency for performance to fall short of high ideals—to banish from Labor Zionism those who opted, for whatever reasons, not to go on aliyah at age twenty or twenty-two.

The question of aliyah remained unresolved. The moderates and hardliners were unable to find a clear, common position in 1934 at Accord. Even the 1935 convention did not take a clear stand on this basic ideological issue.

The most emotional question at Accord that spring, however, was a structural one. Would Habonim would be an integral part of YPZA and the overall Labor Zionist movement, or would it be an independent entity? Those who demanded independence contended that in order to give youngsters a sense of responsibility in shaping their lives as pioneers, they must be allowed the utmost freedom of action. "Only youth should lead youth," was their slogan. Nor should Habonim be tied to party dogmas in whose formulation it had no part. Finally, the autonomy camp pointed to the chalutzic Zionist youth movements already in existence, Hashomer Hatzair in Europe, America, and Palestine, Blau-Weiss in Central Europe, and Habonim itself in England and South Africa. Each was completely independent; none was tied to a specific political party.

In rebuttal, some delegates argued that although Habonim should enjoy autonomy in its internal affairs, full independence would cut it adrift from its parent movement. In any event, the bulk of Habonim's members were likely to come from Labor Zionist homes, schools, and camps. It would be dangerous to cast the youngsters onto the ideological shoals of the 1930s American left, racked by a mortal battle between socialists and communists, especially since both groups were anti-Zionist. Affiliation with the Labor Zionist movement, it was argued, would provide an ideological anchor.

The debate lasted into the small hours of the morning and continued until the Buffalo convention of 1935. In the end, it was decided that Habonim would be governed by a national executive committee, but the committee would be responsible to the national executive of YPZA, which would appoint its members. Habonim was to be autonomous, yet firmly rooted in the Labor Zionist movement.

Dark Skies: Winter–Spring 1935

During the winter and spring months of 1935, the YPZA was laying the groundwork for a Habonim structure in preparation for the national convention in the fall, where the central committee's guidelines would be voted on.

The national secretariat began offering clearer direction to those branches that already had children's groups, and new groups were formed. Plans were made to open Camp Kvutza at Accord for the first time to children as young as ten.

Habonim was scarcely the only item on the YPZA agenda in 1935, however. Socialist Zionism was facing a host of challenges and opportunities that seemed at times to keep the Young Poale Zion fighting on a dozen fronts at once.

In 1935 the Jewish world was haunted by the dark cloud of fascism spreading across Europe like a swiftly gathering storm. Its most virulent form was in Hitler's Germany, but fascist and anti-Semitic forces were putting democracy on the run in Italy, Poland, Romania, Yugoslavia, and elsewhere. Then, too, Stalin's brutality was becoming increasingly evident in the Soviet Union, which had once held out the hope of a new order of economic and social justice. Democrats, especially democratic socialists, felt increasingly fearful of the dictatorial tide.

For Zionists, the worsening situation of European Jewry came just as the British government seemed to be backing away from its support for the Jewish national home in Palestine. In the wake of the 1929 Arab riots, Britain issued a series of commission reports and government White Papers which called for restrictions on Jewish immigration and land acquisition. The World Zionist Organization, the highest body of world Jewry in its efforts to regain a homeland, appeared unable to halt the deterioration.

As Europe sank into nightmare, many frightened Jews were turning to the simplistic answers offered by Vladimir Jabotinsky and his militant, right-wing Zionist Revisionist movement. Jabotinsky called for bold, bombastic gestures in defiance of world opinion. He derided Labor's chalutzic approach of building a Jewish society in Palestine stone by stone and acre by acre. The Revisionists also railed against the Histadrut's social vision, which they called bolshevist and worse. For them, Labor Zionism's twin commitments—socialism and Zionism—amounted to dual disloyalty.

Led by David Ben-Gurion, Labor responded to the multiple challenges with a strategy that called for no less than Labor Zionist hegemony in, or control of, world Zionism. As the most dynamic and best-organized sector of Jewish Palestine, Labor was able to argue forcefully in the world Zionist arena that it was the natural leader of the Zionist movement as a whole. With a combination of careful diplomacy and ideological flexibility, Labor forged a working coalition to isolate the Revisionists, allying itself with such nonsocialist elements as the religious Zionists and parts of the General Zionists. The strategy paid off quickly. When the nineteenth World Zionist Congress convened in Lucerne in August 1935, Ben-Gurion was elected chairman of the Jewish Agency Executive, making him, in effect, the "prime minister" of the Zionist movement.

In America, Labor Zionism drew new strength from the dynamism of its chaverim in Palestine. The YPZA was in regular contact with the movement's institutions in Palestine, and saw itself as the American branch of a movement that was actually leading the Jewish people.

Periodic contact was maintained with Palestine through the organization departments of the Histadrut and the Jewish Agency—both of which were dominated by Mapai, YPZA's sister party in Palestine. The most powerful form of contact, however, was the dispatching to North America of shlichim, who represented Palestine to diaspora Zionism in a function that fell somewhere between diplomat and educator.

One of the earliest shlichim to America was Golda Meyerson, now a rising official in the Histadrut. She came to New York in the early 1930s as shlicha to the Labor Zionist women's organization Pioneer Women. Meyerson was in close touch with the YPZA organization during her New York stay, and in fact played a role in obtaining the site at Highland Mills, New York, for YPZA's first summer camp "Kvutza" in 1932. On her return to Tel Aviv she became chief of the Histadrut's political department.

                              *   *   *

Although its bond with Labor Palestine gave it stature in the Zionist world, American Labor Zionism was still a tiny force. American socialism in general, which seemed to be gaining strength through the bitter industrial struggles of the teens and twenties, faced a sudden and ironic challenge in 1933 with the entry of Franklin D. Roosevelt into the White House. The hope held out to workers by Roosevelt's New Deal had the effect of undercutting socialism's claim that it was the only possible response to the crisis of capitalism.

Among young American Jews, socialism continued to be the most dynamic intellectual and social trend well into the late thirties. But socialists were fractured into a hundred miniparties feuding over the issues of the day: support for the capitalist reforms of the New Deal, the challenge of European fascism and the formation of popular fronts, and the brutality of Stalin's Russia. The debates filled the air on college campuses where Jews attended in large number, and YPZA, with a growing portion of its members now American-born—and college-bound—flung itself into those debates with a passion.

It was in an atmosphere of opportunity as well as crisis, then, that the Young Poale Zion Alliance gathered in Buffalo for its thirteenth national convention on October 10, 1935. Nahum Guttman's report to the movement on the convention, published in the November issue of the movement journal *Jewish Frontier,* gives a feeling of the event.

Buffalo, 1935: "Habonim Was Inaugurated"

Nahum Guttman

New York 1935

Utilizing every means of locomotion at the disposal of impecunious but determined youth—truck, flivver, and thumb—delegates to the thirteenth convention of the Young Poale Zion Alliance descended upon Buffalo in October for four days of sessions, strikingly characterized by a lack of mere verbosity and an abundance of toil. For the first time, YPZA found itself without the need for prolonged ideological clarification. The delegates knew what they wanted—and what they wanted was action!

Why has Socialist-Zionism hitherto been slow to appeal to American Jewish youth? What are the plans that emerge from Buffalo which open the way to wider circles? Two major preconvention developments must be considered.

The metamorphosis of our youth organization from a Yiddish speaking, foreign-born group to an indigenous American movement is completed. In the infant days of the American Socialist Zionist movement, Yiddish was a shibboleth. English was then looked upon as a passing medium that would be gradually replaced by Yiddish. As recently as 1931 the movement could not objectively appraise the culture patterns of American Jewish youth and even endeavored to issue Yiddish material against the odds to an English-reading audience. Most of the delegates to this year's convention were themselves born and raised on this continent and contrasted sharply with the types more common at earlier gatherings. Buffalo, 1935, marks the completion of the adaption of Socialist Zionism to American Jewish youth.

The second of the factors setting the tone of the movement have been developments in Zionist and international affairs. The youth movement, while propounding the ideas of Socialist Zionism and leading a relatively large number of its members to the realization of its philosophy through chalutziut, pioneering in Palestine, is only now able to approach the wider mass of Jewish youth. The Buffalo delegates became aware of the fact that what once was clear to a limited number of devoted comrades is now, thanks to the crisis in Jewish life and the disintegration of the accepted social order, becoming intelligible to others. Crisis is whipping recalcitrants into line.

An ideological war was declared on Jewish youth as yet outside our ranks. Every session was devoted to strategy.

Chalutziut is axiomatically accepted by the YPZA as the core of its program. With scores of its members already pioneering in Palestine as living testimonials to the ability of America to produce genuine chalutzim, and with scores of members preparing to join them in the near future, the YPZA had only to reaffirm its position on chalutziut. The delegates, many of whom were under the eighteen-year age limit for joining Hechalutz, showed grave concern for their proper preparation. The strategy to cope with an already existing situation called for the adoption of a training program beginning in the younger ranks of the movement.

In addition to attending to their own intraorganizational chalutz activities, YPZA are being called upon to set the pace for other members of Hechalutz.

This ideological war manifesto, should it be codified, would read: *"Better chalutzim from America! More chalutziut for America!"*

The second line of our attack is fronted against radical youth "of Jewish origin, indifferent to Jewish problems."

The recent death of Arcadi Kramer, father of the Jewish Socialist Bund, brings to mind the intellectual struggle to reconcile socialism and Zionism in the 1890s. The YPZA is prepared to fight on American soil for the ideas which in Europe are being vindicated by the relentless march of events that pronounces our social ills insoluble save through national redemption. The YPZA at Buffalo threw down the gauntlet to Jewish Socialists and Communists, and challenged their anti-Zionism in the face of contemporary realities.

On the right flank, the YPZA launched a broadside on Zionist and Jewish youth circles. Now Labor Zionism is the recipient of many bouquets and much flattery. True, Zionists generally acknowledge the hegemony of Labor, and profess their sympathies. Zionist youth groups are awakening to the ideals of chalutziut. But the YPZA is not satisfied with the superficial contents of these Zionist youth groups, and will strive to establish mutual relationships that will lead to an intensification of Zionist understanding. "Know thyself—know Zionism—know Labor Zionism"—such was the challenge flung to our Zionist colleagues.

Jewish institutions of learning must be stormed by young Labor Zionists. Jewish education is seeking something vivid and proximate to the life of the American Jewish child. Although Zionism has come up for consideration in more progressive institutions, it has yet to receive its due attention. The embodiment of the Zionist philosophy in Jewish education has become imperative, both because of the weak content of our curricula and because Zionism must begin its training at an early age. The symbiotic relationship between Zionism and the Jewish school is becoming more apparent. Its membership composed largely of Talmud Torah and Folkshuln products, the YPZA is looking upon its alma maters to make Jewish education truly Zionist.

The convention approved the plan of the National Executive for its children's educational organization—the Zionist Pioneer Youth Habonim. Work among children has heretofore been carried on unsystematically. In January of this year, the first steps were taken toward the introduction of a planned program for children, and Habonim was inaugurated as a chalutz scouting movement. To it, the chalutz is the man of productive labor, the socialized being, and the standard-bearer of national renaissance. Habonim is patterned after the Labor settlements in Palestine, and its Hebrew terminology serves to enhance the Labor Zionist environment of the child. Recognizing chalutziut as the spearhead of its educational program, Habonim also incorporates social and cultural elements that provide for a purposeful life in the American Jewish community. It will eventually assist in precipitating Socialism in America.

The successful summer camps of the YPZA have reached the stage where the organization looks forward to having all its members attend next summer. Summer Kvutzot (named after the collective colonies in Palestine, which they emulate) are scheduled to be established in various parts of the country. These Kvutzot enrich the social and cultural life of our youth. The Kvutza, which is operated by its members, has given them their first taste of communal living, and will eventually introduce agriculture as one of their major activities, thus increasing the similarity between the camping experiences and a life of cooperative labor. The singing and dancing, the hauling of wood, the peeling of potatoes, and the construction of a house in the fastness of the Catskills are rehearsals for pioneer life in Palestine.

New York, 1938: "Habonim Was Essential for My Adjustment"

Ruth Halpern Guttman
Jerusalem 1985

I grew up in Vienna between the world wars, in a family that maintained a rich cultural, Jewish, and Zionist life. My father was active in the General Zionist movement, and I began private Hebrew lessons at age five. Later on I studied at the famous Chayes Gymnasium where high level studies were offered in both general and Hebrew curricula. Outside school hours I belonged to Hakoah, the Jewish sports club, and when I was eleven, in 1933, I joined Maccabi Hatza'ir, a Zionist youth movement that combined Labor Zionism with scouting activities.

After the Anschluss, the Nazi annexation of Austria in 1938, my age group became eligible for Youth Aliyah, the Jewish Agency rescue program that took Jewish children from Nazi Europe and settled them in youth villages in Palestine. Almost all the members of my group left for Palestine before the outbreak of World War II the next year, but my parents insisted that I migrate with them to America. My mother's older brother lived in Brooklyn.

And so I arrived in New York in December 1938, a month after Kristallnacht, upset, confused, determined to dislike American life, and resolved to stay no longer than necessary. I was thrown together with my three American teenage cousins, all boys. I knew very little English, and they knew very little about Zionism. They thought I was a queer fish in any case: I wore no makeup and I did not particularly enjoy the Benny Goodman concert I went to on my first night out. For weeks I was lonely and unhappy, certain that my stay in the United States would be continuous misery.

Then one evening, I received a call from another cousin, May Axtmayer. She took me to a meeting of her Habonim group in Brooklyn. I did not understand much of the proceedings, and yet I immediately felt at home. Despite the setting and the language, the atmosphere made me feel that I belonged and that I had a purpose. For the first time I felt that life in America need not be a total loss.

That meeting in Brooklyn was a turning point for me. Soon afterward, May took me to New York City and introduced me to Kieve Skidell, the national secretary of the Young Poale Zion Alliance, Habonim's parent movement. In turn he took me to a German-speaking Habonim group in Manhattan. This group was started by Alex Jakobsohn, who had been active in the chalutzic youth movement in Germany.

Most of the members in the German-speaking group were from Germany, with a few from Czechoslovakia as well. They had been in New York for a while and had passed through their initial adjustment period. With them, my life became at first bearable, then interesting, and eventually exciting. I made friends and learned English quickly. I even began to enjoy New York, despite my earlier determination to hate it. I decided to finish high school as quickly as possible in order to study agriculture before moving to Palestine.

Habonim was essential for my adjustment to life in the United States. On the other hand, my Viennese youth movement experience enabled me to make a small contribution to Habonim activities. I became a leader of a group of twelve-year-olds, first in Brooklyn and then at Camp Kvutza in Killingworth, Connecticut. While still in New York I joined the Haganah, the Jewish Agency's underground defense force. I was a delegate to several Habonim conferences, and, I am proud to say, was on a team that helped the Zionist leader Meir Weisgal at the famous Biltmore Convention in New York in 1942, where the leadership of the Zionist movement first declared the formal goal of sovereign Jewish statehood.

That same year, I was accepted as a second-year student to the College of Agriculture at Cornell University. At that point my direct involvement in Habonim ended. I became active in Kadimah, the Zionist group at Cornell. Its active nucleus consisted of students from the whole Zionist spectrum, including even a few rabid Revisionists. Although there was no Habonim group near campus, I felt I played an important role in bringing the Labor Zionist message to Kadimah.

At Cornell, I also met Kadimah's faculty advisor, Louis Guttman. I married him in 1943 and we made aliyah together in 1947. We have lived in Jerusalem ever since. [Louis Guttman died in 1987—*ed.*]

The Elusive Goal of Labor Zionist Unity

Habonim's successful launching was in part a testimony to the growing appeal of Zionism in America. In part, too, it was an outgrowth of the growing dynamism of Palestinian Labor, which had merged its main Marxist and non-Marxist factions in 1929 into a single, powerful Labor party, Mapai. The new party proceeded to put its stamp on nearly every aspect of the life of Zionism and the Yishuv. The American Labor Zionist parties, Poale Zion and Zeire Zion, followed suit and merged in short order.

Yet unity was still an elusive goal in the labor movement's moral heartland, the kibbutz. The kibbutzim were organized into separate federations divided by mutual suspicion and by a differing approach to the nature and mission of the Palestinian communal farming movement.

The largest of the federations, Hakibbutz Hame'uchad (the United Kibbutz), saw itself as the vanguard of the Zionist working class, and encouraged its member kibbutzim to grow into building blocks of a future socialist society. A smaller federation, Chever Hakvutzot (the League of Kvutzot), clung to the agrarian ideals of A. D. Gordon, and insisted that its member communities limit their size to maintain the intimacy of the early kvutza experience.

YPZA's tradition of militant socialism led it naturally to the class-conscious kibbutzim of Hakibbutz Hame'uchad. The earliest YPZA chalutzim, like Zvi Brenner and the future shaliach Ben Zion Ilan (Benny Applebaum), gravitated to kibbutzim like Afikim. The movement bond was strengthened by the dispatching to America in 1936 of two shlichim whose personalities left a strong imprint on the fledgling Habonim framework: Brooklyn-born Ben Zion Ilan, the first shaliach to Habonim, and Italian-born Enzo Sereni of Kibbutz Givat Brenner, a charismatic shaliach to Hechalutz who later died at Dachau, caught by the Nazis during a daring behind-the-lines mission to save Jews.

At the same time, there was another American Labor Zionist youth movement that remained faithful to the ideals of Chever Hakvutzot and its spiritual father, A. D. Gordon.

Gordonia In North America

David Breslau

Jerusalem 1984

It was on October 14, 1928 that a group of Jewish youngsters from Philadelphia and nearby Camden gathered in the Zeire Zion Labor Zionist center in Philadelphia to form a chapter of Gordonia.

We quickly learned, however, that ours was not the first Gordonia chapter in America. In fact, we began corresponding with chapters in other cities, and soon established a special relationship with the group in Baltimore. Shoshana Kramer, a member of the Baltimore group, wrote: "Our organization was formed on September 6, 1925. The organizers presented a small, unassuming, inconspicuous group: a girl, two boys, and the advisor, the original organizer no more than a boy himself. A small group—but what beautiful ideals, what great hopes and ambitions they represented!"

The advisor, Yaacov Levin, was a dreamer fired with enthusiasm and determined to do his full share in making the dreams of our people come true. Born in 1905 in Riga, Latvia, he immigrated in 1923 to Baltimore, where he enrolled at the Baltimore Hebrew College and the University of Maryland.

While still living in Baltimore, Levin joined Zeire Zion, the diaspora Labor Zionist party that followed the nondogmatic, agrarian socialism of the saintly Aaron David Gordon. Like its Palestinian sister-party Hapoel Hatza'ir, Zeire Zion was a close-knit group with a philosophy of personal example and self-fulfillment through self-sacrifice for the Jewish people. It was well suited to Levin's idealistic character.

In 1926, newly married to Ziporah Handelman, Levin moved to Philadelphia, where he joined with other members of Zeire Zion to form a Zionist commune. The commune, called Kvutzat Gordonia, was committed to making aliyah as a group; in preparation, the members moved in 1927 to Petaluma, California, one of the centers of Jewish farming in America at that time, to undergo hachshara or agricultural training.

Unfortunately, the group disbanded before the planned aliyah date. Levin returned to Philadelphia in 1928 and began teaching across the Delaware River in New Jersey at the Camden Talmud Torah, one of the outstanding Jewish schools of the era. In October, Levin called a meeting of Gordonia, to which he invited his pupils and some young friends.

Gordonia youth groups had been forming in North America sporadically since that first meeting in Baltimore in 1925. Between 1926 and 1928, organizing was coordinated by a National Committee for Gordonia of the Zeire Zion central committee.

Our Philadelphia group, however, was the first Gordonia chapter in America to be organized independently of the Zeire Zion party. After consultations with Pinchas Lavon, then chairman of World Gordonia, a temporary central committee was established in Philadelphia. Yaakov Levin chaired the committee and maintained contact with the world movement and Gordonia groups in other cities. The first national convention of North American Gordonia was held in Cleveland in December 1930. There were twenty functioning chapters at the time.

The Cleveland convention adopted the classic Gordonian principles of self-labor, self-education, and self-fulfillment—meaning pioneering aliyah—as a personal imperative. Education in the movement included the study of Hebrew, elevating the cultural level of the members, and learning about

Labor Palestine. Each member was called on to prepare personally for a pioneering life in Israel. Politically, the convention declared Gordonia an independent organization, but stressed its ideological identification with American Zeire Zion.

Not surprisingly, there were members of the movement who opposed any affiliation with a political party, even a party such as Zeire Zion that followed the introspective, antidogmatic teachings of Gordon himself. For these members Gordonia had to be a completely independent Labor Zionist youth movement. This antiparty trend was strengthened when—following the 1929 merger in Palestine of Hapoel Hatzair with Achdut Avodah to form Mapai— American Zeire Zion amalgamated with the Poale Zion in 1931. Gordonia maintained its independence from the new Labor Zionist organization, establishing its headquarters in Baltimore.

Gordonia reached its organizational peak in 1933. When the movement's national convention convened in Baltimore that December, the movement had 580 members with chapters in ten cities. The convention was dominated by discussions about relationships with other organizations, the question of personal chalutziut—or compulsory aliyah—and the role of the intermovement settlement organization Hechalutz. In the end, the convention came out strongly in favor of compulsory aliyah. The decision proved to be costly: within six months a genuine crisis had developed, as several leading members left the movement altogether. The decline in strength was rapid; by the end of 1934, Gordonia had strong chapters in only three cities, Philadelphia, Toronto, and Baltimore, with several small groups elsewhere.

At about this time, Habonim was formed as the children's section of the Young Poale Zion Alliance. Gordonia was asked to merge with the new movement. The invitation was brought to the Gordonia national convention in Baltimore in 1935, where it was declined.

That 1935 convention committed Gordonia even further to the strict lines it had adopted in 1933. At the urging of Elisheva Kaplan, the Israeli *shlicha* (emissary) to Pioneer Women and a member of the Chever Hakvutzot kibbutz federation, a resolution was passed making aliyah mandatory for all members over the age of twenty-one. More members resigned from the movement. Again, only three chapters, Baltimore, Philadelphia, and Toronto, continued to function.

In March 1936 a new shaliach, Avraham Cohen, was dispatched from Eretz Israel to work with Gordonia. He soon realized that Habonim and Gordonia had more in common than he had thought. He revived discussions to merge the two movements, and by the time he returned to Palestine in 1937 he had negotiated the conditions for unification. The merger took place in Chicago at the "Unification Convention," April 20–23, 1938.

Dallas, the 1930s: "We Became the Outstanding Jewish Youth Group in the City"

Yapha (Ginger) Chesnick Jacobs
Dallas 1985

In 1929, Yaakov Levin, of blessed memory, was appointed principal of The Hebrew School of Dallas, Texas. As was his pattern each time he came to a new city, he formed a Gordonia group with his pupils.

Yaakov would hold weekly meetings where we read A. D. Gordon's essays and the biographies of Zionist and Labor Zionist leaders. We studied the history of the Zionist movement and celebrated Jewish holidays in the framework of the Hebrew School and within the context of Gordonia. On Saturday nights and Sundays we collected for the Jewish National Fund. In 1937 we sold "shekalim"—voting memberships—for the World Zionist Congress.

After the national merger with Habonim, we became a Habonim group. When Camp Bonim, our Habonim summer camp, was established in 1941, our membership grew, and we became recognized as the outstanding Jewish youth group in the city. We were known as having an intense program. People traveled from as far away as New Orleans and Denver to attend. Meanwhile, Yaakov Levin set up Habonim groups in San Antonio and Houston.

Dallas Habonim was a strongly activist group. I spent many days and nights drafting and circulating petitions for Zionist causes. During the trying days of the "Exodus" episode, we conducted a sticker campaign to rally support for the beleaguered refugee ship. In 1946 and 1947, members of Dallas Habonim attended the Habonim Institute in New York and the leadership training seminar at Camp Kinneret, Michigan. As the Dallas delegate to the Habonim national convention in 1946, I proudly took my place with the other delegates when we picketed the British Embassy in Washington, D.C.

In 1949, Yaakov Levin left Dallas, and most of our young leaders left for college and military service. The drain proved to be too great, and Habonim in Dallas declined. Without local leadership, Camp Bonim was also affected, and as stipulated in our charter, it was sold in 1952. The proceeds went to the Jewish National Fund.

Although Habonim has not functioned in Dallas for many years, we still feel its intense effect on us. Several of our members have gone to Israel. Former Habonim members, both those from the local movement and those who have moved here, have become active in the local Jewish community. And there is a special camaraderie among all of us who shared in that very special experience. We still greet each other with a gleam in our eyes, as if to ask: "Are you going to the meeting tonight?"

The First Habonim Kibbutz: Naame, 1939–1940

Shulamit Beitan
Kibbutz Kfar Blum 1985

Standing on the deck waving goodbye to the people who had come to see me off to Palestine, I was—as far as I was concerned—completely cutting my ties with my American past. I expected to see my friends again in Palestine, but as for my family, this was the final goodbye. Travel was just too difficult in 1938.

I had come to this step through my involvement with Young Poale Zion and Habonim, which were a natural extension of my home environment. But the act of actually going to Palestine was a very personal step. I had just gotten married and I was going to my husband's kibbutz, Afikim, where a group of American Young Poale Zion had settled in the early thirties. I was starting a new life, presumably fulfilling the values I had learned in the movement. But I was thinking only of myself.

In those days, those of us who came to Palestine looked ahead, never behind. The movement we had left in America rarely figured in our thoughts or plans. Aliyah was a personal act, and the Americans who came to Palestine did so with the idea of being absorbed into the Yishuv, the Jewish community of Palestine, without setting themselves apart. Once, I recall, Benny Applebaum (later Ben-Zion Ilan) and I called on Golda Meyerson at the Histadrut to discuss future steps for absorbing Americans. One of the earliest American Poale Zionists to reach Palestine, Golda had never asked for special treatment and never offered it to others. After hearing our suggestion, she drew herself up in her most awe-inspiring manner and thundered: "Why should Americans be given preferential treatment?"

Not surprisingly, then, my first year at Afikim was spent trying to become a Palestinian kibbutznik as quickly as possible. I diligently tried to learn the language, and got rid of all my American clothes so I could wear the same rags as everybody else. But at the end of the year, just before I was eligible to become a member of Afikim, I was contacted by a group of American immigrants, the last to arrive in Palestine before the outbreak of war in September 1939.

The Americans, graduates like me of the Young Poale Zion Alliance and Habonim, were preparing themselves for settlement on the land, and were looking for others to join them. Suddenly, it seemed obvious to me that I belonged with them. We held a series of meetings to decide our future. We wanted to maintain our ties with the movement in America but at the same time to join with other groups in Palestine and assimilate completely. We began to scout among young kibbutzim, and groups preparing to settle on the land, for a group that would accept all of our members together and be willing to help serve as a base in Palestine for American Habonim. After visits to Ma'aleh Hachamisha, Mishmarot, and elsewhere, we decided in February 1940 to join with the "Anglo-Baltic Labor Brigade," a settlement group made up of young immigrants from England and the Baltic countries of Latvia, Lithuania, and Estonia. They were living together in the village of Binyamina and pooling their income from day labor.

The group had spent time at Afikim and Kibbutz Kinneret, learning agriculture and communal life, and was now waiting for its own settlement site. The Baltic members were happy to accept our condition to become a focal point for American Habonim, and even welcomed American aliyah to help the kibbutz grow. Thus it was that our kibbutz became the first settlement project of American Habonim. We let the movement know we were expecting them. Naame-Kfar Blum, as our kibbutz came to be known, became the movement's focus.

From Brooklyn to Palestine, 1939: How To Make Aliyah

Engee Caller
Kibbutz Kfar Blum 1985

Coming on aliyah was a complicated procedure during the days of the British Mandate. Some of the roads we traveled to get there were legal, some were not.

The most sought-after route for the would-be *oleh,* or immigrant, was via a certificate of entry, issued by the British and distributed by the World Zionist Organization to potential immigrants around the world. Throughout the 1930s, these certificates steadily decreased in number as Britain sought to appease the increasingly violent Arab opposition to Zionism. In May 1939 the door was practically slammed shut with the issuance of the infamous White Paper, putting a limit of 15,000 per year, or 1,250 a month, on the number of Jews allowed into Palestine. Of course, the plight of European Jewry demanded that the WZO use most of its certificates for rescue.

There were other ways to get in, though. One could enter the country as a "capitalist." A capitalist was someone who could show the British he or she had enough money to avoid becoming an economic burden on the country. Habonim was able to produce several such capitalists. After a member entered Palestine, flashing the appropriate sum in front of the British officials, he or she would return the money to the movement, which would pass it on to another "capitalist" about to enter the country.

People married to Palestinian citizens were allowed to enter the country legally as well. Not surprisingly, more than one Palestinian citizen married a prospective immigrant only to divorce after several months and then re-marry.

Another legal route was available to the children of people who had joined groups intending to take over citrus plantations prepared by the Histadrut citrus cultivation organization. Moshav Bet Herut was founded that way.

And then there were the methods that did not just bend the rules but broke them completely. After World War II, Habonim members would come to the country as students under the G.I. Bill of Rights, or simply as tourists, and then "get lost." Others bought tickets to travel to Greece by boat and then, with the aid of the Haganah, jumped ship in Haifa. And finally, many members of Habonim participated in the "illegal" immigration organized to bring in the refugees from Europe. Those who were caught and banished to Cyprus often would slip into Palestine later on small fishing boats.

I arrived in Palestine in early March 1939, just before the White Paper, drawn there by three important influences—my home, my school, and Habonim. My parents' house in the Bensonhurst section of Brooklyn was strictly religious and served as a community center for those of our neighbors who had come from the same Eastern European shtetl. Many times I felt that I still lived in the shtetl myself. My first language was Yiddish. I learned to read from the Yiddish papers I brought home for my parents. My education included the Sholem Aleichem Folkshul, where we spent our afternoons being introduced to a secularist view of Jewish history and Yiddish culture.

I was introduced to Habonim at a Chanukah party in Manhattan where I was taken by my older sister Bella, who was working in the Pioneer Women's office. Watching children my age singing Yiddish and Hebrew songs, dancing the hora, performing skits about Jewish history and Palestine, fired my imagination.

At my invitation, a few of my friends from school and folkshul met in Bensonhurt for a few Habonim sessions. But the chapter was short-lived, and my *madrichim* suggested I join the Kadima Club of Young Poale Zion, which met in Flatbush, quite a distance from my home. I soon established a regular routine: after sharing a traditional Shabbat meal with my family, I would hurriedly wash the dishes and then dash off to the Kadima meeting and all the Habonim activities that followed.

Oddly enough, despite my deep involvement in the movement, I arrived in Palestine without much thought or planning. I entered on a three-month visitor's visa, but after two months at Kibbutz Kfar Giladi, the kibbutz decided to legalize my status in the country. A young man, a stranger to me, was asked to accompany me to the chief rabbi of Tiberias and "take me as his wife." Ironically, upon hearing my name, the chief rabbi was overjoyed. He knew my parents well, and now he had the honor of marrying their daughter.

A few weeks after the "wedding," en route to a national kibbutz conference near Tel Aviv, my bus was stopped by the border patrol at Rosh Pinah. As usual, the police, on the lookout for illegal immigrants, demanded that the passengers show their identification papers. Since I had neglected to have my papers prepared to reflect my new status, I brazenly showed them my American passport, hoping they would not notice the expired visa. No such luck.

I was yanked off the bus and questioned by the British commanding officer. Fortunately, he accepted my explanation and reprimanded me for not applying for my ID immediately after my marriage. And, since he and his wife were headed for Metulla that very day, he offered to drive me back to Kfar Giladi.

But that presented some problems. Etiquette would demand that I invite them in for tea, perhaps introduce them to my husband. How could I manage that? I had no idea where my husband's tent or cabin was. I mulled on these troubling thoughts as I climbed into their car and headed north.

A few miles from Rosh Pinah, a jeep suddenly came careening towards us and braked just in front of the car. Out bounded the secretary of Kfar Giladi and my "husband." They had been alerted to what was happening by a very effective grapevine.

I introduced the officer and his wife to my husband and thanked them profusely for the lift. After they left, my husband asked, "What would you have done if I had given you a good, resounding husbandly kiss?"

"I would have given you a good resounding slap in the face," I replied, astounded at his audacity. The next day I applied for an ID card.

Years later, when he was ready to marry in earnest, my "husband" and I went to the chief rabbi of Tiberias to get a divorce. The poor rabbi spent hours trying to convince us to make up and give our marriage another chance. He hated to see the daughter of good friends get divorced. And though he saw my parents several times in the years to come, I don't think he was ever told of my fictitious marriage.

Binyamina, 1939: The Birth of Kfar Blum

Shulamit Beitan and Engee Caller
Kibbutz Kfar Blum 1985

During the late fall and early winter of 1939–40, a kibbutz settlement group founded by English and Baltic youth—augmented by an American group—congregated in Binyamina, where we sought out whatever work we could find. We worked in citrus orchards, in a quarry, on private farms, and as shepherds, teachers, and household laborers. At the same time, we established our own small farm. We cut lumber and set up a clothes-pin factory—Israel's very first kibbutz factory. We sent members to work at the Dead Sea potash works and the Atlit salt works.

As a result of the European war that broke out in September, citrus exports had been cut back, and jobs became scarce. We rented a hotel in Metulla to help absorb those members who could not find work. From our base in Metulla, we continued to look for work. By now, however, the group was committed to settling in the Upper Galilee. Nearby, in the vast Huleh swamp, we found a small hill known as Naame, and there we settled.

It took a long time for us to convince the official bodies of the Yishuv to let us stay there. Malaria was endemic; the swamp had to be drained. And there were other settlement groups ahead of us on the waiting list for land. But in the end the Jewish National Fund gave its blessings and on November 10, 1943 we celebrated our Aliyah Day.

We named our kibbutz in honor of Leon Blum, the former premier of France, a Jew, Zionist, and loyal socialist. Those in the settlement group who had remained at Binyamina joined us at Kfar Blum. And there we lived out the story of a young kibbutz. We drained the swamps; we cultivated the land; we built factories; we created a way of life.

Once we were settled at Kfar Blum, we opened an office on the kibbutz to maintain contact with the Habonim movements abroad, and to represent it to the various powers in the country. Those of us who came from America involved ourselves in the problems of American newcomers and let our views be known on the choice of shlichim to be sent to America. In fact, we demanded that prospective shlichim be screened at Kfar Blum and spend some time here with American-born settlers. That system held for several years.

World War II all but ended American aliyah. Most of the Habonim members we expected to join us were drafted or were busy trying to maintain the movement and its *hachshara* farms in America. Still, even in those trying times, Kfar Blum remained the center of Habonim's attention. It even served as a rallying point for Habonim members serving in North Africa and the European theater of the war. They would visit us whenever they could. For our part, we corresponded continuously with America and the Americans in uniform.

When the war drew to a close, most of the members who had committed themselves to aliyah to Kfar Blum found ways of getting here. In the course of time, Kfar Blum began to serve as the introduction to kibbutz life for many who then went on to settle on newer, younger kibbutzim. Today we see ourselves as the first link of a chain that reaches the length and breadth of Israel, literally from the Upper Galilee to Grofit, near Eilat.

Kfar Blum today is known as a "liberal" kibbutz. We have long encouraged our members to pursue higher education even when their field of study was not applicable to the kibbutz economy. Our younger children were free to tour the world, and we were sensitive to the needs of many of our members to visit family in their lands of origin.

Due to American Habonim's influence, our attitude toward traditional

Jewish values was far more tolerant than most secular kibbutzim. We included reading the Torah as part of our Bar and Bat Mitzvah ceremonies. We openly questioned the wisdom of having our children sleep in communal houses at young ages and became one of the first kibbutzim to convert to having children sleep at home. We felt this would strengthen family ties and the bond between the family and the kibbutz.

This attitude has helped to enable a high proportion of our children to settle among us—or to return home after years abroad—rather than feel compelled to leave and find another home. And to this day, we feel that we still have an impact on American Jewish youth. For that we are proud.

Consolidation of a Youth Movement, and Habonim "Under Fire"

David Breslau
New York 1960

"Under Fire" was the phrase used by the movement to describe the period during which the Young Poale Zion Alliance–Habonim convention met in Chicago in April 1938. It was a time when the riots in Palestine and the ever-increasing persecutions of Jews in Europe made it seem as if the whole world had turned against the Jewish people.

Helping the movement chart its course during those early critical years were the first of the *shlichim,* the emissaries sent from Eretz Israel to work with the youth movements overseas. Ben-Zion Ilan (Applebaum) of Afikim was the first official *shaliach* to Habonim. During much of the time he was in America, Enzo Sereni served as the shaliach to Hechalutz. Together, Ben-Zion and Sereni set the tradition for shlichim to North America that has been followed to this day. Ben-Zion was a graduate of the Young Poale Zion Alliance in the Bronx, and rendered yeoman service in all aspects of YPZA and Habonim work. He visited all parts of the United States and Canada, conducted seminars and conferences, and assisted in every aspect of the movement's work.

Wherever Ben-Zion went, he brought with him the message of chalutzic pioneering. But his was a realistic pioneering; he not only impressed the movement's members with the adventure and romance of the chalutz, but he delineated the hard reality of life in Israel. He introduced Eretz Israel into the movement as a living reality with its problems and struggles in the economic, political, cultural, and social fields. He was a disciple of Berl Katznelson, the revered spiritual leader of the Histadrut, and he introduced Berl's techniques into the movement. Through Berl's teachings, published in the pamphlet *Revolutionary Constructivism,* the movement's socialist ideology was freed from certain fetishes and dogmas. The members learned to analyze social and Jewish problems without being afraid of "what the gentiles will say," and learned to associate with Labor Zionist ideology the finer arts, music, Hebrew poetry, and good reading.

Those were dark years for political Zionism. Following the abandonment of the British government's 1937 Partition Plan came the first intimation of a change in British policy in the direction of appeasing the Arabs. American Zionists were called upon time and again to protest proposed changes which, it was feared, would freeze the Yishuv into permanent minority status. The most vigorous of these protest actions was in October 1938, when we first heard that a proposed White Paper would radically constrict Jewish immigration and land acquisition. Our movement played an active role in the protest action. With our active cooperation, the National Emergency Youth Committee for Palestine was convoked in New York, drawing in many Jewish and some non-Jewish youth organizations. Under the committee's guidance, our chaverim in many cities sent telegrams, signed petitions, distributed literature and attended mass meetings to protest the proposed policy. It was the first of many occasions when we would join with the rest of the American Zionist movement to protest British appeasement.

The National Emergency Youth Committee for Palestine gave the first stimulus to leaders of various Zionist youth organizations to plan a program of joint activity. But it took more than a year and a half until something was crystallized in the form of the Council of Zionist Youth Organizations.

Our relations with non-Zionist youth organizations during this period were a complex matter. The 1930s saw the rise of a great many youth groups and federations of youth groups on the American scene, many of them dedicated to high-minded goals of world peace. As the decade progressed, however, the role of the Communist party and its various offshoots in these forums became a controversial matter, for progressive youth movements no less than for conservative-leaning ones. The Youth Division of the American Jewish Congress, for example, disintegrated completely, due largely to the infiltration of several Communist youth groups and individuals. Attempts by the Zionist groups to oust the Communists from the Youth Division and later to check the spread of their antidemocratic influence were futile, often because of a lack of unity among the Zionists themselves. The end of their influence came with the change in the Communist line, following the Stalin–Hitler pact in Eastern Europe.

Our relations with the American Student Union came to a formal end with a decision we adopted in February 1940, instructing all our members to withdraw from that organization. The direct cause of our action was the failure of the union's convention at Madison, Wisconsin, to condemn the Soviet invasion of Finland. Our decision to withdraw, however, was largely a formality, since our chaverim had left the union individually long before, as Communist domination of the organization became more and more apparent.

An attempt was made during this time by the Young People's Socialist League, the youth wing of Norman Thomas's mainstream Socialist party, to bring together a wide spectrum of youth groups in a Campaign for Youth Needs. Our representatives were observers on the provisional committee of the campaign, and our national executive committee weighed carefully whether or not the YPZA should affiliate formally. The purposes of the campaign seemed worthy, but our executive was skeptical about its efficacy, since it succeeded in attracting very few groups beyond its own immediate orbit of democratic socialists. Nonetheless, we continued to attempt joint activities with labor groups on a local level in various cities. Outstanding among these was the Chicago Labor Youth Council in which our members played a prominent role.

A high point in our relations with other youth groups was the Habonim appearance at the second World Youth Congress, held at Vassar College near New York in August 1938. We were represented at the congress through unofficial observers, but we made our outstanding contribution when a group from Camp Kvutza at Accord participated in the Pageant of All Nations at one Congress session. Our chaverim presented a pageant of song, drama, and dance on the subject of the rebuilding of Palestine and our struggle against Arab-German-Italian fascism. The presentation made a strong impression on the large audience, and helped to counteract the anti-Zionist propaganda of the Arab delegation.

Internally, we went through an intensive organizing drive during these early years, stationing organizers and shlichim in various parts of the country and undertaking membership drives, often with the help of the senior Labor Zionist movement. We raised thousands of dollars for the Jewish National Fund and the Histadrut Campaign in addition to soliciting for our own needs.

A magazine for our younger chaverim, *Haboneh,* began appearing regularly. *News and Views,* the publication for the older chaverim, came out every two weeks, and beginning in the fall of 1940 was published in printed form. There were other publications for group leaders and special purposes. In 1938 and 1939 we began holding regular mid-winter seminars. The number of summer camps grew from six to nine, and the end of the summer became another favored time for get-togethers.

One particularly memorable get-together was the national *Pegisha* (conference) at the Habonim camp at Accord at the end of the summer of 1939. It was there that our chaverim first met with the newly arrived shlichim who had come in a single, "large group" of six, and were destined to remain throughout the impending war. The pegisha was convoked as the clouds of war hung heavily overhead. In fact, the pegisha itself commenced with the outbreak of the war in Europe. September 1 and 2, when the news of the invasion of Poland reached us, and even more so the night of September 3, when the British ultimatum to Germany lapsed and the final declaration of war by Britain was announced over the radio, will long be remembered by all the participants in the pegisha. They spent most of that night glued to the few radio sets in the cars parked on the premises.

The *machaneh menahelim* (leaders' camp) convened the following year, in 1940, was the most important educational project undertaken by our movement up to that time. Nearly one hundred chaverim assembled for three weeks at Camp Kvutza in Pipersville, Pennsylvania. For the first time, the national program included not only lectures and discussions but also instruction in handicrafts, singing, dancing, Hebrew, and scoutcraft.

Young Poale Zion Alliance–Habonim activities within the Hechalutz organization intensified during these years. The outbreak of the war placed new challenges before Hechalutz, which was structured to prepare young adults for their future lives in Eretz Israel. With the outbreak of the war, Hechalutz formed what were called *plugot*, or "units," including two that featured aviation training. Immediately after the outbreak of the war, a substantial group of our chaverim left on aliyah, the last group to leave until the war ended.

In February 1940, a group of eighteen chaverim joined the Kibbutz Anglo-Balti at Binyamina. This was the beginning of the concentration of our chaverim in one kibbutz, which eventually became Kfar Blum.

As chalutziut became more and more firmly established at the core of Habonim's program, the children's movement began to have an impact on its "parent" organization, the YPZA. The group leader, feeling a personal responsibility for his work, very often reached the conclusion that there could be no dichotomy between the ideals he was teaching and his own subjective attitude. Basic discussions ensued about the aims of the movement and its organizational structure. The merger with Gordonia in April 1938 only intensified this evolution of YPZA–Habonim in the direction of a chalutzic Zionist youth movement.

In 1939, there were about three thousand members enrolled in the movement, three-quarters of them in Habonim, the rest in YPZA. The movement had functioning units in about thirty cities. Some ten YPZA groups were formally transferred to the senior Labor Zionist movement during these years as their members reached the age of twenty-one.

Finally, at the Cincinnati convention in 1940, Habonim and YPZA were formally merged. Henceforth, Habonim would be a comprehensive chalutzic youth movement, with membership extending in age from ten to twenty-five.

The newly united movement was organized into four age divisions, the oldest being the former YPZA, now known as *Noar* ("youth"). High-schoolers were called *Bonim* ("builders"), twelve-to-fourteen-year-olds were *Tzofim* ("scouts"), and the youngest group became *Solelim* ("pavers-of-the-way"). In each city, each separate age group was led by a *menahel* (counselor) drawn from the *Noar;* all the members in a city formed a single city chapter called a *Machaneh* ("camp"). The terms were changed in 1960.

The Cincinnati convention also adopted a declaration of principles for the new youth movement. The statement, printed on the blue membership cards of generations of Habonim members, has remained substantially intact to the present day.

The Goals of Habonim: Cincinnati, December 1940

1. To strengthen the bonds between American Jewry and Eretz Israel, and actively to support the rebuilding of the Jewish National Homeland.

2. To train young Jews to become chalutzim in Eretz Israel, and, as members of the Histadrut Ha'ovdim, to create a cooperative Jewish Commonwealth.

3. To prepare young Jews for participation in the up-building of a new social order throughout the world, based on the principles of economic and political democracy.

4. To educate young Jews toward the revitalization of traditional Jewish values; for the study of Jewish life, history, and culture; toward a feeling of identification with the Jewish people.

5. To prepare young Jews for the defense of Jewish rights everywhere.

6. To prepare young Jews for active participation in American Jewish community life.

3
The War Years

A Gathering Storm

To most Americans, World War II began on December 7, 1941, with the Japanese attack on Pearl Harbor. For Canadians, of course, as for much of the world, it broke out two years earlier, on September 1, 1939, when Nazi Germany invaded Poland. That invasion, beginning the greatest agony of the world's largest Jewish community, marked the true beginning of the war for Habonim members everywhere, including the United States.

Habonim responded immediately and actively to the war. While most of America was following it in the newspapers, Habonim members studied the war's progress daily, horrified at the nightmare enveloping European Jewry. Special educational programs were distributed, introducing younger members to the Eastern European Jewish world from which most of them had sprung. Some members even crossed the border to Canada, in the hope of enlisting in the Royal Canadian Armed Forces.

In Palestine, the European war created a painful dilemma. As subjects of the British crown, the Jews of the Yishuv had a common cause with Britain in the battle to defeat Nazism. Indeed, the Nazi juggernaut presented the Yishuv with a twofold threat: in addition to Germany's insane war against the Jewish people, the Reich's military successes were bringing Nazi troops eastward across North Africa and southward through Vichy-ruled Syria to threaten Palestine directly.

And yet, despite the common cause against Germany, Palestine Jewry harbored a deep suspicion of the crown.

Britain's attitude toward Zionism had changed for the worse during the late 1930s, under pressure from the ongoing rebellion of the Arabs of Palestine. Beginning in 1936, the Arabs of Palestine had launched into a series of violent attacks against the Yishuv, the British, and each other, spiraling into a three-year uprising against what they saw as Great Britain's sponsorship of the Zionist enterprise.

Britain had responded by forming a commission of inquiry to consider Palestine's future. The Peel Commission met throughout 1937, taking testimony from a broad range of Jewish and Arab representatives. Its recommendation—the parititition of the country into Jewish and Arab states—was greeted with ambivalence by the Zionist leadership. The Arabs, however, rejected it completely and redoubled their attacks. In the end, the partition plan had been dropped, and Britain's policymakers had gone back to the drawing board.

Finally, in May 1939, four months before the Nazi invasion of Poland, Britain issued what amounted to a declaration of war against Zionism in the form of the infamous White Paper, severely limiting the entry of Jews into Palestine just when a refuge was needed most.

The leadership of the Yishuv responded to the dilemma in the only way possible: with the decision, in Ben-Gurion's words, "to fight the Nazis as if there were no White Paper and to fight the British as if there were no Nazis."

As world Jewry prepared to enter its long night of horror, the Yishuv looked more than ever to the Jews of America to provide the moral and physical support needed for survival.

From Chicago to Accord, Autumn 1939: "That Night, We Learned to See the World Another Way"

Lakey Kahn
Tel Aviv 1985

The early autumn of 1939 stands out clearly in my mind in every detail. Above all I remember the night of September 1 when Hitler invaded Poland.

It was the close of our Habonim camping season at Camp Tel Hai in New Buffalo, Michigan, and about twenty of us ended the summer by traveling to Camp Kvutza in Accord, New York, for the *Pegisha,* a national Habonim seminar.

We were young and foolhardy, and we traveled on a shoestring attached to a wing and a prayer. Our conveyance was an open, decrepit truck that broke down repeatedly en route. Perhaps the Habonim songs we sang for hours while our vehicle was being repaired managed to lilt upward through the starlit sky to some divine Guardian who watches over children and fools. It still seems miraculous that we made it to the Catskills. Surely God must have been watching someone that fall.

The first sighting of mountainous terrain, with its greenery and its mountain streams, works magic on the flat psyche of a Midwestern child. Our previous notions of travel were limited to the winter Habonim seminar in Milwaukee. Now we felt like true world-travelers, even though our destination was a campsite with primitive facilities, little drinking water, and no electricity.

I remember becoming obsessed with a compulsion to find the source of the nearby mountain stream. One day I set out on foot. I walked and walked, becoming ever more mesmerized, and then walked some more. I kept seeing it just up ahead but—like a nomad seeking a desert oasis—it never actually materialized. I made it back to the camp at nightfall, bemused by the indignant concern of my chaverim.

On the night of September 1, we gathered around a car radio to listen to the news reports of the Nazi march into Poland. It got pretty crowded bunching up around the car, but this was our only link to the outside world.

Suddenly, as we listened, the world seemed a much more real and familiar place than we had ever known. We, the "intellectuals" of Habonim, had seen it coming. Perhaps "intellectuals" is too high-flown a term, but we knew that through Habonim and because of Habonim, we were infinitely more sensitive to the coming cataclysm than our counterparts in Chicago's Jewish ghetto. For that matter, we were probably more informed than most insular American adults.

When the seminar ended, we proceeded en masse from Accord to New York City, the site of the 1939 World's Fair. We stayed in the homes of Habonim members and wandered around the city, drinking in the dubious wonders of the Big Town. The climax of our trip was our performance for Jewish Day at the World's Fair. We were gloriously proud of ourselves and of Habonim that day: proud, secure in our feeling of belonging, and motivated by our identification with a movement that gave meaning and pattern to our lives.

All the years we had grown up in the movement back home, our parents had always been suspicious of our late-night Habonim doings—to the point where we used to take off our shoes on the landing and enter our homes barefoot in the futile hope of covering up another tardy return. But the truth was we were the paragons of innocence. After Habonim meetings, after the singing and dancing, our evenings would end with strolls through the park until the wee hours, fetching one another home and discussing the woes of the world—all based on our idealistic, romantic view of the world.

On that fateful September night at Accord, though, we learned to see the world in another way, harder and more immediate. My mind's eye still sees the faces of three shlichim, just arrived from Palestine to educate and direct Habonim groups in different parts of America. They were frowning, exchanging worried glances, acutely aware of the danger facing their dream— and by adoption, ours. They knew their lifeline was about to be severed by a world at war. At the time I had no way to understand what it was to have our country facing attack. Now, a half-century and four defensive wars later, I know it only too well.

From Afikim to Accord, Autumn 1939: "We Would Be in a Good Position to Look Out for the Yishuv"

Moshe Levin
Jerusalem 1985

In the winter of 1938, I was asked to join what was known as "the big *mishlachat,*" a special delegation headed for the United States to work with Hechalutz and Habonim.

The mishlachat idea originated with the chaverim in America and was championed by Berl Katznelson. Berl was editor of the Histadrut newspaper *Davar*, but he was much more: he was the teacher, guide, and spiritual leader of Labor Palestine. From his editor's office at *Davar* he would spin out ideas and visions about the future of Zionist labor, and we, his followers—beginning with the head of the Yishuv, David Ben-Gurion—would do our best to bring them to fruition.

In this case, Berl wanted a group of shlichim to go to America and reach out to the Jewish youth there, to draw them into the goals of Labor Palestine through the promising frameworks of Habonim and Hechalutz. In case war broke out, Berl said, we would be in a good position to look out for the Yishuv's emergency needs. We were to leave for America as soon as possible. At the time, I was a member of Kibbutz Afikim and a teacher at the regional school at Degania.

I arrived in America in August 1939, ten days before the war broke out in Europe, with my fellow shlichim Ze'ev Aharon and Shalom Wurm. Our first experience of America was Ellis Island, where we were incarcerated because we had no money and no reasonable proof that we were who we claimed to be. Ze'ev had two dollars in his pocket. I had another two. Shalom was the richest of the group—he had ten dollars. The sums hardly seemed appropriate for the official "educational delegation" awaited by our American youth movement.

Nahum Guttman came from the Habonim office to receive us, and when he learned that we had been detained by immigration, he took immediate action. Within twenty-four hours we were free and on our way to a national seminar at the Habonim camp in Accord, New York.

At Accord we immediately felt at home. Since my Palestine-British English made me "the English-speaking shaliach," I was asked to give a short lecture. Later somebody complimented me, remarking that he had never heard such bad English spoken so fluently.

Over the next few months we were joined by three more shlichim: Mala Gitlin from Hulda, Yosef Israeli from Afikim, and Aharon Remez, a recent youth movement graduate from Tel Aviv, whose father, David Remez, was one of the leaders of the Yishuv. The six of us were assigned to work in various places around the country: Mala, Yosef, and Shalom would stay in New York to try to build up Hechalutz, while Ze'ev went to Chicago, Aharon to Philadelphia, and I to Boston.

The Movement in Wartime

Aharon Remez

Tel Aviv 1985

My participation in the "big *mishlachat*" was, more than anything else, a personal quest. I was a native Israeli, a graduate of Tel Aviv's elite Gymnasium Herzliya high school, a member of the Histadrut youth movement Machanot Olim and active in the Haganah. With all that, I felt a compelling need to learn firsthand about the life of the Jews of the diaspora. I was troubled by the events in Europe and by our own increasingly bitter struggle with the British in Palestine. I needed to clarify my own understanding of the Jewish people and of Zionism. So, just before I joined a group that was to form the nucleus of a new kibbutz, Bet Ha'arava, I agreed with some trepidation in 1939 to join the mishlachat that was about to depart for America.

My knowledge of America, based on casual reading and a few conversations with the Americans living in Palestine, was confused and superficial. I imagined a vast and varied mass of immigrants, each at a different stage of adapting their European-Jewish heritage to the alien ways of America. Despite my ignorance, however, I knew my mission was important. An official of the Jewish Agency gave me some pointers before my departure, and concluded his remarks with these words: "The key to the future of the Jewish people and above all to the future of Zionism will be in the hands of this Jewry."

My first lesson in the American immigrant experience came as soon as my ship docked at New York harbor. Although I held a valid visa, I was interrogated at length by immigration officials and my baggage was searched. Then I was denied entry and shuttled off to the detention center at Ellis Island, which was jammed with immigrants and refugees seeking asylum. America was the last hope for many who had escaped Hitler.

The stories that I heard during those three days on Ellis Island served as my basic training, my introduction to the heartbreaking helplessness of a people dependent on the good will of others. Had I not been one already, my experience on Ellis Island would have converted me into an uncompromising Zionist. At the same time, I learned how little we could actually do to avert the imminent tragedy. If only we had a strong, independent state, a haven for the persecuted, a state that could fight for Jews wherever they were. If only. . . .

During my interrogation, the immigration officers quizzed me about my past. At first they thought I was a refugee, trying to settle illegally in the United States. Then they suspected that I was a terrorist, since I had been arrested several times by the British—once for organizing a demonstration in support of local produce and once for demonstrating against the 1939 White Paper. Then they decided I was a Communist, noting that I belonged to Mapai, the Israel Workers Party, a known socialist party. Even worse, I had lived on a communal farm.

The interrogations were a real opportunity to practice my English. I twisted my tongue trying to explain the meaning of Zionism and kibbutz to those immigration officials. Despite my earnest efforts to explain myself, they eventually decided I was harmless and gave me permission to enter.

New York probably overwhelms all first-time visitors. But the abrupt switch from the misery of Ellis Island to the gaiety of Broadway celebrating the newly opened World's Fair, from the hopeless desperation of the refugees I had met to the boundless optimism of the leaders of Habonim, made me feel as though I landed in another world.

The greatest salve for my spirit was a meeting with a group of Habonim members who were about to leave for Palestine. We did not know it then, but they would be the last group to leave before the outbreak of World War II.

Time and time again throughout my stay, I was struck by America's sharp contrasts. Among Habonim members, I found proud Jews ready to stand up fearlessly for freedom and independence. But they were few in number, and young. The movement was not a decisive influence in American Jewry. Still, it was an unexpected and encouraging phenomenon.

* * *

It is difficult, most difficult, to describe the life of a Zionist youth movement during World War II. The war began in the wake of an agreement between the Soviet Union and Nazi Germany; this pact cast a shadow on American youth and their attitude toward the war. The debate centered on whether the American people should remain neutral or prepare for war.

In those early days, the Communists demonstrated in the streets of cities across America demanding that President Roosevelt cease his efforts to prepare the nation for war. Hashomer Hatza'ir, with its leftist orientation, made an all-out effort to draw the Zionist youth movements away from any public sympathy toward Roosevelt's policy. Within Jewish liberal youth circles the same debate raged.

Habonim, and other youth groups influenced by the movement, immediately adopted a clear stand on the war question. They supported the president, absolutely rejected the policy of "neutralist" circles, and condemned the strange front, ranging from reactionaries to Communists, which supported the Stalin-Hitler pact. The movement's stand was a direct result of its ideological orientation, which was based on absolute opposition to dictatorship in any form whether Communist or Hitlerist; on the assumption that democracy must defend itself and not appear soft or decadent; on complete identification with the problems of the Jewish people; and on a belief that the future of the Jewish people would be assured under a system of true democracy.

Habonim's *madrichim* and *shlichim* throughout North America lived with Eastern and Central European Jewry during that tragic era of their destruction. The news that reached us was vague, but it sufficed to keep each heart hinged to events behind the war front. We searched for ways to help.

It was during those troubled days that we formed what we called The Teheran Group. The U.S. government was subcontracting to large private companies to build certain public projects in friendly countries. One of them was the paving of roads in Teheran, Iran, in order to improve the transportation of vital war materiel through the Middle East. It occurred to us that if we were to send a group of American boys who were well-trained and chalutz-minded to work in Iran, they would be able to help the Palestinian units of the British army who were working in the same area to establish contact with Jewish refugees then gathering on the Russian-Iranian border, and to bring at least a part of them to Eretz Israel.

We searched for weeks for a Jewish contractor engaged in this type of work with experience in huge projects, until we finally found the right person. Through him we were given the opportunity to send a group of boys to work in Iran. To be sure, their contribution to bringing Jews from the Russian border into Eretz Israel was comparatively modest. But for our movement, thirsty for some sort of practical activity, the Teheran Group was a valuable educational force. It enabled our members to feel themselves a partner in the historic events then going on around them.

With the outbreak of war between Germany and Russia, followed by the Japanese attack on the U.S. Navy at Pearl Harbor, ideological differences between the Zionist youth movements were eliminated. Habonim members were drafted to the army, including shlichim. Arrangements were made to continue the movement's activities without them, filling their places with younger members until the end of the war.

The outbreak of war in Europe had an immediate and powerful impact on the Jewish and Zionist communities in America. As isolationism grew, Jews tended to keep a low profile, intent on proving their loyalty to America. The Zionist movement was plagued by internal dissension and ideological confusions. In the face of European Jewry's mounting agony, it pursued a course of quiet diplomacy that would ultimately fail to rescue the Jews. The idea of organizing a Jewish fighting force made American Zionists uneasy, and so did the demand to create an independent Jewish state in Palestine, as formulated by Ben-Gurion in preparation for the Zionist leadership's Biltmore Conference of 1942.

In contrast with the mainstream American Zionist leadership, Habonim identified with Zionism's activist wing, committed to aggressive pursuit of Zionist goals by creating facts on the ground in Palestine. As the war progressed, however, the conditions in which the movement had to operate became ever more difficult. Aliyah was impossible. Educational activities waned as the leadership was called to military service. The training farm at Creamridge became a way station, not on the road to Palestine, but to the U.S. Army.

After countless discussions, the movement leadership and the shlichim decided that despite the shortage of leaders, we would try to intensify our educational program for younger members. In addition, Habonim would provide prearmy training to older members in cooperation with Hechalutz, the umbrella Zionist pioneering organization. Finally, it would try to get people to Palestine in every way possible.

Furthermore, Habonim organized pioneering brigades, made up of graduates of Hechalutz. Brigade members studied first aid, communications, aviation, and other skills that might prove useful in the future. I was the organizer of the aviation brigade. We trained two groups of fliers. Most of us soon joined Allied air forces. Many eventually made it to Palestine and were among the founders of the Israel Air Force.

At its inception, Habonim may have been something of an artificial transplant of European movements. But it quickly became a unique organization in its own right. And the Habonim graduates who have come to Israel represent the best characteristics of progressive American democracy and Zionist idealism. For me, my association with them has been a constant source of renewal for my Zionist convictions and my social values.

Brooklyn, 1941: "We in Kvutza Must Grow Strong in Our Beliefs"

Arthur M. Goldberg
Brooklyn 1941

In 1933, as we were preparing for Camp Kvutza, the Nazi power was sweeping through Germany.

As we packed our bags in 1939, our thoughts turned to the fall of Czechoslovakia. Another nation had crumbled because it believed in truth and decency.

As we returned home from Kvutza that season, civilization was being crushed. War had come to a world that had not known peace.

Last year we came to Kvutza with heavy hearts. France, the symbol of man's hope, had been defeated by the Nazi military machine, and Italy was in the war. The Mediterranean was a war zone and the first bombs had fallen on Eretz Israel.

Now a Nazi band of steel is stretching into the Near East and is tightening about Eretz Israel—a band of steel that reaches around our hearts.

We are again preparing to go to Kvutza. To us, Kvutza never has been an ordinary camp. To us, Kvutza has been a place where the things we believed could be practiced. It is in Kvutza that there is democracy. It is in Kvutza that all are equal. Our Kvutza is a place where we might learn and plan for the day when we could return to Eretz Israel.

In our Kvutza, we could dream and hope together for a day when there would be no war, when men might live a happier life in peace and security.

This is no ordinary season for a far-from-ordinary Kvutza. During this season, we must win new faith in our beliefs. We have not yet had to fight for these beliefs of ours. But others are fighting. The British and their allies are fighting for the same things. The Jews and all others of Europe who believed in freedom have long endured the oppression of the swastika because of their belief in the principles of decency. The chalutzim of Eretz Israel are standing to their guns to defend what they have built and their dreams for the future. We in Kvutza must grow strong in our beliefs and let those who now stand in the front lines know that they can count on us for whatever lies within our power to give in this fight for the future.

Notes on Our Youth Movement, 1942

Shlomo Grodzensky

New York 1942

In the course of more than a quarter century, our Party youth has undergone several metamorphoses. In its first phase, the accent of its program was on Yiddishism. Club activities were conducted in Yiddish and the influence of the extreme Yiddishists was very strong.

In the second phase, the youth movement made an effort to model itself along the lines of party youth in Europe, particularly Poland, from where many of the leading members had recently arrived. Labor Palestine occupied a central place in the ideology of Poale Zion youth, but the values of pioneering Zionism remained foreign to its spirit.

In the early 1930s, under the influence of the Histadrut's overseas representatives, Young Poale Zion added *chalutziut*—pioneering—to its program. But the transition seemed artificial and mechanical. Chalutziut was con-

Reprinted from *Der Yiddisher Kemfer,* Labor Zionist weekly, December 25, 1942. Translated from Yiddish by Akiva Skidell.

ceived as an expression of youthful revolt, socialist self-fulfillment, an anti-dote to the fashionable philistinism of the young generation—anything but what it essentially was: service to the Jewish people. Many people in the youth movement were in the shadow of the radical marketplace of ideas of the 1930s. From about 1929 until Britain's 1938 Munich agreement with Hitler, they were under the illusion that the world was on the eve of the inevitable socialist revolution. During this period the youth movement suf-fered from low morale, from a constant fear that it was not socialist enough. It was not a question of unperformed socialist acts, but of making sure that the ideology was as radical as that of other youth groups.

Today we can clearly state that this soul searching is past. Our youth has found a way for itself that leads to a well-defined goal. Its rootedness in Jewish life and Zionism, and its involvement in *chalutziut* and bonds with Labor Palestine, are no longer subjects for prolonged debate. They are the values that the movement lives by. The aim of Habonim is to deepen the knowledge and understanding of what is happening in the Jewish world.

Several factors led to this transformation. The "revolutionary" market-place of the 1930s has disappeared. Communism no longer holds sway over large masses of Jewish youth, as it once did. The Moscow Trials and the Hitler-Stalin Pact served to discredit communism as a political movement.

Norman Thomas and his followers in the Socialist Party have lost face, too, by their connection with the America First Committee, the isolationist movement whose leading spokesman is the anti-Semite Charles Lindbergh. Our youth is now ready to face reality—the fateful war, anti-Semitism, the need for the reconstruction of the world after the war.

But Habonim has changed in other ways, too, a change which coincided with the change of name from Young Poale Zion to Habonim. The change is in the character of the leadership. Habonim is headed today by young people who have received a good Jewish education, including Hebrew. The sources of their Jewishness are no longer penny brochures or hastily assem-bled tracts. The schools they attend equip them with a true Jewish cultural heritage. The sources of their heritage are accessible to them, as are the sources of the Palestine labor movement. This has put the stamp of authen-ticity and rootedness on the entire movement.

In the course of the past year, I was privileged to spend many hours with these young people in New York and, during the summer, at camp in the country. A true beginning has been made. Finally, some sort of bridge has been built between us, the immigrant generation, and the young generation of American Jews. They are American Jews, products of the American Jew-ish environment, and this no doubt involves some limitations. But the main elements are in place—a naive Jewish wholeness, an absolute identification with the totality of the Jewish people and with the pain of its fate in its dispersion, a readiness to share the Jewish burden, a true willingness to strike root in its cultural heritage, and chalutziut.

About one hundred and twenty-five members of Habonim have already taken the final, fateful step—aliyah. Many of them can be found on the

Anglo-Baltic Kibbutz, now known as Kfar Blum, which is today the central rallying point of aliyah for Habonim. From time to time, I see the small bulletin this kibbutz publishes for its members in the English-speaking countries: America, England, South Africa, and Australia. You will find no high-flown language about heroism and revolution. There is a quiet note of happiness over the effort to strike root once again, to restructure one's life and one's inner being, over the opportunity to serve the Jewish people day in, day out, quietly and without fanfare.

Sometimes these bulletins contain some family news: so-and-so has married, given birth to a child. When I read these bits of news, I think of the grandparents, Jewish immigrants to America who dreamed all their lives of going to the Land of Israel, but never made it. The realization of the dream came only in the third generation and much joy is found in the reports on these Jewish families—the healthy cells in our national body—at a time when blood is streaming from millions of wounds.

The war has, of course, affected Habonim greatly. More than two hundred of its members are already serving in the army and in the coming months many more will join its ranks. The leadership is trying to create the instruments to allow the movement to continue functioning. The younger members have to move into positions of greater responsibility. Efforts are being made to prepare them for their new role. Should the war continue for several more years, their turn to serve in the army will also come.

The present convention of Habonim is far from being an ordinary one. It will be an informal gathering of good friends, several days of spiritual stocktaking, of common learning from one another. For many, it will provide an opportunity to take leave of their friends before they put on a uniform and are sent to some distant military base. They hope to meet again in the not-too-distant future, in the ranks of our own war for Jewish rebirth.

From Washington to New York, 1942:
"Each Individual Had the Responsibility to Struggle"

Arthur Goren
Jerusalem 1985

What follows is not the recollection of significant historical events but the youthful fragments of a larger collective memory—the memory of a Habonim past.

When I joined Habonim at age thirteen, in 1939, it was partly through

fortune, partly by destiny. My mother was an active member of Pioneer
Women and her friends had children my age. Soon after my family moved
to Washington, D.C., I was invited to a meeting.

The meeting was in my home, but I was reluctant to attend by myself, so
I asked a school friend, Hank Meisels, to accompany me. Ephie Bugatch
was there, the son of a Pioneer Woman friend of my mother, as was Moshe
"Itchy" Goldberg, a Habonim organizer from New York. The evening's main
activity was centered around the ping pong table. Hank and I soon joined
Ephie's group, "Nachshon," and met Duvvy Glassman, the group's leader
or *menahel*. Despite the inauspicious start, Moshe, Duvvy, Hank, and I have
lived in Israel for more than thirty-five years now.

Over the next two years I apparently established myself as "leadership
material." I served on committees, went to camp, was tabbed for the leadership course, and then was authorized by the executive committee of Washington Habonim to become a menahel myself. My first task was to recruit
the members I would lead. I don't recall if I succeeded.

I do recall, however, that when the Nachshon group elected me as its
representative to the executive committee, the committee was controlled by
another Habonim group, Kvutzat Brenner, whose members were a year or
two older than us. Duvvy led the Young Turks of Nachshon in a powerful
struggle with the Brenner crowd. I was his loyal lieutenant. We were fourteen
years old.

In the spring of 1941, the national Hechalutz organization organized a
major conference in New York City for Zionist youth movements. No less
a figure than David Ben-Gurion himself, chairman of the Jewish Agency
Executive, was to deliver the keynote address and participate in the sessions.
The national secretariat of Habonim urged its branches across the country
to send delegates.

One evening, after our meeting in the Jewish Community Center had
ended, Tova Siegel and Betty Temin, two leading figures in Washington Habonim, informed me that the executive had selected me as a representative
to the Hechalutz conference. "At the conference," I was told, "you will get
up and say you represent Washington Habonim. You will put us on the
map." The executive had allowed five dollars, half the round-trip bus fare to
New York, for me to put Washington on the map.

As my departure time approached, my pride at being selected as the lone
delegate to speak for Washington gave way to fear and anxiety. How would I
find the courage to stand up and speak before such an august conference, perhaps before Ben-Gurion himself? What if I had nothing to say? Suppose the
debate was over my head? It did not help much even when Tova assured me
that the national office people would tell me what to say. In the end, I had to
get up and make the speech. There was no retreat; I had taken the five dollars.

In New York, I stayed at the home of Dave Breslau, the national secretary
of Habonim. He was friendly in a distant way. I noticed there was nobody
there even close to my age.

As I dutifully sat through the first day's deliberations, I decided that the best time to put Washington on the map would be the last day. And when the final day rolled around, I began framing my speech in my mind. I wrote the first line on a piece of paper.

By mid-afternoon, when the last session began, I knew I had to somehow summon the courage to get up and say something, anything, and yet not bring shame to my leaders—Breslau, Shirley Lashner, and others—who were seated in the row in front of me. Several times, I began to raise my hand to ask for the floor, only to pull it down again in retreat.

Time had just about run out when Tova's and Betty's confidence that I would speak gave me a tiny bit of courage to raise my hand just a little. "Let fate decide," I thought. If the chairman, Avraham Schenker of Hashomer Hatza'ir, failed to see my hand, I could accuse him of political bias.

Schenker looked in my direction but then his gaze seemed to move on. Suddenly, unexpectedly, his arm pointed directly at me. The floor was mine.

I rose in a sweat. Breslau and the others turned to hear what Washington's delegate would say. I read my first sentence and then my mind went blank. I forced myself to ramble on with disconnected thoughts and phrases. The room rocked slightly. I was dizzy. First Breslau turned around again, then Lashner, then the others. With the backs of my leaders towards me, I abruptly sat down in the middle of a sentence. How embarrassed they must be. What shame I had brought upon all.

In later years, that incident has come to my mind several times. Once a line from Ben-Gurion's biography caught my eye. At fourteen, it seems, he was one of the founders of a Zionist youth group called Ezra. Another time I read a eulogy of Hayim Greenberg, the venerable Labor Zionist journalist and editor of *Yiddisher Kemfer* and *Jewish Frontier,* and learned that he was only fifteen when he was a correspondent at the Zionist Conference in Helsinki.

Growing up in the movement, we became increasingly enmeshed in a web of ideas, social ties, activities, and responsibilities. The movement unlocked opportunities for self-expression and forged unique friendships. It sensitized us to others and made us self-confident.

Sometime around the age of sixteen, the strands of movement life blended into a single dominant theme—the question of aliyah. To be sure, Habonim was pluralist. Each individual had the responsibility to struggle with the decision and could come up with his or her own answers. But the movement's subtle and not-so-subtle line insisted that aliyah to kibbutz was the true path.

The interplay between the private and public processes leading to the aliyah decision was filled with nuances and ambivalence. For some, the ambivalence could never be resolved.

Those of us who were uncertain were by the nature of things less articulate than others. At late-night discussions, intimate friends shared their uncertainties. The intimacy forged a powerful cohesion which edged into "movement commitment" and shared dreams. How dangerous dreams can be. Certainly they are more powerful than "ideological clarification."

The path to aliyah consists of small decisions, symbolic acts, and the support of that intimate circle. In 1946, in connection with a forthcoming Hechalutz convention, Habonim launched a membership drive to ensure its control of the organization. The procedure was simple. An applicant filled out a form and mailed it in with one dollar. That made one a declared candidate for aliyah. A chalutz. I was living in New York then.

True, if a person fell to the wayside somewhere between intention and deed, he only suffered the mildest stigma. Still we approached the act of signing the membership form with much soul searching. At meeting after meeting, the leadership implored those who had not yet enrolled to decide soon. I delayed. Days went by, until I was convinced that I was alone in my dallying. Several times I walked that long block in Brooklyn from Eastern Parkway and Troy Avenue to the mailbox on Utica Avenue with a stamped envelope containing the signed application and the dollar.

But I was not at all certain about aliyah. I wanted to go to college. My parents would be unhappy. I was frightened by such a momentous decision.

And now I confess. In front of the mailbox, envelope in hand, I calculated: I would probably be asked to work in the movement, so aliyah was not imminent. Perhaps I could study as I worked in the movement. I would enjoy the prestige of being a chalutz.

I dropped the envelope into the mailbox. For days I felt guilt and shame for my method of reasoning, for not having the courage to face my peers and admit my uncertainty, for masquerading as one of the elect.

That guilt has come back to haunt me from time to time. Years later, when I left Kibbutz Gesher Haziv to study, the guilt gnawed at my conscience for longer than most would have imagined. At age twenty, uncertain as my steps were, I was moving toward aliyah and kibbutz. But the real beginning was further back—at a ping pong table and putting Washington on the map.

Shlichut in Wartime

Despite the confusion and hardships of wartime, the movement continued to grow right through the war years. Events, it seemed, dictated their own pace without waiting for the individual.

Habonim members worked to keep the movement alive, to maintain the *hachshara* farm in New Jersey, and even to expand the movement's range and reach. More summer camps were opened; by 1945 there were eleven, with sixteen hundred youngsters, operating from coast to coast in the United States and Canada.

From the national office in New York, Habonim maintained contact with its graduates at Kfar Blum and with members serving in the Allied forces overseas. At the same time, huge efforts were invested in keeping Habonim at the forefront of fund-raising—particularly for the Histadrut Campaign and the Jewish National Fund.

The six *shlichim* who had arrived in 1939 and 1940 to work with Habonim played a central role in keeping the movement alive and flourishing during the war's early years. By the end of the war, however, events were taking their toll here, too, as Moshe Levin relates.

Boston, 1943: A Shaliach Turns G.I.

Moshe Levin
Jerusalem 1985

When the "big *mishlachat*" first came together in late 1939, we were sent to various parts of the country, working with almost no budget and often sleeping in Habonim members' homes. I had gone to Boston, while Ze'ev Aharon went to Chicago, and Aharon Remez to Philadelphia. Yosef Israeli, Shalom Wurm, and Mala Gitlin stayed in New York.

In early June 1940 I was sent to Los Angeles, which at the time was the second largest center of Habonim activity. I spent the summer of 1941 at summer camps in Chicago and Baltimore. That fall, I received a new assignment: traveling salesman on behalf of the Histadrut Campaign, my unofficial but only dependable source of income. Operating out of New York, I traveled across America. At the end of 1942, I returned to Boston, where my young wife Miriam was pregnant with our first child. In addition to Habonim, I worked with Young Judaea, Junior Hadassah, and the remnants of a Young Poale Zion group.

Then, in May 1943, I was inducted into the U.S. Army. Ze'ev had by now gone back to Palestine, and Remez had gone to Canada to join the Royal Canadian Air Force. For a short time, Shalom Wurm was part of the Free Austrian brigade. Our "big mishlachat" was down to Yosef, Mala, and Shalom.

The army took me to North Africa, Italy, and France. In 1944, following a bout with trench foot, I was assigned to Naples, where I worked as an interpreter and translator. There I met the Palestinian Jewish units of the British army and visited the Jewish Brigade, which was training south of Rome.

When the war ended, I was transferred to Austria, first to Salzburg and then to Linz. I was instructed by the Brigade to visit the concentration camp at Mathausen and to report on the situation. Since no U.S. Army personnel were permitted to visit the camp, I arranged to be sent as a representative of the Jewish chaplain.

At the camp, I had the shock of my life. Although the inmates were free, they could not leave the camp. I walked among hundreds and hundreds of emaciated Jews who, on hearing I could speak Yiddish, gathered to ask if I knew their uncles, aunts, brothers, cousins. . . . Then I was taken to the death factory. Going through those rooms and the gas chambers was an experience I shall not attempt to describe.

Since I was able to write letters without passing censorship, I wrote to the Jewish Brigade to alert them that in ten days Mathausen was to be given over to the Red Army. We had to move as many Jews as we could to the American Zone as quickly as possible. A few days later, a sergeant from the Brigade informed me that the Brigade would send trucks to transport the Jews, but he had to see the camp to devise his plans. I accompanied him, once again as a representative of the Jewish chaplain. At the camp, we made the necessary arrangements. U.S. Army personnel showed great understanding and sensitivity; they knew how to help without being involved.

Somewhat later, I met Simon Wiesenthal in Linz. Together with several Habonim members who I found in a division stationed nearby, we arranged a transfer of food packages from the States, contacted Jews in the Quartermasters' Corps, and began packing food for the thousands of refugees streaming out of Poland, hoping to pass through Austria to get to Italy. U.S. Army authorities knew what we were doing and did nothing to interfere.

In November 1945, I was sent back to the United States. I took up where I had left off, working for Habonim and the Histadrut Campaign until we returned home to Afikim in April 1946.

4

Toward Statehood

The War's Aftermath

At the close of World War II, with six million Jews dead and their communities in ruins, a new era began in Jewish history.

Only a decade before, it was still possible to speak of a world Jewry whose center of gravity was the thousand-year-old Jewish world of Eastern Europe. There, along a thousand-mile strip from the Baltic to the Black Sea, the ten million Jews of Poland and Russia, Hungary, Romania, and Czechoslovakia still lived the vibrant, Yiddish-speaking culture of Ashkenazic Jewry.

True, Eastern European Jewry had been buffeted by conflicting and sometimes brutal social forces for a full century by 1935. In response to the rising nationalism of their Slavic neighbors, rocked by pogroms, restrictive laws and even mass murder, Jews were leaving in ever growing numbers to build a new life elsewhere. For some, that meant Zionism and Palestine; for many more, it meant the inviting shores of America.

But in 1940, when the Nazis' methodical destruction of European Jewry began, the new Jewish communities of Palestine and America were both—in historical terms—still in their infancy, raw and unformed. Both were ideas in the making, and despite the confidence of their leaders and pioneers, it was not yet clear what Jewish life would come to mean in those two still-new lands.

*   *   *

World Jewry faced two urgent tasks after the Nazi surrender: the rescue of masses of displaced persons who had survived the Holocaust, and the struggle for Jewish statehood in Palestine. The two tasks were closely linked. Many of the European survivors could not face returning to their old homes, and most of the free nations had shut their gates to the refugees. As for Palestine, the British had barred large-scale Jewish immigration as a concession to the Arabs, who were increasingly impatient to stop the Jewish drive toward independence. The Zionist movement took the lead in mobilizing world Jewry to the tasks at hand. Zionism was now the best-organized force in Jewish life, with the leadership, the will, and the vision. And, in the Jewish Agency, the Haganah and the half-million Jews of the Yishuv, it had the tools. All over the world, most Jews had come to accept the need for Jewish statehood and were willing to follow Zionism's lead.

*   *   *

Where to lead was no easy question, however. The British, weary from the war, had voted their Labour party to power shortly after the German surrender, and the new government was ready to wash its hands of the intractable Jewish-Arab conflict in Palestine. Under the sponsorship of the new United Nations Organization, a special committee was established in 1946 to examine the options facing the Holy Land. After a year of deliberation, the commission recommended the partition of Palestine into Jewish and Arab states. The recommendation was adopted by the General Assembly on November 29, 1947, and a date was set for the British to hand the country over to its inhabitants. On May 15, 1948, a Jewish state was to be established.

In the meantime, however, British law was still the law of the land. Despite the agony of European Jewry, the British mandatory authorities adamantly refused to admit more than a few thousand Jews a year into Palestine. Anyone attempting to enter without a permit was arrested and placed in a detention camp—first in Palestine and later, when those camps filled up, on the Mediterranean island of Cyprus. At the same time, the land acquisition restrictions imposed on the Jews in 1939 were continued in full force. The Yishuv was not to grow.

As it had during the war, the Jewish Agency under Ben-Gurion attempted to follow a dual policy of cooperation and defiance. The Zionists accepted the notion of partition, and were willing to cooperate with the British in moving the country toward the divided independence planned for it. There would be no cooperation, however, in Britain's cruel restrictions on immigration and settlement. The Zionists began a cat-and-mouse game with the British authorities, smuggling in "illegal" immigrants and establishing "illegal" settlements all over the country.

Nor did all Zionists accept this dual policy. The Zionist Revisionist movement, founded by Vladimir Jabotinsky and now led by Menachem Begin, rejected partition and dismissed any notion of cooperation with the British. As early as 1944—while the war against Hitler was still raging in Europe— the Revisionists had attempted, through their military arm the Irgun Zva'i Le'umi, to launch a full-scale revolt against British rule. Their aim was to drive Britain out and establish a Jewish state in all of Palestine. The leadership of the Yishuv found itself at war not only with the British and the Arabs, but with the Zionist Revisionists as well.

American Habonim had been scattered by the war, struggling to keep the movement alive while many of its leaders were in uniform. With the dawn of the new era in Jewish history, Habonim rose to the tasks of reconstruction and rebirth. As the North American youth movement of the Zionist labor movement, which was now the leader of world Jewry in its moment of greatest trial, Habonim had enormous challenges placed before it, and it rose to the occasion.

Detroit–New York, 1945:
The Story of an Ad

David Breslau
Jerusalem 1985

Habonim held its eighteenth national convention in Detroit December 23–25, 1945. This first postwar convention was like a gathering of the clan: many of us hadn't seen each other for several years. Some were still in uniform, others recently demobilized, and still others were women and younger members who had held the movement together through the war years. Twenty-four of our number had fallen in battle.

We mourned our war dead, including Enzo Sereni, the shaliach to Hechalutz who had parachuted into occupied Europe and died at Dachau. We planned for the future and discussed how the slogan of the convention, "The Conquest of Youth for the Rebirth of the Jewish People," could become a reality.

The highlight of the convention was a closed session with representatives of the Haganah, headed by Ze'ev "Danny" Shind. They discussed the situation of the Yishuv and our responsibilities as Zionist youth. We pledged to dedicate ourselves to the struggle against the British Mandatory power and for the establishment of a Jewish state.

I was elected mazkir of Habonim again—I had served previously (1940–43)—and was chosen to serve as director of the Habonim Institute, the movement's half-year leadership training program in New York, which was about to enter its second year.

My first order of business was to guide the younger members into positions of leadership, as many of my movement contemporaries were in the process of leaving on aliyah. On my release from the army, I came to the national office in New York where, together with Murray Weingarten (now Moshe Kerem) and Artie Gorenstein (now Aryeh Goren), we formed the *mazkirut,* the national secretariat of Habonim.

Those were historic days. Habonim members were called upon to do all sorts of things, many of them secret, to help the Yishuv prepare for the storm that was brewing. We organized and served on the crews of the "illegal" immigration ships, staged demonstrations and protests against British policies in Palestine. We obtained materiel for Palestine, maintained radio contact with Palestine from a clandestine radio station at the Creamridge hachshara farm, prepared to go to Cyprus to work with the refugees interned there by the British, and served in homes for displaced children in France. We served in the Brichah, the Haganah "underground railroad" that smuggled Jews out of Europe. And we continued political work on the American scene. In addition to my own Habonim work, I served as liaison between the North American Labor Zionist movement and the Haganah delegation in New York.

The Executive of the Jewish Agency in Palestine had decided that everything connected with the "illegal" immigration and Haganah activity in general was to be kept a tightly guarded secret. Otherwise, it was felt, the work would be jeopardized. During this time, however, a flamboyant public relations campaign was being conducted by the Zionist Revisionist movement. The Revisionists did little of the actual rescue work at sea, yet they were winning support from wider circles of Jews and non-Jews through their campaign of falsifying the overall picture, exaggerating their own role and derogating the real work of the Haganah.

The mazkirut of Habonim met to discuss the Jewish Agency policy of silence, and we had our doubts. We held seminars, with the participation of Haganah representatives, to discuss the work of the Haganah and determine what could and could not be publicized. But we were told that Zionist discipline must be maintained—we must remain silent. We met with the political committee of the Labor Zionist Organization-Poale Zion, our own senior movement. They, too, insisted on upholding Jewish Agency policy.

Finally, after a particularly vicious attack on the Haganah appeared in a newspaper advertisement placed by the New York delegation of the Revisionists' Irgun underground, the Habonim executive decided it was time to break the wall of silence. The next time a Haganah "illegal" ship approached Palestine, we decided, we would publicize the fact.

A few days later, a delegation from Habonim met with David Ben-Gurion, who was in America at the time, and indicated our opposition to Jewish Agency policy of silence. We came away with the impression that he agreed with us.

That same afternoon, we learned that a Haganah "illegal" ship was approaching the shores of Palestine. We immediately called together the members of the Habonim executive who were in New York, including Dave Goldberg, Artie Gorenstein, Isaac Reisler, and Engee Caller, a member of Kfar Blum who was in America as a shlicha. We decided that Artie Gorenstein would phone Ben-Gurion, tell him we were planning to place an ad about the boat in a New York daily newspaper, and ask him for money to pay for it.

Ben-Gurion told Artie that he had no money and said we should contact Eliezer Kaplan, the treasurer of the Jewish Agency, who was also in New York. We interpreted this as tacit approval. When we couldn't get through to Kaplan, we decided that every member of the Habonim executive would donate one week's income to cover the cost of the ad. We asked Marie Syrkin, a leading Labor Zionist journalist and an editor of *Jewish Frontier,* to write the text for the ad. Dave Goldberg wrote a short postscript describing Habonim, stating that the cost of the ad was being covered by "the lunch and spending money" of our members, and asking for contributions.

The ad was placed in *PM,* a liberal New York afternoon daily. But we still had some doubts about what we were doing, and we called the president of the Labor Zionist Organization, who told us to go ahead. Later in the day, after consulting with other members of the Labor Zionist political committee, he called back and told us not to do it. We decided to go ahead anyway.

The ad appeared on Monday, May 19, 1947. It broke the wall of silence, accurately describing to the American public the Haganah's efforts to bring Jews to Palestine. In the ad, we listed every boatload of refugees the Haganah had sent to Palestine: The *Max Nordau*—1,663 refugees; the *Haganah*—2,768 refugees; the *Theodor Herzl*—2,700 refugees; the *Jewish Resistance*—3,824 refugees; and so on. For the first time, the American public would hear the true story.

And we told that story again and again. As we wrote to Ben-Gurion in late June, ads were placed in *PM,* the *New York Post,* and *The Nation.* Seventy-five thousand copies were circulated at meetings of the American League for a Free Palestine. A copy was sent to every chapter president of Hadassah; ten thousand copies were distributed in key districts of the Zionist Organization of America. The ad was reprinted in ten newspapers around the country, and the response of the rank and file of the Labor Zionist movement and broad sectors of the General Zionist movement was overwhelmingly enthusiastic. As a result of our action, we were able to force all the Zionist youth groups to join in sponsoring additional advertisements that described "the positive achievements of the responsible Jewish community in Palestine."

Not everybody was happy with what we did. Even as favorable letters and cables were arriving—including one from the Haganah in Palestine—the official leadership of the Labor Zionist Organization decided to call us on the carpet, and convened a closed hearing to review the entire incident. Marie Syrkin appeared in the dock with us, and after lengthy deliberations we were let off with an official reprimand from the movement. At the same time, positive reactions continued to pour in, from leading Labor Zionists, from Zionist rank-and-file around the country, from the Haganah and from leading members of Mapai, the labor party in Palestine.

In the aftermath, donations began to pour into the office. They more than covered the cost of the ad. And we had enough money left over to issue a record album, a 78 rpm three-disc set that we called "Songs of the Haganah."

From Kfar Blum to New York, 1945: ## "I Concentrated on Telling the Truth"
Engee Caller
Kibbutz Kfar Blum 1985

Even before World War II came to an end, Habonim was already planning its postwar activities. The movement demanded a large and competent delegation from Palestine, including at least one shaliach from the movement's own kibbutz, Kfar Blum.

I was asked to join the mishlachat, but I refused, fearing my inability to fulfill the task. For months I held out. Finally I agreed to go, but only if the Habonim leadership, which was of my generation, accepted me.

I was still serving at the time in the Palmach, the Haganah's underground mobile strike-force. One day, Yigal Allon, the commander-in-chief (and later foreign minister), came to me to say that he had received a request to demobilize me so I could join the mishlachat. "Just say what you prefer," he said, "and I will act accordingly." But I had no choice. My movement conscience would not allow me to refuse. So I was released from the Palmach, spent a week in Jerusalem at a training course that consisted of two lectures and four lessons on Bible, and set out on my new task.

Since I insisted on traveling on my Palestinian passport, I refused to take the first U.S. bound ship, which was reserved for American citizens only. The second was an old, dirty Portuguese tub that wended its weary way to Alexandria, Marseilles, and Lisbon where it was confiscated by the government. After a month in Lisbon, I boarded another Portuguese boat bound for Philadelphia, only to be greeted by a national dock strike on arrival. The next day I disembarked and was met by Leon (Ari) Lashner and Leo Krown. We piled into their jalopy and headed for New York. During the trip, the car broke down. We arrived in New York at 3:00 a.m. My journey from Haifa to New York took only two months.

After a steaming hot bath and a few hours of sleep at my sister's apartment, I was reading the Sunday newspaper when I noticed that the Histadrut Campaign convention was being held at a hotel just a few blocks away. Naturally, I decided to go. As I entered the hotel lobby, I ran into friends from the Creamridge training farm, from Habonim, and from the senior movement. The word spread that I had arrived, and the chairman of the session invited me to speak.

I was stricken with stage fright and just plain scared. But on my way towards the platform, I spied my uncle.

"What should I say?" I asked him.

"The truth," he replied. And so I began to speak, and all the familiar faces before me—people I had met at so many lectures, activities and celebrations—responded warmly to my simple story about Kfar Blum and the role their children, siblings, and friends had played in its founding.

From then on, I concentrated on telling the truth—the truth about the Jewish settlements, about illegal immigration, about the Haganah and the Palmach, about Kfar Blum. I steered clear of politics, which I felt the other representatives could explain more clearly.

I discovered what Kfar Blum meant to Habonim in America. To them, Palestine and Eretz Israel were Kfar Blum. They ate, drank, and slept Kfar Blum. They knew everything that had been done and was being planned in our/their kibbutz.

An especially moving experience for me was a personal meeting with Leon Blum, the proud Jew and former socialist premier of France in whose honor our kibbutz was named.

Blum had come to the United States in March 1946 to seek a loan for French postwar reconstruction. The Jewish National Fund sponsored a luncheon for him at the Waldorf Astoria. Since I was a member of Kfar Blum, they asked me to address the gathering. In response to my story of our kibbutz, Blum promised to visit what he called *"mon village."* He never made it, but members of his family did.

The dedication of the members of Habonim could be most clearly seen in their day-to-day activities—their fund-raising for the Jewish National Fund and the Histadrut Campaign, their demonstrations against Britain's closing of the gates of Palestine, their local educational activities, the discussions, seminars, lectures, and Camp Kvutza, the apex of Habonim activity, where campers acted out night defense activities, or the disembarking of "illegal" immigrants as if they experienced them personally.

The depth of the members' commitment could be measured when the request came to work on the boats transporting "illegal" immigrants and to pack arms and ammunition for the Haganah. The request was spread in secret sessions, by word of mouth, hint, and wink. Despite the threat of jail sentences in the United States for illegal gun running or deportation to Cyprus by the British should a boat be intercepted on the shores of Palestine, members of Habonim and other Zionist youth movements were the first to volunteer.

It was difficult being a shlicha in America in those days—not physically or materially, but because I was away from the kibbutz during those most trying times. I had promised two years of service. At the end of two years, I was asked to stop in England to discuss the possibility of organizing World Habonim, and I was asked to stop in France to meet again with Leon Blum. But on the very day that my two-year term ended, I boarded a boat in New York and headed home.

The Habonim Institute

Jerry Reichstein

Herzliyah 1960

A youth movement's leaders are a sort of catalyst between the aims and purposes on one hand, and the membership on the other hand, causing an interaction that produces the body of deeds. In a youth movement such as Habonim, where, in addition to everything else, personal values and personal realization of the aims are so important, the type, the training, the knowledge, and the conduct of the leadership and each individual leader are so much more crucial. Therefore, in Habonim, there has always been a great deal of thought and attention devoted to the selection, the preparation, and continued nourishment of leadership. The Habonim Institute, which functioned in the United States from 1945 to 1949 and continued in Israel until 1951, is one of the finer accomplishments in this pattern of intense concern for leadership.

In 1945, World War II was drawing to a close. It was clear that, in the immediate post-war years, tremendous tasks and responsibilities would fall on world Jewry, especially on the Zionist movement. Firstly, there was the growing realization of the ghastly destruction of six million Jews in Europe. Of more immediate importance was the problem of caring for and even settling the remnants of this community. In Palestine the community was rapidly strengthening itself and approaching the day when statehood would be practicable. American Jewry would have to be mobilized.

Habonim would have its role to play. The war, however, had made great inroads into the leadership ranks of the movement. The situation called for a radical departure, something comprehensive that would provide a group of leaders who could be counted upon to see the movement through what looked like years of expanded membership and responsibilities. Thus the idea of the Habonim Institute was created: to train this corps of new leaders.

There was another factor that led to the creation of the Habonim Institute. This was dissatisfaction with many of the existing institutions of Jewish learning. A positive, forward-looking philosophy, combining Jewish values, national inspirations, and a concern for social welfare, was missing. Missing also, in most places, was an understanding of the dynamic, creative process that education and learning can and must be. These approaches and values became the very bases of the Habonim Institute. Therefore the Institute can be seen as the opportune fulfillment of two concepts and needs: a leadership-training school and a unique approach to Jewish education. That it contributed to American Jewish educational thought can be gleaned from the fact that similar institutes were organized by other Jewish youth organizations in America and that its program served as the basis for all sorts of courses organized after the creation of the state of Israel. When the Institute moved to Israel, it became the pioneer of the concept that American Jewish education is complete only if some time is spent in Israel.

A survey of the courses and instructors and techniques of the Institute reveals the uniqueness of form and content. This list of courses and hours is based upon the report of Shalom Wurm, who was the director of the first year of the Habonim Institute in 1945. (David Breslau was director of the Institutes from 1946 to 1948, and Yehuda Messinger was director of the Institute in 1949.)

The first subject studied was Jewish history, which included the period of the emancipation of the nineteenth century, ending with the history between the two World Wars. The final part of the series consisted of several lectures on Jewish immigration and prospects for post-war rehabilitation. A second series of studies concerned the American Jewish community, which consisted of a brief history of American Jewry, the organization of the community, the Jewish labor movement, a statistical survey, and cultural and religious trends among American Jews. The third series was on Zionism and Palestine and included Palestinography and Jewish colonization in Palestine, the history of the Zionist movement, the sociology of the community in Palestine, its political and economic organization, and Arab-Jewish relations. The final part of this series was a study of the Jewish labor movement in Palestine. (One clearly remembers that, in a discussion of problems of the Histadrut, the situation of overpaid Egged bus drivers was mentioned. This same *shaliach* is probably one of those still working with this problem fifteen years later).

A special course was devoted to a study of the texts and personalities of Labor Zionism. Another series was devoted to the study of labor movements and socialism, including a survey of the history of socialist thought, modern trends and theory, a survey of the socialist movement in principal European countries, and the American socialist movement. Six lectures were delivered on Soviet Russia, and several on American labor unions.

There was a series on Yiddish literature, twenty hours; ancient Hebrew literature, fifteen hours; modern Hebrew literature, twenty hours. A special curriculum dealt specifically with the history of the youth movement, as a sociological phenomenon, its origin, and its development in various countries, particularly in Western Europe. It also dealt with the Jewish youth movements in the diaspora and in Palestine. This series included a series of lectures and discussions on the psychology of youth-group work and youth leadership, cultural programs, and summer camping. There were also two classes in Hebrew, one intermediate and one advanced.

A study of the list of lecturers and discussion leaders reveals a fascinating and able group of personalities. This list, taken at random, includes Dr. Ben Halpern, Dr. Ira Eisenstein, Dr. Benjamin Schwadran, Dr. Weinryb, Shlomo Grodzensky, Mark Starr, Daniel Bell, Professor Simon Halkin, Baruch Zuckerman, and the late N. B. Minkoff, Reuven Shiloach and Hayim Greenberg.

It certainly cannot be claimed that even the best-planned and best-executed curriculum could have adequately covered all the material in the major areas in three short months. Nor did the Institute try to accomplish this. What it wanted to do was to expand the horizons of the eighteen students, to attempt to provide as much material as possible, to arouse an interest in further study both during and after the Institute. In other words, in its academic aspects the Institute did more than just create and pass on knowledge. It also aimed at being a stimulant to the further intellectual growth of the students, an important aim in itself.

Many of the educational forms and techniques of the Institute were geared to this double process of information and intellectual development. Instead of being lectures, many of the courses and classes were planned as seminars, in which the atmosphere was one of give and take rather than the traditional teacher-student relationship. From time to time students had to prepare and present papers. In every course outlines and bibliographies were prepared, and books were put at the disposal of the students to encourage reading.

This enlightened educational approach was only one aspect of a broader concept of learning held by the planners of the Habonim Institute. They knew that education and learning are measured not only in academic terms or in the content of subject matter. Equally important is the general development of the individual, his emotional as well as intellectual growth. This includes such things as the creation of a set of basic values and an appreciation of people and ideas. This concept of the process of education views learning as a dynamic process that occurs not only in the classroom but in every activity. Specifically, this meant that the aims of the Institute and the ideals of Habonim were taught and reinforced not only in the study material but in every aspect of life in the Institute.

One important aspect of this approach was the communal life of the student body. All the students lived in the building, sharing similar facilities. Most aspects of daily life and learning were communally controlled by the group, acting as a whole through weekly meetings and committees. These meetings handled the needs of individuals and reviewed the activities of the group and the study material covered during the week. It had the privilege of making recommendations for modification of the studies. There was a *kupa,* a common treasury, set up by the contribution of the spending money of the students, which was then shared equally by all. Evening and other special programs were prepared by the group. This included traditional Friday-night observance of the Sabbath with candle lighting, readings, singing, and the communal meal.

There were numerous special activities, such as a nine-day visit to the Hechalutz training farm, during which time the student body combined study with work. There were also trips to various Jewish and cultural institutions in New York City. Many times the Institute was visited by guests and personalities. The atmosphere in the Institute many times reached a high pitch of excitement and interest.

In addition to an analysis of its structure and contents, there are a number of other criteria by which to judge the Habonim Institute, Class of 1945. All the graduates were active in the movement, locally and nationally, for a number of years. About half of the class have settled in Israel. Practically all are better Jews one way or another. For years, notes taken in lectures were circulating around the movement helping in the planning of discussions and seminars.

After the first Institute, "more and better" Institutes were held in the same building; and eventually it was transferred to Israel. With each year the approach, the curriculum, the content were changed to suit the specific needs of the time. But that is another story.

"Illegal" Immigration: Laying the Groundwork

Akiva Skidell
Kibbutz Kfar Blum 1985

On January 15, 1946, I disembarked in New York from a ship that had left Marseilles two weeks before. The next day I was discharged from the U.S. Army. I had spent the last sixteen months overseas, mainly in defeated, occupied, and embittered Germany. It had been probably the stormiest period of my life.

In December 1944, I had participated in the bleak days of the Ardennes offensive, Nazi Germany's last military gasp. I then marched eastward across northern Germany in pursuit of the disintegrating Germany army. I celebrated V–E Day in Braunschweig, where I came closer to being hit by the wild shooting of celebrating G.I.s than I had in eight months of service as radio operator for a front-line armor division.

Then I visited Buchenwald in search of my family, which I had left behind in Poland fifteen years before. No luck. I followed that with a trip to "Kibbutz Buchenwald," where Holocaust survivors were training to go to Palestine. I went to Berlin, where I served as a translator in German and Russian and met some of the surviving remnants of the Berlin Jewish community. I sent the first postwar report on the Berlin Jewish community, a list of five hundred survivors. It went out under my own name through U.S. Army mails. That was completely illegal but hardly dangerous under the circumstances.

That fall, I was just as busy. I was posted in Germany, where I had continuous contact with the people at the Kibbutz Buchenwald training farm. At the same time, I came to know more and more displaced people. In September, I attended the first congress of displaced persons in Bergen-Belsen. I followed that with a furlough to Palestine to visit my sister, and to see Naame-Kfar Blum, Afikim, and other places. In November, during a delay en route in Paris, I met with Nahum Guttman and Benny Applebaum (Ben-Zion Ilan) of Afikim. Together we met with David Ben-Gurion in preparation for the Congress of Jews in Allied Fighting Forces.

When I finally arrived home that January, I was determined to embark with my family on the great adventure of aliyah as quickly as possible. But not everything happens as quickly as we wish. At the Poale Zion convention in Atlantic City, several days after my discharge from the army, I met my old friend Joe Boxenbaum, who told me he was working with the Mossad le-Aliyah Bet, the Haganah's underground organization for "illegal" immigration.

Within days, I met Ze'ev "Danny" Shind, head of Mossad operations in

America, who proposed that I recruit the crew for the ships he proposed to buy. Leon (Ari) Lashner was in charge of recruiting at the time, but he insisted on shipping out on one as a radio operator. I went to work with Pinchas Rimon, who was then known as Paul Milgrom. After he left for Palestine on a student visa, I worked with Shmuel Halpern. Both live at Kfar Blum today.

The work was not covert. We operated on a strictly commercial basis through registered shipping companies. But the British government was pressing U.S. authorities to make things difficult for Aliyah Bet, as the Haganah called "illegal" immigration. Since the Jewish and even Zionist leadership was not entirely behind the project either, we tried to attract as little attention as possible.

Getting skilled sailors to volunteer for duty was one of the toughest chores we faced. We set up a front organization called the Palestine Vocational Service on the premises of the Jewish Teachers' Seminary, a Labor Zionist-oriented college on East 70th Street in Manhattan. We placed small, cryptic ads in the newspapers, promising adventure. We also met with small groups of people—Zionist youth groups, demobilized service personnel—who we thought might be willing to help.

Our call was first answered by the members of the chalutzic Zionist youth organizations, many of whom were in line to make aliyah. With immigration nearly at a standstill, and what few British permits there were going to refugees in European D.P. camps, the chalutzim saw service in the Aliyah Bet fleet as the most direct way to get to Palestine. Others were military men who had served in Europe and seen the destruction of European Jewry with their own eyes. They wanted to do something concrete, even at personal risk, to help the survivors. We offered difficult conditions, terrible overcrowding, high tension, the possibility of legal complications and danger, and no financial remuneration, glamor, or glory in return for the chance to help the displaced persons of Europe. About three hundred people were accepted out of the one thousand we interviewed.

The induction of our first batch of sailors into the Haganah was a dramatic moment. It took place in a Manhattan office building, in a nearly dark room, in the presence of a few Haganah leaders and some of the major funders of the operation. There was something cloak-and-dagger about the ceremony. Each of the inductees took an oath on a Bible. There were a few speeches which few of the boys understood. Then it was over and we were ready to begin.

From late 1945 through the second half of 1947, we bought nine ships, which transported thirty thousand refugees to Palestine. Our little fleet became famous. The two corvette-class boats became the Israeli Navy after independence. The *Pan Crescent* brought in over fifteen thousand refugees. And, of course, there was the *Exodus,* which we first knew as the *President Warfield,* a Chesapeake Bay excursion boat.

Interestingly, in our first attempt to take the *Exodus* across the Atlantic, she ran into stormy seas at Cape Hatteras and had to turn back for repairs.

Despite its inauspicious start, however, we know what the fate of the *Exodus* was to be.

Finally, the time came for me to make aliyah. In those days, the only regularly scheduled transportation from New York to Palestine was a boat called the *Marine Carp,* which sailed once a month. The *Marine Carp* went from New York to Beirut, to Haifa, to Athens, and then back to New York. That meant a person could obtain a visa for Greece and then jump ship at Haifa, which is exactly what Sam Halpern and his wife and son did, as did I with my wife Ettie and our four-year-old daughter, Sema. When we reached Haifa, we were met by an Aliyah Bet man who provided us with day passes to visit the city. We were then taken to Haganah headquarters, which issued us identity cards establishing our residence at Kfar Blum. The same day, the kibbutz truck picked us up.

New York Harbor, 1946: "Here Goes the Jewish Navy!"

Joe Boxenbaum
Tel Aviv 1985

The day after I was discharged from the U.S. Army, Leon Ari Lashner came to me and said there was a delegation from Palestine that needed my help. We walked to the New York headquarters of the Jewish Agency, where I met Ze'ev "Danny" Shind of the Haganah. He briefly described what he intended to do: establish a company to purchase and refurbish boats for use in "illegal" immigration activities in Palestine. He had problems, both minor and major. Even opening a bank account was proving problematic.

I said, "Come."

We took the subway to the Delancey Street Station on Manhattan's Lower East Side, and entered a branch of a bank I knew. I knew the manager, a Mr. Green, from before the war. I told Green that the man with me wanted to open an account.

"What is it all about?" he asked.

"Believe me," I said, "it's better you don't know, in case you get investigated."

He objected that he couldn't open an account unless someone introduced him. I told him the man's name was Mr. Eastman, the cause was worthwhile, and that someday he would be proud of the part he played.

He then asked Mr. Eastman to come to the bank the next day to introduce the members of the firm, so the account could be opened formally. The next day, the account was duly opened, with a note appended to the effect that no information was to be given out without his—Green's—approval.

When we got outside, I told Danny: "There you are. Now leave me alone."
But there was more, and before I knew it, I was deeply involved. One day,
Danny told me he was negotiating to buy two corvette-class ships. (They
would eventually be called the *Wedgewood* and the *Haganah*.) He asked if
I would help close the deal.

The owner of the ships was in the jewelry business, and had an office in
the Empire State Building. He had bought the ships as war surplus from the
U.S. government, and was eager to sell. But he didn't know how.

He asked Danny whom he represented. Danny, who usually sat with his
mouth and eyes closed, opened both and said: "The Jewish people."

The man, who was Jewish, asked no more questions. He reduced the
price, and we quickly finalized the purchase. Now I thought I could get on
with things. I had been out of the army for several days already, and was
ready to go to work.

But another question came up: What to do with the boats? They needed
repair in dry-dock. The man who sold them to us might have known jewelry,
but he didn't know ships.

We asked around for a Jewish-owned shipping firm, and ended up downtown, near Wall Street, at the American Shipping Company. We spoke to
Morris Ginsburg, the younger brother, and explained to him frankly what
we meant to do. On the spot, he decided to help us. He went to the shipyard,
checked prices, checked quality. Without him, I doubt whether those boats
could have crossed the Atlantic.

The night the ships sailed, there was an odd incident. We had moved the
ships from one shipyard to another, and they were now in Staten Island. The
captain of one of them, a Jewish boy named Lichtman, disappeared. We
found him drunk at about 2:00 a.m. I slapped his face and locked him up
on board until the ships sailed.

I was standing on top deck when the tugboats arrived. The tug captain
shouted: "Here goes the Jewish Navy!" And all that time, we had thought
everything was top secret. It was no wonder the secret got out, though.
Danny had brought a number of people to the docks, people connected with
the Jewish industrialist Rudolph Sonneborn, others who had helped us,
given money and so on, to cultivate them and get them more involved. With
Cadillacs coming to the wharf, nobody could have kept the operation a
secret. If the FBI had ever seriously looked into the matter, they would have
had no problem uncovering the whole scheme.

I. F. Stone, a respected journalist, became very interested in our project
and wanted to accompany the men across the Atlantic. I advised him not
to. There was no way to tell how long the crossing would take. Instead, he
flew to Europe and boarded the *Wedgewood* there, along with the "illegal"
immigrants.

Ironically, I hadn't served with the Navy during the war, but with the water
division of the Army. Still, I had learned something about ships. Perhaps the
most important thing I knew was that there was no way a ship in the condition ours was in would reach her destination without full cooperation from

the crew. They had to know the importance of the mission. We had to give them more than just the bare necessities. Since we could provide no luxuries, we had to give them a sense of purpose. They had to feel they were part of one devoted team. We knew London was pressing Washington not to allow boats to be sent from America to help us.

With all the various companies we had established, names became something of a game. One time, I had just come back from Panama, where I was trying to get back two ships the British had confiscated. We needed to register some new companies. Our attorney asked me for some names. I said to give first priority to F.B. Shipping. The initials, I explained, stood for Fanny Barnett, whose husband owned the Hotel Fourteen where our Palestinian hush-hush men used to stay. In actuality, they were in honor of England and its prime minister, Ernest Bevin. They stood for "F——— Britain" and "F——— Bevin."

Another time, Ehud Avriel of the Jewish Agency and I were called at 6:00 a.m. to meet with Shaul Avigur, the commander of the entire "illegal" immigration operation. Ehud was dog-tired. He had been getting calls all night from Yugoslavia, Bulgaria, and Romania, and he was fed up. Ehud told Shaul that he and I had to leave—we had a meeting with "the Colonel." Shaul didn't dare ask which colonel. We went to a cafe and ordered some drinks.

Ehud toasted, "F——— Britain."

I replied, "F——— Bevin." From that day on, we always signed our telegrams to each other "F.B." No matter what the last name was, there was no doubt as to the identity of the sender. And the two largest ships in the Aliyah Bet fleet, *Pan York* and *Pan Crescent,* were owned and operated by F.B. Shipping Co.

We had two European embarkation points for Palestine. The one in Marseilles was run by Shmarya "Rudy" Hatzameret from Kibbutz Beit Hashita; the one in Italy was run by Yehuda Arazi, a born underground man.

I remember one operation in which we were transporting a group of youngsters to a boat that was to leave for Palestine the next day. The night was cold and damp. I was helping the children onto a truck when I saw a little girl shivering in the night. She didn't even have a sweater.

"Are you cold?" I asked.

"How could anybody be cold on a night like this?" she replied.

The big, corvette-style ships that we brought from the United States created a revolution in the "illegal" immigration. Instead of several hundred immigrants, we could think about transporting several thousand at a time. But that meant a great deal of planning. None of the boats was meant for carrying passengers—most were either former warships, fruit boats, or cargo ships. They had to be prepared for human beings: kitchens had to be installed, sanitary facilities provided, considerations for children and the elderly.

When the Jewish Agency's aliyah workers in Europe saw our big boats, they wanted to load as many people as possible. Instead of beds, they hung cloth hammocks, tier upon tier. At that time Europe lacked food, and every conceivable necessity for the voyage—soap, towels, flour, eggs—was a problem. The overriding consideration was how to take on the maximum number of people with the minimum amount of necessities.

Thinking about the revolution caused in "illegal" immigration by the arrival of the big ships, I recall an incident in Paris in 1946. In those days, except for restaurants that bought on the black market, most places served only rationed food. After June 29, 1946, the "Black Sabbath," when the British rounded up most of the leaders of Jewish Palestine, those who escaped the dragnet had fled to Paris.

One night, several of us who were working on Aliyah Bet decided to treat ourselves to a good meal at a black market eatery. We must have been celebrating something. The eatery was empty except for a table at the far end. There sat David Ben-Gurion, David Remez, Eliezer Kaplan, and Moshe Sneh—practically the entire top leadership of the Jewish Agency, the Yishuv, and the Haganah. I think it was the birthday of Kaplan, the Jewish Agency treasurer. We kept our distance, sitting by the door.

A few minutes later, David Ben-Gurion walked over to me. He said that an English admiral had told him our tactics concerning "illegal" immigration were wrong. The admiral felt we should send many small boats, so the British navy could not cope and some might reach the shores of Palestine.

I told Ben-Gurion I thought the admiral was wrong and that he didn't know the facts. Ben-Gurion got angry and started shouting. He insisted that I see him to discuss the matter before he left for Switzerland. I told him I had to go back to the United States. He told me to do what I had to do there and then come back. I refused, saying the trip was too long. Then he really got angry and started giving me orders and raising his voice.

Moshe Sneh came to my rescue. He suggested that we meet the next day, and he would share my views on the matter with Ben-Gurion later. I don't know if he ever did.

On the Mediterranean I, 1946: "They Told Us We Were Illegal"

Shimshon Belman
Moshav Bet Yanai

Avraham Weingrod
Moshav Bet Herut 1985

We were at the training farm in Creamridge, New Jersey, when we first heard the details of the Aliyah Bet operation. Four of us volunteered immediately: Mendy Mendelson, now of Kibbutz Ma'ayan Baruch, Elliot Kaufman of blessed memory, and ourselves. It was January 1946.

During the winter we moved to New York and began repair work on the boat we would sail on, the *Wedgewood*. The ship was in bad shape, so our first job as sailors was scraping and painting. Shortly thereafter, we were officially enlisted in the Haganah by a short, eagle-eyed Palestinian named Dostrovsky. After independence he would be known as Yaakov Dori, first chief of staff of the Israel Defense Forces.

Within six weeks, the ship was in good enough shape for a maiden voyage up the East River. To our surprise, it moved. In addition to ourselves, the crew consisted primarily of demobilized Jews who had seen what was happening in Europe. Joe Boxenbaum, the American organizer, had recruited professional sailors for key jobs like captain, chief engineer, and first mate. Two Norwegians also signed on, as did four members of Hashomer Hatza'ir.

In April, we were ready to go. We said goodbye to our families that Passover. A few nights later, we slipped away from Creamridge to the harbor and were on our way.

After a few uneventful days, we ran into some very heavy weather and our troubles began. One after another, the motors, pumps, and other equipment failed. At one point we had to work the rudder manually. Ironically, as the boat began to fall apart, it was only the experience of the Norwegians that pulled us through. We made it to the Azores, where we put in for repairs.

From the Azores, we went to Savona in Italy, near the ancient port of Genoa. We spent a month there, preparing to take on refugees. Savona was a Communist city and very anti-British. As a result, the people were very friendly to us. Yehuda Arazi came to give us a talk, and we met the Palestinians who would take charge of the ship once we sailed for Palestine. They seemed very professional and went about their job with a cool efficiency.

At last we were ready to take our "passengers" to Haifa. The departure was at night. We sailed along the coast for a few hours and then were directed to the embarkation spot by the lights of Italian fishing boats. In the distance we could see the headlights of the trucks loaded with refugees approaching the shoreline. Later we would learn that they were British trucks, driven by members of the Royal Army's Jewish Brigade.

In the dead of night, we began to load our passengers. And then, in a moment, the operation stopped. The Italian police, under pressure from the British, had ordered us to cease our activity. The left-wing American journalist I. F. Stone was on shore, as was Ada Sereni, the widow of the legendary shaliach. After protracted negotiations, the order was rescinded and we proceeded. We boarded about one thousand two hundred refugees. As soon as they were all aboard, we quickly cast off and sailed away under full steam. As we began to move, the Italian police began to shoot at us. We felt it was just a symbolic protest and they had no real intention of interdicting us. We were on the last lap of our journey.

The conditions on the *Wedgewood* were indescribably bad. Everybody was issued a small bag in which to vomit. When the bags were used, there was nothing else. Sanitation broke down completely within days. People were packed in, with no place to move, and since we were traveling under the guise of a cargo ship, nobody was allowed on deck where they might be seen. Despite the problems, we managed to keep going.

We lost track of the days, but it must have been less than a week when, in the late afternoon, a British fighter plane appeared suddenly in the sky. It circled us at low altitude. The game was up; we had been caught. Shortly thereafter, a British destroyer pulled up along side. The drama between the Royal Navy and the refugee ship began.

By loudspeaker, they asked us to identify ourselves. We told them we were bringing Jewish refugees to their homeland. They told us that we were illegal and that if we entered Palestinian waters, we would be boarded. We said that nothing could prevent Jews from returning to Palestine. As if to punctuate our point, we ran the Jewish flag, the Star of David, up the mast for the first time.

The British replied by firing a shot across our bow, which terrified everybody. Then they boarded us. Our orders at that point were to mingle with the passengers. There would be no crew and no officers. There would be no resistance, either. Under a British hand, we floated into Haifa bay.

The next morning we were towed into Haifa harbor. Our first view of Palestine was the city of Haifa rising up the hill in the early morning sunshine. We were greeted by the shouts of the men in fishing boats. The port itself was filled with British army personnel ready to take us to detention. At this point, we were swept up in a common surge of emotion and broke out in song. We sang the "Song of the Partisans" and then "Hatikvah." This was our moment of victory. The full power of the British empire could not stop us, though we did not know where we were going next.

Our destination, it turned out, was Atlit, a detention center established by the British. It was two days before Black Sabbath, June 29, 1946, when the British would try to break the back of the Haganah by arresting the most prominent personalities of the Jewish community.

We spent a month in Atlit detention camp. Toward the end of July, we were released and returned to Haifa. After a few days at the Hotel Carmelia, we headed for Kfar Blum.

On the Mediterranean II, 1946:
"We 'Disappeared' into the Streets
of Palestine"

Ralph Banai
Kibbutz Ma'ayan Baruch

Dave Fendell
Kibbutz Kfar Blum 1985

We were recruited to sail on a corvette-class cruiser, the *Norsyd*, which had accommodations for about seventy-five sailors. In the spring of 1946, under a Panamanian flag, we left New York for Marseilles. There we stripped the ship of all its remaining military equipment to make room for as many refugees as possible. We renamed her the *Haganah*.

We sailed to Sete, where one thousand refugees were waiting to come on board, and then set off. Despite the deplorable conditions, the spirits on the boat were high. We were a hardy band of pioneers going home. When we were less than a day's travel outside Haifa, we began to transfer our passengers to a small Greek tub we called the *Biriya*. Everybody, even pregnant women, left our boat by rope ladder. They were transferred to the *Biriya* by Haganah lifeboats. Since each lifeboat could hold no more than thirty people, it took us a full day to complete the transfer.

Though the seas were high and the winds rising, luck was with us, and no one was lost in the transfer. As the *Biriya* headed for Palestine, we turned back toward an island near Athens. We learned that we were to meet our second load of passengers on the coast of Yugoslavia.

We sailed to Split, where a pilot boarded to guide us through the Yugoslavian islands to the small port of Bakar. It was there that our misadventures began.

The first night, some boiler pipes broke. The Yugoslavs were so anxious to get rid of the refugees that they sent some cadets from their naval academy to repair the damage. It took a day to fix the pipes.

Then the refugees were brought in by boxcar, guarded by Yugoslav soldiers. The Yugoslavs insisted that we take all twenty-seven hundred refugees on this boat, which had been built for seventy-five at most. Our passengers approached the boat loaded like pack horses, with everything they owned strapped to their backs. They were stripped of their possessions by their erstwhile guards. As the soldiers stole the goods, they drove everybody on board at bayonet point.

There were more people than our ship could hold, but we sailed. It was hopeless even to try to keep the deck clear or conceal the fact that we were carrying refugees. There were just too many people. All we could do was keep the people evenly dispersed, so the boat would not list at a dangerous angle.

The night before we were to reach Haifa, our engines died. It seems the Greeks had sold us fuel mixed with water. If the sea had not been as calm as a pond, we surely would have capsized. For a day and a night, the engineers tried and failed to refire the engines. That night, we sighted a ship and signaled for help. As it began to approach us, the lights of another boat, much closer, pierced the night, signaling that it had the situation in hand. It was a British destroyer.

We hailed the destroyer by megaphone and requested to be towed to Haifa. The destroyer then shut down its lights and sailed away. Still, we were not worried as we expected it to return or send help. It did neither. We were in a desperate situation.

Then our Danish engineer had an idea. We could convert our oil-burning boiler into a wood-burning one, and shift the good fuel to the other boilers. Using wood from the makeshift bunks, we were able to get up enough steam to get going again. We sailed, with the British destroyer tagging along behind us.

As we approached the shore, a second destroyer approached us, this one equipped with boarding equipment. As we crossed into Palestinian territorial waters, they boarded us. Our pilot, an ex-paratrooper and a veteran of the Normandy invasion, had been making the boarding as difficult as possible. When the British rushed the pilot house to grab the wheel, the pilot jumped through the open windshield of the wheelhouse into a throng of refugees, who succeeded in concealing his identity.

The refugees and crew used tin cans and staves in an attempt to ward off the British. Needless to say, it did not work. As the boat and its cargo were towed to Haifa, small boats with provisions approached. Each time one left, it took a few more crew members with it. The following day, as the refugees were being taken to the Atlit detention center, we were photographed in a shop in the Hadar Hacarmel district of Haifa and given British-stamped identity cards. And so, like our pilot, we "disappeared"—into the streets of Palestine.

Cyprus, 1947: "The British Scarcely Provided Red-Carpet Treatment"

Shimon Kaufman
Los Angeles 1958

The *Lanegev* had been an Italian fishing boat. She originally had cabins for the crew of eight above the deck, and one large hold below. But like every ship of the Aliyah Bet, she had been refitted for this voyage, and now held about six hundred fifty immigrants. We sailed into the Mediterranean in January 1947.

Using sails and auxiliary engine, the *Lanegev* arrived within sight of the Palestinian shore on the night of the twenty-first day after it had put out of the port of Sete. We hoped to elude the British navy and land on the beach near Caesarea. But, as fate willed, we were sighted by a British destroyer as we attempted the final run to shore. There followed a minor battle against three ships of the Royal Navy. British marines boarded our ship, to be met by a hail of stones and broken bottles. Raking machine-gun fire from a destroyer finally cleared our decks (casualties: two immigrants wounded and one of the English Habonim killed); and, with the marines in control above deck, we were taken in tow to Haifa. There we were forcibly disembarked and put aboard a British troopship, which immediately set sail for Cyprus.

Although the British were our "hosts" in Cyprus, they scarcely provided red-carpet treatment for our arrival. The military had cordoned off the port area, and waiting army trucks whisked us away to the camp for "Illegal Jewish Immigrants." There we were searched and questioned, then released inside the barbed wire enclosure among the immigrants who had arrived on Cyprus before us. About seven hundred immigrants already occupied the camp. In a way, it was a minor homecoming, for the other immigrants were anxious to know all about our trip, our battle with the British navy, and whether or not there were more immigrants waiting to sail from France. We, in turn, were anxious to know what sort of life they led in this British prison camp, what ships they had sailed, and how long we might have to remain here in Cyprus.

We soon learned that we were in the "summer camps," a makeshift tent city that the army had set up a few miles outside Famagusta. The rising tide of immigration had quickly made this area inadequate, and work had started several months before on a second, more permanent, area about twenty-five miles distant. There, German prisoner-of-war labor had erected five adjoining Nissen-hut encampments, sufficient to accommodate another ten to twelve thousand people. It was to these "winter camps" that the passengers of the *Lanegev* were transferred within a few days. Little did the British then dream that the stream of Aliyah Bet would grow so large as to require the construction of several more encampments.

In one sense the Cyprus internment camps were prisons. They evoked painful memories of Nazi concentration camps, from which many of the immigrants had "graduated." The camps were surrounded by high, barbed-wire fences. British soldiers manned the machine guns that were mounted on watchtowers at set intervals along the fences. Armed soldiers were stationed at the gates through which we received our food supplies, mail, etc. On several occasions, when panicky guards thought that people within were attempting to mob the gates, shots were fired, wounding a few of the immigrants. These episodes gave rise to feelings of hatred toward the British soldiers.

But, in another sense, the camps were autonomous Jewish republics. There arose camp "governments," composed of representatives of all the groups and movements living within the camps. These governments acquired considerable responsibility and authority. They organized sanitation and food distribution. They acted as representatives of the immigrants whenever there were dealings with the British army authorities. And they were responsible for various cultural activities, holiday celebrations, and demonstrations.

The only outside organization that was officially permitted to help the internees was the American Jewish Joint Distribution Committee. The "Joint" sent one of its ablest field directors to Cyprus shortly after the establishment of the camps. The director, Mr. Morris Laub, brought quite a large staff of doctors, nurses, social workers, and teachers from Palestine and began to administer to the needs of the camp population. The fact that the "Joint" staff members were Palestinians raised the morale of the immigrants and helped create a Hebrew atmosphere.

Unofficially, Haganah people were also smuggled into the camps. A comprehensive system of military training was set up, and thousands of people learned the elements of soldiering under the watchful eyes of British soldiers. The reply to British inquiries was that these were organized sports activities, intended to keep the internees occupied. The sports activities consisted of marching, fighting with clubs, throwing (rocks being substituted for grenades), calisthenics, negotiation of obstacle courses, etc.

Among the immigrants were numerous groups of orphaned children, who had been organized by the various youth movements in Europe into aliyah groups. Each group traveled with a *madrich,* who tried to be both parent and teacher. With the help of the "Joint," the British officials finally consented to house all of the children in one encampment.

Teachers and emissaries of the youth movements came from Palestine as members of the "Joint" staff, and a serious effort was made to provide for the education and well-being of these children. In walking through the children's camps, one had the feeling that this might almost be Ben Shemen or some other children's institution in Palestine.

The typical pattern of organization of the immigrants was the movement pattern, an extension of the political fragmentation that plagued the life of the Jewish community in Palestine and of the Zionist movement in Europe. Each movement had its own living quarters and its own communal kitchen and jealously guarded the interests of its members. But, aside from kitchen and other work details, there was not enough activity to keep people busy. The more active movements organized Hebrew classes and handicrafts, but most people had too much time on their hands. Here, too, the "Joint" stepped in. Teachers were brought from Palestine to conduct seminars for adults. Tools and materials were supplied to craftsmen. One could shop in the camps and buy buckets, teapots, tables and chairs, trousers—all made by various craftsmen inside the camps.

The key factor in our morale was the monthly aliyah of seven hundred fifty persons. When the British learned that a ship had run the blockade and landed immigrants on the coast of Palestine, the quota for that month was arbitrarily suspended. In the camps, bitterness was rife, and morale fell to a low ebb. On one occasion, doctors recommended that all infants and pregnant women be transferred to Palestine at once. This could be accomplished, said the British, only by giving them the next monthly quota and postponing the regular transfer. To this the immigrants agreed. Later, the same arrangement was made for the children's camp; again, the adults agreed to a postponement.

In this manner a whole year passed before the turn of the *Lanegev* passengers came for aliyah. In January 1948, British army trucks again carried us to Famagusta, where we boarded the *Kedma,* at that time the only Jewish passenger ship in service. On the *Kedma* we were treated as honored guests and had a comfortable overnight trip to Haifa. There we were met by some of our chaverim from America, who had, by means of experiments, found chinks in the British wall and had reached Palestine before us. At last our long journey was completed. It had taken us almost a year and a half to travel from the United States to Eretz Israel.

When the passengers of the *Lanegev* arrived in Cyprus, in January, 1947, there were seven hundred internees already there. When we left, one year later, there were over thirty thousand, despite the monthly transfer of seven hundred and fifty to Palestine. Mr. Bevin's attempt to discourage aliyah by opening Cyprus internment camps had been turned into a massive demonstration showing that the survivors of European Jewry would not be stopped in their determination to reach Palestine.

Europe, 1946: Working with War Orphans

Naomi Handelman
Tel Aviv 1985

During World War II and its aftermath, a number of international Jewish relief agencies came into being to care for the children left orphaned by the Nazi horror. Three such organizations were operating in France, where tens of thousands of Jewish orphans were stranded, but few of the people connected with those organizations had strong Jewish backgrounds and few could transmit Jewish traditions to their young charges.

After the war, representatives of the organizations came to the United States looking for help. The Jewish Education Committee (today the Board of Jewish Education) in New York offered its facilities, and nine people were chosen to go to France. Three of the nine were from Habonim, one from Chicago, one from Camden, and I was from Philadephia. Since I could speak both Hebrew and French, I was selected.

I went to France on an almost unconverted troop ship. The men slept in the dormitories and the women in the six-berth officers' cabin. The other passengers were mainly Europeans who had been caught in America during the war and a few students.

Among the passengers were a young Mexican man and his two teenage sisters. He watched his sisters during the day, but did not want to be bothered by them at night. Since I spoke some Spanish, they asked me to tour the deck with them at night.

Yom Kippur came. Services had been scheduled for the same time I usually took the girls for their walk, so I explained that it was a Jewish holiday and I would arrive later that night. When I finally arrived at their cabin, their mother embraced me and called me "sister" and "cousin." She explained that they were Arabs from Lebanon living in Mexico.

In France, I was sent with another girl to Moissac, a village near Toulouse in southern France. The Jewish scouts ran a boarding school there, teaching basic academic subjects and manual professions. The program's Jewish content consisted of "le bentch" and "le bracha" and Hebrew lessons. The Hebrew teacher was an Alsatian Jew married to a Protestant; her idea of a lesson was to present the word *sus,* horse, in all its forms—horse, horses, mare, mares, his mare, and so on.

The director of the institute was a Frenchman from Normandy. The only Jewish word he knew was "goy." Another member of the staff was a talented actor who had given up his career when he began to observe Judaism. By the time he came to us, he would no longer work on the Sabbath.

During the war the institute had been able to disperse the children among farmers, maintaining contact throughout the Nazi occupation. After the war they managed to gather them together again without the loss of a single child. Unfortunately from our point of view, the staff's orientation was strictly French, and they rejected an opportunity to transfer the children to Spain and then to Palestine.

In late 1946 I left the institute to attend the Zionist Congress in Basel, the first one to convene since 1939. Afterward, I went to work near Paris in a children's home operated by Youth Aliyah. Most of the children there had spent part of the war in the Soviet Union, and the teachers quickly learned that to call a child's work "original" was taken as severe criticism.

Before long, it was decided that this group of children would be included on the next "illegal" ship to Palestine. I was asked to escort them to Marseilles. When we reached the port, we learned that there would be some delay. I stayed to help care for the children. In the course of my activities I met several Palestinians, some members of English and American Habonim, and Yitzhak "Antek" Zuckerman of Warsaw Ghetto fame, who asked me to go to Germany to investigate the conditions of the displaced persons there.

It was impossible to obtain a visa for Germany, so I flew to Prague, arriving just before the Communist takeover. From there, I bought a series of train tickets that would ostensibly take me back to France. The first stop was Pilsen, where I enjoyed some of the world-famous beer. The next stop was the German border and then Regensburg, where I was supposed to change trains. I did change trains. But the one I boarded was bound for Munich, not Paris.

Once in Munich, I left my passport at the Jewish Agency and was given a displaced persons identity card. My name was now Bluma Bilgroid. To explain my English, I made up a story that I had spent a few years with an uncle in Philadelphia.

I spent a month in Germany. There I met the kibbutz movement leader Yitzhak Tabenkin, attended a world convention of Mapam youth and helped arrange a jamboree for a delegation sent to the United Nations Relief and Rescue Agency to request supplies. I hated being surrounded by Germans though, and a month later—to the day—I crossed into France.

The youngsters I had met in Germany arrived in Paris shortly after I did. They were on their way to Marseilles and an "illegal" ship. I accompanied them and after some delay they boarded the *Exodus*. As they boarded, the famous Tour de France bicycle race passed a kilometer away. All eyes were fixed on the bicycles, none on the port.

When the people of the *Exodus* were transferred to three British ships anchored outside Port du Bouc in the hope that the people would disembark, I was among those asked to go. A French coast guard cutter visited the ships several times daily with a doctor. Our people insisted that somebody join the cutter who could speak their language. Our purpose at this point was to reassure them that we were with them in spirit. In between trips with the coast guard, I spent my time knitting booties for the babies born on board.

After that, I decided to take a look at Palestine rather than return to America. The Joint Distribution Committee, the international Jewish agency with overall responsibility for overseas relief work, agreed to the request, and their Marseilles representative arranged my cabin passage. I had little money and few possessions except for a fur coat given to me by my relatives in Paris.

The ship's first stop was Beirut. I was invited by a local resident to visit, but I decided to stay on board with the Palestinians. When I arrived in Haifa, I was met by my cousin.

It was then that I got my first compliment in Palestine. An Arab customs inspector said to my cousin, "Why don't you marry her?"

My cousin replied, "I'm married already."

The customs officer said, "How about your brother?" Upon hearing that his brother was married as well, he mused, "It is a pity to let a beauty like that out of the family."

It was a beautiful day: November 15, 1947.

New York, 1946: "We Knew That We Differed From Non-Jewish Children"

Janet Ades
New York 1986

Through the activities of its small groups, Habonim instilled in us a deep identification and pride in our people and a visceral interpretation of Zionism as inclusive rather than divisive, as within and flowing from our history. It taught us to view Zionist activity as the development of a tradition, not a sectarian rebellion. And it gave us a sense that we were in charge of our own destiny, not victims. In 1946 and 1947, it did this in the teeth of the death camps and their corpses.

In the days before Israel's independence, instilling these revolutionary ideas in Jewish youngsters was a huge task. Habonim did it by making Zionism fun, using songs, dances, hikes, and the group experience itself. In my particular Habonim group, a major feature of the educational program was storytelling.

The stories had a Samsonian strength that I remember forty years later. Their passion came from our stoop-shouldered, sixteen-year-old leader, Artie.

We were a small group of rambunctious nine-year-olds who had entered school as the war ended. Before Israel's independence we were formed into a *kvutza,* the basic unit of Habonim organization. At the same time we were becoming aware of the world outside our neighborhood, of the story of our dead, of our statelessness and our helplessness. We met on Friday evenings in the furnished basement of the home of one of our more affluent members. We accepted our membership and our meetings as natural. We sang the songs of pioneers in Eretz Israel, we learned to dance the hora and we played spin-the-bottle, and it seemed as natural to us as the Brownies or the Girl Scouts must have seemed to our contemporaries. But we knew that we differed from non-Jewish children. We had heard and overheard just how different we were.

Even as we learned to read the headlines in the daily newspaper, the story of Buchenwald and Ilse Koch broke. Now we could read what had happened: how Jews were melted down and made into soap; how Ilse Koch, the head of the women's section who was known as the Bitch of Buchenwald, had selected tattooed people, had them killed and their skins made into lamp-shades. During morning recess, after lunch in the schoolyard and on the way home, we talked about Ilse Koch and what she had done with the matter-of-fact curiosity and directness of children.

It said something very powerful to us that the world press, "their" press, now acknowledged what had been until then a whispered and fractured reality. In each home the specific details, the family's particular insight on the huge panorama, differed, however slightly.

Sometimes, because we were children, we had been given only hints and fragments. Perhaps we had found a hidden envelope of snapshots or seen displaced persons and refugees in the movie newsreels. Now we all knew what had happened, and we knew that if we had been there, it would have happened to us. Even in our nine-year-old minds, it posed the inchoate question: What destiny for us?

We were humiliated to imagine ourselves helplessly led to the gas chambers, and horrified at the notion of bodies melted down for industrial products. I still shudder to imagine a person showering with a piece of such soap.

Artie led us through the anguish. With his stories, he met the danger that we might turn away from our own suffering, perhaps even despise it. He would plead with us to remain quiet until the story itself could take over.

My favorite was the story by the Yiddish writer I. L. Peretz, titled "The Three Gifts," a fable about the Jews' nobility of spirit and timeless commitment to values, even in the face of cruelty. The meaning was not lost on us.

Yet fairy tales in the end are just fairy tales. After the victory in Europe and before Israel's independence, we perceived the refugees' plight, the postwar Polish pogrom at Kielce, the intransigence of the British. Artie validated that knowledge. Yes, he told us, Jews have always been persecuted everywhere we have dwelled. In Yemen and the other Arab countries, Jews had to step into the gutter to allow a Moslem to pass.

Artie sat us around him in a semicircle on the basement floor. His problem and Habonim's task now was to teach a generation that had seen half their people made into soap, who knew that the world offered no refuge, to believe that we could prevail.

He began with the truth. "We did not go like lambs to the slaughter," he said. "It is a lie. Listen: when the Germans marched across Czechoslovakia, Prague fell without a shot. When they marched into France, Paris fell without a shot. But when they drove their tanks into the ghetto of Warsaw, Jewish youth fought back."

Artie's account was full-bodied, detailed, and attentive to our concerns. He told us how Mordecai Anilewicz had worked to unite the bickering Jewish youth movements, to plan the uprising, sneak couriers outside the ghetto wall, and smuggle in guns and ammunition. How they dug bunkers, hid food, and made Molotov cocktails, even though they must have known it would not be enough.

April came, Artie told us, and the Germans drove their tanks into the ghetto from which the Jews had gone to their death, their heads shaved like shorn lambs. Still, it took a month of fighting before the ghetto was no more. "We did not lose," Artie said. "We fought back." Never say there is only death for you.

Classic Jewish dreaming is what stooped Artie's shoulders. With the wonder of his Zionist dreams, he taught us of the Holocaust. He taught us that we could know what happened and that knowledge could give grace and meaning to our lives because we have the power to act. He taught us the meaning of the Holocaust and the Warsaw uprising—to honor our people and to be for ourselves.

Letters from Palestine, 1946: "The Attitude Is One of Quiet Waiting"

Whether as sailors in the Aliyah Bet, as war-refugee relief workers, or simply as young American Jews heading for the Jewish homeland, Habonim members began moving to Palestine in relatively large numbers on the eve of independence. Some registered for studies at the Hebrew University or other institutions; others went to Kfar Blum, the movement's own kibbutz in the northern Galilee.

One group of new *olim,* about fifty strong, joined together with two other groups of South African ex-soldiers and Israeli Gordonia graduates to found a new kibbutz. In March 1947, they settled at Ma'ayan Baruch in the Galilee not far from Kfar Blum. The kibbutz was a "Tower and Stockade" settlement, thrown up literally overnight to thwart British efforts to slow the Zionist effort.

The Palestine that the young newcomers found was a nation in all but name, anxiously waiting for its fate to be decided. In New York, the United Nations was considering proposals to partition the country into Jewish and Arab states, and the outcome of the deliberations was far from certain. In the neighboring Arab states, leaders were vowing to stop the Jewish state and were preparing for war. In Palestine, the British mandatory government had dropped most pretenses of neutrality in the Jewish-Arab struggle, stopping "illegal" immigrants boats, arresting Zionist leaders, breaking up land-settlement attempts, and trying to destroy the Jews' military preparedness as the showdown approached.

For the six hundred fifty thousand Jews of the Yishuv, life was a delicate balance of preparing for war, absorbing newcomers, expanding the bounds of Jewish settlement—and still trying to live a daily life.

One of the first Habonim members to reach Kfar Blum after the war was Avraham (Alvin) Weingrod, who went on to become a member of Moshav Bet Herut, near Netanya. In these letters to his fiancee, Blossom Allentuck of Washington, he describes the mood on the kibbutz and in the country as Palestine moved inexorably toward statehood.

* * *

June 17, 1946

We have been here only three weeks and I can only write about the physical appearance of the part of Palestine I have seen—the Galilee. As you know, I usually remain unperturbed while others rave, but I can tell you that Palestine—certainly the Galilee—is beautiful beyond anything you ever imagined. That first ride from Haifa to Kfar Blum is something you will never forget, especially when you climb to the top of a high hill and suddenly below you lies the blue Kinneret. It is a shockingly grand and magnificent country. When you see it, you feel only a great people are worthy of it.

When I say beautiful though, I do not mean rich. Despite the best efforts of the Jewish National Fund, Palestine still sadly lacks trees. The valleys are cultivated but the hillsides are barren. As you drive along the road, the settlements seem like islands in a large and barren desert. There are plenty of Arabs and Arab land, but the Arab villages are so ugly they spoil the beautiful countryside.

* * *

July 24, 1946

About Naame, or Kfar Blum, as it is known around here. It is not at all the primitive or crude-looking settlement we had expected. The children's houses and the permanent homes are neat and reasonably well furnished. There are four rooms to a house and each room houses a family. The newer settlers live in temporary housing. Temporary here is a term that can stretch for a considerable period of time. This housing is not as nice and the kibbutz would be better off to build permanent housing. But they simply cannot find the time or labor to do it. There is a tremendous labor shortage everywhere. At Kfar Giladi they told us that they are short fifty people every day and could use one hundred more. In the Galilee, there are only 8,000 Jews and 40,000 Arabs.

* * *

July 31, 1946

The Yishuv is living through an extremely difficult period. Tel Aviv has been completely closed off and being subjected to a block-by-block, house-by-house search. At the same time, the British plan has been announced to hand the Palestine question to the United Nations.

Out in the provinces, up in our corner of the Galilee, we are far away from the business and events of Tel Aviv. We cannot even get a newspaper. While the situation seems serious and grim, the atmosphere is surprisingly quiet and unexcited. Of course, when the news is broadcast on the radio, everybody in the dining room listens intently. Occasionally you can even hear it.

But so far, the day-to-day life, the work, the time after work, has been unaffected. The attitude is one of quiet waiting. I think the reason is—and this is one of the most positive things about Kfar Blum—that except for the new arrivals, the people here are thoroughly rooted in Palestine, the kibbutz and their work. For the majority, this is their way of life. There is no other. They feel that this is their kibbutz and their land and that nothing could change that.

* * *

September 24, 1946

I divide my time between the vegetable garden and irrigation. Water is the most precious element in Palestine. Without irrigation you cannot do anything. The irrigation system is quite crude and imperfect but it is all we can afford. Eventually, over a period of years, pipes will be installed. But now you have ditches and furrows and water is pumped from the Jordan to flood the ground.

* * *

October 23, 1946

You may not have a clear idea about how kibbutzim start. A group of people does not settle on the land simply with whatever money it happens to have. Some groups have no money at all.

Colonization is a national plan and run, ultimately by the Jewish Agency. When each kibbutz starts, it has a budget from the Agency. With this money they put up the first buildings and buy heavy equipment such as trucks and tools. The budget these days is around 20,000 pounds. In addition, the kibbutzim get all sorts of loans from various institutions. That is the most popular word in Palestine—institution.

A great deal of the support you receive depends on the kind of kibbutz you are and where you choose to settle. It is no secret that many sites are chosen primarily for strategic or political reasons, regardless of the possibilities for self-sufficiency. These places have to rely on outside funding for a long, long time. It doesn't make for a high standard of living but that is how the country is built. Menara, which is a three hour walk from here, was built for those reasons. It is on the top of a mountain, practically on the Lebanese border. It overlooks the entire Huleh valley. That is also why the eleven settlements in the Negev were established.

* * *

November 4, 1946

By now you may have heard about the new settlement activity in the Upper Galilee in which two Jews were killed. The new point is directly behind Kfar Blum and all of us were involved in one way or another. I was deeply impressed by the spirit of cooperation within and among the kibbutzim. People worked together hard and willingly, yet quietly and efficiently. This was not the usual, more simple type of settlement. Eventually a fight developed between Arabs and us which ended up in firing. The firing wasn't heavy but ended only when the British police arrived.

The British army has occupied the new point until the matter can be resolved in the courts. But forty members of the kibbutz have refused to leave, even though they cannot work. On principle, once Jews have established a settlement, they do not leave it. Everybody is certain that in the end, we will have another settlement in the Huleh.

Ma'ayan Baruch, the Upper Galilee, 1947–49: "The Work Went On"

Asher Gray

New York 1949

Ma'ayan Baruch is now two years old. It has about one hundred forty members and sixteen children. It is situated at the foothills of Mount Hermon, looking down on the Huleh Valley at a point where the present Israeli frontier meets those of Syria and Lebanon. It is in the old biblical province of Dan. During the War for Israel's Independence, Ma'ayan Baruch became an important link in the borderline chain of settlements whose endurance helped stake out the present boundaries of the country. At Ma'ayan Baruch is a group of close to fifty Americans who were once members of Habonim and Young Poale Zion.

The settling of Ma'ayan Baruch was a middle-of-the-night "tower and stockade" operation: A convoy of trucks loaded with everything needed to make up the kibbutz and stock it for the next three months set out under an armed Palmach escort for the point of settlement on March 11, 1947. In a few hours and before dawn, there were a stockade of barbed wire, a network of trenches and sandbag gun emplacements, the first of three prefabricated huts, an additional number of tents, the water tank, and searchlights.

The settlers were of three distinct groups. There was a South African group of *"Chalutzim Chayalim"*—soldier-pioneers—who had visited Palestine while on leave from the South African army in Egypt during World War II. The second group was made up of members of American Habonim and Young Poale Zion who had received agricultural training at Creamridge, New Jersey, and in Israel at Kfar Blum and Kfar Giladi. The third group was a young native Israeli group of the Gordonia youth movement.

This mixture later proved to be so successful from the social point of view that efforts are being made to duplicate it with younger groups from each of these three countries.

Ma'ayan Baruch was soon to be drawn into the war and to play a proud role in it. The sabra group went into the army as a complete Palmach unit and served together throughout the heavy campaigns of 1948. The Americans and the South Africans, because of their experience in the armed forces of their respective countries, served in many important capacities in the technical trenches of the Israeli army where, as did most "Anglo-Saxon" elements, they played a role much greater than their numbers might indicate. They became pilots, bombardiers, and navigators in the Air Force, where some of them are still serving. They went into the tank corps, the jeep commandos, and mine-laying and communications.

Out of a present population of one hundred forty, about fifty-five served in the armed forces outside the settlement. Forty-five more, both men and women, served as a local garrison, guarding their stretch of the border and serving quite often when called to do so in tactical operations outside their sector.

All in all, Ma'ayan Baruch lost fifteen chaverim, by sniper fire and in offensive action. In the legendary conquest of the fortress of Nebi Yusha, six members of the kibbutz lost their lives.

In spite of all this, combined with daily air raids and artillery shellings which drove the chaverim and their children to the musty air raid shelters at all hours and for hours at a time, the work of building the kibbutz went on. Fields were plowed, an irrigation system laid out, a dairy and sheep herd built up, orchards planted, and fish ponds dug. Though the settlement is still within its barbed wire confines, its green fields stretch for miles, right up to the Syrian frontier.

New York, 1947:
Buying Arms for Palestine

David Glassman
Herzliyah 1985

In the fall of 1947, I arrived in Brooklyn to lead a Habonim group in Borough Park. I did not want to do it, but my good friend Artie Gorenstein had just become a member of the movement's national secretariat, and he made me do it.

One day, I got a mysterious phone call from Kieve Skidell. He wanted to know if I had any drafting experience. I had attended Yale University on the G.I. Bill and told him that I did. He insisted that I cancel a *kvutza* meeting I had scheduled and immediately go to a small apartment on West 114th Street in Manhattan. I did as I was asked.

At the apartment I met Phil Alpert, who was also a recently graduated mechanical engineer, and Haim Slavin. On the table in the center of the room was a pile of very odd-looking pieces of metal. They were the object of all the urgency. I was told curtly that each piece had to be measured, drawn, and recorded, so they could be returned by the next morning to where they belonged, before their absence was noted. I worked through the night and for several days more.

That episode began my involvement with the Haganah's military purchasing mission, an involvement which lasted for eighteen months. The mission was headed by Haim Slavin, whom I regard as a genius. Our main project was to produce a small light machine gun, the *Dror*. Haim supervised the operation from a small apartment. One room was his office, the other his bedroom. A barefoot girl typed all the purchase orders, which went out under fictitious company names.

Phil and I did the leg work. We would visit the people and companies with whom we did business. We could not invite them to our office, since we had no office. But we did succeed in shipping to Israel the blueprints and the tools necessary to make the *Dror,* and when I arrived in Palestine, I was involved in its production. The gun never became fully operational in the Israel Defense Force because it was too complicated to work easily in the desert. Eventually it was replaced by the Uzi.

Our mission also handled transporting arms and munitions to Palestine. One time, we secured twenty tons of dynamite at an army surplus sale in Denver. We said we planned to use it for blasting mines. We didn't say where those mines were.

The scheme called for us to transport the dynamite east, re-crate it, and ship it to Palestine labeled as farm machinery. We needed a site to re-crate the stuff without being easily traced. We decided on Habonim Camp Galil, outside Philadelphia. The camp was in the center of a woods and virtually inaccessible. Philadelphia Habonim agreed to help out.

The dynamite was transported from Denver on two tractor trailer trucks. My job was to meet the drivers at a certain crossroads in Pennsylvania and guide them to the camp. We didn't want them to know exactly where they were going.

I left New York in a rented car at about 10:00 p.m., in the middle of a severe snow storm. Everything that could go wrong did go wrong. I had engine trouble; I got a flat tire; I skidded on an icy road and smashed into another car. Fortunately, the damage was light and neither the other driver nor I was in a mood to argue.

Cold, tired, and desperate, I arrived at the designated crossroads an hour late. No trucks. I suffered through one very anxious hour before the first truck arrived. The driver told me that he too had hit bad weather. An hour later, the second truck arrived and we set off.

I led the truck through a maze of back-country roads, partly to confuse them, partly because I was confused as well. When we arrived at Camp Galil, we were greeted by a half-dozen frozen Habonim boys and the warehouse crew from New York. They leaped upon the trucks and unloaded the cargo. I led the drivers out of the camp, paid them, and told them to forget that the night before had ever happened. They were happy to oblige.

We repacked and restenciled the crates in record time. I phoned New York and they sent down some trucks from a firm we used regularly. They were very trustworthy people. Italians, I recall.

But luck was still against us. As the ships were being loaded, one crate labeled "farm machinery" slipped from an icy sling. When the stevedores saw the boxes were full of dynamite, all hell broke loose. They did not care if it was dangerous or not. They were not going to fool around with it. It was impossible to keep the accident quiet.

The police and the FBI swung into action. They quickly traced the merchandise to our warehouse, which they then raided. Fortunately, we had been alerted to the raid and had been able to remove most of the more sensitive and incriminating documents, which we stored for a time in my cousin's garage. Still, the raid ended our operation in New York in that form.

Our warehouse crew was arrested. I was ordered to go into hiding with Eli Shavit, who had replaced Slavin by then. I was to stay in a different hotel every night. I had never stayed at a hotel before in my life, so it was quite an experience. I was also told to wear a hat. There I drew the line—I could not stand hats. But orders were orders, and I bought a hat.

When the political climate improved a little, I was ordered to give myself up. With our lawyer, Eli Shavit and I went to police headquarters where we were booked, fingerprinted, photographed, interviewed by the press, and released. Our trial took place just after Black Sabbath, when anti-British and pro-Jewish sentiment was running strong. We had an Irish judge who gave us a one-year suspended sentence.

Not long after that, I found myself on a boat to Palestine.

* * *

Although the terrible, wonderful events of the 1940s called up deeds of great heroism and sacrifice, there was another side to those years—modest, even ambivalent, but every bit as human. Many Jews in North America, including many members of Habonim, experienced the historic drama going on around them more than anything as a backdrop to their own continuing drama of day-to-day survival.

Montreal, 1947: "We Danced the Hora in the Middle of the Street"

Mordecai Richler
Montreal 1964

War. "Praise the Lord," my father had sung, demanding more baked beans, "and pass the ammunition." My brother wore a Red Cross Blood Donor's badge; I collected salvage. One of the first to enlist was killed almost immediately. Benjy Trachstein joined the RCAF and the first time he went up in a Harvard trainer the airplane broke apart, crashed on the outskirts of Montreal, and Benjy was burned to death. At the funeral my father said: "It's Kismet, fate. When your time comes your time comes."

Mrs. Trachstein went out of her mind and Benjy's father, a grocer, became a withering reproach to everyone. "When is your black-marketeer of a son going to join up?" he asked one mother and to another he said: "How much did it cost you the doctor to keep your boy out of the army?"

We began to avoid Trachstein's grocery, the excuse being he never washed his hands anymore. It was enough to turn your stomach to take a pound of cottage cheese from him or eat a herring he had touched. It was also suspected that Trachstein was the one who had written those anonymous letters reporting other stores to the Wartime Prices & Trade Board. The letters were a costly nuisance. An inspector always followed up because there could be $20 and maybe even a case of whiskey in it for him.

Benjy's wasted death was brandished at any boy on the street hot-headed enough to want to enlist. Still, they volunteered. Some because they were politically conscious, others because boredom made them reckless. One Saturday morning Gordie Roth, a long fuzzy-haired boy with watery-blue

From "My Sort of War." Reprinted with the author's permission from *The New Statesman,* September 4, 1964.

eyes, turned up at the Young Israel Synagogue in an officer's uniform; his father broke down and sobbed and shuffled out of the shul without a word to his son. Those who had elected to stay on at McGill, thereby gaining an exemption from military service, were insulted by Gordie's gesture. It was one thing for a dental graduate to accept a commission in the medical corps, something else again for a boy to chuck law school for the infantry. Privately the boys said Gordie wasn't such a hero, he had been bound to flunk out at McGill anyway. Garber's boy, a psychology major, had plenty to say about the death-wish. But Fay Katz wrinkled her nose and laughed spitefully at him. "You know what that is down your neck," she said. "A yellow stripe."

Mothers who had used to brag about their children's health, making any childhood illness seem a shameful show of weakness, now cherished nothing in their young so greedily as flat feet, astigmatism, a heart murmur or a nice little rupture. Only Tansky, the communist who ran the Corner Cigar & Soda, questioned the integrity of Britain's war effort. Lots of ships were being sunk in the Battle of the Atlantic, true, but how many people knew that the U-boat commanders never torpedoed a ship insured by Lloyd's or that certain German factories were proof against air raids because of interlocking British directorates?

If Tansky was concerned about capitalist treachery overseas, French Canadians at home gave us much more cause for alarm. Maurice Duplessis's Union Nationale party had circulated a pamphlet that showed a coarse old Jew, nose long and misshapen as a carrot, retreating into the night with sacks of gold. The caption suggested that Ikey ought to go back to Palestine. Mr. Blumberg, our teacher at the Talmud Torah, agreed. "There's only one place for a Jew. Eretz. But you boys are too soft. You know nothing about what it is to be a Jew." Our principal was a Zionist of a different order. His affinities were literary. Achad Ha'am, Bialik, Buber. But I managed to graduate from the Talmud Torah uncontaminated. In fact, I doubt that I ever would have become a Zionist if not for Jerry.

Jerry, who was in my classroom at Baron Byng High School, represented everything I admired. He wore a blazer with JERRY printed in gold letters across his broad back and there was a hockey crest sewn over his heart. He had fought in the Golden Gloves for the YMHA, and he was high scorer on our school basketball team. Jerry went in for rakishly pegged trousers and always carried condoms in his billfold. One day he came up to me in the school yard, bounced a mock punch off my shoulder, and said, "How would you like to come down to Habonim with me tonight? If you like it, maybe you'll join."

Jerry, chewing on his matchstick, picked me up after supper and then we went to call for Hershey and Stan. Walking to the Habonim meeting house with Jerry, Hershey and Stan, my chaverim, became a Friday night ritual which was to continue unbroken through four years of high school.

Then the war was done. We read in the *Star* that in Denver a veteran had run amok and shot people down in the street; the *Reader's Digest* warned us not to ask too many questions, the boys had been through hell; but on

St. Urbain Street the boys took off their uniforms, bought new suits, and took up where they had left off. Sugar, coffee, and petrol came off the ration list. The Better Business Bureau warned housewives not to buy soap from cripples who claimed to be disabled veterans. An intrepid reporter walked the length of Calgary's main street in an SS uniform without being stopped once. Ted Williams was safe, so was Jimmy Stewart. Joe Louis promised to fight Billy Conn again. Our prime minister, McKenzie King, wrote: "It affords me much pleasure both personally and as Prime Minister to add a word of tribute to the record of the services of Canadian Jews in the recent war." Nice, very nice. Pete Grey, the Toronto Maple Leafs' one-armed player, was made a free agent. A returning veteran took his place in the outfield.

Hershey's father, gone into the war a scrap dealer, a rotund good-natured man whose sporting life had once been confined to cracking peanuts in the bleachers at Sunday afternoon double-headers, now flew army ordnance corps colonels and their secretaries by chartered plane to his hunting lodge on a lake in northern Quebec. He emerged as a leading dealer in army surplus tanks and other heavy equipment. Hershey's family moved to Outremont. Duddy Kravitz drifted away from us, too. Calling himself Victory Vendors, he bought four peanut machines and set them up on what had clocked as the busiest corners in the neighborhood.

Jerry and I became inseparable, but his father terrified me. He ridiculed Habonim. "So little shmendricks, what are you gonna do? Save the Jews? Any time the Arabs want they can run them into the sea." I can no longer remember much about our group meetings on Fridays or the impassioned general meetings on Sunday afternoons. I can recall catchwords, no more. Yishuv, White Paper, emancipation, Negev, Revisionist, Aliyah. Pierre Van Paassen was our trusted ally; Koestler, since "Thieves in the Night," was out. Following our group meetings we all clambered down to the cellar to join the girls and dance the hora. On Saturdays we listened to speeches about soil redemption and saw movies glorifying life on the kibbutz. Early Sunday mornings we were out ringing doorbells for the Jewish National Fund, shaking tin boxes under uprooted sleepy faces, righteously demanding quarters, dimes, and nickels that would help reclaim the desert, buy arms for Haganah, and, incidentally, yield 35 cents each off the top—enough for the matinee at the Rialto. We licked envelopes at Zionist headquarters. Our choir sang at fund-raising rallies. And in the summertime, those among us who were not working as waiters or shippers went to a camp in a mosquito-ridden Laurentian valley, heard more speakers, studied Hebrew, and, in the absence of Arabs, watched out for fishy looking French-Canadians.

On the night of November 29, 1947, after the UN approved the partition plan, we gathered at Habonim and marched downtown in a group, waving Israeli flags, flaunting our songs in Anglo-Saxon neighborhoods, stopping to blow horns, and pull down streetcar wires, until we reached the heart of the city where, as I remember it, we faltered briefly, embarrassed, self-conscious—before we put a stop to traffic by forming defiant circles and dancing the hora in the middle of the street.

Our group leaders went off to fight for Eretz, and in the febrile days that followed we gathered nightly at Habonim to discuss developments. A distinguished Jewish doctor was invited to address the Canadian Club. To our astonishment, he said that though he was Jewish, he was, first of all, a Canadian. Israel, he said, would make for divided loyalties, and he was against the establishment of the new state. The chaverim, myself included I'm sorry to say, took to phoning the doctor at all hours of the night, shouting obscenities, and hanging up. We sent taxis, furniture removers, and fire engines to his door; then, as one event tumbled so urgently over another, we forgot him.

Abruptly, our group began to disintegrate. We had finished high school. Some of the chaverim went to settle in Eretz, others entered university, still more took jobs. Hershey entered McGill. I had to settle for the less desirable Sir George Williams College. Months later I ran into Hershey at the Cafe Andre. He wore a white sweater with a big red M on it and sat drinking beer with a bunch of blond boys and girls. Thumping the table, they sang loudly, "We are little black sheep, who have gone astray. Baa-baaa-baaa."

My companions were turning out a little magazine. I had written my first poem, all in lower-case letters. Hershey and I waved at each other, embarrassed. He didn't come to my table, I didn't go to his.

The Eve of Statehood: Habonim Mobilizes for War

David Breslau
Jerusalem 1960

On November 29, 1947, the United Nations General Assembly met in Lake Success and voted to partition Palestine into two states, one Jewish and one Arab. The bare two-thirds majority that passed the historic resolution, turning on the joint support of the Soviet Union and the United States, ushered in a new age of Jewish history.

Habonim's national executive committee, the *Merkaz,* captured the feelings of Jews everywhere in a resolution adopted days later:

> For two thousand years our people dreamed. For two thousand years Jews remembered Zion and prayed for deliverance. In song, in prose, in their hearts and thoughts, Jews kept alive the dream of the Return to Zion—and the dream kept them alive. For two thousand years Jews piously hoped that the Return would take place "quickly in our time."
>
> It has happened and is happening in *our* time. Ours will be the time written of, sung about, talked about as long as the Jewish people will live. Ours will be the generation of the Third Temple.

How fortunate we all are! How happy we all are! The hopes, longing, sacrifices, struggles against persecutions, battles for the sanctification of the Lord and our people—all stir around and well up in one tremendous, joyous cry: the Jewish State, *medina ivrit, b'yameinu,* in our time!

It was made possible by the combined efforts of Jewish people everywhere, by the translation into practical action of the latent hopes and energies that the Zionist movement brought to the surface and directed into creative channels. It was made possible, most of all, by those young people who themselves journeyed to Palestine, to plow and sow, to drain the swamps, to create gardens out of the wilderness, to build and to be rebuilt.

We call upon all Jewish youth in America, but upon the members of Habonim first and foremost. Let us rise and accept the challenge of history! Ours is the chosen generation! We dare to believe that a new code of ethics will blaze forth from Zion, a new life based on the principles of equality and social justice, the code of the prophets themselves.

The new Eretz Israel calls upon us. Let us go and rebuild Zion. Our help, our support, our selves are needed.

Let us arise and build!

The turbulent months following the partition vote were for Habonim anxious months of waiting for direction. Overnight, the heady celebrations of partition had turned into a sober realization that the Jewish state would have to be established in battle.

The cost of the growing war, the immensity of the task ahead, and the knowledge that this was a total war, with the entire Zionist effort at stake, aroused our chaverim. How could we participate most effectively in this struggle? Could we be content with business as usual? In that terrible moment, when the question at hand was survival or destruction—for Eretz Israel, and, we believed, for the Jewish people—a movement which educated its members to feel personally responsible for the creation and defense of Eretz Israel could only consider one course of action: one that paralleled the path chosen by the Jewish community of Palestine.

This sense of urgency penetrated wider and wider circles and aroused elements that had been far removed from the Zionist struggle. There were plans being discussed for a broad call to action to American Jewish youth, and our movement prepared itself for an active and leading role.

A program began to evolve, based on the emergency needs of Eretz Israel. In this light, an urgent *mo'etza,* a national council of the movement, met in Cleveland in March 1948 and laid the groundwork for a national mobilization of Habonim—a *giyus.*

"Recognizing that the Jewish people are at war," the mo'etza declared, "recognizing that our enemies are bent on the destruction of the achievements of the past fifty years of constructive Zionist effort, recognizing that in the last analysis our own strength will be the decisive factor, the national council of Habonim declares a state of emergency in Habonim in order to effectively mobilize the manpower of Habonim for the service of the Jewish people."

The mo'etza resolution went on to "call upon all chaverim over eighteen years old to submit to the discipline of a national *va'ad giyus,*" or mobilization committee, which was given a four-part plan to carry out. The plan called on all Habonim members in the Hechalutz organization to prepare for immediate aliyah or *hachshara* farm training ("individual cases to be brought to the va'ad giyus for personal consideration"), reiterated Habonim's commitment to chalutzic group aliyah, called on other members to participate in a "limited service corps for Eretz Israel," and decided to assign a limited number of members to stay on "to continue the important organizational and educational work of the movement in recruiting additional chaverim."

There were serious doubts within the movement. Our mission extended beyond the war in Israel. Would not this mobilization detract from this central role of Habonim? Would it not alienate considerable numbers who were not yet chalutzim? And would it not affect the entire approach and nature of Habonim?

As an educational youth movement, we concerned ourselves with the individual, his development, needs, and personality. We attempted to rear well-rounded, self-sufficient individuals, capable of making decisions. In speeding up aliyah, would we still be true to these purposes? Moreover, did we have the personnel for the va'ad giyus, for our hachshara farms, and for the guidance and orientation that would be necessary once our chaverim arrived in Israel?

Those entrusted with carrying out the mobilization were no less aware of the obstacles and implications than were its sharpest critics. But the forces which had impelled the mo'etza in its solemn, calm, and overwhelming determination were all too clear. And, in the first weeks following the mo'etza, the newspaper accounts of mounting death tolls and ever larger military actions in Israel fortified the conviction that we were being true to our movement's largest mission.

Now we had to bring the call to mobilization to every individual. To begin with, there were the members of Garin Aleph, the large group that was preparing to make aliyah together to kibbutz in the near future. It would have to compromise its elaborate plans for agricultural training and equipment purchasing in order to work toward the larger goal. And in the same moment that the movement proclaimed its mobilization, a new garin was called into being.

Selected madrichim and shlichim toured the country, interviewing all chaverim age seventeen and over, Hechalutz members and nonmembers alike. In the course of two months, approximately six hundred chaverim were interviewed. Eighty members of Garin Aleph, fifteen members of the new Los Angeles-Montreal aliyah group, and one hundred five other chaverim left on aliyah. Ninety chaverim went on hachshara. Thirty-five chaverim agreed to take on assignments in movement work. Altogether, an aliyah of two hundred left in nine months. Another thirty volunteered for a limited service corps, which did not materialize. Altogether, 60 percent of the chaverim interviewed responded to the mobilization.

The main chapters were written by those who went on aliyah, joining the settlements and the fighting forces of the new Jewish state. Scattered throughout the army were Habonim chaverim, some of them riflemen and sappers, others in senior technical and administrative positions.

Those who stayed behind struggled mightily to prepare the movement for the new era that was about to begin.

In Battle: Machal, the Volunteer Warriors for Israel

Akiva Skidell
Kibbutz Kfar Blum 1973

To fight the War of Independence, the newly created state of Israel urgently needed specialists with skills and experience: pilots, tank commanders, doctors, technicians, administrators. Thousands of overseas volunteers responded, among them close to two thousand Americans and Canadians, many of them veterans fresh from World War II. They fought valiantly on all fronts, in all three branches of the Israel Defense Forces, in any assignment they were given or took the initiative to create. Together, these Overseas Volunteers—in Hebrew, *Mitnadvei Chutz La'aretz*—were known by the Hebrew acronym *Machal*.

Over one hundred of Machal were killed in action, including the American West Pointer, Colonel David "Mickey" Marcus, who led the fight to break the siege of Jerusalem and link the eternal city to the Jewish state.

After the war, most of the Machalniks returned to their homes, but several hundred stayed on to found kibbutzim or work in their professions in settlements and cities throughout the country. Today, several wars and decades later, they, and others who came back, are still here. Now their children and even grandchildren are serving in the Israel Defense Forces.

Despite the passage of time, it seems as if those days are still with us. I recall vividly the late afternoon hour one Tuesday in July 1948, when a man in civilian clothes, armed with a pistol, drove up in an old jeep to the tomato field at Kfar Blum and ordered me to be ready in half an hour to go along with him to army headquarters. This is how my association with Machal began.

Actually, it will be recalled, I had begun having something to do with volunteering for the War of Independence (in the broader sense) in 1946 in New York, through my association with Ze'ev "Danny" Shind of the Mossad Le'Aliyah Bet, who had called on me to recruit volunteers for the ships

Adapted from ACCI Bulletin 1973.

transporting "illegal" immigrants. The several hundred men who passed through the portals of our recruiting office, which we called the Palestine Vocational Service, were the first Machal volunteers, long before there was a formal Machal and before there was an Israel Defense Force.

But to get back to the summer of 1948. At army headquarters in Tel Aviv, I was given my assignment: I was to proceed back north to Nahariya, to Seventh Brigade H.Q., to act as liaison between the commanding officer of that unit, Ben Dunkelman, formerly of the Canadian armored corps, and the minister of defense. I arrived in Nahariya on the eve of the battle of Nazareth, and Dunkelman had no time for me. Once the action was over, it turned out he had little use for a liaison officer anyway. If he wanted to see Defense Minister Ben-Gurion, he knew damn well where to find him and needed no go-between. Instead I was to have another assignment: the Seventh Brigade, especially its 72nd Battalion, was full of Machal people, and it became my job to act as their spokesman, welfare officer, education officer, and what have you.

My experience with the boys in the field may have been of some help when I was asked, in November, to take charge of the Machal Section in the Manpower Division of the General Staff. Thinking back on the Machal office, one recalls quite a range of activity that emanated from it: production of educational material in several languages (our chief product—a fine monthly in English, "Frontline"); welfare activities, with the help of volunteers from the local community and in very close contact with officers from abroad; social activities, in the later stages centered in the Machal Club on Hayarkon Street in Tel Aviv; representing the needs and problems of the Machal people to the Army H.Q. and the Ministry of Defense; contact with the units where the boys and girls were serving, to help straighten out any problems, from requests for leave or a transfer to a miniature rebellion in one of the units; assistance in some especially difficult medical problems or intervening in all sorts of legal entanglements with the Israeli authorities and especially with the foreign consulates.

As the war was winding up, emphasis switched to repatriation of the boys who wanted to leave; working out conditions of service of those who intended to stay on in the army—especially in the Air Force—as needed specialists; and assisting those who planned to make Israel their home after discharge from the service.

It was a cooperative effort of considerable proportions. At one time there were as many as seventy soldiers, and a good number of civilians besides, attached to the Machal office. But I cannot conclude this account of the Machal office without mentioning one who, alas, is no longer with us: Shimon Gafni, better known as Sunny Weinstein, the boy with the perpetual smile on his face, whose devoted activities on behalf of the Machalniks who tried to make their way in the new land of Israel, deserve long to be remembered.

On the Battlefield, 1948:
"We Were a Nation, But We Would
Have to Fight for It"

Engee Caller
Kibbutz Kfar Blum 1985

After lengthy discussions, Kfar Blum permitted me to join the Palmach, the mobile striking-units of the Haganah. It was early 1943, and the Palmach was then organizing its fourth company, the first to include city people. The unit was to have only a sprinkling of kibbutz members, who formed the core of the Palmach's highly trained force.

We were based at Kibbutz Givat Haim on the coast, where we worked fourteen days each month. This paid for our upkeep, plus ten days of training and bus fare home once a month. The Haganah could not afford permanent bases, so the kibbutz movement had established these sites to give the Palmach a base to live, work, and train.

During the training period, we were up at dawn. We began the day with a long run, which I found difficult, and a swift dip in the swimming pool. Sessions in the use of small arms, stick-fighting, physical exercises, Morse code, and topography followed. Then there were lectures on Jewish history, Zionism, Israel, and other topics. Our lecturers included some of the Haganah's top commanders, such as Moshe Sneh, Israel Galili, and Eliyahu Golomb. They used to stay and discuss with us the problems ahead until the late hours of the night.

Our most important task at the beginning was to learn the countryside. At night, we would be sent alone into Arab villages, where we had to mark such important points as the *mukhtar*'s home and the visitors' center. I won't forget the night I went through my Arab village. It was pitch dark and mongrel dogs were barking. The rustle of every blade of grass increased the palpitations of my heart. Despite the fact that I totally lack a sense of direction, I finally made it back to the Palmach tents on the kibbutz.

Because the Palmach had been outlawed by the British, we posted guards around our training sites to alert us to unexpected visitors. One night, my unit officer woke me and told me that two British army officers had come to the kibbutz. They said they were curious about kibbutz life.

As the resident American, I was assigned to accompany our English-speaking visitors, show them around the kibbutz, and steer them away from the base and the arms cache. I was given a room on the kibbutz and spent a week with these suspect "visitors." The whole time they were photographed from every angle by our people, who then checked on them with Haganah intelligence. On the day they were to leave, one of the officers reached into his pocket and produced a letter of introduction from the Jewish Agency asking that Givat Haim welcome these good friends of Zionism, all members of the British Labor Party. They had forgotten to present the letter when they first arrived. For years, the officers sent me New Year's cards at Givat Haim.

We always lacked training equipment. Once, when we were to have a lesson in the use of pistols, another girl and I had to travel to a kibbutz, an hour and two bus rides away, to get two pistols to use. They only had one holster, so I wrapped my pistol in a light summer scarf.

On the return trip, the only open seat on the crowded bus was next to a British army officer. I had no choice but to sit next to him. I noticed that he seemed enchanted by the countryside, so I struck up a conversation, explaining where we were and what we were seeing. Suddenly the bus stopped and was boarded by British and Arab patrols making a routine search for arms and other contraband. Everybody was ordered to get off the bus, but as I got up to leave, the British officer motioned for me to stay seated. He told the policeman that I was with him. The pistol was lying on my lap, wrapped loosely in a summer scarf.

It was crucial that each Palmach member know the countryside. Every ancient tree, every ruin, rivulet, hill, and settlement was marked out for us on maps, and we hiked unceasingly to ensure that we knew the land from every angle, blindfolded, in every type of weather, from every approach.

The culmination of these hikes was the annual march to Masada on the shores of the Dead Sea. At the time, the British forbade Jews to travel that far south into the Negev, but that didn't stop us. Loaded with food, water, blankets, some disassembled arms, and other equipment, we set out on a ten-day trek from Jerusalem to Masada and back. Once we passed through the potash works on the Dead Sea. Another time we visited the new settlement of Revivim and the wild canyons of Ein Gedi.

At Masada we would meet up with other Palmach companies, and on the eleventh day of Adar, the anniversary of Yosef Trumpeldor's heroic last stand at Tel Chai in the Galilee in 1920, we would ascend Masada. There were no steps, no path, no cable car. We climbed on our hands and knees, aided only by ropes we tied to heavy rocks. At the top, we were met by a glorious sunset. After a ceremony in the evening, we spent the next day exploring the ruins.

Our Palmach unit participated in every aspect of Haganah activity. We smuggled illegal immigrants in from Syria and Lebanon. We met immigrant ships that came across the Mediterranean. We freed our captured comrades from Atlit prison.

It became clear, however, that I was not to be a fighter. Instead, I was the company clerk. That meant long nights peering at lists in a headquarters tent lit by a kerosene lamp. It meant long bus rides visiting units throughout the north, checking on their provisions and the transfer of arms. It meant rising at dawn for Safed and getting off the bus at the snow-laden slopes of

Hermon to await the group that was settling Biriya at that ungodly hour in the morning. It meant transporting secret maps from point to point, clenching my teeth and fists but remaining silent as I was subjected to humiliating and degrading body searches. But the maps, hidden in a secret compartment in my briefcase, were never found.

In the late summer of 1945, I was sent as a *shlicha* to American Habonim. Upon my return in early spring, 1947, I was assigned to the commander of the Haganah for the Upper Galilee. Although I was officially a clerk once again, one of my first tasks was to act as translator for Hillel Landesman of Kibbutz Ayelet Hashachar, chairman of the Galilee Regional Council, on an official visit to the British army commander at Rosh Pinah. I seethed inside when the official representative of the British crown could not see fit to offer a chair to the white-haired representative of Galilee Jewry. His Christian chivalry was his undoing, however. He offered me a chair, and I offered it to Hillel while I stood at his side.

Like its military representative in the Galilee, the British empire was trapped in Palestine, caught between its native good manners and its disdain for the Zionists. In Palestine, the Jews and the Arabs were moving toward confrontation, with Jews ready to right for our statehood and the Arabs ready to fight to prevent it. Britain could not make peace between the sides, and was unable to decide that one side should be made to submit.

By 1947 Britain was more than ready to wash its hands of the whole problem. The world waited in anticipation for the upcoming United Nations vote in the fall on the plan, submitted by the special UN commission appointed the year before, to partition Palestine into Jewish and Arab states.

In Rosh Pinah, our British commander demanded that the Jews withdraw from the Galilee. Britain was of the opinion that the Arabs would attack and pillage all the Jewish settlements in the region, he said. With quiet dignity, Hillel told him we would never leave our homes. If necessary, he said, we would defend ourselves with our meager resources. We were determined to build the Galilee for ourselves, he said, and for our children and the rest of our Jewish brethren streaming into the country.

Only a few weeks later, the British left Rosh Pinah. We occupied the police station before the Arabs could get there and used it for our headquarters. On the way, we peeked into the barracks where Hillel had met the commander. On the wall was scrawled: "Welcome to the Haganah." At least one British soldier understood our right to exist.

On November 29, the United Nations voted. Partition was approved. The Jewish state was to arise alongside an Arab state, with the border between the two drawn in a crazy-quilt pattern. Parts of the central Galilee were to go to the Arab state, most of the western and northern sections to the Jewish state. The Arabs of Palestine began attacking Jewish settlements everywhere.

I continued to serve as a translator. On the night of one of the fiercest attacks on Ramot Naftali, I was glued to the wireless at Ayelet Hashachar while the Ramot Naftali nurse reported on the wounded. Despite my meager knowledge of medical terminology—in both English and Hebrew—I translated her words to an American Jewish doctor who had come to help us. I then translated his advice and prescriptions back to the nurse.

In addition to translating, I would distribute wireless messages to the appropriate officers, according to the instructions of the wireless operator. The operator knew I was from Kfar Blum, but he did not know that I had grown up in Habonim with Ari Lashner. And so it was that the operator was deeply embarrassed at my emotional reaction when I read the message he handed me on March 16, 1948: Ari Lashner killed by a sniper from a neighboring village while working on Kfar Blum's electrical poles.

The United Nations had set May 15 for Britain to hand over Palestine to the new Jewish and Arab states. As the date approached, we came under heavy attack by Arabs from across the Lebanese and Syrian borders.

Finally, after refusing for months to do so, we realized it was time to evacuate the children, women to care for them, and older parents to safer places. Twice I had to say goodbye: once to my comrades at Kfar Blum and once to my family at Kfar Giladi. Members of Kfar Blum went to our old home at Binyamina, returning to Kfar Blum only at the end of 1948.

On May 14, 1948, at 4:00 p.m., on the eve of the Sabbath in Tel Aviv, David Ben-Gurion addressed Jewish Agency Executive and the Vaad Leumi, the Yishuv's national council, and declared the independence of the Jewish State of Israel. We were a nation at last, but we would have to fight for it. At midnight, when the UN partition plan legally took effect, five Arab nations around us invaded Palestine, joining forces with the Palestinian irregulars who had been fighting since the fall.

The war was fought with tricks and cunning as well as force. One night, we sent a caravan of trucks and other vehicles south to Tiberias with their lights off. They then turned around and headed north, with their headlights on. The next day the Arab radio reported heavy reinforcements had arrived for the Jewish forces in the Galilee.

After we had secured the Galilee, my brigade went south and took part in the battles around the Gat/Gal-On area, and then north again to the Western Galilee. In November 1948, my army career ended—if, indeed, an army career ever ends here.

Kfar Blum, 1948:
The Death of Ari Lashner

Rose Breslau
Kibbutz Kfar Blum 1948

It happened yesterday between 10:30 and 11:30 in the morning. He was helping to set up electricity for some of the houses and so strapped himself to a pole in the fashion that such work is done. While he was working, a trigger-happy Arab from Salchia shot him in the back.

The entire kibbutz was shocked and stricken by his death. People gathered and stood together in small groups for comfort. No one said anything. The quietness and stillness were uncanny. And all the time, various pictures of Ari flashed through my mind, but the one that was the clearest was that of Ari standing on a flat stone near the stage of the amphitheater of the Habonim camp at Killingworth, Connecticut, lecturing at the seminar . . . That picture of Ari, young and vital, will always remain with me.

I cannot really describe the great feeling of despair that took hold of us at his going and the manner of his going. It is still incredible. His body was taken to the Mazkirut building, and from there, carried and driven to the little cemetery near the garden. The people followed near and behind the coffin. There was an escort of men with guns to protect us. Only the clump-clump of hundreds of boots walking through the mud could be heard. Kieve said a few words before the coffin was lowered into the ground. He spoke about the conflict in Ari's nature: How he loved beautiful things—a good book, music, art, a glass of wine—and how he had, on the other hand, the desire to come to Eretz Yisrael and take part in its upbuilding. Kieve spoke about his years in the movement, his years at sea, and his work with the ships. . . . He spoke simply and beautifully.

Part II

5

In the Era of Jewish Nationhood

"We Did Not Know That We Were Our Parents' Children"

Leonard Fein

Boston 1988

May 14, 1948, when statehood happened, was almost an anticlimax, the climactic event having taken place months earlier, far from the swamps and the desert, in a place called Lake Success, New York. There, on November 29, 1947, the United Nations had voted to partition Palestine and to permit two states, one Jewish, one Arab. Perhaps we danced on the streets in May of 1948: in November of 1947, we danced and we wept, for there was no getting away from the fact that on the morrow of our unspeakable tragedy, we were reborn.

And we, of course, had a piece of it. We of Habonim were part-owners. We'd met real Jews from Palestine, and some of our own *menahelim,* group leaders, had gone off to till the soil and fight the war, to experience what we knew as *hagshama atzmit,* self-fulfillment. (There's a critical clue there: We were never taught that the life of the *chalutz* was a life of self-sacrifice; on the contrary, it was the good life, richer in its satisfactions than any other.)

With what envy we young ones had watched as our seniors (themselves in their late teens) demonstrated in front of the British embassy, or packed arms for illegal shipment to Palestine. With what admiration we bade farewell to the volunteers of Machal, the volunteer diaspora corps of the new Israeli army. With what resolve we sought to speed our own adolescence, so that we could join them in the work of building.

Ah, we were filled with ourselves. We were the silver salver on which Jewish statehood would be reborn, and we were the pioneers of the new social democracy that was sure to come here in America, too.

141

Builders and Dreamers

I do not know whether the "we" numbered more than several hundred—several hundred, that is, for whom Habonim was truly a movement, not merely an "organization" (the contemptuous term we used to dismiss Young Judaea and the other bourgeois entities our peers belonged to). I know only that from the age of eleven, our endless debates on the ideal society so obviously marked us (to ourselves) as serious (not somber) that we may well have been insufferable to those denied the Labor Zionist dispensation.

It is difficult now to recall the issues that inspired and aggravated us, or even those that marked us off from the generation of Habonim (every two years in the movement was a generation) that had come before. In August of 1945, when I was eleven, Miriam Falk Biderman, then *rosh* at Camp Moshava, informed us at flag-raising that a terrible new weapon had been dropped over a place called Hiroshima, a weapon that would change the world and our lives.

In the early 1950s, as McCarthyism took hold, we debated endlessly the question of how explicit we ought to be in declaring ourselves socialists. Might such a declaration, expressed in our statement of principles and inscribed on the back of our membership card, not alienate the parents of the ten-year-olds we were so desperately trying to recruit? In 1948, as the rest of the country was deciding between Truman and Dewey, we, too young to vote, debated the choice between the Democrat Truman and the Progressive candidate Henry Wallace, between pragmatism and principle. We quarreled over the Korean War, our radicals insisting that we should condemn both sides for their imperialism and resist the draft, our pacifists, newly inspired by Gandhi, demanding that we refuse to carry arms, most of us way over our heads; we were still kids, more comfortable with abstract utopian ideas than with immediate policy questions, not yet aware, so long before the 1960s, that kids—read "students"—could change the world. We were more at ease debating the relative merits of the kibbutz and the *moshav shitufi*, the collective model versus the cooperative model. And because our debates were so intense, we prided ourselves on being, in a gray-flannel, conformist era, cut from a very different cloth.

But the point (or so it now seems to me) of all the quarrels and debates was less in their substance than in the very fact of them, the indication that young people (including very young people) could profitably spend a Saturday night talking big talk. Whether the talk was bloated, whether it was well- or ill-informed, I cannot say, I do not know. But it marked those of us who engaged in it for all time: We took not only ourselves, but also ideas, seriously, and we learned to float comfortably from idea-talk to kid-talk and back.

Around us, there swirled all the events that have since entered the history books. We knew of them, but only at a vast remove. What, for example, could it mean to us, chalutzim-in-the-making, that David Ben-Gurion, prime minister of Israel, and Jacob Blaustein, president of the American Jewish Committee, were making agreements on the meaning of Zionism and its implications for American Jewry? *We* were the vanguard, and it was *our* debates and *our* decisions that would shape the Jewish reality. Was it not, after all, but a tiny vanguard that had brought the Jewish state into being, and were we not the agents of that vanguard here?

How much a period-piece the Blaustein-Ben Gurion agreement now seems, how tangential to the real issues that have defined—and clouded—the Israel-diaspora relationship these past decades. And yet how important a clue it offers. For the agreement, specifying the limits of Zionism's claims on American Jewry, was struck with a leader of an explicitly non-Zionist organization. We, part of Zionism's inner family, were bypassed—and, as time went by, we began to realize that under the new circumstances of Jewish sovereignty, the explicit identification as "Zionist" was an identification of declining value and significance. Soon enough, all American Jews would fall under Israel's thrall. The only distinction we could claim was our commitment to aliyah itself. But it did not take long to learn that for all that aliyah remained our formal purpose, few of us were moving beyond purpose to practice. What, then, was our special claim, what our distinguishing quality? Pro-Israelism became the mass commitment of all America's Jews, and the capacity of others to express that commitment in politically more potent or financially more generous ways than we were able to, would lead Israel to reassess the relevance of American Zionism.

But all that was off in the troubled future. During the still-glory years, we were sure of ourselves and of our role.

I say, "we," though for the thousands of people who passed through the movement, ephemeral success stories of our sporadic organizational efforts, the heady arguments and the fixed purposes made little difference. It is the radically smaller number for whom Habonim was home that I have mostly in mind in these reflections. And even for that hardy band, it is probably a mistake to say that the ends of the movement were more important, or even as important, as its means. I cannot now say with any confidence just how political we were, even though we took our politics, domestic and Israeli, quite seriously. My impression is that our ideological intensity was principally a device for rationalizing, justifying, extending the core experience, which was psychological rather than political. Perhaps it is ever thus, politics—as Harold Laswell put it—as the displacement of private motives onto public objects. The curious and possibly distinctive element of our experience, however, is that we were gathered up at a young age, when private motives are just taking shape, and what we were taught was to internalize the public motives of Labor Zionism, to make them our private motives.

That is what we were taught and what we in turn taught. The teaching reflected socialist optimism regarding human nature; it drew on the precedent of the chalutzim, who quite clearly had made the nation's agenda their own; above all, it spared us the effort of defining private motives for ourselves, for so readily at hand and so insistently pressed upon us were sanctioned motives of historic consequence and revolutionary possibility.

At this remove, the rest of it is a blur. We sang the Spanish Civil War songs without knowing much about the Spanish Civil War (I speak here of my own generation, of course); we marched with the NAACP (this was in Baltimore) to desegregate the one legitimate theater in what was still, by law, a Jim Crow town; in Union Square in New York we eagerly debated with the Marxists, citing Arthur Koestler on the corruption of the revolution, and went home to sing folk songs the Weavers were later to make famous. We knew that Adlai Stevenson was Jewish and Dwight Eisenhower was white bread ("bourgeois" was our universal dismissive word until Lenny Bruce came along) and that folk dancing was more honest than the cheek-to-cheek stuff and a hundred other things that no one else knew, or so we believed.

It seems to me now that the one thing we did not know at all was that we were, after all, our parents' children. We supposed that we were making a decisive break from the bourgeois habits of our immigrant parents, that it was we who were described in the Hebrew song, "A song of youth, a song of our future, a song of renewal, building and ascent." In truth, however, we were a generation of continuity, and our Jewish/leftist sensibility was not significantly different from our parents'. Nor, for that matter, was our Zionism, at least in the case of those of us—a decisive majority—who did not make aliyah. We were, as our parents had been, *chovevei Zion,* lovers of Zion. And the adjustments, the compromises, the bargains we eventually made with ourselves and with history were not so very different from theirs.

Nor, I suspect, have the disappointments been, whether in the world or in ourselves. The internalization of public motives is a mixed blessing, especially in an environment where that is neither the practice nor even the norm. Asking what you can do for your country makes greater inaugural rhetoric, but is hardly the conventional American standard. And as we have watched Israel unfold, an Israel so very different from the one we imagined, loving Zion—from a distance—has become ever so much more complex than we had thought. The experience of Israel has raised questions about our optimism, now rendered quaint, naive, as also about ourselves, questions best left unspoken here.

In 1950, the kibbutz was a harbinger of the future; by 1960, it was, as Buber described, an experiment that had not failed. In 1950, for reasons I cannot now comprehend, we were still persuaded that the world was manageable and that human nature could be changed, whether by a more enlightened and less exploitive economic system or by the power of rational persuasion or by progressive education; by 1960, the shock of the Holocaust had worn off, and the lessons had begun to take. In 1950, we were witness to what voluntarism could accomplish, for that was Israel's story. By 1960, *mamlachtiut*—statism—had become Israel's method for accelerated development, and the mystique of pioneering was on its way to the museum of sweet/quaint memories.

In 1950, and still in 1960, the prospect of American Jewry seemed grim at best. We would not be able to prevail against the temptations of the open society. By 1970 and 1980, the Jewish community here had become more vigorous, more ambitious, more satisfying. In 1950, America seemed a dull place; serious culture meant European culture, and serious politics was surely not possible without a social democratic party; by 1960 and 1965, America was at the very least interesting, and its blessings of freedom increasingly noteworthy and praiseworthy. In 1950, we who shared in the Labor Zionist dispensation felt ourselves quite alone in our insight into the Jewish condition, into the human condition. By the mid-sixties, whether because of the rise of countercultural expressions or because of the greater centrality of Israel in American Jewish life, our perceptions were no longer so distinctive.

Still, it seems to me that the answers with which we began have, over the years, given rise to the questions with which we now live, and they are, for all that they disconcert, healthy questions. The words of the songs we sang have faded from our memories, and that is likely as it should be; new lyrics are now required. But the melodies linger on (and, as that phrase itself demonstrates—"*hamangina nisheret*"—snatches of the lyrics, as well). And why not? "Arise" by any other name would sound as sweet, so long as it is to build.

Gesher Haziv, the Western Galilee, 1949: "To Settle the Land Immediately and Permanently"

Mikey Duvdevani and Kieve Finkelman
Kibbutz Gesher Haziv 1959

The time: Chanukah 1946. The place: New York. The purpose: a gathering from across North America to create Habonim's first organized settlement group, or *garin*.

The ideas were nebulous, the approach fiery and idealistic. Our main goal was just to establish a framework for the garin. We succeeded in doing just that, and forty members joined.

Over the next six months the executive committee enunciated the garin's basic principles of membership. Problems of *kupah* (communal fund), higher education, vocational training, and equipment lists were tackled by letter and personal contact. To make executive meetings easier, and to create a center for garin activities, a *bayit* was formed.

The bayit was truly the turning point. Twenty chaverim living together in one house, pooling their lives and living as a kvutza in anticipation of aliyah, converted intent into reality. The house was opened in October 1947 in Brooklyn's Seagate section. It became a meeting center for the movement in general, as well as a favorite inn for wandering movement people. Of course, we also remember the notorious chaver who came for a weekend—not a garin member—and stayed for three months because the atmosphere was so congenial.

But the bayit played a vital and varied role.

When the Jewish State decision was accepted by the United Nations General Assembly, the whole movement gravitated that night to the bayit and celebrated the event there. Literally hundreds of our chaverim—and dozens of residents of staid Seagate—joined us at the bayit.

Large-scale, organized aliyah from Habonim emanated from the house. The planning, the purchases, the meetings, and aliyah seminars were all centered there.

At the time of arms purchases for the Haganah, the members of the bayit were active. The Seagate bayit was one of the first addresses investigated when the authorities discovered dynamite being shipped to Palestine through New York harbor.

There is no need to talk of the many fond, personal reminiscences, such as one dollar for a week's allowance and how to spend it, the search for inexpensive recreation, the furnishing of the house, the Silver's Steam Baths on Friday nights, the Sunday morning ritual of cleaning the bayit, which consisted of moving all portable objects in the house (including our three-month visitor) onto the sidewalk, and many more such items.

The first large aliyah group of Garin Aleph arrived for training at Kibbutz Ramat Yochanan, outside Haifa, in April 1948. The kibbutz was attacked that very same day. The group joined a small group of Americans who had come earlier to form a focal point for the garin. More aliyah followed rapidly, and in a period of a few months more than eighty members were concentrated at Ramat Yochanan.

This was the period when the largest need in the country was settlement. Israeli officials wanted to guarantee the army's gains on the ground, and the only effective way to do that was to settle the land immediately and permanently. We had been at Ramat Yochanan a mere nine months, and were far from achieving our basic and essential training needs, when we began clamoring for settlement. Jewish Agency people were reluctant to give us our way. They wanted to pamper and protect this American Habonim garin. After weeks of wrangling, we finally won.

We then decided that we would not go out alone and thus become an American island in a sea of Israeli culture. Language problems still beset us; our reading of the Hebrew press was perfunctory; discussions were carried on in English; the vocabulary of the radio news was way above most of us. The solution we envisioned was uniting with a group that had a strong Israeli background. We found such a group in the people from Bet Ha'arava.

Bet Ha'arava was a kibbutz on the north shore of the Dead Sea, founded less than a decade before. Some months earlier, in the first May onslaught of the Transjordanian Arab Legion against the newly declared state, Bet Ha'arava fell and its members were evacuated. They were now preparing to resettle on a new site, within the borders of Israel.

The site chosen for us, on the Mediterranean seacoast north of Haifa, was a British army camp overlooking the Arab village of Azib. Near the end of spring the Arabs, who had watched the encirclement of Hanita, Matzuba, and Elon, fled their village for refuge in Lebanon. They went over the rock of Ras en-Nekura—Rosh Hanikra—in the wake of one of those inexplicable Haganah victories.

On January 27, 1949, the garin arrived, and from that moment, the hill became ours. It rained that day, and the sky was sullen and heavy. The stripped cement-block buildings stood roofless, windowless, and doorless. There were large streaks of gray from the rain. The ceremony was impressive and well attended, but the guests left before dark. The chaverim had covered one of the buildings half with flat tin and half with canvas. At an odd assortment of tables, Gesher Haziv ate its first supper.

Urim, the Negev, 1950: "We Wanted to Strike Out on Our Own"

Shimon Kasdai
Kibbutz Urim 1985

A generation in the movement is only about five or six years. In the period after World War II, it was the generation of Garin Aleph that ran Habonim. These were the chaverim who participated firsthand in the struggle for Jewish statehood.

We, the members of Garin Bet, had been spectators more than participants in the historic events at the close of World War II. We watched as the victorious Allied powers squared off into a Cold War, culminating in the Korean conflict. More important for us, we watched as the Zionist struggle in Palestine reached a decisive phase. We avidly monitored the news of illegal immigration, arms-smuggling, and the political struggle in the United Nations. When the state of Israel was declared, Habonim danced in the giant hora in Times Square and celebrations were organized in every Habonim chapter. But as the Independence War broke out, Garin Bet was still on the sidelines.

Shortly after the founding of the state, Garin Aleph departed for Israel. There they joined with a group of Israelis who had left Kibbutz Bet Ha'arava after it fell to the Jordanians, to found Gesher Haziv on the Mediterranean coast.

When our time came for aliyah, a year or two later, we were loath to follow blindly in the footsteps of Garin Aleph. Although they encouraged us to join them at Gesher Haziv, we wanted to strike out on our own and make our own unique contribution.

Our first discussions about the possibility of group aliyah took place in 1947 at the Habonim Institute, the half-year leadership training program in New York. Just over a year later, at the hachshara farm at Smithville, Ontario, Garin Bet held its founding meeting. In short order we had more than one hundred twenty members.

Under the press of events in the Middle East, the members of Garin Aleph advanced their aliyah dates. Consequently, the members of Garin Bet were forced to sacrifice their personal plans to fill leadership positions in the movement and to keep the training farms running.

In retrospect, Garin Bet turned out to be the link between the pre- and post-Independence periods in the movement. We were the last to participate in Habonim Institutes in New York and the first to participate in Institutes in Israel. We were the generation that implemented the decision to establish the Workshop program in place of training farms in America. Our first wave of settlers was the last to come directly from America, with no prior living experience in Israel.

The first groups of settlers from Garin Bet arrived in Israel in the spring and summer of 1950. We spent a year training at Kibbutz Geva. During that year, eighty of our members arrived at Geva and finally we were ready to decide where we would settle permanently. Many of us wanted to establish our own, new kibbutz. The kibbutz movement and the other settlement authorities pressured us to join one of the many weak and struggling kibbutzim. Finally, we decided to join Kvutzat Urim, in the Negev.

Urim lies in the western Negev desert, about thirty-five kilometers northwest of Beersheba. Settled by Bulgarian refugees brought out of Europe in 1943 and 1944, it was one of eleven kibbutzim set up literally overnight in a dramatic operation that took place the evening after Yom Kippur in 1946 in defiance of a British settlement ban.

Some of the Bulgarians had done their training at Kibbutz Geva, before Garin Bet had arrived. In 1948, the site of the kibbutz was moved slightly to the north, to a strategic point controlling the Gaza-Beersheba-Hebron road. The new spot had been a British police compound and a school for Bedouin children.

When the eighty Americans of Garin Bet joined Urim's forty veteran settlers, it seemed as if we were at the end of a dust brown world. Writing to our members still in North America, one person said we lived in a dust hole.

The early years were far from easy. The radically different cultural backgrounds of the members, combined with the primitive living conditions, led to endless misunderstandings and conflict and a steady exit of both Bulgarians and Americans. By the mid-1950s, however, our economic situation began to stabilize. And at this point we were joined by the third element of population—native-born Israelis.

In the years that followed, four Israeli garinim came to Urim. Garin Bet proved to be only the first of several American Habonim garinim. But our garin, the group that oversaw Habonim's transition from the pre-state period to the era of Jewish nationhood, was to be the last massive settlement group from North American Habonim.

Habonim and the Great Israeli Labor Schism

Almost as soon as Garinim Aleph and Bet came to Gesher Haziv and Urim respectively, they were caught up in a raging debate that was cutting through the heart of the Israeli kibbutz and labor movement at the time. It was a debate that would lead ultimately to a painful schism—the *pilug*—that would leave Labor Israel divided and bitter for two generations.

The roots of the split went back almost twenty years, to the period of the early 1930s when the Mapai labor party first arose. The new party had brought together nearly all the factions of Labor Zionism, aside from the sectarian Marxists of Hashomer Hatza'ir, in one big party of labor under the sole leadership of David Ben-Gurion. It was to serve as a political parallel to the single trade union founded earlier in the Histadrut.

The unity, however, masked some basic differences of belief. These continued to fester under the surface. One of the most important was the question of socialist militancy. Was Labor Zionism part of an international socialist movement or of world Zionism—or both? How closely could it work with the parties of bourgeois Zionism, whose vision of Israel conjured up private enterprise and economic inequality?

By the early 1930s, Ben-Gurion and Mapai had decided the question firmly in favor of close cooperation with the non-socialist wings of Zionism. According to some historians, the key reason for the decision was the rise of Zionist Revisionism, the ultra-right wing movement of Vladimir Jabotinsky. The Revisionists seemed to have taken on as a sacred mission the breaking of the Histadrut and the defeat of Labor Zionism.

In response to the Revisionist rise in the 1930s, Ben-Gurion's strategy called for the labor movement to forge an alliance with some of its nominal enemies, the capitalists. Labor, of course, was to be at the helm, allowing it to set the priorities of the Jewish state-in-the-making. But leadership implied that Labor's agenda must become, first of all, a national agenda uniting all Zionists toward the building of a Jewish state. As a result, Labor's once militant economic and social agenda began to soften.

By the early 1940s, a group of labor leaders centered in the kibbutz movement began to rebel against Ben-Gurion's moderate new social program. Led by Yitzhak Tabenkin of Kibbutz Ein Harod, the ideological center or "mother of Hakibbutz Hame'uchad," the rebel group began as a dissident faction within Mapai. It was known simply as *Siah Bet*—Faction B.

Toward the end of World War II, Siah Bet left Mapai altogether and formed itself as a separate party, to be known as the *T'nuah le-Achdut Ha'avodah*, the Movement for the Unity of Labor. "Unity" might seem to be an ironic term for a schismatic sect; it must be remembered, however, that Tabenkin's larger goal was to press for the unity of the working class in the face of Israel's growing capitalist sector. From 1948 to 1954 they joined with Hashomer Hatza'ir to form the United Workers' Party, or Mapam.

For most Jews in the diaspora, even most Habonim members at the time, the schism seemed like distant hair-splitting based on a clash of personalities. For those who had settled on kibbutz, however, the emergence of a new labor party—led by the top leaders of Hakibbutz Hame'uchad—produced a wrenching crisis of loyalty.

The kibbutz in 1948 was much more than a village with a collective lifestyle. Kibbutzim were political units, identified with a political party, and they saw themselves as building blocks of a new type of society. The rise of Achdut Ha'avodah forced every kibbutz, and every kibbutz member, to choose sides. They had to decide whether they stood with the leadership of the kibbutz movement or with the leadership of Mapai.

The choice, moreover, cut deeper than simply how to vote on election day. For most kibbutzim, this was a question of basic identity. There was little tradition in Hakibbutz Hame'uchad of freedom of conscience, of leaving party loyalty to the individual. And so, entire kibbutzim began choosing sides. In the process, angry confrontations arose. Families were divided. Friends stopped speaking. On some kibbutzim, white lines were drawn down the middle of the dining hall floor: Mapai members sat on one side, Achdut Ha'avodah members on the other.

Finally, in the early fifties, kibbutzim began to split in two. In some cases, one group would leave to join another kibbutz, leaving behind the farm in which they had invested their lives. In other cases, the kibbutz was actually carved up, as one group went to a far corner of the fields to build a new village with its half of the farm's property. In September 1951, the kibbutzim loyal to Mapai joined together with the old Chever Hakvutzot, the band of smaller communes that had long since outgrown A. D. Gordon's agrarian visions, to form Ichud Hakvutzot Vehakibbutzim—the Union of Kvutzot and Kibbutzim. Habonim's first Workshop, newly arrived in Israel, was present at that historic gathering.

The Ichud would prove to be a very different type of kibbutz movement from the Me'uchad. From the beginning, it refused to demand party loyalty from its members. Although it retained formal ties to Mapai, winning formal representation on various party bodies and institutions, it left its members free to join any party they chose.

For American Habonim graduates in Israel, choosing sides in the schism was almost a foregone conclusion. The socialist militancy of Achdut Ha'avodah had little appeal for Americans raised in a two-party system of compromise and cooperation. Beyond that, the promise of liberalism and freedom of the individual, implicit in the Ichud's formation, had a powerful appeal to the Americans. In time, as we shall see, American Habonim graduates would take the lead in pushing the Ichud to new levels of personal freedom, giving the member more control over personal budgets, bringing children home to sleep with their families, even permitting the establishment of synagogues on secular kibbutzim.

The *pilug,* the split in Mapai and the kibbutz movement, was little more than a distant echo to most Habonim members in America. Yet, it had two immediate side-effects on North American Habonim. One was the creation by the Me'uchad of its own youth movement in America, known as Dror (liberty). The other was the formation, after ten years of failed attempts, of a World Habonim organization uniting the separate Habonim movements in the countries of the English-speaking diaspora.

Dror-Hechalutz Hatza'ir: A New Labor Zionist Youth Movement Comes to America

Yehuda Paz
Kibbutz Kissufim 1985

Dror ("Liberty") did not last long in America as an independent youth movement. It was formed in the years immediately following World War II in the wake of the split in the Israeli labor movement between Mapai and Achdut Ha'avodah, and more specifically after the polarization of Hakibbutz Hame'uchad into pro-Mapai and pro-Achdut Ha'avodah camps.

The Mapai faction in the kibbutz movement left the Achdut Ha'avodah majority in 1950 and 1951, joining with the Chever Hakvutzot movement to form a new federation, Ichud Hakvutzot Vehakibbutzim.

Historically, American Habonim had strong links with Hakibbutz Hame'uchad: Kibbutz Kfar Blum, the first American Habonim kibbutz, for example, was a full-fledged member. But Habonim also had strong ties with Mapai, through its historic association with the Labor Zionist Organization of America-Poale Zion. And so Kfar Blum, Ma'ayan Baruch, Urim, and Gesher Haziv, all with American Habonim graduates as members, joined the new federation.

Dror-Hechalutz Hatza'ir (the movement's full name) was founded by those loyal to Hakibbutz Hame'uchad. Throughout its history it was the American youth arm of that kibbutz movement. And when Hakibbutz Hame'uchad reunited with the Ichud in the 1980s to form the United Kibbutz Movement, Habonim and Dror-Hechalutz Hatza'ir merged as well. All in all, Dror existed in America for over thirty years. And if its achievements were not monumental, it did succeed in bringing significant numbers of Americans on aliyah, founding Kibbutz Kissufim in the western Negev, and contributing to the development of several other kibbutzim. At its zenith, Dror reached out to significant numbers of American youth. Dror was the creation of a small group of shlichim who set out with the specific aim of founding a new movement after it became clear that Habonim would remain entirely in the Mapai camp. This was a first foray to North America for all but one of them. They lacked financial resources and had to take full-time jobs to support themselves. They were snubbed by Zionist institutions and by the shlichim of different political persuasions. Still, they were able to establish the nucleus of a new movement.

It truly was an outstanding delegation. Between 1947 and 1950, it included Yaakov Eshed, leading ideologue of Hakibbutz Hame'uchad; Yehiel Shemi, who later became one of Israel's leading sculptors; Dov Meisel, who went on to create the Museum of the Diaspora in Tel Aviv; Aharon Megged, later one of Israel's best-known novelists; and Hadassah Diner, one of the early American pioneers in Palestine and a founder of Kibbutz Afek-Mishmar Hayam.

This intense, talented, and spirited group established a communal home and movement center in the Borough Park section of Brooklyn, where they attracted a growing number of American youngsters and an ever-changing parade of visitors from the kibbutz movement, the Palmach, and the labor movement.

In the heady atmosphere of those early days of Israeli independence, Dror expanded rapidly, opening branches throughout New York City, Toronto, Montreal, Chicago, Detroit, and elsewhere. Summer camps were established, each bearing the name of a kibbutz. The central camp, in Liberty, New York, not surprisingly was called Ein Harod, after the mother kibbutz of Hakibbutz Hame'uchad.

In 1949, in cooperation with the Hechalutz organization, Dror bought a training farm in Verbank, New York. This marked a coming of age for the movement. It meant that among its ranks were people serious about making aliyah, for whom agricultural training and experience in communal living were crucial. They were kibbutzniks-on-the-way.

Garin Aleph, the first Dror settlement group, completed its American-based training in 1949 and the following year settled first at Kibbutz Kabri and later at Kibbutz Na'an. Garin Bet, the second and largest settlement group Dror ever organized, filled Verbank beyond capacity during 1950. By the end of the year, they were all at Kibbutz Na'an. There, a joint settlement group of North American and South American Dror gathered and in the middle of 1951 founded a new kibbutz, Kissufim, less than a kilometer from the Egyptian-held Gaza Strip.

During the next few years, more settlement groups were formed and passed through Verbank on their way to Kissufim and other destinations. But as the stream of settlers trickled down, the need for a training farm passed as well. Settlers began to go directly to Israel for training, and like the training farms of the other movements, Verbank was closed down and sold.

Yet for those of us who sojourned briefly at Verbank; those of us whose
first experiences with nature were as awkward young Jewish students trying
to look and act like farmers; for those of us who spent our evenings in long,
intense discussions and then forced ourselves to awaken at dawn to go to
work; for those of us who huddled together not only to keep warm during
a winter when we had no money for fuel but also to keep out the cold
world which regarded our en-route-to-Israel life as a strange cross between
idealistic foolishness and adolescent rebellion—for us, Verbank will always
remain a crossroad in our memories, the place from which we set out to
live our dream.

In the best tradition of Hakibbutz Hame'uchad, Dror regarded itself as an
activist movement. Every member was required to make aliyah. It held that
the kibbutz was the only framework for full socialist Zionist self-realization.
It was radically socialist, at times occupying the very edge of the left flank,
and radically Zionist.

Its message, if simplistic, was crystal clear: our greatest privilege is the
opportunity to participate personally in the Jewish national renaissance in
Israel. Participation means linking the struggle for new and revolutionary
social justice and socialism with the struggle for national liberation. As the
kibbutz is the most complete juxtaposition of those two aims, the kibbutz
is the overriding moral imperative for which the movement exists.

Dror attracted a group of intellectually and culturally sophisticated
members. For example, long before almost any one had heard of the land-
mark fragment of young Karl Marx called "Alienated Labor," the movement had discovered a mimeographed translation which was dutifully
discussed and slotted into the educational program. Dror was known for its
surplus of experts on the more arcane aspects of socialist Zionist theory,
and its leaders were often invited to address the ideological seminars of
other movements.

When Achdut Ha'avodah and the old Left Poale Zion faction merged in
Israel, inevitably the union was extended to North America as well. This
led to a strange marriage: Dror with its young American-born pioneers-on-
their-way coupled with the largely foreign-born, Yiddish-speaking, commit-
ted-to-America leftists of Left Poale Zion. Although the differences in thinking and life-style were too great to be overcome, the union did not fail
entirely. Common political positions were hammered out, particularly in
Canada, and the Left Poale Zion Yiddish schools became bases for Dror.

Despite its small numbers, Dror played a role on the youth movement
scene in America. For example, when I was the national secretary of Dror,
I was also deputy chair of Hechalutz and for a time chaired the Young
Zionist Actions Committee. That I held these positions was not an exception
but the pattern. Perhaps the intensity of our commitment attracted our colleagues in other movements.

In sum, if today the kibbutz is not only my home and that of my wife and
family, but the basis and expression of my worldview, the wellspring of my
activity, and the root-source of my beliefs, it is from Dror-Hechalutz Hatza'ir

that I first learned those truths. It was a brief, bright, hard flame; a dream, a vision, a hope; a small, tightly bound group; a road and a direction.

The Founding of World Habonim

Yola Lee
Kibbutz Gesher Haziv 1951

The founding of an international Habonim organization climaxed a long process of evolution, and was a triumph of reality over slogan. The Habonim movements in each country began independently, on different platforms and in differing circumstances; each evolved its individual traditions. Yet despite all the surface differences, they were really one movement.

Habonim movements were united, first of all, by a common cultural heritage. Each evolved within a Jewish community rooted in a free, "Anglo-Saxon" culture—in England, Ireland, Australia, South Africa, and Holland as well as the United States and Canada. In every country where it was active, Habonim based its outlook on a sense of responsibility for the Jewish community and of identification with the whole Jewish people and tradition. In each country, Habonim oriented itself gradually toward chalutz-centricity, educating its members to self-realization in Israel's cooperative settlement movement. In every Habonim movement, that process was one of free choice, never compulsion.

Habonim everywhere based its chalutz education on attraction to the positive values of creativity and collective living in Israel rather than on a negation of the diaspora. Habonim in all countries rejected dogmatic ideological collectivism, just as its vision of society rejected dictatorship. We sought to build a society based at once on socialist economics and morality, and on personal freedom and the democratic process.

This basic identity of the Habonim movements provided a basis for common action during the ten years that Lishkat Hakesher, the Contacts Office, existed. These same educational values and goals were the underlying reality of World Habonim.

For all that united us, though, our unity evolved slowly. It began with the first joint settlement of chalutzim from British and North American Habonim at Kibbutz Anglo-Balti, the forerunner of Kfar Blum. In 1941, while the group was still in training at Binyamina, a conference was called of Habonim graduates in Israel. It set a long-range goal of unifying the Habonim movements in the English-speaking countries. As the first step, Lishkat Hakesher was established.

Its immediate task was to make contact among the various movements and to link the movements with Kibbutz Anglo-Balti in Eretz Israel. The central tools were the typewriter and the mimeograph machine, and its first institution was the periodical *Hamekasher* ("The Link").

The Lishka, as conceived at Binyamina, was to evolve into an office "to represent the interests of the Habonim movements before the national institutions in Eretz Israel; to negotiate with these institutions on all questions affecting the work of the Zionist youth movements in the English-speaking countries; to assist the national movements in the sphere of cultural activities, information on Eretz Israel, etc.; to deal with the question of shlichim to the various movements; to arrange for the absorption of Habonim *olim* [immigrants]; to keep their obligation toward Eretz Israel before the attention of the movements in the various countries; and to unite the movement in support of Kibbutz Anglo-Balti."

The ultimate task of Lishkat Hakesher was "to pave the way for the amalgamation of the Habonim movements into a world-wide organization, at a world conference to be called at the earliest opportunity."

Ten years passed between the Binyamina declaration and the convening of the world conference, a delay that was the legacy of war. The job of maintaining contact began well, and the first issues of *Hamekasher* were filled with discussions on the nature and task of Habonim. But they bore little fruit for the war caused an aliyah gap of more than five years. This drove a deep wedge between the movement generation that first built Kfar Blum and the later generations to reach Israel.

The long-awaited postwar aliyah brought life and drive to Habonim in Israel and reestablished the lines of contact between the chalutzim here and their movements at home. At the same time, the new aliyah brought with it an atmosphere of suspicion between the veterans and the newcomers. The newcomers brought with them the outlook of the movements overseas, each jealously preserving its own local traditions. For the veterans, the differences among home movements paled in comparison with the daily challenges of chalutz life.

There was one very real ideological issue dividing the movements: the "political affiliation" of the American movement. At Binyamina, the American movement's affiliation with the Poale Zion party had been dismissed as a minor point, or characterized as "greater political maturity" on the part of the Americans.

The matter became more complicated after the split of Mapai and the emergence of the left-wing Achdut Ha'avodah splinter. Now the question was not just whether Habonim should formally identify with Labor Zionist politics, but which Labor Zionist party one followed. Moreover, the split in Mapai had all the viciousness of a divorce, and the children were not spared. In Eretz Israel, party branches, kibbutzim, and even families were divided. In its wake came splits overseas that nearly finished off the chalutz youth movements of Europe. English Habonim in particular responded with revulsion toward any whisper of party affiliation in the youth movements.

During the war years English Habonim had experienced a unifying process of its own that confirmed its abhorrence of party affiliation. Wartime refugees to Britain from the Continent had recreated their various chalutz splinter movements, but they managed to link them in a union known as Mishmar Habonim. Mishmar, in turn, united with English Habonim on a "general" platform of conscious nonaffiliation. Then, too, the English youth movement's experience of Labor Zionist politics was a senior Poale Zion party intimately identified with the British Labor Party.

For all these reasons, the English movement cherished its political neutrality as a core principle. Despite all the postwar efforts of English Habonim graduates in Israel, the movement refused to amalgamate with American Habonim as long as the Americans retained their affiliation with the Labor Zionists.

This, then, was the "ideological" problem that took center stage when Lishkat Hakesher convened for a conference at Kfar Blum in the spring of 1947. And yet the mood was upbeat, for underneath the divisions ran a substratum of the movements' basic similarity and the pressing need for concrete action. The old leadership still believed that acquaintance and mutual experience would soften the new generation as it had the old, and that a formula would emerge in good time. For this reason, they rejected the compromise proposal to establish a "Federation of Habonim Movements." Instead, they decided to postpone World Habonim indefinitely, and to continue practical work within the loose framework of Lishkat Hakesher.

From a purely practical standpoint, the need was immediate and pressing. Aliyah was growing, raising new problems of absorption. The new phenomenon of *garinim*, organized settlement groups, had blossomed in several countries, bringing special problems of training, absorption, and the need to find suitable partners in the founding of new settlements. All this added to the work of the Lishka.

Then there were postwar shlichim to be recruited, trained, and put through the formal processing routine of the Zionist roof-institutions that would employ them. Soon afterward, the American Habonim Institute moved to Israel and became international in its makeup. And there were the after-effects of Israeli independence: absorbing those who had come to Israel as volunteers during the War of Independence and wanted to settle there, the activity connected with various summer courses and institutes, and much more. There was the problem of gaining influence in the various national institutions—the government, the Jewish Agency, the kibbutz federations—to achieve the cooperation we needed for all of this. Lishkat Hakesher moved from Kfar Blum to Tel Aviv and steadily increased in scope, prestige, and activity.

Almost imperceptibly, the Lishka became an informal international executive committee. The movements began to work smoothly in harness, and the suspicions gradually disappeared. The leadership training courses were an important factor in this process for they provided a constant, living link with the movements overseas. Certain differences would linger, but now we understood the underlying similarity of our approaches, our goals, and our needs.

What was gained by the changeover from the informal Lishkat Hakesher to a formal world movement? Probably the first practical effects were felt in Israel, and touched the average movement member overseas only very indirectly. After all, most of the practical powers of a world executive had been wielded by the Lishka for some time. Nor did changing the name permit any major action to be taken without the agreement of the national movements.

Still, there are various areas in which the establishment of World Habonim marked significant progress. First in significance was the fact that the world movement gained an Israeli wing in the youth movement Tnuah Me'uchedet, with all that this meant both practically and psychologically; this could not have been done under the tenuous arrangements of a contacts office.

Then, too, the existence of a world movement was a powerful lever in our delicate but important relationships with various Israeli institutions. It increased our status in negotiations—for shlichim recruitment, for placement of visiting groups, and much more—with the various settlements of our own movement.

In any case, the movement in Israel was too big a business to work through informal understandings and traditions. Even by the time World Habonim was founded, we boasted ten Habonim settlements plus garinim in Israel. In addition, the movements overseas had begun to lean more and more heavily on Israel in such matters as leadership training, "work-study" courses, and so on. A clear, efficient, integrated structure was essential.

Questions of Adaptation: Zionism in the Era of Jewish Statehood

The birth of the state of Israel would in the long run pose a profound challenge to the Zionist movement in the diaspora: having accomplished the urgent goal of nationhood, the movement's reason for existing would become less and less clear. Even for the chalutzic youth movements, committed to mobilizing young Jews for personal self-realization by settlement in the young state, much of the drama was gone. The very nature of the call to youth to join in the salvation of the Jewish people lost much of its urgent appeal once the deed was done.

In the early days of statehood, the challenges were mostly joyous ones. Travel was now open and unhindered, making possible a much freer exchange of people and ideas between the youth movements in the diaspora and their graduates and leaders in Israel.

One of the first decisions of American Habonim after the establishment of the state was stunningly obvious: the transfer of the movement's leadership training course, the Habonim Institute, from New York to Israel. Now that the state existed, there was no reason for the movement's would-be leaders to spend an extended period after graduating high school in New York, discussing what Jewish nationhood might be like, when they could experience it directly.

Starting in 1949, then, the Institute ceased its operations at the Jewish Teachers' Seminary on East 70th Street in Manhattan and was transferred to the labor college at Beit Berl, near Tel Aviv.

Within a year, however, even that began to seem outdated. If the movement's future leaders could come to Israel to experience it, rather than talking about it, why were they sitting at Beit Berl and talking about kibbutz, the highest expression of the movement's ideals?

The Launching of the Habonim Youth Workshop in Israel

Yehiel Sasson
Kibbutz Kfar Blum 1985

I was the first of the post-World War II American immigrants to Kibbutz Kfar Blum to return to the United States as a shaliach. That may be because I was one of the first Americans to go to Palestine after the war. I had been stationed in the United States throughout the war. Each time I was to be sent abroad, something came up to spare me, and when V.E. Day came, I was promptly demobilized because I had a son.

I made it to Israel in a very prosaic fashion. Using the G.I. Bill of Rights, I obtained a student visa and was registered at the Hebrew University. I entered Palestine in June 1946 with a group of olim, mostly women and children holding precious immigrant certificates and a few men with student visas. My student visa, however, was just a way to get me into the country; once there, I "got lost" in Kfar Blum. Since I had a solid Hebrew education and some experience in business, I was swiftly absorbed into kibbutz life and served as treasurer before and during the War of Independence.

With many misgivings, we went on shlichut to Habonim in early 1951. As Americans, we hoped we would understand American youth better than our European-born counterparts, and so might be able to accomplish more despite our relative lack of experience.

After several meetings with the leadership of Habonim and some contact with Jewish youth in general, it became apparent that the foundation of the state of Israel had created no great revolution or revelation among American Jewish youth. The few thousand members of Habonim—the same number as always—included some very bright, articulate, and inspired young people. But the vast majority of young Jews, even the university students and the intellectuals, were completely indifferent to the dramatic events in Israel. In retrospect, the Six-Day War seems to have had a much greater impact on the Jews of America than the creation of the state.

Those shlichim who had European backgrounds set out to convert the masses of Jewish youth to Zionism. They preached doom and growing anti-Semitism in America. Like Ben-Gurion, they believed in the percentage theory: with more dedicated effort, we could convince 1 percent of American Jewish youth to move to Israel. The American-born shlichim, by contrast, realized that to enlist American youth as Zionists and convince them to move to Israel would require a long, difficult process, involving more intensive Jewish education as well as youth movement techniques.

Based on the success of training farms in Europe prior to the war, the European-born shlichim felt that if Hechalutz, the umbrella Zionist pioneering organization, could expand its network of training farms, thousands of people would go to Israel. Ironically, the farms then in existence, including the two largest, Habonim's in Creamridge, New Jersey and Hashomer Hatza'ir's in nearby Hightstown, had survived the war only with great difficulty. They were underfinanced and severely short of people. To me, and to the national leadership of Habonim, it seemed an anomaly that the members of the training farms in America should live in conditions worse than those of the settlers in Israel. Moreover, it was not clear that those who passed through the training farms in America were more successful in adjusting to kibbutz or Israel than those who came by different routes.

Following this line of thinking, we decided to sell the farms and use our assets in a more productive fashion. We conceived of the Youth Workshop in Israel. For the first time in many years, the gates of Israel were open. Modern transportation made the trip feasible.

Zvi Opher, then shaliach to Hechalutz, was very skeptical about our approach. But being a responsible and forward-looking person, he was prepared to accept the decisions of the Habonim leadership and the "American" shlichim. The Jewish Agency's Youth and Hechalutz Department was more reluctant to change the traditional modes of training. It took several trips to Israel to persuade them.

Since we had very little money at our disposal, the trips to Israel were not easy to arrange. On one trip I managed, with the help of Aharon Remez, then with the Israel Defense Mission in New York, to hitch a ride on a Catalina amphibian plane being flown to Israel for the Israel Defense Forces. The plane stopped for repairs in Iceland, London, Rome, and Athens before we arrived in Israel, three days after takeoff. We had several meetings, and in the end, Ben-Zion Ben-Shalom, the director of the Youth and Hechalutz Department, made a special trip to New York to convince us of our errors. Instead, with many reservations, he agreed to the plan.

Thus, in September 1951 the Habonim Workshop was launched as a program of work and study, based on kibbutz, for a selected number of Jewish high school graduates, primarily members of Habonim. That first year the program included extensive touring, experience in kibbutz and moshav life, ideological seminars, leadership training, and more. It was too much. Even in a year, the program could not achieve all its objectives. Subsequently we narrowed it to include long stretches on kibbutz, punctuated by educational touring and seminars.

During my stay in the United States, we sent two Workshops to Kfar Blum. And like most pathfinders, the program encountered many difficulties. But by the time we came home to Israel in 1953, it was an established form, and its basic pattern still exists.

The First Habonim Workshop, 1951: "The Chance to Travel to Far-off Israel"

Fradle Pomerantz Freidenreich

Ridgewood, New Jersey 1985

The creation of the Habonim Workshop truly opened a new path in Zionist youth education. The State of Israel was barely three years old, and the notion of a comprehensive, year-long work-study program in Israel for American Jewish youth was unknown. The Workshop, in fact, set the pattern that is still felt today in American Jewish education.

Not surprisingly, then, the departure of the First Workshop was an occasion for public recognition, even fanfare. On the evening before our departure, we had what looked to our adolescent eyes like a fancy reception at a hotel in New York City. The leading officials of the senior Labor Zionist movement attended and saluted the program, the participants, and our parents for allowing us to be part of such a "radical" venture. After the speeches, we sat for a formal photograph that appeared in the next day's Yiddish and English newspapers.

The forty-two people on the First Workshop formed a motley group. Most were active leaders in Habonim, but several had no previous connection to the movement or to organized Zionism (although, in those days, it was difficult to be completely unconnected to things Jewish). Some of us had completed one or two years of college; others were fresh out of high school. Some had had an intensive Jewish education, while others could not read a Hebrew letter. Some had already declared an intention to settle on kibbutz; others barely knew where Israel was.

To complicate matters, the group had not been screened for emotional maturity, work and study habits, or the ability to live in a group setting. As it turned out, the people in the group had extremely divergent capabilities in these areas.

Still, the chance to travel to "far-off" Israel seemed, in our minds, to combine romanticism, uniqueness among peers, idealism, and the chance to escape everything that local life represented. Even those of us who had attended college were still living at home.

We left New York on a small KLM charter plane to Paris. With stops at Gander, Prestwick, and Amsterdam, the trip took more than twenty-four hours. We slept overnight in Paris and then had a few hours to run through the Louvre and stroll down the Champs Elysées. For a group of unsophisticated teenagers, it was pretty heady stuff.

From Paris, we stood like sardines on an overnight train to Marseilles. After a brief day exploring the city, we boarded the S.S. *Negba,* one of the infamous trio of Israeli ships that carried passengers across the Mediterranean. Our five days aboard that vessel, and I use the term advisedly, provided a unique entry experience into group living. We were housed as one unisex group in steerage, and we slept on canvas cots in a room adjacent to the boiler. Dim bulbs burned day and night so people could find their clothes, beds, and toilet facilities, such as they were.

The ship carried three hundred people too many, mainly immigrants from Morocco and Eastern Europe. Most of them slept on the deck, where a warm September provided respite from the close conditions below. There was an air of urgent expectancy, despite substandard health conditions that left twenty-one Workshoppers suffering from food poisoning.

The S.S. *Negba* was our first encounter with the new state. The Israelis working on the ship, besides flirting with the Workshop girls, gave us an opportunity to hear about life in Israel from a point of view other than that of a diaspora Jew. These were not intellectual discussions but the perspectives of young adults not much older than ourselves who were living what was for us the Zionist dream. Until then, our role models had been our shlichim and those members of the movement who had gone to the hachshara farms and then to kibbutz. Now, for the first time, we were meeting Israeli citizens, not necessarily idealistic or committed to what we felt was a holy mission. The interchanges were enlightening, and sometimes a rude awakening. When we docked at Haifa five days later, one small group of immigrants on our ship was found smuggling diamonds in their chasidic-style fur hats. The discovery was a shock to the country, and to us.

Our first sighting of the Israeli coastline was classic Hollywood fare. We arose before dawn, rushed to the ship's railing, and kept our eyes peeled for the memorized pictures of the Haifa oil refineries. When we saw them, some of us unabashedly shed tears while others assumed a more poised and sophisticated posture, trading pleasantries about the view. Some of the new immigrants broke into the strains of "Hatikvah." At that point, we all gave in to our emotions.

My memories of our early weeks in Israel often seem linked to other movement-related events. I recall that as I stared at the stars after our first kibbutz dinner at Gesher Haziv, I remembered how impressed I had been when I first visited the Creamridge farm and the Seagate bayit, the Habonim communal house in Brooklyn. Each had evoked images of communal living in action: young adults taking responsibility for their destinies without the comfort and familiarity of parents and home. Idealism come true. Arise and build.

But we were not at Camp Moshava, Yad Ari, or the local Habonim center. We were in a Habonim kibbutz in Israel, where babies had been born, and where security and the work schedule were the primary topics of conversation. It was simultaneously exhilarating and sobering.

After Yom Kippur, we moved to our first home away from home at Beit Berl, the Mapai party's ideological study center near the village of Kfar Saba. That year, 1951, was a year of austerity, and although we lived institutionally and were sheltered from the worst of the shortages, we still felt deprived compared to what we were accustomed to at home. We conditioned our stomachs to dozens of variations of eggplant and cauliflower. We made a nightly routine of sneaking out to the citrus groves of a neighboring moshav to fill our wastebaskets with oranges. Little did we know how grand our diet was then, compared to what we would not have by the spring, when, living at Kibbutz Urim, a pat of margarine would be the Sabbath treat.

But 1951 was also a time of strong idealism, when Zionism was not a word to be sneered at. It was thrilling to feel a part of the nation building experience. We were awed by the unbelievable absorption efforts. The countryside was dotted with tent and tin hut transit camps housing tens of thousands of immigrants. A visit to a flooded immigrant camp after a major rainstorm in November helped us put our own shortages in a more realistic perspective.

Reaching out to meet others, we found that our Israeli peers were serving in the army, founding new kibbutzim, and working with new immigrants, and they still looked strong, healthy, and pleased with life. We were proud to be identified with Mapai and the kibbutz movement. When we traveled, we tried hard not to look like tourists and insisted on wearing our blue Habonim shirts. We found a society that wanted to receive us.

As a special group from abroad, unique opportunities were created for us. In addition to our studies of Hebrew, Bible, and Israeli geography and culture at Beit Berl, we heard guest lectures by outstanding personalities such as Abba Eban. We visited Ben-Gurion in his garden and talked at length with Golda Meir at her office in the Labor Ministry. Our talks touched on all aspects of Israeli life.

We were watched over by David Breslau, the "dean" of the Workshop at Beit Berl. When we let him, he was a combination of teacher, mentor, warden, and surrogate father/mother. Dave did much to shape our course of events and interpret our impressions. He laid the groundwork for the new Workshop model. It was at Beit Berl, under Dave's tutelage, that we began to accept the reality of being away for a year.

After Beit Berl, we went to Kfar Vitkin, a well-established moshav north of Tel Aviv, for five weeks. Each of us lived with a family in their modest, two- to three-room homes (my family's shower was a roped off section next to the hot water heater in the living room, where I slept on the sofa).

Each family had a chicken coop, a barn with two or three cows, a garden, an orchard, and fields. Most of us had a chance to try our hands at a little of everything. I learned to milk, to deliver the milk in cans to the central dairy by horse and wagon, to dig irrigation ditches for the citrus trees, pick fruit, gather eggs, cut beet-sugar, and help care for my family's three young children. One of the highlights of my Kfar Vitkin stay was helping the veterinarian when he artificially inseminated our cows. Who knew you could immobilize so large an animal by pinching her nostrils?

Our Workshop group had a choir that enjoyed a modest reputation. As a farewell to the moshav, we offered a dance/choral presentation that caused quite a stir in the village. Our musical repertoire included some Yiddish songs, and as we performed, the secretary of the moshav, a crusty old bachelor, stormed out of the hall in protest over our use of the "ghetto language." We carried on undeterred, and were later praised by moshav members for our brave "galut perseverance" in standing up to the secretary.

By January, winter was in full swing, and what better time to move to Kfar Blum in the northern Galilee for four months of mud, rain, and cold. The concrete buildings especially built to house our group had a capacity of thirty, so ten of us were moved in pairs into small tents at the opposite end of the kibbutz, overlooking the Jordan River. It was a shock to open the tent flap, look out at the trickling stream and think of the image we had once held of the Jordan.

It was a hard winter, and our living arrangement did not contribute to group cohesion. My work was especially isolating, since I worked on the kitchen's special-diet crew, which required me to be at work by 4:30 A.M. to clean fish and pluck chickens.

Some Workshoppers got to know members of the kibbutz by working with them and being invited to their homes. It was hard, though, partly because there was a ten-to-fifteen year age difference between our group and the kibbutzniks—not enough to be like parents, but not close enough to be like big brothers.

Toward April, we were offered choices for the last three months of our year. Most opted to extend the kibbutz experience, and so thirty of us went to Urim, a new, undeveloped kibbutz, made up largely of American Habonim graduates. Many of them were people we had known from home, two, three, or even six years older than us, just a step or two ahead in life. It was easy to identify with them, and I remember those months as the closest thing I could imagine to what I thought my own future might be like.

In fact, the Urim period was the closest thing to real kibbutz living that we had experienced. The Workshoppers were interspersed among the unmarried kibbutz members and social interaction was far greater than it had been at Kfar Blum. Because the kibbutz was so young and short of manpower, we had a great opportunity to work in all areas and take on responsibility. We even stood armed guard at night, keeping an eye out for Bedouin infiltrators who came to steal the irrigation pipes.

When Passover came, we joined in the kibbutz seder, held in the shell of what was to be the kibbutz dining room. Sitting with the kibbutz members and their guests, reciting the kibbutz *haggada* to the accompaniment of the Negev breezes, underscored the deep differences between us. It was our first Passover away from the family table and its familiar traditions. The large kibbutz gathering with its lack of intimacy, the sense of distance from loved ones, was pervasive. And yet, we were in a kibbutz mood, wearing the embroidered Yemenite shirts we had all bought that year, still flush with the excitement of the agricultural Omer festival held in the fields that afternoon. We felt young, pioneering, infused with our living Zionism, and yet homesick. I felt a bittersweet ambivalence.

Even now, more than thirty years later, it is hard to assess the Workshop experience. The group was not cohesive, had been poorly selected, and was not well prepared for that which it was to encounter. Yet, we were afforded undreamed of opportunities, and learned skills and facts firsthand which were out of reach to most of our American peers. We had a chance to participate in a dynamic period of Jewish history and to make headway into our own search for a Jewish identity as adults. There is no doubt that the Workshop was a significant adventure for us all and that its impact would remain with us for a lifetime.

Five marriages were a direct result of that year. One of our group died a few years ago. The rest are aging gracefully, entering the time of life where one is a parent to two generations—our children and our parents. Most of us have married, some have divorced, and all have entered the usual professions and businesses. Six of us, to date, have made aliyah; one is living on a kibbutz. Many have been frequent visitors to Israel; some have children living there and others have attended a variety of Israel-based programs. Some of us are very active in our local Jewish communities and synagogues; others are totally uninvolved with anything Jewish. Some are still active in the Labor Zionist movement. There are about fifteen of us about whom nobody seems to have any information.

Given the demographics and average probabilities, it could be argued that all of us might have ended up doing what we do concerning Israel and Jewish communal life anyway. I suppose that is probably true, especially since we hardly fulfilled Habonim's mandate for us to return as movement leaders and then settle in Israel. But when I speak with a few of our group who are far removed from Jewish life in any organized form, they say that the Workshop made a deep and important impression on them. It forged a living connection with Israel, kibbutz, and the Jewish people. The year provided a frame of reference so that when they reflect on their Jewish roots, they feel a certain specialness about the year. That is no small measure of the effectiveness of the program.

For me, personally, it was a year of maturation and personal bonding with the young and idealistic country. It was also the beginning of a pervasive, personal, mental aliyah syndrome that still affects my own plans and my children. For all the difficulties this has caused me, I am grateful. Because of it, my life has a dynamism, a greater sense of purpose, and a heightened sense of the centrality of Israel in my own Jewish weltanschauung. Although such ideas were first nurtured by my family and deepened by my Jewish education and experience in Habonim, they were reinforced by my year on the First Workshop.

Screening Applicants for Workshop

Sarah Lederman
New York 1985

In 1952, Billy Goldfarb, then the national secretary of Habonim, called me at my office at the Jewish Vocational Association of New York. At the orientation sessions, two days before the Second Workshop was to leave for Israel, a serious problem had emerged: Could I please see a young lady for an evaluation?

Working out that problem convinced me that a program sending young people abroad from all parts of North America needed concerted and professional screening. As a product of Pioneer Women's early experiment with adolescent young women, I had learned directly from Sophie Udin, our leader, that professional know-how could and should be put to use in behalf of the movement. I therefore assumed responsibility for organizing a screening procedure for the Workshop program.

Supported by my friend, the psychiatrist Dr. Lillian K. Kaplan of blessed memory, we rallied a group of psychologists and social workers, former Habonim members in various cities and the shlichim to the movement. A systematic approach was developed for interviewing potential Workshoppers. When significant doubts arose, we could implement a full psychological profile. A central screening committee in New York reviewed every application. This effort challenged the awareness of those in the Habonim leadership eager to fill quotas and enlist numbers for the Workshop as to what it meant for some young people to live this closely to others so far away from family and home. On the other hand, the Habonim leadership helped standardize the relationship between the screening committee and the people "out there."

During the year, those of us in New York began to believe that the Israeli counselors could use some coaching about the needs of these American and Canadian adolescents, especially those who proved to be fragile, homesick, or have problems with separation. To that end, I was inveigled to accompany the Third Workshop on its trip to Israel in September 1953. It was my task to oversee this inordinately large group—more than sixty young people, including ten between the ages of twenty-one and thirty—across the Atlantic, through the port of Naples, and across the Mediterranean to a safe haven in Haifa. There, I met with the Israeli counselors for the Workshop from

Kibbutz Geva and Kibbutz Kfar Blum. One of the most poignant and satisfying chapters of my life was the exchange and study of the screening
process with Pinchas Rimon during the week I spent with him as he took
that Workshop to Kfar Blum. I like to think this was one of the hardy
seedlings that eventually led to the flowering of the North American tenth
grade program for which Kfar Blum is now famous.

The screening process developed and was honed by my experiences along
with those who took the work seriously. If the use of an idea is evidence of
its worth, this system was reviewed and adapted by Aryeh Nesher for the
Jewish Agency's Sherut La'am national service program. Moreover, our
screening program allowed for the inclusion in the Workshop program of
newcomers to the movement. We found that newcomers could be successfully chosen and integrated if a Workshop was composed of about 10 percent
nonmovement members. They challenged our own members to assess their
values and demonstrated that nonmovement members could assume responsibilities and become bona fide members of the Workshop as well as respond
to the movement's philosophy.

For me personally, by staying in touch over the years via the Labor Zionist
movement's CHAY Commission (Commission on Chalutziut and Youth),
through interviews and added committee work on a variety of levels, I have
found my thinking constantly refreshed and stimulated. Moreover, seeing
these young people grow into leadership roles here and in Israel has enriched
me. I have been moved by and proud of the caliber of person that Habonim
and the Workshop have nurtured. The Workshop builds an everlasting bond
between its members and the deepest tie to our common destiny.

New York, the Early 1950s:
"It Was Inefficient, Gentle and Decent"

Marion Magid
New York 1962

To confess that one belonged to Habonim Labor Zionist youth movement
is to invite silence from all sides; it is not accounted a significant error and
does not even appear in the ledger of important disappointments of the age.
To "radicals" and/or ex-radicals it is, of course, a betrayal of the real, the
only, cause; to members and/or ex-members of the more dogmatic Hashomer
Hatza'ir it is sissy stuff—*they* had real court martials, group analysis, the

This essay first appeared in *Midstream,* September 1962, as an appreciation of the
book *Arise and Build.* Reprinted with the author's permission.

girls were not allowed to wear lipstick. Worse, it is square. To the free spirits who were never even tempted, it connotes every kind of retrospective badness: group activity, uniforms, socialist realism, bad prose, calisthenics. To the uninformed it is no different from the boring concerns of their parents. To non-Jews who came to New York from the midwest, it has a certain quaintness, but it is not really as colorful as a childhood in Brownsville, or eight years at the yeshiva. To Israeli sabras, preferring girls from Stockholm or at least Iowa, it is, of course, squarest of all. (I had not been on Tel Aviv's Dizengoff Street long before I learned to keep a discreet silence about the sources of my racy, Russianesque Sephardic Hebrew.) Finally there is nothing to do with this book [*Arise and Build*] but read it in guilty secret, savoring everything—the incredible Anglo-Hebrew prose, the line drawings of Bat Sheva at the pump and Dan at the *Ohel,* the smell of mimeograph ink which still seems to hover about the outsize pages. Prepared to be bored, beguiled, condescending, nostalgic, one is yet not prepared for the avalanche of memories that comes bucketing down. In the end there is a curious maternal impulse to shield the book from the gaze of the cosmopolitan outside the art cinema. "Are you returning to your origins?" he asks cleverly, brandishing his own Gallimard paperback.

I was a member of Habonim from the late forties to the early fifties, and the reason was that it appealed to my sense of the heroic. The alternatives seemed out of the question. My friends put their hair up in bobby pins and taught each other dance steps; it was not enough. I longed to be a girl in khaki who accompanied a jeepful of men across the African desert. I longed to be Ludmilla Pavlichenko, the Yugoslav partisan girl who parachuted behind German lines (starring Philip Dorn) and would not talk. I loved her name and her accent. I used to lock myself in the bathroom, draped in a sheet: "Yes, my name is Ludmilla Pavlichenko; do your worst, you swine!"

My friends went to the Loew's Paradise on Saturday afternoons. They formed a club called "Les Amies" (pronounced, *Les Ameez*). They asked me to join but respected my decision not to—our family was different. We had penholders and camels made of olivewood; paintings from the Bezalel Institute of Rebecca at the Well on black velvet; views of the Old City in Jerusalem bound in leather and veiled by tissue paper. We had *Are the Jews a Race?* by Karl Kautsky and the complete works of I. L. Peretz. The parents of my friends questioned me extensively. "How come you aren't kosher?" They thought we were excessively Jewish, yet we did not go to Shul on Yom Kippur. We must be some kind of Bolsheviks.

A girl in my class joined the A.Y.D. She tried hard to recruit me. It seemed more feasible than Les Amies, but not quite right somehow. Every summer Gilda went off to interracial camp where she was taught never to say "God bless you" when anyone sneezed, and the words to "I Dreamed I Saw Joe Hill Last Night" and "Bandera Rosa." I liked the songs well enough but was doubtful about the overall style. My aunt was "progressive." She and her cronies from the boardwalk at Brighton Beach wore wooden beads, gypsy earrings, peasant skirts, and blouses; most of them had moustaches and were badly in need of dental work. Gilda and her friends were only twelve, but well on their way to that style. They took modern dance classes from Negro teachers and marched, in sturdy Foot-Saver shoes, in the May Day parade. I went to a few meetings of the A.Y.D. but the square dancing put me off. It was not really foreign; it was not really heroic; it did not have that Ludmilla Pavlichenko quality. When I became a Zionist, Gilda and I stopped being friends for a while; then in 1947, when Russia voted in favor of the establishment of Israel, we reconciled. I called for her at the headquarters of the A.Y.D. A huge sign was strung across the meeting hall. *"Shalom Aleichem, Chaverim,"* it spelled out in Hebrew letters. At the interracial camp, Gilda learned to dance the hora.

I lived in the Bronx, but the first Habonim meeting I went to was in Manhattan. The geographic factor was crucial—Manhattan seemed much farther away from the Bronx than Palestine did from America. We had a large family in Palestine and photographs of all of them arrived regularly: innumerable barefoot children in white sunhats, tractors, wooden bungalows, on special occasions they were photographed in Russian blouses in green or brown rotogravure. The landscape of those photographs was as familiar to me as my own block—but we had no relations in Manhattan. A few years later, a sizeable portion of my generation was to see the East Side for the first time on the way to psychoanalysis; I discovered it through the Labor Zionist movement.

The Manhattan *machaneh* (unit) met in a baronial town house on 70th Street between Third and Lexington Avenues. It had a marble stairway, fireplaces, a panelled library, stained glass windows. I had never seen anything like it. The boys wore white shirts, open at the neck. To me they looked like scions of a noble house, singled out for heroic action of some sort. I can remember nothing that was said at that first meeting—only figures silhouetted against those patrician windows. (Even today, any group of two or more in a room seems to promise an ideological outcome; I cannot have dinner at a round table without secretly expecting someone to read the agenda.)

A few weeks later they took us by truck to the Hechalutz training farm in Creamridge, New Jersey. In the failing light of a late November afternoon, the farmhouse was sad and beautiful. It did not look Jewish. Night fell. We lay on the floor, propped on our elbows, while stumps of candles burned in overturned ashtrays. "My sister," the narrator continued, "leans against a lamppost in Shanghai—purer, still, than any virgin." The Jeremiah symphony revolved seventy-eight times a minute. Someone asked me to go for a walk. I was dazed, the blood pounded in my ears. American dogs from nearby farmhouses barked as we walked down the long black country road. "Woe unto them that are at ease in Zion," he said. I could hardly breathe. I had never heard a midwest accent before. Gates seemed to swing open. The noble empty truck was parked near the noble farmhouse. The next day they let me sort socks in the *machsan* (clothing storeroom). Tenderly I separated the warriors' sad, noble socks into twos and plotted the course of my life: I would leave high school immediately and become a *chalutza;* I would ride on the back of open trucks with a rifle at the ready and eat out of huge cracked plates with big tin forks and spoons. I would be Ludmilla Pavlichenko in Palestine.

Poor in-between generation that missed all the good parties and came a little too late for this one also. Nobody asked us to man barricades or smuggle arms or even leave the university for agricultural school. We were too young. An arms cache was discovered, it was whispered, at the Seagate *bayit* (Habonim clubhouse), but we had nothing to do with it. We collected money for the Jewish National Fund on the Independent subway and pasted stickers saying "Boycott British Goods" all around town. We hoped to be arrested, but weren't. When partition was voted in November 1947, we danced a hora around the Times building; all the Zionist youth movements turned out for the occasion. The Hashomer Hatza'ir members had snappy dark blue shirts with red strings at the neck—they made a better showing than we did.

I was sent to a seminar camp for prospective *menahalim* (leaders) in the summer of 1948. A *madrich* (instructor), specially imported from Detroit, sat at the head of a long table. "The Boy Scouts," he said, "are an organization designed to maintain the status quo." It was an eye-opener. We learned to cook shish kebab Israeli style, to roll cigarettes out of Bull Durham tobacco with one hand, to spring to our feet in case of sudden ambush. Every morning a shaliach with curly hair and a Roman profile stood before a map of Palestine with a pointer: noble sand-colored parallelogram: Latrun, Bab-el-Wad, Nebi Yusha. The camp was in the hill country of Vermont—Ethan Allen and the Green Mountain boys. There was no contradiction: Socialist-Zionism was a metaphor for every kind of gallantry. On Shabbat we carried around Borochov, Achad Ha'am, A. D. Gordon, but we read Kafka, Thomas Wolfe, Dos Passos.

What there was of ideology went down easily enough. It was socialism of the most natural kind, and brave Judaism. Neither I nor the people I knew then had a particular gift for dialectics—if they had, perhaps they would have been elsewhere than in the Labor Zionist movement at that time. In any case the old days of argument were in that past which had already become legendary: Kfar Blum, Ari Lashner, Enzo Sereni; arguments about Marxism at City College and movement strategy during World War II—"Fight the White Paper as though there were no war, and the war as though there were no White Paper." We listened dutifully to the *sichot* (talks) that were arranged—out of nostalgia one almost felt for the early days—but they were not the main thing. The main thing was the energy. For the first and perhaps the last time, there was an arena in which to act, a community to be addressed. No one wanted privacy yet. The kibbutz movement, we were told, had rewritten the Haggada to its own specifications and there were no holds barred on creative synthesis.

We synthesized everything we could lay our hands on. The reigning art form was the *Oneg Shabbat;* with a fine disregard for the formalities we combined Bialik with Bartok and fused them in a rich prose that owed a lot to Norman Corwin. When in doubt we lit more candles, turned up the phonograph, and instructed the narrator to pause ominously here and there. Nature was our ally; the wind in the trees, the rising of the moon, the rustlings in the diaspora night. Armed with enthusiasm we ventured where piety might have counseled reticence. We put Spinoza on trial for apostasy; he was acquitted, though not without a few bad moments. We conjured Herzl from behind the kitchen door and assured him of our wholehearted support; we chastised Heine for his ironies. For Tisha B'Av we walked by torchlight down to the lake and set the raft afire. The burning raft floated down to join the Neversink River and forty fourteen-year-olds dressed in their pajamas looked on in wonder. Transfixed at what we ourselves had wrought, we mourned the Second Temple as never before.

We worked together, ate together, went on scouting expeditions together; we did not sleep together. It has become, I believe, a cliché of youth movement sociology to note the discrepancy between the rebellion that was preached and the actual code of puritanical behavior. Sighs and furtive gropings rent the night at Camps Hiawatha and Laughing Water, designed to maintain the status quo, but at the kvutzot of the Labor Zionist youth movement, widely reputed among neighboring communities as centers of "free love," sex was sublimated to the larger attempt.

There were intimations of disorder. The war was won and the Zionist youth movement suffered the slight embarrassment of fulfillment. At the Creamridge *hachshara* an ideological struggle was in progress. The culture bloc was for Achad Ha'am and the anticulture bloc was for the egg route. The movement, it was being said, had for too long harbored bohemian elements with no intentions of "ascending." Alien ideologies reared their heads—sociology, group psychology. "Did you ever notice," a defecting chalutz suggested, "that pretty girls from non-Zionist backgrounds seldom remain long in a youth movement?" In the summer of 1950 the leadership was reading Karen Horney and David Riesman. A new jargon was heard around the campfires: ego ideals, group attitudes, interpersonal relations. The apple had been plucked and eaten. "You're basically a marginal person," the head of the kvutza told me in the clearing near the lake. I thought it had to do with sex. "You're only what people think you are, Nora," I replied, "so be careful whose mind you get into." I was in the grip of Djuna Barnes.

Leaving was sadly painless. I wore eyeshadow and was taken to the Thalia on Saturday nights. I learned that Yeats was not pronounced "Yeets." I forgot about Ludmilla Pavlichenko and wanted to be Rebecca West or at least Ursula Niebuhr. In the spring of 1951 the Creamridge farm was sold at auction. The movement, recognizing the changing times, had abandoned the idea of hachshara in America in favor of a more "normalized" approach—training institutes in the state of Israel. Red-faced farmers in sport jackets bid callously for the livestock and equipment; the noble farmhouse stood empty and haunted.

The main thing about ceasing to be a child is learning to forgive the past. It is curious, in retrospect, how little Habonim requires forgiveness; how much there is to be grateful for. It spared us, above all, the ignominy of the "Jewish Question"—in all the infinite variety and ingenuity of its forms. It was a way of being Jewish which was not problematic. We were saved from the primitive longing to shed our identity and the more complicated necessity for reiterating it at every turn.

We were never really as alienated as we pretended to be, and that, undoubtedly, is why most of us stayed in America. We longed to find danger in the streets of New York as our fathers and grandfathers had found danger in Polish and Russian streets, but it was no use. We were still too close to the "golden" America of our parents, and besides, nearly everyone was Jewish. Marshalled from the all too ignoble safety of our homes, it was all we could do to keep ourselves honed for the apocalypse; we established bivouac in the big houses of Flatbush, stood vigil outside the Museum of Modern Art.

Curiously, the first service of this parochial time was to make us cosmopolitan. Products of P.S. 105 and the Grand Army Plaza Public Library, we learned about the map of America—not only Detroit, Pittsburgh, and Chicago, but Akron, Dallas, and even New Orleans. Our friends went to dances at the 92nd Street "Y" and knew all the songs on the hit parade, but we had mail from Paris, Jerusalem, and San Francisco. It was not considered *de rigeur* to look at scenery in those days, yet not infrequently, in the midst of the seminar or the scouting expedition, on the surprisingly beautiful grounds provided by parent organizations, nature was upon us. Through the courtesy of the Labor Zionist movement, we looked at trees.

We were touched by history and felt sorry for those condemned to living out their merely sociological destiny. If Labor Zionism could not wholly save us from the suburbs, it made us less easy there; and permanently unamused by Jewish jokes badly told by members of the second generation.

We learned to love mimeograph machines. Let him who has never savored the faintly acid reek of duplicating fluid not scant this. Antique typewriters with flaking oilcloth covers and bulletin prose hortatory and mangled—how sweet they were! Having collated our ideological weapons, we met in the 14th Street Automat to plot further strategy. Thus did we learn the intrinsic dignity of the political: that an action has consequences, that things can be changed, that an idea is as powerful as a wish.

The astonishing thing is not that more of us did not settle in Israel, but how those who did not were rendered permanently uneasy in America. They were not more than twenty, those who taught us, and their lessons remained curiously difficult to unlearn. Of all feelings, the provisional quality of existence in the United States remains hardest to shake off—a slight skepticism about the things of this world—Cinema 16, the first stirrings of Zen, the latest in Scandinavian household furnishings. Later, boarding gangplanks for Paris and Athens, it always seemed the wrong gangplank; engaging with cathedrals, ruins, and etchings, there was always the suspicion that we had landed on the wrong littoral of the past. Later, when the Guggenheim became our aliyah and the Ph.D. our hityashvut, it was not without a certain guilt which even our own finest ironies did not serve to mitigate.

As ideological movements go, it was—in New York at least and in the period of which I speak—moderate. It did not deform personality and left fewer scars than most of the alternatives I have since heard about. It was a reasonable movement—inefficient, gentle, and decent. In an age lacerated by extremes, these virtues are not to be minimized.

Detroit, the Early 1950s: "Habonim Was Looked at as a Bit Wild"

Daniel J. Elazar
Jerusalem 1985

For most of my years in Detroit, from 1949 to 1953, which were also my last two years in high school and my first two years in college, I was a member of Habonim. I was not yet in the movement when the state of Israel was established. In fact, at that time I was in the hospital recovering from viral pneumonia. But if I missed the initial celebration, the new state was still a fresh experience for all of us. As young people, we were less engaged by the wonder of it all than by the struggles over aliyah and particularly aliyah to kibbutz. A number of the movement's senior members had rushed off to Israel in 1948 and early 1949. Unfortunately, many from Detroit returned, disillusioned, a few years later. That had an impact on us.

In some respects, my involvement in Habonim was unexpected. I was a strongly committed Zionist and I sought a strong Zionist youth movement. An earlier experience in Young Judaea convinced me that a movement under the thumb of its parent organization, especially Hadassah, was doomed to be *pareve;* it could never take stands on the crucial issues that mattered to young Zionists, particularly aliyah. I was one of those who seceded from Young Judaea in 1949 when an effort was made to establish an American branch of Hanoar Hatzioni, a chalutzic youth movement with a centrist, nonpolitical approach. The effort failed. I was the only member of Hanoar Hatzioni west of the Appalachians.

In Detroit, I could not find any kindred spirits committed to my brand of intensive Zionism. What I did find was Habonim, which combined chalutziut with an equal commitment to socialism, or at least to that dimension of socialism represented by the kibbutz. And that is where I diverged from Habonim. Even then I was not a socialist and Labor Zionism did not hold that kind of ideological appeal for me.

Moreover, I was observant. By choice, the Habonim center was off limits to me on Friday nights. I spent Sabbath evenings with my family; even if I had not, the secular character of Habonim's Shabbat was not to my liking. To compound matters, Habonim in those days was still tied to the Eastern European origins of most of its active members. It still placed an emphasis on Yiddish culture. I, a Sephardi and a Hebraist, had little sympathy and less affinity for that aspect of the movement. Finally, I took my Jewish and Hebrew studies seriously. My peers in Habonim viewed the movement as a surrogate for serious Jewish study.

Nonetheless, I plunged into Habonim affairs and became a wholehearted member. I think my successful integration had something to do with the particular group I encountered. It was more Americanized than some of the other Habonim groups in Detroit.

Detroit Habonim in the late 1940s and early 1950s was on the fringes of radicalism in a city famous for its radicalism in the 1930s. We grew up in the shadow of the United Auto Workers, the Reuther brothers, sitdown strikes, and militant unionism.

We were influenced accordingly. We sang the right labor songs. The Spanish Civil War, which had ended just ten years before, was probably a greater force on our lives than the Holocaust, even though Habonim itself absorbed a number of survivors who had settled in Detroit. We had regular contact with a panoply of radical groups that existed in Detroit, not only Zionist radicals like Hashomer Hatza'ir, but Communists, Trotskyites, Socialist Labor Party people, and even a few surviving Wobblies. Of course, we were at the vanguard of the folk song revival. Pete Seeger and The Weavers were number one on our hit parade.

Perhaps equally important, Habonim provided me with a social group in a city where I was notably alone. My family had moved to Detroit in 1948, when I was in the ninth grade. I found it difficult to fit into a new school framework. It did not help that most of my classmates had been together since kindergarten. And though 90 percent of the students in the school were Jewish, few had serious Jewish interests. Even at Hebrew High School and the College of Jewish Studies, there were not many like me and the few I found were not my age or did not share common interests outside the classroom. Habonim filled an important gap in my life.

My parents were tolerant of all this. They recognized my need though they did not encourage my participation. In those days, and perhaps at other times, Habonim was looked at as a bit wild; young people who did not want to accept the discipline or learn from the experience of their elders. We wanted to do everything ourselves, from building our camp to advocating aliyah in the face of a lethargic Labor Zionist movement, to choosing the way we dressed and staying out all hours of the night. Ironically, I took to building the camp with great relish although I never attended, opting instead to travel or to attend a Hebrew-speaking summer camp. Also, my group tended to dress more neatly, a point in their favor in my parents' eyes.

By the early 1950s, there was a great dampening of sentiment for aliyah and kibbutz in Detroit. Habonim began to grope its way toward different goals. It was then that I went away to the University of Chicago, where I had little connection with Habonim.

Aliyah in the 1950s:
Garin Gimel and Beyond

Meir Hurwitz
Kibbutz Kfar Hamaccabi 1985

One of the unfortunate side effects of the departure of two large aliyah groups from American Habonim, with the birth of the state of Israel, was a crisis of leadership in the movement. The first group, Garin Aleph, had founded Gesher Haziv. The second group, Garin Bet, joined Urim.

Garin Gimel was a completely different kind of group. It was smaller, and the aliyah of its members stretched from 1951 until the late 50s. Most went to Gesher Haziv, although a few joined Urim, and others scattered to other kibbutzim and the cities.

I was a member of Garin Daled.

Like many others, I had come to Habonim through my family. My parents had been members of Hechalutz, and I was born in Haifa during their two-year attempt at aliyah. In 1946, when I was ten years old, my parents sent me to a Habonim group being formed in Pittsburgh, but it didn't work out, and I did not hear about the movement again for four years.

The second time around was more successful. I was particularly impressed with the seriousness with which international topics were discussed, as if it really mattered what the few of us decided. I spent the summer at Camp Kinneret near Detroit and came to appreciate that the leaders of Habonim were members of the movement and not hired staff.

The large-scale aliyah in the late 1940s and early 1950s hit the movement in Pittsburgh hard. By 1952, it depended mainly on one person, Ben Frank, and when he went on Workshop, activity ceased completely. The following year, however, after Ben returned, we slowly reorganized the movement. Ben convinced me to attend Workshop in 1955. On the boat back to the land of my birth, I had already mapped out my next few years: I would get a degree and then return to Israel to live.

The Fifth Workshop was run well, thanks to the dedicated members of Kfar Blum, especially our *madrich,* Eddie Parsons. Our group, however, had a low proportion of Habonim members, another indication of the movement's precarious condition in those years. Of the thirty-two participants, only nineteen had previous contact with Habonim. Among the boys, only three out of twelve were from Habonim.

The Workshop spent a week at Urim, and I spent a week of my free time at Gesher Haziv to check out the possibility of returning on aliyah, but I was unable to make up my mind about my future plans. When we returned to America, Danny Mann, then the *mazkir* (national secretary), met us on the boat and talked with us about our tasks in the movement. It was decided that from my base in Pittsburgh I would help organize the movement in Cleveland.

During that year, we were approached by one of the rabbis in Pittsburgh who offered us a free hand to organize the children of his temple. We discussed the offer, but realized that we did not have the strength to open a second center—the most we could offer was to accept the children into our existing groups.

Toward the end of the school year, at a national meeting of *merakzim* (city organizers), Danny Mann raised the question of army service. The U.S. Army had introduced a new program that allowed for a half year of active duty, followed by five-and-a-half years of active reserves. Danny said it would be a good idea if we tried this program, to see how it might affect aliyah. I enlisted.

During my long reserve service I offered my services to the movement. This had been common a decade earlier, but it was now difficult to find more than one or two people willing to put themselves at the movement's disposal. I told the national secretariat I would work wherever they needed me, but that I planned to study agricultural engineering. I asked them to take that into account.

The leadership asked me to work in Detroit. There was no agricultural engineering program there. Instead I studied civil engineering. I stayed in Detroit for two-and-a-half years. In addition to Habonim, I helped organize the Student Zionist Organization and the Zionist Youth Council. Cooperation between movements was at its height in this period, and all the movements except Hashomer Hatza'ir were represented on the council. Even LTF, a Conservative synagogue youth group, decided it was Zionist and sent a representative to the council.

During this period, Habonim had no clear-cut aliyah program. At national meetings various groups would discuss the gamut of possibilities from kibbutz and moshav to city life. It was at one of these meetings that Garin Daled was born. Seven members who were interested in kibbutz decided that Urim would be our destination. I was chosen to coordinate the group, and contacted other members as well. Eventually, five of us moved to Urim, trickling in one at a time.

My absorption into Urim was ultimately unsuccessful. I knew that after a year, but I decided to stay ten years before I made any decisions. That ten years eventually stretched to nineteen before I actually left, moving to another kibbutz. I moved to a place where I felt I could contribute more for I still believe the Habonim philosophy that insisted self-realization and pioneering do not stop when a member moves to kibbutz. Indeed, it only starts then.

America in the Fifties

During the 1950s, American society was undergoing a quiet paroxysm of conservatism, which history remembers under various names: the Eisenhower Years, the Baby Boom, the Cold War, and most of all, McCarthyism.

As disturbing as it seems in the hindsight of history, America's air of complacency in the 1950s had very real roots. The nation was, first of all, in a state of national exhaustion in the aftermath of World War II. Most Americans wanted to settle down and enjoy life. Then, too, life for most Americans was easier to enjoy in the 1950s than it had been in living memory. The war was followed by a burst of industrial growth, fueled by America's new dominance of the world economy, and nearly every economic class benefited. It was, as a later generation might have put it, a rising tide of economic success that was raising many boats, and many more hopes. The growth of the suburbs in particular, fueled by the low-cost housing of building visionary William Levitt and his Levittowns, was making home ownership accessible to millions in the working class.

The American dream appeared to have arrived, for Jews no less than for non-Jews. Criticizing society fell out of favor as did movements built on such criticism.

Even as radical movements were in retreat, moreover, they were dogged from the rear by a resurgent American right wing, which was wildly flailing the broad brush of McCarthyism to brand as Communist virtually anyone on the left, even mainstream liberals within the Democratic party. Here, too, there was an underlying motive, in the aggressive foreign policy of the postwar Soviet Union. As soon as the war ended, the Soviets under Josef Stalin shut Eastern Europe behind the Iron Curtain of dictatorship. Soviet Communism was at its most aggressive stage of expansionist paranoia, stirring unrest and challenging the West from China to Greece. The West indeed seemed to be on the defensive.

From 1950 to 1954, the junior senator from Wisconsin, Joseph McCarthy, exploited Americans' real fear of Soviet expansionism to spread a terror of his own across America. Through congressional hearings, FBI investigations, blacklisting, and more, McCarthy and his minions managed to intimidate into silence broad numbers of people whose crime was having spoken out for a progressive vision of society.

All of this had its impact on Habonim. To be sure, the militancy that once characterized the social platform of Labor Zionism had long since been put on the back burner. Since the thirties, Labor Zionism had focused nearly all its energies on the overarching battle for the Jewish state. Now that the state was won, Zionism as a whole faced the perplexing question of its own future as a movement.

In the face of all those challenges, Habonim's old commitments to socialism, economic transformation and workers' rights began to seem to some members like unnecessary, and unwelcome baggage on the movement's already overburdened journey to a new identity.

By 1957, the critiques of Habonim's socialist heritage reached the point where they were submitted formally to the *ve'idah,* the national convention, in the form of several resolutions on Habonim ideology.

Resolutions of Detroit Habonim to the 1959 National Convention

Over the last few years, Habonim has undergone a change from its ideological origin. We, the members of Detroit Habonim, feel that the time is long past due to examine our Labor Zionist orientation and our values in relation to pioneering aliyah and the workers' settlement in Israel. We bring these resolutions to the national convention.

Resolved: That Habonim Labor Zionist Youth examine the principles and ideology on which it was founded.

Resolved: That our attitude towards pioneering aliyah and the workers' settlement in Israel be reexamined and redefined.

Resolved: That if, as a result of our reexamination of our principles and ideology, we find we are not a Labor Zionist movement, our name be changed accordingly.

Resolved: That our attitude toward socialism be reexamined.

If we find that pioneering aliyah and the workers' settlement in Israel have meaning for our movement, then we resolve to educate our members to join the workers' settlements in Israel, with the Habonim Workshop as the goal for all high school members and aliyah the goal for all college members.

Arise and build ourselves.

The resolutions did not pass the convention. Remarkably, the convention chose instead—as it had at previous conventions in the fifties—to pass resolutions that *reaffirmed* Habonim's commitment to progressive social justice.

The following resolutions were adopted by Habonim conventions between 1953 and 1957. They do not mention socialism; still, they reaffirm the Labor Zionist tradition of justice at home and moderation abroad with a forthrightness that seems, in the context of their times, to be remarkable. And, as we examine the turbulent social activism of what was to come in the 1960s, it is worth recalling that Habonim was, in many ways, ahead of its time.

Civil Liberties

America has two ways of meeting the challenge presented by a divided world: it can choose the prospect of atomic destruction, or it can inaugurate an era of unparalleled progress. It can meet this challenge by force of a powerful army only, or it can meet the threat of Communist aggression by battling it with ideas, as well as with a determined effort to raise the standard of living of people the world over through technical and financial assistance to underdeveloped and impoverished countries. Only if people the world over will be convinced of the positive values of the democratic way of life and of the sincere desire of the democratic powers to advance their welfare, will they join in the rejection of Communist totalitarianism.

Should America choose the road of military superiority alone, it may well defeat itself. The danger of Communist subversion must be met internally as well as in foreign affairs. Unless we conduct this battle with a continued development of a positive democratic program, fear, tension, and suspicion will continue to mount.

The forces of reaction are exploiting the fear of the Communist menace to suppress every liberal thought and every progressive idea irrespective of its inherent value. Liberals have themselves been infected with the fear of expressing their views and have paralyzed themselves, silently standing by, hoping that they will not be affected.

The fight against McCarthyism must become the personal responsibility of every American if he desires to retain his American heritage. Under the guise of fighting Communism, McCarthyism may well destroy the basic tradition of democratic America and negate the spirit and the letter of American constitutional rights. The assumption of guilt by association; the smearing of a man's name before his guilt has been proven; the use of television, radio, and newspapers to satisfy the publicity hunger of the investigators without regard to truth—all contribute to an increasing hysteria which is dangerous to the continuity of our country as we know it. This is what we are fighting abroad. We must fight it at home as well.

—1953

Labor

As chaverim of Habonim our orientation is twofold: as Zionists we are concerned with the welfare and progress of our fellow Jews; as Labor Zionists we are concerned also with the welfare and progress of our fellow men. We assert and affirm our belief in the right of every individual to life, liberty, and economic well being.

As Habonim we are not content merely with paying lip-service to these ideals. We call upon every chaver actively to support the work of unions and cooperatives which strive for the benefit of mankind and to interpret the activities of these groups to the community at large. We call upon our chaverim to observe picket lines and to influence others to do likewise.

We greet the International Confederation of Free Trade Unions, in which both the AFL-CIO and the Histadrut play an active role. Habonim commends the work of the AFL-CIO Ethical Practices Committee. We must lend our support to those forces working honestly and democratically for the economic and social progress of our society and give the lie to those who would discredit all unions on the pretext of corruption or malpractice.

—1957

Civil Rights

Nearly four years ago the Supreme Court outlawed segregation in the public schools and in other areas of American life. The court's decision was welcomed by the members of Habonim, but its results have greatly disappointed us. The manner in which the decision has been carried out by the South has generally been a series of measures ranging from indefinite delay to violence, all of which have as their aim the separation of Negroes and whites as much as possible. The exceptions to this pattern, though praiseworthy, have been much too infrequent.

The North, for all its back-patting, has been as guilty as the South of failing to demonstrate its sincere belief in those ideals of brotherhood, equality, and freedom of opportunity that America says it considers the finest heritage a nation could have.

That white Northerners have paid only lip service to these ideals is shown by their movement, en masse, from neighborhoods in which Negroes have settled to all white areas, their often making life as unpleasant as possible for a Negro family which moves into a white neighborhood, their establishment of gentlemen's agreements designed to keep neighborhoods racially pure, their arrangement of their lives so that social intercourse with Negroes is impossible, their repetition of the untrue clichés which belittle Negroes, and their passing on of these attitudes to their children.

We Northern Jews have shown as much selfishness and cowardice in this area as our gentile neighbors. Our weakness in failing to face the dangers in this area of civil rights has paralleled our being unable to meet the dangers facing us as Jews, in another area of civil rights.

The danger lies in the field of religious freedom. In recent years there has been a growing pressure in America to inject Christian religious practices in many areas of American life, especially public education. This pressure has had such results as Christmas trimmings and celebrations in many public places, even in stores and businesses owned by Jews, and the singing of

Christmas carols, the injection of "nondenominational" prayers, and the teaching of religion in the school program.

The constitution guarantees religious liberty and the separation of church and state. The above-mentioned practices represent infringements of these guarantees. Their influence is not offset by such practices as celebrating Chanukah and Pesach in the schools as well as Christmas and Easter or by teaching the ethics which are common to both Christianity and Judaism. These methods serve only to cover both faiths with a false blanket of similarity and, by ignoring their differences, to tailor them to fit a pattern of conformity.

We, as members of Habonim, as Jews, and as citizens raised in the spirit of freedom, must fight these practices of segregation and religious restriction and the attitudes which they represent, both individually and by joining those who are fighting for freedom and the defense of civil liberties in schools, on the political scene, in the Jewish community, in our own neighborhoods, and in every area of our lives.

—1957

Kfar Blum and Gesher Haziv, 1958–59:
Letters from the Workshop

En route to Kfar Blum
September 26, 1958

Dear Fagey,

Today is my ninth day at sea and I am a seasoned sailor. I have not gotten sick at all and I am an expert at keeping my balance on a rocking deck. The S.S. *Zion* is really a beautiful boat. You could probably best describe it as a miniature luxury liner. Each cabin has four double bunks, three sinks, and eight closets. There are also two portholes which up to now we have kept closed because we have had some pretty rough weather in the Atlantic, and if we had kept them open we would have been flooded out. There are lounges with bars on all three decks but you don't have to worry about the bars. The Workshop made a ruling that there would be no drinking of hard liquor on board, so we only take a shot of wine every once in a while.

Let me describe a typical day to you. We get up at five minutes to nine, leaving us plenty of time to get dressed and washed for breakfast, which is served promptly at 9:00. At 10:00 we have a discussion. We invited the ex-general secretary of Hashomer Hatza'ir, who is on board, to speak to us about her movement. Of course the discussion ended up about her feelings toward the Soviet Union. Another interesting discussion was with a boy from Betar, the right-wing Zionist Revisionist group. We really chopped him down to little pieces. I honestly don't understand how a political party with that kind of ideology can be the second largest power in Israel.

In the afternoon there are Hebrew classes. At 4:00 we have what they call tea time. Afterwards there is dancing on the deck and this is really a sight to see. When it was rough waters on the Atlantic, the circle would start on one side of the deck and within ten minutes it would be on the other side. The rail of the deck is packed with old folks watching the young pioneers doing Israeli dances. We make our usual wisecracks, such as "Don't applaud, throw money."

The group feeling so far has been pretty good but not as good as I had hoped. The ones who are causing the most trouble, I hate to say, are a few boys who were not members of the movement before they went on Workshop. I hope that these people will work out for the sake of the group. We saw land for the first time in nine days yesterday. We saw Spain and the Rock of Gibraltar. I will be in Israel on Wednesday. I will write from there.

Love, Ilana

Kfar Blum
October 21, 1958

Dear Dave and Zelde,

How are both of you doing? I am just fine. I am on my first vacation and that is why this letter was delayed.

Our arrival into the port of Haifa on board the S.S. *Zion* is something that I will always remember. We arrived at noon on October 1. It was a beautiful and clear morning and excitement penetrated the entire ship. Everyone was on the decks about two hours before we actually sighted Israel. As our ship entered port, about a dozen small rowboats came out to meet us. These boats were filled with relatives and friends of those on board ship. They shouted and waved and bid us a general Shalom. It was one of the warmest moments I have ever known. I felt at home even before I was on Israeli soil.

I can now begin to say that I am beginning to feel at home here on Kfar Blum. We have been working very hard and I believe we have established a reputation as being good workers. This has made us very happy and has inspired us to work even harder.

I work in the infirmary, helping the nurse. I wash floors, clean up, and do minor first aid. I like the job because I am in constant contact with people and I am always learning something new.

My Hebrew is progressing in a normal pattern although sometimes I think my English is becoming poorer because of it. Some of the people speak a little Hebrew and a little English. In order to speak with them, I break my English into its simplest form. I guess they do the same with their Hebrew for my sake.

Regards, Francis

Kfar Blum
October 1958

Dear Zelde,

I don't know how much you have heard so far about the Workshop but I have been requested to fill you in on the dope. Virtually the day after we came to Kfar Blum, we started on our program of orientation to kibbutz life. Our madrich showed us around and then we went on a short walk to the shoemaker where we all got sandals.

We postponed our first vacation because we felt that we weren't yet familiar enough with the country to spend five really worthwhile days by ourselves and also because we were anxious to get to work. Two weeks later, when our vacation was due to come, we were approached and asked to postpone it again because a field of cowbeets needed thinning and there wasn't enough help. We unanimously agreed to meet the request and to postpone our vacation indefinitely until we were not needed so badly.

Most of us are working in the vegetable patch or the children's houses. Some are in the fish ponds and others elsewhere. I am in the chicken coop. Our Hebrew program is strong and our discussions have all been great. The kids in the older grades are wonderful friends. In a nutshell, it is the best year of our lives.

Keep in touch, Barry

Gesher Haziv
November 3, 1959

To: Menucha Kraines
Central Shlicha, Habonim, New York
Dear Menucha,

Well, now that a month has passed since the gang arrived here, I guess that I am able to give you a few general impressions on behalf of the kibbutz. The group, our first Workshop here at Gesher Haziv, is without question a good one. Because it is a large group with a solid backbone it can overcome some of the internal weaknesses. The group has made an excellent impression. In work, many hold responsible positions in agriculture and the services.

I would say that one of the shortcomings is that the educational aspect of the Workshop was not stressed before they came. That is, each kid should be given a bibliography to complete and be tested on it before he comes—especially the nonmovement members. There is no excuse for anyone coming without knowing how to read and write Hebrew. This lack of prior preparation slows us up no end.

The discussion groups have been good. One of my major projects is getting the whole group to come regularly. The ones who are most lax are precisely the ones who need it most, the nonmembers. Once again, please stress to those in charge of preparing next year's group that the prospective Workshopper must be studying Hebrew all year and he must read and be tested on a number of books before he is accepted. Without this kind of preparation, new members and nonmembers are apathetic to the educational aspects of the program.

The days are very full. On a typical day, one group studies Hebrew from 6:30 to 9:30 in the morning and then works from 10:00 to 3:30. The other group works from 6:30 to 11:30 and studies from 12:30 to 3:30. We have discussion groups three times a week from 4:30 to 5:30.

As far as extracurricular activities in the first month, there has been a trip to Montfort and we participated in the lighting ceremony at Shlomi, a nearby development town. They put in electricity before the elections. Today is election day and the Workshop has been sent out to Nahariya and to various precincts to act as observers. About ten who know Hebrew will be messengers.

The gang has really brought life to the place. The kids at Gesher Haziv are a little in awe of the group. They are older and more worldly, so there is a barrier which probably cannot be overcome this first year.

With warm spirits, Temi Goldwasser
Madrichat Workshop

6

The Sixties: Revolution
in the Air

Entering the 1960s, Habonim was a small organization clinging to the Labor
Zionist tradition in the face of an unsympathetic American Jewish environment.

Beneath the surface, however, changes were taking place in Habonim and
among American youth at large that would transform the movement almost
overnight. By the mid-1960s, Habonim would again be widely acknowledged
as a significant force on the American Jewish youth scene and a dynamic
part of the landscape, in a decade that has become synonymous with social
upheaval.

* * *

In 1960, the movement celebrated the twenty-fifth anniversary of the Buf-
falo convention with the publication of a retrospective volume, *Arise and
Build,* compiled and edited by the indefatigable David Breslau. Also in 1960,
World Habonim united with another worldwide chalutzic youth movement,
Ichud Hanoar Hechalutzi ("Anach"), which was active mainly in the Span-
ish- and French-speaking countries. The new, merged body was called Ichud
Habonim.

The creation of Ichud Habonim had an immediate impact on American
Habonim in the adoption of a new movement vocabulary to conform with
usage common in Israeli youth movements. Henceforth, the city chapter,
the *machaneh,* was to be known as the *ken* (plural, *kinim*), and the redoubt-
able figure of the *menahel* (group leader) would be addressed as *madrich.*
The age groups were renamed as well: the youngest members, *solelim* ("pav-
ers"), were renamed *amelim* ("toilers"). Junior high schoolers, or *tzofim*
("scouts"), were renamed *chotrim* ("strivers"). The high school group, the
core of movement activity, retained the name *bonim* ("builders"). And the
college-age group, previously known as *noar* ("youth"), received the honorable title of *ma'apilim,* "those who dare," that once belonged to the prestate
"illegal" immigrants. Finally, the name *machaneh* was now given its literal
meaning, "camp," and applied to the venerable institution of Camp Kvutza,
which would henceforth be known as *machaneh Habonim.*

The Toronto Convention, 1962:
The Radicalization of Habonim

Meir Ciporen
New York 1988

In the late 1950s, two things happened to Habonim that paralleled something taking place in the country at large. One was the rise of the civil rights movement; the other was the birth of the peace movement.

Most histories date the birth of the modern civil rights movement from 1954, the year of *Brown v. Board of Education,* the U.S. Supreme Court ruling that banned segregated schooling. The victory for Negro rights fired the imagination of black America, and segments of the liberal community with it. Across the nation large-scale activism was ignited, beginning in 1955 with a bus boycott in Montgomery, Alabama.

Habonim's involvement was immediate, and immediately controversial. In Baltimore, in particular, Habonim people ran into friction from the local Jewish community when they took part in sit-ins and demonstrations against segregated businesses. Some of the picketing was directed against stores owned by Jewish merchants—including one who had discriminated against Yemenite-Israeli sailors on shore leave, mistaking them for blacks. Habonim took to the streets in protest, but Baltimore Jewry was not sympathetic. "How does this look," people in the community asked, "for a Jewish youth group to be picketing Jews?" Habonim was undeterred, however. In October 1958, national Habonim was the only Jewish youth group to join officially in a national Youth March for Integrated Schools in Washington, D.C., together with more than ten thousand other young Americans.

A minor incident that took place in 1959, at the twenty-fifth anniversary convention of Habonim in Washington, was typical of the mood in the movement at the time. It was a festive event, a sort of milestone for the movement, and our guest speakers included the Israeli ambassador (Avraham Harman, a British Habonim graduate) as well as labor leader Victor Reuther. In between sessions a group of us who kept kosher stopped in at a lunch counter, looking for a dairy meal. While we were waiting for our food, a black man came in and sat down, forcing the manager to do a little reshuffling of the seating in order to keep us segregated. When we figured out what was going on—we were all from the North, and we were not used to seeing segregation on a daily basis—we told the manager to forget it. We weren't hungry anymore, we said. Besides, we told him he might be making a mistake putting us with the whites. We were Jewish, we said.

The second process of the 1960s, the peace movement, arose more slowly. In retrospect, however, it might be seen as the truest expression of the generational change that created the youth revolution of the Sixties—and perhaps the youthful nihilism that succeeded it.

For those who grew up in the post-World War II era, one of the central facts of life—a subconscious basis for understanding the world—was the knowledge that an atomic bomb was detonated over Hiroshima. Unlike generations before, the postwar generation grew up in full awareness that the world could be destroyed in an instant. In the late 1950s, as these children were coming of age and the Cold War was dragging on, fear of nuclear holocaust began changing to anger. On campuses around the country, groups of students began a crusade for disarmament. The slogan was "Ban the Bomb," and the symbol was the famous inverted Y in a circle, originally drawn from the semaphore-code flag positions of the letters "N–D"—Nuclear Disarmament.

For Habonim members on college campuses, the peace movement reignited an old Labor Zionist tradition of socialist internationalism that had been submerged years earlier into the movement subconscious.

In 1959, at the time of the Cuban revolution, I was *rosh ken* (chapter chair) of Brooklyn Habonim. Together with several other chaverim, I went down to the Jewish Community Center on Eastern Parkway for a joint activity with the United Synagogue Youth. Intermovement activity was very much in vogue at the time, and we were meeting to discuss what our movements had in common, and what divided us. When we got to the question of political positions—or lack of them—the Habonim people brought up our feelings as socialists about the Cuban revolution. At that point even the stutterers among the U.S.Y. stopped stuttering and joined in to attack us.

In time, campus activists for civil rights and disarmament would coalesce into a single movement calling itself the New Left—to distinguish itself from the old, dogmatic, socialist left of the 1930s. As early as 1960, however, the incipient change in young America was already forcing many of us in Habonim to reexamine the "labor" part of our identity as Labor Zionists.

This reopened for us the age-old Zionist and Labor Zionist debate over our relationship to the community. Since our movement is other-directed—to Israel—what was to be our role here in the diaspora? Should we isolate ourselves, or express our positions while we are here? How far should we go to express these positions? Was Habonim ultimately—renewing the old YPZA-Habonim debate—an educational youth group or a political movement?

The debate came to a head in 1962 at *ve'ida*, the Habonim national convention, at Camp Kvutza in Lowbanks, Ontario, with the unsuccessful candidacy of Max Langer for *mazkir* of the movement. Max lost the election, but in a sense he won the movement.

Max Langer was a physician from Vancouver who came to Brooklyn in 1960 for his medical residency and became *merakez* (organizer) of the Brooklyn ken. In addition to working with the ken, I recall, he became involved on a peer level with a cadre of older, college-age people.

During the course of 1961–62, Max began articulating a radical critique of the Zionist youth movement itself. The movement, he said, had been transformed into a children's organization for recruitment to Israeli kibbutzim, rather than a vehicle for challenging the reality of diaspora Jewry. His thinking, as it appeared in articles he published in various Habonim journals, was drawn not from the literature of classical socialist ideology but from progressive social scientists like Erik Erikson and Margaret Mead. For many of us, it was deeply compelling.

In order to recreate a challenging, politically aware Zionist youth movement, Langer urged that the movement drop the younger age-groups and focus its attention on youth over the age of fourteen. The top leadership, he said, should be in its twenties, not in its late teens. The movement should declare its independence, or at least full autonomy, from the Israeli establishment with which it was identified, the Mapai party and the kibbutz movement. Outreach, he said, should be based on ideology rather than on the social experience of "adolescent cliques."

The most controversial aspect of Langer's proposals related to *shlichim*. By 1961 Habonim had sixteen shlichim from Israel, working with a movement of fewer than two thousand members. To Langer, the dominant role of the shaliach suppressed the growth of indigenous youth leadership.

These ideas—politicization, autonomy from Israel, limiting the shlichim's role, eliminating the younger age groups—were brought to the Lowbanks convention as the platform of Max Langer's candidacy for the position of mazkir Habonim. The other candidate, nominated by the national secretariat, was Aaron Shoirif (now Sharif) of Washington, a talented leader and a powerful intellect in his own right.

The experience of the 1962 convention was a bitter one for those of us who supported Langer. The shlichim were unanimously opposed to him and his ideas. It seemed that they, and the world movement behind them, were afraid the North American movement was about to rip itself apart. Support for their position was brought in from Israel, including the head of World Habonim. In the end, though, it was American Habonim that made the decision: outside the New York area, most of the movement supported Shoirif, and he was elected mazkir.

Ironically, Shoirif quickly built up a working secretariat in the national office made up largely of Langer people. Artie Schneiderman took a year off from school, I came in as *rosh chinuch* (education director), and for a short time Max himself was put on the secretariat as well. By the time the movement was ready to convene at the 1964 national convention to elect the next mazkir, we were back to one agreed candidate; this time, it was Abba Caspi of Baltimore—a Langer supporter.

During the years that Shoirif was mazkir, a certain blending took place of people and ideas from both sides. Part of the reconciliation had to do with personality. It was simply impossible to view Aaron Shoirif as an enemy for any length of time. There were bitter fights during the first year, leading to at least one mass resignation from the secretariat, but Shoirif always found a way of healing the differences and bringing the sides back together.

In the end, Habonim did not drop the younger age groups, and the shlichim were retained at full strength as partners in the movement's leadership. But at the same time, we plunged into an intense engagement with the world around us.

In the summer of 1963—following a decision of the 1962 convention—
Habonim opened a national leadership training camp, to give a strong dose
of ideological and leadership training to chaverim entering their last year of
high school. The camp, Machaneh Bonim, became a central element in the
movement's program and a proving ground that would introduce hundreds
of members to activism on a national scale.

That December of 1963, Habonim's winter bonim seminars around the
country were devoted to civil rights. Those seminars, bringing our teenage
members all over the country into contact with active leaders of the civil
rights movement of the day, put American politics on the Habonim agenda
to stay. More than a few parents would have the experience of seeing their
children, fresh from a summer at a Habonim camp, watch a news broadcast
of civil rights marchers singing "We Shall Overcome," and then being asked:
"Why is the TV singing the Habonim song?"

Not all of the transformation was without controversy. While civil rights
was accepted almost universally as a legitimate item on the Habonim agenda,
the question of peace—which by 1965 had become the question of Vietnam—would remain divisive right up to the end of the decade.

*   *   *

One of the most profound legacies to Habonim of the Sixties revolution
was one least expected by the fearful shlichim: a renewal of large group
aliyah to kibbutz from Habonim.

Beginning in 1964 with the aliyah to Urim of the second Garin Daled,
Habonim began sending an almost constant stream of garinim to our kibbutzim in Israel—and within a decade, founding new ones again.

Another old movement structure was revitalized in 1964, when Garin
Etgar, scheduled to leave for Gesher Haziv the following year, opened a
communal house in Chicago. In 1967, Garin Ma'or to Urim opened its own
bayit in Philadelphia. By the mid-1970s, communal living in a bayit had
become the norm wherever groups of college-age Habonim members could
be found.

It may well be that this was part of the larger process of radicalization.
The formation of a garin was not simply about moving overseas; it was a
political statement as well. That became part of the groundswell of change
in Habonim. By focusing more clearly on the reality of Jewish life in
America, the movement was becoming more Israel centered.

Habonim in the 1950s had been one of the few progressive alternatives
available in a quiescent American society. Moshe Kerem (Murray Weingarten) of Gesher Haziv once said that when "young Jewish kids started to
become aware of things, they were doing it by writing papers in school about
kibbutz."

By the mid-1960s, it might be said that America had caught up with Habonim.

From "The Zionist Youth Movement in America"

Max Langer (Michael Livni)
New York 1964

The Political Nature of the Youth Movement

Perhaps no self-image has had a more damaging effect on the Zionist youth groups than the image they have built of themselves as an "educational youth movement." The word "movement" in the context of educational youth movement has become quite meaningless—all that is really meant is that individuals are being educated to have a certain individual response to problems of Jewish identity. These responses range from giving serious consideration to your Jewish education and Hebrew background, to varying degrees of identification with Israel, including aliyah. There is today a definite trend to a general ideological convergence among the major Zionist youth groups, and nowhere is this more apparent than in their self-image as the educational youth movement creating some kind of liberal-Jewish-Zionist personality type.

Movement implies social change. The Zionist youth groups are primarily concerned with changing individuals. Admittedly, this is a prerequisite to social change, and let no one construe that I am denying that the individual within the group has to be educated. But more is involved than just creating a general personality type with a positive Jewish outlook or even an individual that will live on the kibbutz. A movement has to mobilize the personality type it creates to change the social order to which that movement relates. A movement has to see itself as affecting the affairs of man. Those who actively concern themselves with the affairs of man are concerned with politics. In other words, a movement is a political entity. Of course a political entity in this sense by no means implies affiliation with a political party. Such an affiliation may or may not be part of the movement.

As a movement, Zionism has been the decisive force in the affairs of Jewry for the past sixty years, and the Zionist youth movements of Eastern Europe were instrumental in shaping the contemporary social structure in Israel. To speak of a nonpolitical Zionist youth movement, a term sometimes employed by the Student Zionist Organization and Young Judaea, is a contradiction in terms. No movement is nonpolitical, certainly not a Zionist youth movement. To speak of a Zionist youth movement as a political movement which uses education as one of its chief techniques is valid, and this was in fact the sense in which the term "educational youth movement" was first used.

Of course, a nonpolitical children's organization sponsored by various adult Zionist groups is also a possibility. Under the cover of "educational youth movement" all Zionist youth groups have in fact moved in this direction to a considerable extent.

The slogan "educational youth movement" has become one of the rationales for the emphasis on the younger age groups. The relative success of Zionist youth groups with very young members is a mixed blessing. To a large extent the best energies of Zionist youth leadership are dissipated in "babysitting," doing the job that the educational system of every Jewish community should be doing.

Summer 1963: The Opening of Machaneh Bonim

In the summer of 1962, Habonim operated eight summer camps: in New York, Pennsylvania, Maryland, Michigan, California, British Columbia, Ontario and Quebec. The following summer, to cope with the movement's growth in the New York area, the movement opened a second New York camp serving New Jersey and upstate New York. The new camp, in the Catskills resort town of Hunter, was named Tel Ari in memory of Ari Lashner, the New York Habonim graduate who had fallen at Kfar Blum during Israel's War of Independence.

While Tel Ari continued for several years to serve parts of the New York region of Habonim, it most stands out in the memories of two decades of Habonim members as the home of an experiment, which opened in 1963 in a tent camp up the rocky hill from Camp Tel Ari: Machaneh Bonim, the national leadership training camp of Habonim.

The goals of the new camp—and its ethos as an expression of the changing mood of Habonim in the 1960s—are clearly summed up in a message to the members of the sixth Machaneh Bonim in 1968 from that summer's rosh machaneh (camp director), Abba Caspi.

The Goals of Machaneh Bonim

Abba Caspi
New York 1968

Machaneh Bonim was born at the *ve'idah* (national convention) of Habonim in August 1962, when a dissident group of movement radicals—yours truly included—began pushing a program to change Habonim and turn its attention outward to the challenges facing us in the Jewish community. The major objectives of our program were:

1. To change Habonim from an "educational" children's organization into an activist youth movement.
2. To raise the age level, quality and ideological sophistication of the leadership of Habonim, and create a national *chevrah* (cadre) of young adults capable of implementing the reform program.
3. To strengthen and emphasize the (older) age groups of *bonim* and *ma'apilim* and stress their peer-level activities, as opposed to what we considered at that time to be an overemphasis on leading (younger) *amelim* and *chotrim*.

The idea of a Machaneh Bonim clearly is relevant to all three of these objectives, and for that reason Machaneh Bonim was one of the innovations in Habonim that we worked hard to have approved by that convention. Fortunately for Habonim, and, I think, fortunately for the chaverim of Machaneh Bonim, we were successful.

The Goals of Machaneh Bonim

I would define Habonim's goals in sponsoring Machaneh Bonim as follows:

1. To develop chaverim who will be able provide dynamic leadership for Habonim. In my opinion, the qualities most important for a leader in Habonim today are:

a) *Ideological commitment.* In Habonim terms, ideological commitment does not mean slavishly following a set of rules and answers handed down from on high, but it does mean understanding and identifying with a certain frame of references: concern for Jewish survival, for the quality of Jewish life, Jewish thought and culture, for Israel, for the quality of human life in general, for political, economic, and "participatory" democracy; active involvement in the world and Jewish life, and belief in the possibility of improving them through personal effort. Most important, it means having the knowledge and ability to develop and change Habonim's approach so as to maintain its relevance to present and future problems in an ever-changing world.

b) *The ability to express Habonim's approach* not as a collection of slogans, but as an approach to the problems of Israel, Jewry, and the world.

c) *The ability to communicate Habonim's approach* to other Jewish youth, both to high school age youth in the community at large and to younger children in Habonim and outside it.

d) *The desire and enthusiasm* to get involved in doing something about these problems through undertaking leadership responsibilities in Habonim.

2. To develop the nucleus of a national chevrah of movement leaders who

will help and support one another, and will have the ability and direction to change and develop Habonim as a national movement relevant to and involved in this and future generations of Jewish youth.

Chinuch Program at MB

The chinuch (education) program at Machaneh Bonim Vav, 1968, has been designed to help accomplish many of the above goals. Most of the program has been aimed at attempting to think through, understand, and develop solutions to the central problems facing Habonim and the Jewish people today:

1. The economic future of the state of Israel, the future of its collective sector. What kind of society will Israel be, as reflected in its economic organization?
2. The political future of Israel, its position in the Middle East, the confrontation with the Arabs of Palestine. What kind of society and culture is Israel to be?
3. The future of the North American Jewish communities and their relationship to Israel. The future of aliyah from North America.

In each of these cases, we have not expected chaverim to parrot back the "right" answer or slogan; rather, we have attempted to give a fair presentation of various points of view on each of these issues and to enable chaverim to acquire the knowledge and tools necessary to think through these questions in a real way and arrive at their own conclusions.

Aliyah in the 1960s: The Resurgence of the Garin

"Habonim Strengthens Aliyah Framework"
From a movement newsletter 1964

In October of this past year, seventeen members of Habonim boarded a plane for an important flight—a flight to the realization of years of Habonim education. The seventeen were members of Garin Daled, a group that was formed three years ago and has been preparing since to settle at Kibbutz Urim, in the northern Negev. Most of the members of Garin Daled are university graduates, holders of a variety of academic and technical degrees.

Next October, another group of Habonim members, formed two years ago, plans to settle at Kibbutz Gesher Haziv. This group, which has thirty participants, is called Garin Hei. These members are currently finishing their university studies while sharing the leadership responsibilities throughout Habonim.

Finally, a third group of members are beginning to organize Garin Vav. They plan to leave for Gesher Haziv in 1967. It is heartening, and a credit to the educational program of Habonim, that after some lean years, its members are once again organizing themselves into group frameworks for aliyah to kibbutz.

The catalog of garinim appearing in a movement newsletter in the spring of 1965 represented a remarkable achievement. For more than a decade, Habonim had been hard-pressed to produce more than a trickle of individual emigrants who were willing to leave America and settle on kibbutz, along with two small garinim—Gimel and the first Daled—that settled slowly at Gesher Haziv and Urim. But the mass aliyah of Garin Aleph to Gesher Haziv in 1949 and of Garin Bet to Urim in 1950–51 appeared to have been a one-time phenomenon.

When garinim again began forming regularly, a decade later, the life of American Jews had undergone an evolution that greatly complicated the process of organizing a kibbutz settlement group. The most important change was college attendance. Between 1950 and 1960, college attendance became the norm rather than a privilege among young American Jews. Where a garin's choice of a target date for departure once had to work its way around security problems or British restrictions, it now was increasingly dependent on divergent graduation dates.

Beginning in the late 1950s, nonetheless, returnees from the Habonim Workshop began bonding into groups committed to returning to kibbutz—after graduation—and fulfilling the movement's highest goal. The first such group was Garin Daled, which chose its name to continue the Hebrew numeration begun with Garin Aleph in 1949. It was an unfortunate choice, since there had already been a seven-member Garin Daled in the fifties.

The next garinim were Hei and Vav. In choosing Gesher Haziv as their settlement target, they were establishing a new pattern: returning to the kibbutz where they spent their Workshop year.

The system of numbering the garinim according to the Hebrew alphabet quickly broke down, however. Garinim Hei and Vav, both headed for Gesher Haziv, were separated only by their origins in different Workshops and their disparate graduation dates. In 1966, the two Gesher Haziv groups combined to form a single garin, which called itself Etgar—"Challenge." From that point on, Hebrew names became the order of the day. In 1967, graduates of the Fifteenth Workshop at Urim declared their intention of returning to the Negev, and took as their name Ma'or, a play on the Hebrew name Urim ("Lights"). The next garin to declare its intention, Negba ("To the Negev!") was made up of graduates of the Seventeenth Workshop, and it, too, was bound for Urim. It would be the last organized American garin to settle in the movement's pre-1960 settlements.

The early sixties also saw the first attempt by Habonim members to address another problem raised by the near universal college attendance. Many young Jews, including Habonim members, were simply unwilling to devote themselves to a life of physical labor on a farm, no matter how socially just the farm's structure. Discussions among movement members began to focus—reprising discussions among the founders of Hakibbutz Hame'uchad in the 1920s—on finding a way to apply the kibbutz model to urban life in Israel.

The result of these discussions was the formation of Garin *Shaal,* which was determined to forge a new pattern of Israeli collectivism by settling together in a development town and living as a sort of urban kibbutz.

The eighteen members of Shaal settled in 1968 in the development town of Carmiel in the Galilee. The experiment, discussed at length in a later chapter, lasted only four years. But it had a profound impact on Carmiel, on the kibbutz movement, and most of all on generations of American Habonim that came after.

The Bronx, the Late 1960s: "We Were Filled with Ideas of Revolution"

David Twersky
Kibbutz Gezer 1985

There were times, sitting in the small apartment where I lived on kibbutz, when I would watch the winter rains outside and listen to my stereo playing hard-rock music like "Streets of Fire," to remind me of the American city streets where I grew up. Most often, I thought about a peculiar street gang I used to belong to, Habonim.

In the late 1960s and early 1970s, as the New Left started turning in on itself in sectarian battles, the ideological debate on the American campus sometimes resembled an old-fashioned turf war. And for a time, we in Habonim almost ruled the streets—at least in our part of town.

I joined the movement at the relatively late age of fourteen and a half. Since I had never attended camp, I didn't feel much like part of the movement until the bus ride to the 1964 winter seminar in Toronto, where I met Charlie Shidlowsky and Sydney Nestel. They are still my friends and sometimes neighbors. In the movement I found warmth, intelligence, good times, and girls. Many of my closest friends today are those I met when I started to go to Bronx Habonim.

When I joined Habonim, in 1964, the sounds on the street were those of America changing. The civil rights movement had reached its first peak with the great 1963 March on Washington and the Civil Rights Acts of 1964. Vietnam was still a little known corner of Asia, although peace played a role in the election that year. According to one of the Democrats' 1964 television commercials, Lyndon Johnson had to crush Barry Goldwater in order to keep a little girl in a field of flowers safe from the threat of nuclear war. I didn't know then that Johnson's victory would be the last presidential race for two decades in which I could support a winner. Within two years of Johnson's election, we were denouncing him as a "fascist" because of his policies in Vietnam.

The year 1965 was probably the turning point. In the civil rights movement, young black leaders like Stokely Carmichael were announcing that the black movement had to make its own way without its white liberal allies. "Black Power" was the new slogan. In Habonim newsletters around the country, articles began appearing that compared black power to Zionism and reasserted Labor Zionism as a movement of "Jewish national liberation." We rediscovered Ber Borochov, with his militantly socialist approach to Labor Zionism. And we discovered Max Langer, by then gone on aliyah to Gesher Haziv, who we believed had reasserted Habonim's birthright as a political movement.

In Vietnam, President Kennedy's police action was turning into President Johnson's war, and young Americans were being drafted in growing numbers to fight the Cold War-turned-hot.

On the campus, the Students for a Democratic Society—formed in 1962 as a breakaway from the social-democratic League for Industrial Democracy—was at the height of its influence, just before its deterioration into Marxist sectarianism. During the winter of 1966, SDS chartered its first two high school chapters, one in the Bronx and one in Washington, D.C. Both were founded by Habonim members.

During the fall of 1965, the executive committee of Bronx Habonim drafted a resolution condemning the mounting Vietnam war, and submitted it for adoption by *Merkaz* Habonim, the central committee of the national movement. Knowing that it represented a controversial issue even among the members of Habonim, we first circulated our resolution among chapters around the nation. The resolution touched off a lively debate; most Americans were still convinced that the Vietnam War represented a national effort to save southeast Asia for democracy. The nature of the South Vietnamese regime was still not clear to most people. Neither was the commitment of the Vietnamese to getting us out of their country—nor the national agony that was in store for the American people, especially its youth.

Those aspects of the issue were secondary in the Habonim debate that fall and winter, however. The advocates of the antiwar resolution tended to speak in terms of the national rights of the Vietnamese people, which they compared with some naivete to Zionism. The opponents spoke mostly not of communism or national rights, but of Habonim's role as an educational organization dedicated to Israel and kibbutz. The most articulate expression of opposition came from Los Angeles, where the *rosh ken* (and later city councilman) Zev Yaroslavsky wrote an open letter to the movement, insisting that Habonim had a commitment to the Jewish community and should not divert itself into divisive attacks on U.S. foreign policy.

During the summer of 1966, the principals in the Vietnam debate met for the first time when we arrived as campers at Machaneh Bonim in Hunter,

New York. It was Machaneh Bonim's fourth summer—Machaneh Bonim Daled—and we took the saucy step of contracting the name to "M.B." Our slogan was "M.B. Daled—really solid." But it wasn't terribly true.

It was a stormy summer, probably one of the wildest in the history of Habonim camping. We, the sixteen-year-old-campers, were filled with ideas of revolution and students' rights. We wanted free speech and personal autonomy, which in our case meant the right to skip swimming lessons and ignore lights-out. Some of us even refused to stand for the raising of the American flag, which got a couple of us expelled from camp.

Our ideas were a heady mixture of anarchism, semidigested Marxism, and SDS new leftism. We quoted Borochov at length, and studied the writings of Max Langer, whom most of us had never met. At our meetings, which lasted until the wee hours of the night, we debated camp rules and societal values. And we drove our counselors crazy.

There was some sad irony in that. Our camp director that summer was not some young Republican, nor even a Habonim-as-an-educational-group traditionalist, but Artie Schneiderman, the incoming mazkir Habonim and one of the leaders of the Langer revolution of four years earlier. Artie wanted nothing more than to run a reasonably safe summer camp for a group of fifty-odd unruly high school seniors. But we were implacable, and we did not trust anyone older than us.

Some of our self-assured cynicism about those older than us came out in a song we wrote that summer. We adapted a tune by Phil Ochs, the popular left-wing folksinger, about the hypocrisy of liberalism. Our version went like this:

> Sure, once I was young and impulsive
> I joined Hashomer Hatza'ir
> And each time I thought of Tel Hai
> I was prompted to shed a small tear.
> Ah, but I've grown older and wiser
> And that's why I'm staying right here
> So love me, love me, love me
> I'm a Zionist.

It would be a mistake to suggest that our unruly, hard-core radicalism was shared even by most of our fellow campers at Machaneh Bonim Daled. Many, perhaps most of our chaverim that summer, were faithful Habonim members who saw the movement's mission in more sober terms that we radicals did. But many of us who went through that summer together—even those who disagreed bitterly over the rules of camp and of society—went on to share a militant commitment to applying Habonim's ideology in every aspect of our lives. Today, many of those who spent that summer of 1966 together at Machaneh Bonim have become important leaders in a wide variety of endeavors: Raphie Goldman in kibbutz movement work, Yehuda Rubin in the West Bank settler movement Gush Emunim, Zev Yaroslavsky in Los Angeles city politics, Marty Karp in Israel-diaspora community work in Jerusalem.

In time, too, the radicalism of some members would be toned down by the growing alienation of the American left toward Israel. We had been fastidious about demonstrating our allegiances to both. We attended antiwar rallies with banners that declared us proudly as Zionists. In the great 1969 Washington Mobilization to End the War, we mobilized other chalutzic youth groups to march with us under a Socialist Zionist banner, and turned the "Mobe" into a national movement activity with dozens of chaverim from around the country camped out at J. J. Goldberg's parents' house.

It soon became clear, however, that our "comrades" on the Left were rebuffing our overtures. Israel, our so-called allies told us, was a white settler colonialist state, guilty as sin. As Zionists, we were not their comrades.

In those days, everybody seemed intoxicated with the idea of revolution. Our dispute with the left over Israel forced us to stand back and reconsider a wide range of issues. Suddenly we saw all kinds of flaws and excesses. If the left was wrong on Israel, maybe that was no accident. By 1969, the student left was busy breaking into minifactions and sects, vying to see which could have the least grounding on any plane of reality.

There was pressure on us from the mainstream Zionist organizations as well. In the wake of a miraculous military victory, the Six-Day War brought the occupation of the West Bank and other territories. The case for Palestinian self-determination was made not only by the left against Israel, but by us within the Zionist community. That position brought us into conflict with the Israeli government, headed at the time by Golda Meir, and with most of the American Jewish and Zionist establishment. Because of our direct ties with the kibbutz movement and the Labor Party in Israel, we were expected to show more restraint. We did not.

The twin forces acting on us came to a head in April 1970. The United States had invaded Cambodia. Four students had been killed protesting at Kent State University in Ohio. Shortly thereafter, we began to organize our contingent to march in the Israel Independence Day parade, an annual New York mega-event. We notified the parade headquarters that we would be carrying signs referring to the tragedy in Ohio. The most militant one read: "Grant us peace, O God—and Mr. Nixon." We figured we were being responsible and didn't want to overdo it.

On the day of the parade, we were about one hundred strong, marching between B'nai B'rith Youth of Queens and Young Judaea of New Jersey. We were feeling a little small and out of place. It was almost the end of the parade, at 86th Street, when a parade marshal demanded that we remove our sign. We politely but firmly refused. He responded that either we remove the sign or he would. We pointed out that he was only one, however enthusiastic and determined, while we were one hundred.

He held his ground. He grabbed the placard. A few of us grabbed him. Later, he claimed that the sign called for the assassination of President Nixon.

The episode led to a meeting with Yitzhak Rabin, then Israel's ambassador to the United States. We explained to him that Kent State had changed everything. For Rabin, four dead was a tragedy but not a turning point. He asked why we couldn't celebrate Israeli independence without mixing in other issues. In retrospect it seems like a good question, but at the time it only got us mad.

Habonim was of the left, it was Zionist, it was activist. That was a difficult combination of commitments to hold together, and over time it began to break apart. By the 1970s, Habonim members would be focusing most of our attention on specifically Jewish frameworks.

Still, it was a special time. Muki Tsur, one of the leading intellectual lights of the kibbutz movement, a shaliach to the American movement in the late 1960s, saw parallels between our situation and that of the Second and Third Aliyah—the young radical Zionists who arose in Russia during the 1905 and 1917 revolutions. Maybe that was making too much of it; then again, maybe not enough. Everything was in motion then and fair subject for critical reappraisal. If we were the victims of fads and trends, we were saved from intellectual and moral feebleness by the need to confront the contradictions in our situation rather than ignoring them.

California, the Mid-1960s: "The Neshef Is What We Remember Most"

Ronnie Cohen
Los Angeles 1990

Ask people who were active in Los Angeles Habonim in the fifties and sixties what they remember most about Habonim—aside from camp. They will tell you in a single word: the *Neshef.*

The Neshef (literally "soiree") was an annual performance put on by Habonim—usually in the spring—to raise money, to present ourselves to the community, to take up every moment of free time for every member for at least six weeks; to put in serious jeopardy the academic standing of three-quarters of the movement; in short, to drive ourselves, our parents, and everybody around us crazy. But the funny part is that once having been in a Neshef, you would never want to miss it for the world.

The Neshef format changed from year to year, in several dimensions. I remember Neshafim that were written and directed by professionals—some of them outstanding professionals, such as Elyakum Shapiro, who went from our Neshef to the New York Philharmonic (not directly, you understand). At other times, our own members wrote, produced, and directed the entire production.

There were Neshafim where most of the performances were done by a small group of high school-aged kids, and the younger chevre did very little; on other occasions, the stage was rampant with eleven year olds.

The location of the Neshef also changed from year to year. I tend to associate Neshafim with the Wilshire Ebell Theatre, but I also remember high school auditoriums, and various temples (such as Temple Isaiah or the Scottish Rite Masonic Temple, *lehavdil*). For a time in the 70s, it was even staged in the prestigious Greek Theater, high in the Hollywood Hills.

And, of course, the content of the program changed from year to year. Israeli singing and dancing were always present in every Neshef. Some Neshafim were only that, tied together with a loose narration. But we also had plays, skits, Greek choruses, modern dances, slide shows, and other experimental media.

For all this variability, though, certain things were always true of practically every Neshef. For example, every Neshef was accompanied by an ad book, for which we had to sell ads, collect money, lay out the book, and finally—usually very late in the night (or early in the morning) before the Neshef—collate. I probably put on more miles walking around tables in the Institute of Jewish Education, the Labor Zionist center in West Hollywood, collating ad books than in all the hikes at camp.

Another thing—every Neshef always brought out a cadre of dedicated members of the senior movement and/or Habonim alumni. But—being Habonim—we were always very careful to make sure that these adults could not put too much input into the performance, thereby endangering our amateur standing. I remember one chaver who was a real actor: we only let him on stage during the dress rehearsal, so all he could do was "polish" the performances. In practically every area of the Neshef, we had help from these chaverim: they sewed the costumes, helped us with the scenery, applied make-up to us on the night of the performance, and taped the Neshef, so we could listen to it later.

Speaking of listening to it later, every Neshef always ended in a Neshef party; and listening to the tape of the Neshef was a central part of the party. As for what else we did at these parties, I'll leave that to your imagination.

Another thing about all Neshafim—there was always a conflict between the demands of putting on a Neshef, and the educational program of the movement. In some years, we tried to push ahead—ostrichlike—with the educational program and pretend that the Neshef did not exist. Most of the time we tied the content of the Neshef into our educational program for the year (or vice versa).

The ironic part is that from my perspective today, the Neshef was probably the *most* educational part about Habonim in the city. During the course of our experience in Habonim Neshafim, we learned to sing, dance, act, write, direct, and choreograph. We learned to be responsible for property, to live up to deadlines, to work together as a group for a common goal, and to be proud of what we could accomplish. We afforded every single child in the movement an opportunity to be on stage in a real live performance, with a supportive audience in a positive experience. And we gave a lot of chav-erim opportunities to do more. It is no wonder that the Neshef is what we remember most about Habonim in Los Angeles.

California, the Late 1960s: "Commitment to Ideals Was the Core of Our Being"

Janet Vogel Shultz

Los Angeles 1985

We were the youth of the Sixties. We came from San Francisco and Van-couver, from Los Angeles and its "valleys"—and from cities and suburbs like them all over North America.

In our Habonim educational programs, the theme of social justice was our intense and impassioned refrain. Commitment to ideals was the core of our being. On weekends, when we met for fun, we sang along with Bob Dylan and Joan Baez and protested the world's injustices. At camp we sat up late at night, pondering the Special Days and *sichot* (group discussions) that would transmit a meaning of equality and the pain of discrimination to young campers growing up in plenty.

Our generation began with a new Workshop location, Kibbutz Urim, re-placing the previous site at Gesher Haziv. There in the Negev in the fall of 1965, we were faced with the sudden need somehow to win the hearts of kibbutzniks who laughed at our strangeness. Eventually, we did win their hearts, and that first Urim Workshop, the Fifteenth, left its mark as a group that cared about both ideals and farm practicalities, about work and fun, about old ways and new.

Our generation had to say good-bye to three different campsites in South-ern California alone: Naame, our cornerstone in the high desert; Malibu, our transition site near the coast; and Gilboa, our new camp in the mountains of Big Bear, protected at last by Ginchy, that fearless, devoted mythical mascot of the *medurah,* the campfire.

Many of us began Habonim as shy, self-conscious, homesick campers. And yet, almost all of us ended our youth movement years feeling tried-and-tested, capable in areas that school and family had never touched and tempered in the same, intense, intimate way.

By the time Habonim was through with us, we had become creators, innovators, singers, dancers, writers, storytellers, artists, hikers, nurturers, organizers, risk-takers, educators, leaders, and friends. They were *chevrah,* those friends. They had created with us, laughed with us, questioned with us, entered into commitments with us, and cried along the way through it all. Our chevrah were those who grew up with us in Habonim, traveled with us along the way through summer camp, seminars, Neshef, and Workshop.

Along the way, we prepared countless *onegei Shabbat,* the unforgettable secular rituals by which we welcomed the Sabbath, celebrating Judaism in our own way. We prepared the medurah, the rollicking summertime Saturday-night campfire that ended the Sabbath. We prepared thousands of discussions and activities to pass along to those younger than us the ideas and values we had received, and new ones we had found.

Along the way, we were moved together in silence as we stood and watched the Friday sunset from *Givat Shabbat,* our Sabbath hill.

Along the way, we struggled to maintain a shaky control over kids we led who were only three or four years younger than we were. We struggled to master our camp kitchens, too, sometimes succeeding more than we could know.

Along the way, we survived the pained good-byes at the end of the summer, when the buses boarded to take away the kids from San Francisco and the kids from Los Angeles. Oh, we all vowed to write through the winter, and a few actually did and we all counted the days until Winter Seminar, when the cities would be reunited for three brief days.

Along the way, our Habonim chevrah was forged into a solid chain of shared experience and trust, of friendship that has remained vivid through all the years since we were done with the movement, and the movement with us. Like generations before us in Habonim and like those that came after, our Habonim friendships usually stood the test of time, remaining the realest bonds we would ever know, even when the movement itself had become just a youthful memory.

Our Habonim chevrah became rich, vital extensions of ourselves. They were then as they are now.

On the Eve of the Six-Day War: Some Excesses of the Sixties

By the spring of 1967, Habonim was being transformed by the forces of "the Sixties" into something barely recognizable to movement veterans of a generation earlier. There were several large garinim preparing to make aliyah to Gesher Haziv and Urim. In the cities, members were studying the early socialist Zionism of Borochov and Syrkin with an intensity that was unimaginable six years earlier. Through all this, the movement had grown to a size rivaling its 1947 prestate peak: between three thousand and four thousand members active in nearly forty cities.

No other American Zionist youth movement had thrown itself open to the changes of the new American youth culture with the enthusiasm of Habonim. But the infusion of counterculture carried with it a dark side, as well: drug use.

As the Zionist youth movement that was arguably the most autonomous and the most American of any American Zionist youth group, Habonim had always swung with youth trends on the left. In the 1930s, for example, Habonim members jumped to the forefront of support for the Spanish republic. In the 1950s and early 1960s, Habonim was enthusiastic in its embrace of folk music. And in the late 1960s, the latest trend was the use of marijuana.

By no means was all—or even most—of Habonim drawn to drugs, nor indeed to any of the radical trends of the youth culture, the antiwar movement included. Indeed, the movement continued to avoid taking a formal position on the war in Vietnam until the summer of 1969, when the national convention at Camp Galil in Pennsylvania adopted an antiwar resolution only after a bitter fight, and then by a narrow margin.

In fact, the influx of the counterculture into Habonim was largely regional at first. In most of the movement's regions, the ambience of Habonim life in the city and at camp remained largely unchanged right into the 1970s: folk music, moderate politics, and orderly activities. It was in the Northeast, and to a lesser degree on the West Coast, that the impact of drugs (meaning marijuana), rock 'n' roll, and the glorification of rebellion first began to make itself felt. When it did, however, the impact was profound and deeply divisive.

In the spring of 1967 the *mazkirut,* the national secretariat, heard reports that members of the *Merkaz,* the movement's central committee, had been smoking marijuana with some regularity. The two members were confronted and asked to stop smoking or resign from the Merkaz. They refused. In a heated debate, the mazkir, Artie Schneiderman, pointed out the danger of marijuana use in a movement that educated children and depended on adults both for community sponsorship and for parental permission to draw members in. In reply, the accused members and several others pointed to Habonim's long tradition of individual autonomy and personal freedom. Marijuana use was harmless, they insisted, and its illegality merely one more example of the repressiveness of American society. The demand for the members' resignation was brought to a vote, and failed. Artie Schneiderman resigned as mazkir.

A heated transcontinental telephone debate ensued, and in the end a formula was reached that allowed Artie to return as mazkir. The Merkaz voted to ban the use of marijuana at Habonim activities. This now raised an impossible question: What constituted a Habonim activity? Habonim members spent most of their time with other Habonim members. Movement activity was virtually nonstop during waking hours. If a Habonim member could smoke, but not at a movement activity, when *could* a member smoke? The solution was a talmudic one: movement activities were defined as organized activities involving three or more movement members. There was to be no mechanism for policing members' behavior. All members were put on notice that the future of the movement was in their hands.

*   *   *

For American Jews, the summer of 1967 was the summer of the Six-Day War. For American youth, it was also "the Summer of Love," when tens of thousands of young people descended on San Francisco and youth all over the country were drawn into the new spirit of the age. Marijuana use became a virtual sacrament among some sectors of young America, and Habonim was not spared. It was also the largest summer in the history of Habonim camping: Na'aleh in New York had 240 campers, and other camps were not far behind.

In the years to come, the Middle East war of June 1967 would come to be seen as the watershed event in the modern history of Israel and world Jewry. For a few Habonim members, though, its most immediate side effect was the opening of Arab East Jerusalem to the Israeli consumer.

The Seventeenth Workshop, which coincidentally included many of the unruly veterans of Machaneh Bonim Daled of 1966, reached Kibbutz Urim in September 1967. Almost immediately after arriving, they (and other American students in that first post-June wave of volunteers) discovered something that most Israelis would not realize for years to come: the newly acquired Arab streets of East Jerusalem harbored a society where hashish— a potent derivative of marijuana—was generally tolerated and cheaper than anything the Americans had ever seen.

It would be months before Israel at large noticed the acrid smell wafting out of the volunteers' quarters on kibbutzim all over the country. At that point, and for years to come, Israelis' attitude toward American Jewish youth became one of deeply mixed emotions. There was deep gratitude that so many youthful volunteers were ready to drop everything and come to stand with Israel in its time of trial; at the same time, Israelis were repelled by the American youth culture of long hair and hedonism, of "drugs and sex and rock 'n' roll." They wanted American kids, but to a growing degree, they did not want the ones they saw.

The mutual suspicions generated between Urim and the Seventeenth Workshop by the presence of drug use among the Workshoppers would return to haunt almost every Workshop for decades to come.

7

The Six-Day War and Beyond

In May 1967, Israel faced its greatest crisis in nineteen years of statehood when Egyptian President Gamal Abdel Nasser ordered the withdrawal of United Nations peacekeeping troops stationed along the Egyptian-Israeli border in Sinai.

The UN troops had been patrolling the border for ten years, stationed there in 1957 at Israel's demand as a condition for withdrawing from the Sinai after the Sinai Campaign of October 1956. Now Nasser, in a show of nationalist defiance, was ordering them out. The UN quickly complied, over Israel's protests.

In the days that followed, a circle seemed to close around Israel. Nasser ordered the Straits of Tiran at the mouth of the Red Sea closed to Israeli shipping. This effectively blockaded the port of Eilat, Israel's lifeline to Africa and Asia. At the same time, Syria ordered its troops up to the edge of the Golan Heights. The Syrians had been shelling Israeli settlements in the Galilee on and off for fifteen years. Both Egypt and Syria staged mass rallies amid blood-curdling cries for Israel's liquidation.

For much of May, Israel's army was on almost full alert. The economy slowed to a halt as reservists were called up. Psychologically, Israelis were preparing for an Arab death blow. And in communities around the world, Jews waited for the axe to fall.

Finally, on June 5, Israel struck first, eliminating the Egyptian and Syrian air forces in one stunning blow. Over the next six days, Israeli troops moved into the Sinai, onto the Golan and—after Jordan's King Hussein refused discreet entreaties to stay out of the war—into the West Bank and Jerusalem. The six-day victory is remembered in history as the Jewish state's finest military hour, and as a textbook example of modern surgical warfare.

The legacy of the Six-Day War changed the face of Israel and world Jewry. When the war ended and the Israel Defense Forces found themselves in control of the West Bank and other territories, Prime Minister Levi Eshkol declared the occupation to be a temporary evil. The territories were to be held as a bargaining chip in return for a future peace treaty with the Arab states, except for East Jerusalem. Then, the following November, the Arab heads of state met in Khartoum and announced their famous "three no's"; no recognition of Israel, no negotiations with Israel, no peace with Israel.

Those events—the war, the Khartoum summit—set in motion two decades of crisis that continue to rivet the world's attention: the rise of the Palestine Liberation Organization, committed to Israel's destruction, and its recognition by the Arab states as the "sole legitimate representative" of the Arabs in the territories; the ascendancy of the religious-nationalist settler movement Gush Emunim, committed to permanent Israel presence in the West Bank as a step toward messianic redemption; Labor's 1977 fall from power in Israel, leading to a decade of Revisionist ascendancy under Menachem Begin and Yitzhak Shamir; and, finally, the collapse of the consensus on the meaning and mission of Israel.

Over the years, North American Habonim would be transformed—sometimes painfully, sometimes exuberantly—into a militant oppositionist movement within the Zionist community. Often, to the chagrin of its sponsors and senior allies, it would become closely identified with the Israeli peace camp, opposing the government in seeking to maintain a flexible negotiating position and opposing any actions that might ultimately lead to the territories' annexation.

*   *   *

In the spring of 1967, however, none of that was apparent, as Israel and world Jewry sat braced for the worst—and then celebrated the stunning victory.

In June 1967, the Sixteenth Workshop was winding up its year at Kibbutz Urim in the Negev. The following letters home from an anonymous Workshopper tell the story of those fateful days. The world was a more innocent place then; even the true nature of the war remained unclear, as these letters demonstrate.

Tuesday, June 6, 1967

Dearest folks,

As well you know, the war which so many hoped would not come began yesterday. Of course, by the time you receive this letter it may already be over, and I may be touring the Old City of Jerusalem. All that, however, is part of the future.

This is what I began to type yesterday afternoon:

June 5

Today the war began. Egyptian tanks approached and possibly crossed the Israeli border, and we sent our planes to meet them.

I was in the children's house cleaning up after breakfast when I heard over the radio that Israeli planes were firing on Egyptian tanks. Immediately after, Dani Kerman entered, calm, unmoving, and told us to take the kids down to the shelter.

We moved into the shelter, where we stayed for about two hours. Then we went back to our regular schedule, except that the children were kept in the classrooms and not allowed to move around. Our main activity seemed to be the radio. At 1:30 the non-Urim children were sent home, and I went to my room to take a break to begin this letter to you.

At 2:15 p.m., the air raid bell rang. I rose from the typewriter and ran nearly half a mile to the other side of the kibbutz to be in the shelter with the children I take care of.

The children came out of the shelters around 4:00 and had their afternoon snack, and we prepared to stay with them as late as necessary. At 6:00, however, they were sent home.

In the background to all this was the sound of distant shelling and of overflying planes. In fact, just before we heard the radio announcement, we heard planes flying low over us on their way to the Sinai border.

* * *

June 6

Last night we slept in the trenches. Mothers and children slept in the shelters, and all men were on guard duty because of the danger of Egyptian fedayeen (infiltrators). It was a crowded and uncomfortable night, but brilliantly starlit. The darkness of the kibbutz was a complete one, however. We are under blackout tonight also.

As it turned out, the precautions were well taken. A fedayeen mine was discovered and exploded by us at the edge of our fields.

At 7:00 this morning, we were released from the trenches and went off to work on our regular schedule. There was another alert around 9:00. We were again in the children's house when we heard explosive noises and the doors shook. The windows had all been removed or taped. We dropped under the tables. Then when there was a silence a second later, and as the siren began to ring, we moved the kids, who had been sleeping, down into the bomb shelter. It lasted only a few minutes. The noise had been a sonic boom.

Most people, incidentally, had slept little or none during the night, me among them. So I went out on a break during the afternoon and got an hour's sleep. Tonight the blackout is still in force, but people are sleeping at home, although fully dressed.

I just heard the 9:00 news. Syria, Egypt and Algeria have broken diplomatic relations with the United States. We are fighting in Kalkilya [on the West Bank], which has been shelling Tel Aviv. We have taken the French Hill in Jordanian Jerusalem and now have land contact with Mt. Scopus, and the advance in Sinai is moving along well.

I realize how scary all this seems to you. We are, of course, worried, frightened at times, but we are working and playing a valuable part here, which gives us a great feeling. We are all so thrilled at the way we are smashing the Arab armies. Rumor has it that we may take the Old City of Jerusalem in the near future. We are shelling Bethlehem and have conquered Gaza and a number of other places.

We are all very concerned about the casualties, but it is not something that is spoken of. Most people have friends or relatives in areas that have been shelled or bombed.

None of us want to return home. The Workshop at present is going very well, and we are performing a useful function here. I repeat, it is a great feeling.

I'm too tired to go into the political situation now. My dearest love to you. I may be part of the first Workshop ever to tour the Old City of Jerusalem.

* * *

June 7

We woke up today, Wednesday, after sleeping in our clothes, to an almost normal day. The sound of distant shelling, which had been constant on the first two days, was almost completely absent and the only other noise was of our airplanes on their way to the rapidly receding front lines in the Sinai Desert.

At breakfast, one of the people with whom I work passed along some wild rumors about Jerusalem, which we both assumed to be perfectly true: "Jerusalem will have to be rebuilt. The shelling undergone by new Jerusalem was horrible. The museum, the Knesset, the University, all badly damaged."

Israeli radio does not announce anything until it has become fact. Some say this is because the Arabs listen to our radio to gain information, the Arab radio being unreliable. At the same time, some of what I was told did pan out. "Our soldiers have been asked to respect holy places, which means that we are most likely in the process of taking the Old City."

At 10:45 an alert was sounded and we took the kids down to the shelters. It was a very short one; just a precaution until a couple of unidentified planes in the area had been checked out. Throughout all the alerts, the children were constantly in good spirits and never grew hysterical. Incidentally, the Tuesday alert in the morning which I said was called because of a sonic boom was actually some trigger-happy gunner out in one of our fields who thought he was seeing something. That is all.

About 4:30, the mother of one of the kids I take care of walked in with her daughter and told me that rumor had it we had taken the Straits of Tiran and were attacking Shechem [Nablus] in Jordan. And we had taken the Old City. At 5:00, the radio announced all the rest, but said only that we had broken into the Old City. It's apparent though that we've really taken it because the radio has been playing Jerusalem songs for the past half-hour.

At 5:20 I heard that Hussein had agreed to surrender but that his army refused. Radio Egypt is still claiming they will throw us into the sea. "Jewish armies, you have been betrayed. Your prime minister has run home to his young wife. Moshe Dayan, we will put out your other eye." Every so often, though, they have to be interrupted by military music. Hussein's latest word is that he will fight to the last drop of blood.

On the 7:00 news it was announced that we had liberated Jerusalem at 10:30 this morning.

* * *

June 10

Dear folks,

It seems that I owe you a full report on the war. I'll try to make it a decent one, but I'm sure you realize the impossibility of telling so much in detail and letting you know the emotion as well.

You should have received a telegram from me, and one from the Habonim national office, on Wednesday. The crisis was truly over at Urim by the time the telegrams were sent. We have been unbelievably lucky. We were at no time shelled or bombed, in spite of the shelling of kibbutzim in areas closer to the Gaza Strip.

Back in America, Habonim was preparing for camp. Still, Israel's crisis was Habonim's crisis, and hundreds of chaverim sought to go over as volunteers, to help keep the economy going and bring in the spring harvests on the movement's kibbutzim. In late May the world movement stepped in: instructions were sent from Tel Aviv to New York to limit the number of Habonim members volunteering in Israel. Someone had to stay behind to open camp.

In the years since that fateful spring, Jewish historians and publicists have described the Six-Day War as a crucial watershed in modern Jewish history. It was June 1967, it is said, that cemented the bonds of total solidarity between Israel and a heretofore hesitant world Jewry. The Six-Day War created the identity of interests by which the Jews of the world see Israel's fate as their own. Since 1967, we are told, we are all Zionists.

Readers looking for some sort of expression of that millennial transformation in the literature of Habonim at the time will not find it, for a simple reason: unlike most diaspora Jews before 1967, Habonim was already Zionist. Still, as is evident in the following memorandum from the national secretariat, sent to the movement's leadership at the end of June, the Six-Day War had a profound and immediate impact on Habonim.

From the national office, June 1967

Our generation in Habonim has never fought for survival in the ghettos of Eastern Europe; we have never personally felt the sting of anti-Semitism in America, though it still exists elsewhere in the world; our generation did not have to physically build a Jewish homeland in a Middle Eastern desert.

Instead, our task in the 1960s has been to excite Jews about their heritage and their future as a people centered in Israel. Our task has been to demonstrate the personal relevance of a Jewish way of life—to make Jews feel Jewish, to show Jews they are personally tied to Israel, and through our own personal example, encourage meaningful aliyah. We have often been alone in this task.

In the last few weeks, however, we have witnessed the real emotional commitment that hundreds of thousands of Jewish youth and adults have for Israel. More than 4,000 young people from thirty-two countries have arrived in Israel as volunteers as of June 28. Of the first 200 American youth to drop everything to race to Israel's aid before a travel ban was imposed, forty-five were members of Habonim.

Many thousands of Americans were preparing to leave for the Middle East when the war erupted. Most would have assumed non-military roles to keep the economy going. At the same time, the American Jewish community raised millions of dollars for aid. Other communities rallied as well. The 30,000 Jews in Belgium managed to give $30 million.

The crisis, which turned from a terrifying fear for the very existence of the state of Israel, to a great military and psychological victory, proved to us that we are not alone in our love for Israel. Now we must keep this spirit alive in times of peace as well as times of war.

A Shaliach's Mission: Habonim after the Six-Day War

Yaakov Gali
Kibbutz Ma'ayan Baruch 1986

It was my luck to be sent out as central shaliach to North American Habonim just a few days after the Six-Day War. It was the beginning of an era that was by all accounts entirely different from anything that had gone before. It was a time when a shaliach who was willing and able had a unique opportunity to contribute in any number of fields. The Jewish world was open at our feet, waiting for the message of Israel.

In American Habonim I found, somewhat to my surprise, a chalutzic youth movement with a Zionist tradition of many years' standing. I found a special character in the movement, too, which I came in time to know and value.

The movement I came to was very caught up in the spirit of the times in America. The New Left, the debate over the war in Vietnam, campus unrest, and even drugs had their impact. At the same time, though, I found the movement very closely connected to the reality of Israel, and particularly to kibbutz life. The movement had deep bonds to the kibbutz movement—far deeper than I had realized before—and it educated its members quite openly to the goal of moving to Israel and settling on kibbutz.

As I came to know Habonim better, I found that the older members of the movement, most of whom had spent a year in Israel on the Workshop, were actually a living, organic part of the kibbutz movement of that time.

In my own work and in my supervision of the work of the other shlichim who were active during that post-Six-Day War period, I tried to develop new guidelines that would focus our efforts on specific areas of operation. Our first priority was a concentrated effort to work with older members. My aim was to obtain the highest possible enrollment in the movement's two main ongoing programs: Machaneh Bonim, the national leadership training camp, and the Habonim Youth Workshop on kibbutz.

We also worked hard to increase registration at the movement's summer camps, drawing both from movement members and from the general public. These three programs—camp, Machaneh Bonim, and Workshop—offered us the most concentrated opportunity to work with a youngster and bring our message home in an intimate setting.

Our second priority was organizing the activities of garinim, kibbutz settlement groups. With the increasing popularity after the Six-Day War of kibbutz volunteering and other types of short-term kibbutz experience, we began to view returnees from kibbutz programs as a potential source of membership for the movement's garinim. Accordingly, we began to reach out to kibbutz program returnees, and with some success: former volunteers proved to be a fruitful source of recruits for our garinim, and some even entered the movement as camp counselors and organizers in the city.

Alongside those activities, we worked with students on the college campuses around North America, with the goal of recruiting them into the various frameworks in which we were active. Partly this was a response to the increasing prominence of the college campus as a forum for political debate on the Middle East, which seemed to offer a pool of young Jews looking for a liberal Jewish framework of the sort Habonim could offer.

Partly, too, our campus work was a simple recognition of the changing sociology of American Jewish youth. While Jewish families continued to live in cities and suburbs, the Jewish college student—the key target for our Zionist message—was now to be found away from home on campus. And so we went where our youth were; we even opened a campus desk in the national office in 1969, staffed by a full-time shaliach, Muki Tsur.

Another activity that was crucial to my agenda was nurturing our relationship with the senior Labor Zionist movement in the United States and Canada, including the Pioneer Women, Poale Zion-Labor Zionist Organization, and the Farband Labor Zionist Order as well as the evolving Habonim Alumni organization. Our goal was to mobilize them to work together on behalf of the youth movement in which their young people were educated, in order to strengthen and enlarge it.

As noted, the Six-Day War changed American Jewry's relationship to Israel in a very fundamental way. One result of the war was an enormous sense of openness toward Israel on the part of the mainstream institutions of the Jewish community. We sensed at the time that if we did not find a way to act on this new reality, we were likely to miss an historic opportunity. The solution, as it turned out, was the Kibbutz Aliya Desk.

The desk functioned simultaneously as an arm of the Jewish Agency's aliyah department and as New York representative of the kibbutz movement's short-term labor bureau in Tel Aviv. Its first task, therefore, was to respond to any and all inquiries from the public—whether from an individual or an institution—indicating an interest in visiting or working for Israel or visiting in a kibbutz framework.

It was clear to us that the more people who came to Israel and kibbutz, the more would want to settle there. Working with money and personnel underwritten by the Jewish Agency and the kibbutz movements, we organized new kibbutz programs to meet a wide variety of needs: short summer visits, touring programs, year-long work study programs, and more. By the end of my shlichut, we had managed to establish a network of Kibbutz Aliya Desks around the country, directed and staffed by the shlichim of Habonim and the other chalutzic youth movements.

We were flooded with inquiries. We recommended to many applicants that they consider involvement in the many kibbutz-oriented programs of Habonim in North America—and, indeed, more than a few young people actually did join the movement's *kinim* and garinim.

One more area of activity that grew out of the Six-Day War deserves mention: the decision by the Israeli government and the Jewish Agency, at the earnest urging of the central shlichim from all the Zionist youth movements, to reach out to the general Jewish community of the United States and Canada with the message of Zionism.

After lengthy lobbying, the shlichim of the Zionist youth movements were able to bring about the institution of what became known as "the American Plan," aimed at broadening Zionist activity and increasing aliyah consciousness in the widest possible circles of American Jewish community life.

The Jewish Agency and the government agreed to raise one million dollars and recruit one hundred new shlichim to carry out the American Plan. The result was an entirely new category of shaliach: the community shaliach. These shlichim were assigned not to the branches of the traditional Zionist youth movements, but to local Jewish federations and community centers that had never before seen an Israeli shaliach. In due time, too, shlichim were added to the general Jewish youth groups sponsored by the synagogue movements and B'nai B'rith.

A good part of my personal time in America was devoted to touring the country, visiting the movement's camps and kinim in order to get to know the members personally. I tried to get across the message that the greatest contribution a Habonim member could make would be to work in the movement and join a garin to settle on kibbutz. I was not always successful, but I managed in the process to build a network of strong personal ties with individuals who have remained a part of my life ever since—some in Israel, others who stayed behind in North America.

Those three years of my shlichut to Habonim remain one of the most fascinating and rewarding positions I have held in all my years of public service to Israel and the kibbutz movement.

New Goals for Aliyah

The years following the Six-Day War were a time of rapid change in Habonim, as the younger members who had grown up during the 1960s moved into the leadership of the movement.

In 1969, the members of Garin Maor—graduates of the Fifteenth and Sixteenth Workshops—began departing on aliyah to Kibbutz Urim. The members of the Seventeenth Workshop prepared to take over the reins of the movement, and to consider their own aliyah plans. This would prove, however, to be a complicated and painful process.

A few weeks before leaving Urim, the Seventeenth Workshop met and discussed its aliyah plans. The members, no more than thirty in all, agreed that they wanted at some point to form a garin and return to kibbutz. Virtually all planned first to return to North America and finish college. Many expected that over the next four years it would be possible to expand their numbers vastly, to one hundred or more, given the revolutionary mood they believed existed on the American campus.

There was no agreement on where this garin would eventually settle, but this seemed amenable to resolution over time. In the meanwhile, the group agreed to form not a garin, but a *misgeret*—a "framework" for creating a future garin.

The misgeret's difficulties in making up its mind over where to settle would ultimately prove to be its undoing. The division involved differing experiences of Urim; some liked it and some did not. But there was a deeper division: the chaverim of the Seventeenth Workshop remained divided—as they had been at Machaneh Bonim in 1966—in the degree to which they were influenced by the 1960s and the American "counterculture."

For a group that was centered around New York, and grew to include numbers of members in Montreal, Toronto, Washington, and elsewhere, the spirit of the sixties appeared to breathe new life into forgotten aspects of early Labor Zionist ideology. Their language was a mixture of Borochov and

SDS, while their ambitions tended toward a romantic, revivalist chalutziut mixed with a strong dose of New Left communitarianism. They were unhappy with Urim, based on their Workshop experience. They wanted the misgeret to start its own kibbutz or choose a small one on which they could leave their stamp—a new Habonim settlement, the first since Urim was founded almost two decades earlier.

At the other pole was a group centered around Habonim's Midwest leadership, based in Chicago. Their concerns were much more practical ones. The likelihood of starting a new kibbutz—even of receiving permission from the appropriate Israeli institutions—seemed hopelessly far-fetched. They wanted to achieve the possible, without turning the movement, the kibbutz federation and themselves inside-out in the process.

Much of the sentiment of the Midwest group was captured up in a letter sent to the misgeret by members of Urim, urging the group to join the existing kibbutz.

April 28, 1969

Dear chevrei hamisgeret, shalom,
About a week ago, Zvi [Miller], Dani [Kerman] and I were drinking coffee in Tel Aviv after a meeting. The result is this open letter.

We have often discussed the misgeret and its future. It is no secret that we would very much like to have you with us at Urim. Whatever you do, and wherever you go we will retain a deep interest in you and a sense of responsibility for you. The garin that will emerge from the misgeret has a great deal to offer to whatever kibbutz framework you eventually join. Urim will continue to grow and develop with or without you. The three of us feel, however, as do many other chaverim at Urim, that considering both what you want and what we want, we will come closer to success together than separately.

We products of American Habonim have always distinguished ourselves by a lack of discipline, a big portion of individuality, and very often by a lack of historical perspective. It is a futile but nonetheless interesting exercise to wonder what might have been had Garin Aleph of American Habonim joined Kfar Blum rather than Gesher Haziv. Or what might have been had Garin Bet gone to Gesher Haziv rather than to Urim. By the time we grasped the possibilities, there were no longer large garinim coming from the movement. Today, all of us are proud of our own kibbutzim—but none of us have succeeded in preventing problems.

All of us have seen and concluded that a small kibbutz is a non-viable entity. Our experience has shown that the individuals who make up any group, and by extension any kibbutz, develop all sorts of approaches, all sorts of interests and all sorts of problems. These have constantly to be weighed, compromised with and taken into consideration. If there is a lesson to be learned from experience it is that no one is likely to be spared the necessity of grappling with reality. The question is always in what framework do you grapple with reality and with whom?

Urim as such does not require pity. We will do all right for ourselves. The question is, what will we be able to do for the movement in America, for the area we live in—what will be the nature of the community we will develop? I ask the same questions of the misgeret. It is our feeling that with you, we will be able to do much more.

There is nothing certain in life. No one can guarantee what will be the result of the misgeret going to Urim or to any other point on the map of Israel.

For the misgeret, there are many opportunities inherent in a decision to join Urim. But more than opportunities, there is a very real, a very tangible and a very im-

portant challenge. It is my feeling that if both we and you face this challenge successfully, we will be capable of doing some very, very important and satisfying things
together.

Shimon Kasdai.

* * *

When the misgeret met for its second *kinus* in the spring of 1969, the
decision was made. The chaverim from the East Coast continued to insist
that an attempt be made to find a target that would be open to the innovations
of Habonim's Sixties Generation. The Midwest group announced the
formation of its own garin to Urim, Garin Negba—"To the Negev."

During the fall of 1969, Garin Negba took over the *bayit*—the communal
house—founded in Chicago four years earlier by Garin Etgar and later used
by Garin Maor. In New York, meanwhile, the group that had held out for a
new kibbutz continued undaunted in its hunt for a new kibbutz.

After some of its members toured Israel to review prospective targets, the
group decided to set its sights on Kibbutz Tel Katzir, on the shores of the
Kinneret. A garin was founded in New York, choosing the name Omer (a
synonym for *katzir,* or harvest). It had only nine members.

Garin Omer lasted less than a year before disbanding. It left a vital legacy,
however. From their bayit in Brooklyn, members of Omer struck out on a
path of campus activism that would lead to a steady expansion of their circle,
and four years later—in 1973—many of the same people would form the
core of another garin with the same determination to start their own kibbutz.
That garin, Garin Gezer, would succeed where Omer had failed.

Entering the 1970s: Habonim and the Jewish Student Movement

David Twersky

New York 1988

In the space of one week in November 1969, two unrelated events took
place that would later come to be seen as the beginnings of a watershed
change in American Jewish life. They created, for a period of time, a space
in which Habonim and a few other youth movements were able to establish
an agenda that has shaped American Jewry's self-perception ever since.

In Boston, a group of Jewish students entered the annual General Assembly of the Council of Jewish Federations—which was already coming to be
acknowledged as the central body, for all intents and purposes, of organized

North American Jewry—and disrupted the proceedings. Seizing the microphone, the students presented a list of demands to the assembled leadership of American Jewish philanthropy. The demands centered on the redirection of communal spending priorities toward Jewish education. The demonstration was unprecedented, and was written about in *Time* magazine.

The following weekend, in Washington, D.C., several hundred young Jews marched as a Zionist contingent at the massive rally known as the Mobilization to End the War in Vietnam. Among their other activities during the mobilization weekend, the Zionist marchers prepared and handed out several thousand peanut butter and jelly sandwiches, labeled "Socialist Zionist," to their cold and hungry fellow demonstrators. They also helped organize a first-ever "Jewish movement center" during the mobilization, which held debates and forums on the Middle East, Jewish social concerns, and more. The sandwiches were written up by Pete Hamill in his column in the old New York Post, although their message was omitted.

These two events were linked by more than an accidental proximity in time.

Among politically aware Jewish college students in America, the dominant mood was undergoing a profound shift in the late 1960s. Students as a group were now well to the left of the post–World War II liberal consensus that had united many of their parents. The war in Vietnam was at its height; the civil rights revolution seemed woefully unfinished. There were frequent protest demonstrations on campuses and in cities across the nation, and young Jews were playing a central role.

At the same time, several factors combined during that period to produce an extraordinary proliferation of specifically Jewish-oriented activist groups on campuses across the country. This development came to be called (perhaps somewhat pretentiously) the Jewish counterculture. While its impact seemed small at the time, many of the leading figures in Jewish community life of the late 1980s had their first experience during that period in combining organized Jewish life with the politics of the larger society.

The growth of the Jewish counterculture—or, as it was more modestly called, the Jewish student movement—resulted from several historical factors.

Chronologically speaking, the first impulse for the rebirth of a separate Jewish activist movement came from the rise of black separatism in the mid-sixties. The turning inward by black activists, under the slogan of "Black Power," pushed the civil rights movement's Jewish elements to the margins of the struggle. For some Jewish liberals, black power forced an awakening of identity.

The second factor was the Six-Day War, and the intense fear in those fraught days of May 1967 that the Jewish state might be destroyed. For those of us born after the Holocaust, this was our first direct experience with fear for Jewish survival. When Israel won its remarkable June victory, the tremendous surge of pride among Jews around the world produced an unprecedented wave of identification with the Jewish state.

A third factor that helped shape the new Jewish politics was the increasingly hostile attitude of much of the black movement, and of the ever-more-radical New Left, toward Israel in the post-1967 period.

Given the tenor of the times, it was hardly surprising that many young Jews instinctively gravitated toward a political line that combined their two most pressing impulses: a Zionist and pro-Israel outlook and a left wing, often naively Marxist political approach. Jewish students in large numbers felt driven to fight for their own political breathing space on the noisy ideological battleground of the late sixties American campus, between the status quo pro-Israel line of the organized Jewish community and the left's hostile Israel-bashing. As a result, a generation of young Jewish activists was schooled in the complex dialectics of political positioning and coalition-building.

There was a fourth factor at work as well in the creation of the Jewish student movement: the renewed activity of the American Zionist Youth Foundation (AZYF). At the World Zionist Congress that convened in Jerusalem in 1968, the chairmanship of the World Zionist Organization's Youth and Hechalutz Department—the international parent-body of the AZYF—was given to a charismatic young colonel who had recently stepped down as chief educational officer of the Israeli army, Mordechai Bar-On. Morele, as he was known, instituted a policy of responding to the New Left's noisy anti-Zionist rhetoric not with attacks on the left, as some of his Zionist colleagues urged, but with a vigorous reassertion of the traditional progressivism of Labor Zionism.

Beginning in the fall of 1968, the AZYF began flooding American college campuses with reprints of assertive left wing Zionist manifestos that declared Israel's right to survival and security in terms acceptable to the campus left. Zionism was presented as it had first been framed by the pioneers of Labor Israel: as the national liberation movement of the Jewish people.

Nor was the counterattack limited to pamphlets. Aided by the financing and know-how of AZYF staff, Jewish students were encouraged to organize independent campus organizations—the old national framework of the Student Zionist Organization was dissolved—and to develop their own approaches and strategies for responding to the anti-Israel propaganda of the New Left. Funds were provided for student groups to publish their own monthly (in one case weekly) newspapers. National conferences were subsidized for students to meet and refine their views.

An essential component of this reborn Labor Zionist ideology was a sharp critique of Israel's new relationship with the Palestinian Arabs in the occupied territories. Within a year after Israel's 1967 victory, student activists were coming to Zionist gatherings around North America and presenting resolutions—always roundly defeated—demanding Israeli acknowledgement of Palestinian national rights. Today, twenty years later, with so many people in the Jewish community, in Israel, and in the West at large sharing this position, it is worth noting for the record that this was the general position of the emerging Jewish student movement from its beginning, hammered out in countless Jewish student conferences and campus newspaper editorials.

Members of Habonim played a decisive role in this configuration. As a veteran youth movement committed to the very principles that had suddenly come into vogue, Habonim provided a ready source of cadres for the newly emerging Jewish student movement.

It was Habonim's unique character, however, that gave it its central role in the emergence of the Jewish student movement. Because its educational philosophy stressed kibbutz as the ideal society, and drew on the rich vein of labor and socialist Zionist tradition, Habonim was "left" enough to retain some credibility—or at least to maintain a dialogue—with many of the assorted sects and "vanguard parties" that dotted the political landscape.

At the same time, as a movement committed to aliyah—and with a proud record of building kibbutzim from the upper Galilee to the Negev—Habonim had the Zionist credentials to work closely with mainstream Zionist and pro-Israel Jewish groups. In many cases, coalitions of Jewish students chose Habonim members to represent them to the adult Jewish community, knowing that acceptance was more likely if the approach came from a chaver of Habonim.

Finally, Habonim was Jewish enough—in the broadest sense of the term—to cement strong links with a broad spectrum of Jewish viewpoints on campus, from the Orthodox to the right wing to the reborn socialist Bund.

One alliance is particularly worth noting: recall that week in November 1969 which saw the Vietnam mobilization in Washington and the Jewish education demonstration at the General Assembly in Boston. Habonim was, for the most part, in Washington. The disruption in Boston was carried out by a group dominated by graduates of Conservative Judaism's summer camps and youth programs, young intellectuals who took the lead in founding the early *chavurot*, the counter-culture prayer groups in Boston and New York.

Over the next year, groups of Habonim members and *chavurah* activists joined forces and assumed leadership in building (with enormous help from the AZYF) the North American Jewish Students Network. From its founding in 1969 until it lost its independence in 1976, Network served as a kind of Union of Jewish Students across the continent. It brought under one umbrella the entire spectrum of campus Jewish activists from B'nai B'rith Hillel to the full range of Zionist youth groups, and from Lubavitch youth to new age mystics, the Jewish Student Bund and much of the Jewish new left.

Much of the cultural and intellectual tone in the new Jewish student movement was set by the chavurah activists who came out of Conservative Judaism; much of its political tone and organizational leadership came from Habonim. For a while, the national chairperson, the secretary-general, the fieldwork-outreach worker, and the editor of the Network newsletter were all from Habonim.

Members of Habonim were central, too, in the short-lived but heady experience of the Radical Zionist Alliance (RZA), an umbrella of left wing Zionist campus groups and youth movements. Still, it was through Network—and such Network offshoots as the Coalition for the Advancement of Jewish Education (CAJE), the Jewish women's movement, and the Jewish Student Press Service—that the Jewish student movement had its most profound and lasting impact. Indeed, many of the personal and working relationships developed during that period, particularly between Habonim members, RZA recruits, and chavurah activists, continue to play a role in the life of the organized American Jewish community two decades later.

The Network and RZA experiences allowed Habonim not only to play a central role at a moment in history—out of all proportion to its minuscule numbers—but also to recruit new members for itself at the college-age level. Many of these new recruits, who first came to Habonim as camp counselors or as garin members, found their lives forever changed by the experience.

On the down side, those Habonim members who devoted time and energy to these larger frameworks tended to abandon the routine and discipline of Habonim work in the local chapters. It may well be that the internal life of the movement suffered as a result. Still, had they not been permitted to go on expressing themselves on the national level as members of Habonim and its leadership bodies, these members might well have drifted away from the movement in any event.

In the end, the issues and contradictions that we addressed in the Jewish student movement, and the political space that we created, anticipated many of the contemporary problems confronting Israel and American Jewry today. Within the world as it appeared to us then, Israel could be criticized openly and forthrightly, but it also had to be defended. Zionism, we insisted, was just. Indeed, it was the proper analysis of the Jewish condition. Jews, we insisted, deserve their own state in the Land of Israel. We insisted that Zionism as such did not necessarily imply a denial of Palestinian rights, any more than the espousal of those rights automatically entailed the repudiation of Israel.

At the same time, our conception of American Jewry was fundamentally group oriented. We had no intention of serving as "the Jewish wing" of the American left; rather, we saw our responsibilities in terms of the communal life of the organized American Jewish community—such as it was. Indeed, our agenda went beyond mere defense of Israel, or the broader issues of the Middle East. We were involved in Soviet Jewry work; we fought for changes in the spending priorities of local Jewish federations, demanding more money for Jewish education, more attention to the plight of the Jewish poor and elderly; we fought for a more cohesive, democratic, and self-assured Jewish communal and political life. In much if not most of our agenda, history has borne us out.

Perhaps we were a bit too naive, too facile in insisting that Zionism—Jewish self-determination—must lead inexorably to support for Palestinian self-determination. On the other hand, it could be that all those (including most of the Labor party leadership) who at the time denied the very existence of the Palestinian Arab people were the naive ones.

It was an exciting time, and it saw a large group of movement members reach political awareness. The sociologist Daniel Bell once remarked that everyone on the left has his own Kronstadt—a betrayal of principles by the larger forces on the left, forcing the believers to reevaluate their convictions. Bell's Kronstadt was the original Kronstadt, the 1921 Soviet sailors' uprising brutally suppressed by the Bolsheviks. For us, the New Left's hostility to Israel and Zionism forced that painful reevaluation. It also helped us to grow up quickly and see the world more clearly.

Through the activities and leadership of many Habonim members, Labor Zionism played an important part in the reawakening of Jewish consciousness in this country over the last two decades. In this sense, too, that November weekend in 1969 closely resembles the present moment in American Jewish life.

Behind the Green Line: The Debate over Settling the Territories

A Memorandum from the Mazkir

Avi Ben-David
New York 1972

Three years ago, the Merkaz made the decision that there would be no settlement by Habonim garinim in "the territories." This decision was made in the presence of Senta Josephthal, then the secretary-general of the Ichud kibbutz federation, and caused quite a ruckus in Israel and the kibbutz movement.

There were several reasons why this decision needed reconsideration. The past decision stated what we would not do as far as the territories were concerned, but it did not answer the crucial question, "Why not?" Indeed, Habonim, which prides itself on being an educational force, had a decision on its books which came like a commandment from Sinai: "Don't ask why, just don't go!"

A more immediate reason that decision must be reevaluated is the informal relationship that now exists between Habonim and Garin Hagolan, which plans settlement in the northern Golan. The mazkir of the garin, Roy Belzer, is merakez [organizer] of the ken in San Diego. We could not encourage active involvement in the garin as long as the prior decision was on the books.

Finally, English Habonim is planning a settlement at Mevo Hama in the Golan Heights, and they are looking to Habonim in other countries to join with them.

These points are important to us, because we are in need of a new settlement site since our last garin, Maor, has left for Kibbutz Urim. The world movement is putting a good deal of emphasis now on settlement of the Arava in the southern Negev. Until a decision is made, both by the movement and by the people interested in settling in the Arava, the movement should investigate as many alternatives as possible.

The Merkaz discussion of the problem was opened by Roy Belzer, presenting the view of Garin Hagolan. In the discussion that followed, the general feeling was that each territory should be considered individually and there was a need for military settlements for defensive purposes.

The first proposal, which was altered twice, was:

Habonim does not support and will not participate in civilian settlement of the Sinai, Gaza Strip, or the West Bank, because:
1. Arab land is being expropriated for such settlement.
2. Arabs from these areas are not allowed to settle in Israel.
3. The Jews settling in these areas will not be willing to live in an Arab state if return of the territories is necessary as a part of an overall peace settlement satisfactory to the Israeli government and the people of Israel as a whole.
4. Settlement in the territory may block very real peace possibilities with Israel's Arab neighbors.

The resolution was modified twice, and finally accepted with 13 votes in favor, 1 opposed, 3 abstaining.

The second proposal was: "We support the aims of Garin Hagolan, since the Golan is in a different category from the other territories."

Chaverim were reluctant to bring the question to a vote. There was strong feeling that the members of the garin should examine their own future in light of point 3 of the first resolution. A question was then raised as to the nature of the treatment of the Druze on the Golan Heights. The question could not be answered conclusively by anyone in attendance at the Merkaz, and it was decided to table the proposal to the next Merkaz, when Ken Bob (who will be in Israel) and Alisa Belinkoff will respond to the question and the proposal will then be dealt with. The vote to table was 8 for, 5 against, 3 abstaining.

*   *   *

The question of whether or not to accept settlement in the Golan remained an open question for most of the following year. The members of Garin Hagolan—most of whom were not Habonim members, but former kibbutz volunteers recruited to the garin by a movement core—lobbied hard for recognition as a movement body, but the opposition was equally impassioned.

In the end, the issue was brought to the national convention in the summer of 1973, where settlement in the Golan was rejected. Garin Hagolan was denied recognition as a project of American Habonim. The decision caused a minor furor in Jerusalem, where stunned Jewish Agency officials began scratching their heads in wonder at the contrariness—some had far harsher words—of a Zionist youth movement under the umbrella of the World Zionist Organization.

In the meanwhile, more headaches were on the horizon as another garin began to take shape, like Garin Hagolan, outside normal movement channels: Garin Gezer.

The Formation of Garin Gezer

In the spring of 1972, discussions began in New York over forming a nonagricultural settlement group. The original members were a group of friends who had long been active in New York Habonim, joined by former members of the short-lived Garin Omer and activists in the North American Jewish Students Network.

The group, which began referring to itself as a garin long before any firm decisions were taken, was a combination of would-be kibbutzniks and young professionals—academics, therapists, and others—who wanted to live in a communal framework. Most members agreed that the two goals could be combined. Once the right spot in Israel was found, they believed, those members who so wished could farm, and the others would work in their own fields and pool their salaries. Given the small numbers, they expected to look for a small kibbutz where they could have a group impact, thus avoiding the burdens of starting a new settlement.

Other aspects of the group's future life together engaged far more of its interest in the early stages. Inspired in part by the all-embracing Jewish atmosphere then popular in the Jewish Students Network, the garin wanted to devise a standard of Jewish practice that would allow any Jew who wished to, to join the group. At a minimum, all agreed this meant a kosher kitchen; other questions remained open, amid mutual assurances of good will.

The question was, where to go? Settling in Israel was nearly unanimous. Some consideration was given to a city commune. Based on their understanding of the short-lived Garin Shaal experience in Carmiel, however, the group decided it needed a self-contained community with an independent economic base. That seemed to mean a kibbutz.

In the summer of 1972, contact was made with Gezer.

Gezer, on the Tel Aviv-Jerusalem highway, was founded as a kibbutz in 1946 by German Jewish youth. It fell to the Jordanian Arab Legion in 1948 in one of the lesser known tragedies of the War of Independence, and twenty-nine were killed. The rest were taken captive.

Kibbutz Gezer reassembled in 1949, but the trauma of the massacre never healed, and in 1961 the kibbutz dissolved and dispersed. For the next decade, the Ichud kibbutz movement sent in one group after another in attempts to restart a kibbutz. All failed. In 1970, the land was given over to a group of young Americans who had been involved in an experimental *chavurah* in Boston, and Gezer-America was launched.

Gezer-America was a loosely knit group with few rules and little stability. By 1972, when the New York Garin first made contact, it was estimated that five hundred people had passed through Gezer-America "on the way from Berkeley to Katmandu," in the parlance of the time.

The New York Garin sent a delegation to see Gezer-America in January 1973. What they found was a run-down village, its buildings suffering from a decade of neglect. The delegation met with economists and officials from veteran kibbutzim who told them the garin's central dream was impossible: there was no way to build a kibbutz economy if half the members from the beginning worked outside and donated a salary.

On the other hand, there was land, and there were buildings, and a few tractors, and apparently it could be had for the asking. One afternoon during the week long visit, two garin members, veterans of Garin Omer and the Seventeenth Workshop, climbed to the top of Gezer's old grain silo and looked out over the land. From high up, it appeared completely green. Off in the distance loomed Tel Gezer, the remains of the ancient Canaanite city of the same name. It seemed very near and real, after years of hoping.

On February 22, 1973, at the Hashomer Hatza'ir meeting hall in the Bronx, forty members of the garin reconvened to discuss the delegation's findings. Marty Salowitz, secretary-general of the Jewish Students Network and a former *rosh* of Na'aleh, reported the good and bad news: Gezer could be had for the asking; the New York Garin could be, ironically, the stabilizing influence in a troubled community; but there could be no guaranteed work in the free professions for the foreseeable future. After an all-night discussion, the garin voted to adopt Gezer, and nearly twenty professionals left the garin. The evening would be remembered for years as "the Bronx Massacre."

Over the next months Garin Gezer began a furious outreach program. Thousands of letters were sent to Habonim members, Network activists, former kibbutz volunteers. Conferences were held around the country, applicants were screened. In Tel Aviv and Jerusalem, meanwhile, political storms were brewing for Garin Gezer.

The first problems came from Habonim and the kibbutz movement. North American Habonim, at the behest of the Ichud federation and with the encouragement of the chaverim at Urim, had adopted as a settlement target a small kibbutz near Eilat, called Grofit. Now the movement was being asked to support, with money, manpower, and future garinim, a kibbutz in the center of the country. Gezer had no priority on any government list: it was not in the desert, not in the Galilee, not in the territories. It was a virtual suburb of Tel Aviv. Moreover, the garin requesting recognition had a majority of members with no Habonim background. Why, the Ichud asked, should we supply the full-time staff of farm advisers you will need for years in order to get off the ground?

After long negotiations, the garin won the movement over. Gezer was recognized alongside Grofit as a project of Habonim and the Ichud. Arrangements were made for the garin to receive a half-year's agricultural training at Afikim, where their *madrich* was to be YPZA veteran and twice-shaliach Ben-Zion Ilan (Benny Applebaum). Efforts were begun to find a kibbutz that would "adopt" Gezer and guide it through its formative years with advice, guidance, training.

The other set of problems would prove far more troublesome, hovering over Gezer for years to come. In the offices of the Jewish Agency and the Ministry of Housing, Gezer was listed as having been founded in 1946. Its entitlement to start-up funding had long since expired. But after a decade of neglect, it needed almost everything redone: the houses were collapsing, the electricity dated from 1949, the tractors were run down, the roads and sidewalks were all but nonexistent.

If Gezer would prove capable of confronting these problems and surviving, it was because the garin was built around a remarkable group of young activists including several top leaders of the Jewish Students Network, with years of experience between them in Zionist politics.

By the fall, the outreach had succeeded in building the garin to thirty-seven members. In the interim, however, Gezer-America had disbanded. The land was empty. The aliyah date was moved forward to January 1974. The kibbutz movement could not promise to keep the space open longer than that.

And while the members of Garin Gezer were planning their aliyah, the leadership of North American and World Habonim continued their efforts to build an American garin to Grofit. They were supported actively by the most recent American *olim* at Urim, which took on responsibility for nurturing the struggling young kibbutz to its south.

The debate was not one of left versus right. Partisans of both target kibbutzim agreed that North American Habonim had no business settling in the administered territories. The debate—to the extent that it was an open debate—centered on the conflicting goals of seeking personal fulfillment for the members (at Gezer, a stone's throw from Tel Aviv) versus serving Israel's national priorities (at Grofit, in the distant south).

The Yom Kippur War

Yom Kippur, Saturday morning, October 6, 1973, while Jews around the world were in synagogue praying on Judaism's most sacred and most universally observed holiday, the armies of Egypt and Syria crossed the frontiers into Israeli-held territory in a massive surprise attack.

Unlike the Six-Day War, there was no lightning Israeli victory to be had this time. For two weeks, Israel appeared to be fighting for its very life, and losing ground for the first time since the 1948 War of Independence. Only in the war's third and final week did Israel rally and regain some of the ground it lost. At no point did the battle zone enter the pre-1967 borders of Israel proper; still, the war was a profound shock. In 1967, fighting from the "suicidal" borders of the Green Line, Israel had lost fewer than seven hundred soldiers; this time, with Sinai, the Golan, and the West Bank providing "ideal" buffers, she lost more than two thousand six hundred.

The Yom Kippur War was a surprise in more ways than one. For six years, since the Six-Day War, Jews had come to regard Israel as virtually invincible. It was inconceivable that the Arabs would dare to attack, and even more inconceivable that Israel could lose the upper hand even for a moment. As in 1967, Jews were stricken with fear for Israel's survival, but this time the fear was accompanied by a profound disorientation. Reality had been turned upside-down.

Part of Israel's military disadvantage in 1973 was political in origin. For the first time in its history, Israel was seen to be entering a war without allies and without the sympathy of world public opinion. Six years of occupation had turned many of the world's "neutrals"—particularly Africa, Asia, and most of the communist bloc—into active enemies. Even Israel's closest friends, in the United States, western Europe, and in the free trade-union movement, were for the first time finding it awkward to appear too friendly toward the "Zionist occupier." That, in turn, limited Israel's freedom of action in the field, since the Israeli military is completely dependent on a steady flow of spare parts from the West.

In the years to come, the conflicting emotions that arose during the Yom Kippur War—anger and suspicion toward the Arabs on the one hand, questioning of Israeli actions on the other—would evolve into two conflicting camps dividing Israel and world Jewry roughly in half. In 1973, however, they were still entirely contained within the torn emotions of Jews caught unawares on Yom Kippur, as reflected in the following letter to members from the Habonim national office, written at the end of October.

The War

Letter to Movement Members
From the National Office

This has been a very tough period for the mazkirut (national secretariat). The question, "What do we do?" has been primary in our minds. We have had discussions, arguments and more.

The first thing that one has to overcome is the terrible feeling of "Oh no! War again!" Of all the lives being lost. The next thing is the lies of our enemies. When one watches the treatment that Israel gets in the U.N., one wonders how the hell Israel tolerates it. When [Jamil] Baroody, the representative of Saudi Arabia, goes on a witchhunt, full of anti-Semitic, Hitlerian thought, no one in the Security Council takes the time to object. It is Israel who must object. When Israel is speaking, many are the countries willing to interject and chastise on the most minute of points.

After taking these things in stride (if that is possible—it is a stark realization that so much of the world hates Israel outright or is willing to hate Israel for oil or money), one realizes that we must help Israel in every way possible, and that there are three basic ways: Education, money and aliyah.

Education is our main reason for existence and must be our main direct effort. We must continue our own education so that we know what is really the situation and have the facts at hand to refute the arguments of the Arabs and their sympathizers. More than that, we must publicize Israel's case. We must seek new members willing to learn systematically about what Israel is and what her needs are. For those that are not so inclined, we must give them as much information as they will tolerate.

In this effort, we must be fair and not fall into the ways of our enemies. We must also in some way deal with those who, on Israel's behalf, distort the truth. There has been exploitation along these lines, and it is a terrible shame on the Jewish people.

Money is an immediate priority. With the big fund-raisers that are around, Habonim will never be a prime factor in this field. Still, is important to participate. Israel's financial losses have been extreme during this war, and will continue to be as long as a sizeable number of Israelis are mobilized in the reserves.

Our last way of helping is aliyah. Many *chevre* have already gone to Israel as volunteers to help kibbutzim that are very short of manpower, and more want to leave. This is an immediate way of helping, but this is not enough. To really be a viable state, Israel needs many more chevre. It is a pretty blunt statement, but if Israel had five million Jews instead of less than two-and-a-half million, the Arab states would be much less ready for war. It is their conception of Israel as a very small state surrounded by their mass which helps to incite them into war every few years.

Of course, if it were only a question of getting Jews to Israel, we could all become aliyah agents and just send people over. That's not it. There are enough aliyah shlichim taking care of this. What Israel needs in aliyah are groups of chevre who are ideologically motivated, who will set up the Gezers, join the Grofits, maybe reestablish the urban collective, which shall be the building blocks of a strong, ideological society capable of dealing with the hate on every side and making it into peace. True, this is a dream, but a dream upon which we are already embarked. The only way to live through the insanity and hatred of the present is to build and develop the dream. ALEH UVNEH.

Gezer, 1974:
"Does This Mean We Were Pioneers?"

Karen Charnow
Kibbutz Gezer 1985

In October 1973, at the apex of the Yom Kippur War, I left the United States for Israel. I traveled with my sister, who lived in Paris, and on January 15, 1974, I met on the steps of the Ichud kibbutz movement headquarters with thirty-four other members of Garin Gezer. We were about to leave for Kibbutz Afikim, near the Kinneret, to begin the training that would culminate in the reestablishment of Kibbutz Gezer. Two more members would join us a week later; they had stayed in America to attend a Bob Dylan concert.

The path that had led me there began in Washington, D.C., in 1959. My parents thought it would be a good idea for me to get out of the house for the summer and meet some new friends. My grandfather had fought in the Jewish Legion in World War I and my mother had attended Camp Kvutza at Accord. I was sent to the nearest Habonim camp, Moshava, in Annapolis. From then until 1967, I went to "Mosh" every summer and was deeply involved in the movement in the city. After high school I went to Israel, first on a summer tour, then as a kibbutz volunteer.

While I attended the University of Maryland I kept up a low level involvement in Habonim, but I found myself more drawn to the new Jewish student groups on campus. One summer, I decided to taste the reputed "radicalism" of New York Habonim, so I joined the staff at Camp Na'aleh, where I renewed some old friendships with people I had known in high school. It turned out they were organizing a garin, with the idea of founding a new kibbutz. I was intrigued. The alternative was law school in Boston. And so it came to pass I was on the steps of the Ichud that day in January 1974.

We spent our first six months at Kibbutz Afikim, on *hachshara*. We learned how to get up for work at ungodly hours; how to share one toilet among twenty-five people; how to throw great parties. We learned about group living and collective decision making. Most of all, we learned a lot about ourselves. The tension at Afikim was almost as high as the expectations. Our physical quarters were lousy. We were bewildered and far from home. At length, the training period drew to a close.

On July 4, 1974, we set out for Gezer. The site was about as ready for us as we were for it. We left a crew behind to salvage and kosher the kitchen, while the rest of us dispersed for a much needed two-day vacation.

We got back in time for the melon harvest. That was the first time most of us had ever seen a melon in a field. Organizing a harvest was an interesting operation. We got back, too, to find chicken coops ankle-deep in mud. Sprinklers that should have been turned on for only a few minutes had been left on all day. And we came back to a kitchen whose roof leaked when it rained and whose floor oozed mud when it was washed. Only one or two houses had hot water. Does this mean we were pioneers? Maybe for our time and our backgrounds, we were. There were no Chinese restaurants around, and no Bloomingdale's for seven thousand miles.

We began to learn. We learned how to farm; how to organize a work day; how to run the place with a population steadily declining for the first six months. We had eggs to collect, chickens to inoculate, cows to milk, and fields to prepare and plant.

And we got help. Kibbutz Tzora, a South African Habonim kibbutz a few miles away, adopted us and sent us counselors whose advice proved invaluable. And the Jewish Agency, after much prodding, rehabilitated the housing, built a new dining room, and finally supported us down the entire road.

While there was a steady attrition of garin members, there was an even stronger inflow of new people. In the first year, several dozen members of Habonim came over for shorter or longer periods, to join us in our grand adventure. A dozen-and-a-half or so ended up settling in; since we had a second garin coming in 1974, Garin Bet, this first wave of volunteers who settled in became known as Garin Aleph-and-a-Half.

Then there was the constant flow of volunteers you could only call "members of the Sixties generation." The old Gezer had won international renown as a prime way-station on the Berkeley-to-Katmandu express, and word of its breakup had not gotten around—especially since for much of the world, replacing one Gezerful of American hippies with another was no change at all. There seemed to be a certain category of potential volunteer that the kibbutz movement was intentionally steering our way, or maybe these people were asking for us.

We had our fair share of eccentric characters. A woman in charge of irrigation did not believe in using chemical pesticides and herbicides, but did not want anybody to think she was lazy. Every day she went to the fields and sprayed water. No one could understand why the weeds were out of control and the corn was infested with bugs. The kibbutz barber, for a while, was a woman who was legally blind. She married a man who had thrown hot tea on her in anger. She was a woman of much passion and depth, but she couldn't really see your hair.

Somehow, with all the slightly and not-so-slightly crazy people, we managed to lay the foundations for a kibbutz and begin to build the type of community we envisioned in those late-night conversations in New York and at a dozen conferences before we came to Israel.

We had agreed upon several guiding principles. We wanted to establish complete sexual equality by shunning traditional stereotypes and raising our children in a nonsexist environment. We wanted to build a creative Jewish community that merged the traditions we had brought with us and the traditions of the kibbutz movement. We wanted a kosher kitchen, so any Jew could feel welcome at Gezer. We refused to hire workers to do our menial labor. That means for six weeks every year, every member of the kibbutz has to put in tens of hours of overtime to weed the cotton crop and prepare the vineyard. As children of the sixties, we envisioned an open community based on trust.

And the truth is that many of these principles do guide our lives today. While we have not completely conquered sexual stereotyping, nobody is bound by traditional kibbutz divisions in the choice of work. We try to maximize the number of men working with the children. Our little store is open twenty-four hours a day to all permanent residents, and each person is trusted to record his or her own purchases. The *moadon* (clubhouse) is always open for people to get a cup of coffee or read a magazine. The library, arguably one of the best English-language collections of light reading in the Israeli countryside, is always open and people check out and return books freely.

We have developed our own approach to celebrating the holidays as well. Unlike most kibbutzim, which have one large gathering on Passover, for example, we divide the community into small groups, to foster a more intimate atmosphere. We hold High Holiday services in our synagogue. Every week, people meet there to welcome the Sabbath and conduct their own, very innovative service. For several long periods we have had young rabbis living with us, dividing their time between standard work branches and cultural work for the Gezer community. We make potato latkes as well as jelly doughnuts on Chanukah.

And in our own contribution to Israeli culture, we have built Hambo Field, one of the most beautiful baseball fields in the entire Middle East. It is dedicated to the memory of Velvl Lehr, former head of the Na'aleh Camp Committee and a staunch friend of American Habonim. It has become the nerve center of the Israel Softball League, a lasting addition to the Israeli sports scene that was born at Gezer.

Although it still has problems, although it still has a shortage of trained people and still lacks members willing to take on certain jobs, Gezer has grown into an attractive and viable community. Gezer learned to live together, to help each other in crisis and to share each others' joys.

Grofit, 1976: "The Arava Is Not an Easy Place to Live"

Muki Telman
Kibbutz Grofit 1985

The idea of sending settlement groups to Kibbutz Grofit was the result of a meshing of our own interests as movement members with the interests of the various Israeli authorities responsible for settling the Arava, the arid desert in the far south of Israel.

Garin Grofit grew out of a core of people who attended the Twenty-Second Habonim Workshop in 1972. The Workshop that year was a large group, and the movement split us into two groups. At first, the plan was to send some to Kibbutz Yotvata, near Eilat, and some to Kibbutz Gesher Haziv near the Lebanese border. We were already interested in settling in the Arava, however, since it appeared to us as the greatest pioneering challenge we could find. We convinced the national office to send us all to the south.

The reason our demands were met, I think, is that somewhere in the Habonim-kibbutz movement bureaucracy, a decision had already been made to make the Arava a high priority target for Habonim and other American youth movements. In the years that followed, both Young Judaea and the

Reform movement sent groups here, and both movements have founded kibbutzim that are our neighbors today.

The Arava is not an easy place to live. Our settlements sit in a broad, dusty valley about ten miles north of Eilat and the Red Sea, along the border with the Kingdom of Jordan. It is the hottest and driest region in Israel. Annual rainfall is measured in millimeters. Temperature often tops one hundred degrees Fahrenheit during the summer for days at a time. Even with air conditioning, life in the Arava is a daily challenge for all who choose it. But in the early days we did not have air conditioning.

While we were still on Workshop, we went to the kibbutz movement and presented it with the idea that we would start our own kibbutz in the Arava. When they finished laughing at us, they told us to come back when we had seventy members in our group, and then they would be willing to talk. At the time we had six members.

We never got up to seventy members; in the end, we reached a total of twenty-five members, coming to Israel over a two-year period beginning in the fall of 1976. Since starting a new kibbutz seemed beyond our grasp, the movement suggested that we join a struggling kibbutz in need of reinforcement. Our influence, they argued, would be almost as great in a kibbutz in need of members as it would be in a new kibbutz. They proposed that we consider Grofit. And indeed, Grofit seemed to be what we were looking for.

In 1973, Grofit was six years old and had twenty-eight members and twelve children. It had been extremely unstable throughout its history. The founding garin was made up of members of the Israeli youth movement Noar Oved; it was soon joined by another, younger Noar Oved group, but the two groups ran into serious social conflicts. After three years, the first group left and the kibbutz had to be started anew. At that point, Grofit entered what we still call "the railroad period." People would come, stay for a short time and then leave.

At the time that we came along, development of the Arava was just beginning, and we felt we could have a powerful impact on the kibbutz and the entire region.

When the first group of our American garin arrived in 1976—only seven people in all—Grofit had forty members and fewer than thirty children. But there were signs of an incipient stability. Some of the older members had finally, truly decided to stay and make Grofit their home. When I arrived in the second wave of our garin, there were fifty members. Today we have one hundred members, twenty candidates, and scores of children—with more on the way every day.

We had wanted to found our own kibbutz because we wanted to be involved in every aspect of building a kibbutz. But when we arrived in Israel, I don't think we really understood what that meant. Soon after we arrived at Grofit, it was obvious that our greatest contribution could be to help the kibbutz establish a functioning economic infrastructure. Many of our members had university degrees, and we added a missing level of expertise.

One of us was an electrical engineer. Although his job as kibbutz electrician was far below the level of his training, he played a crucial role in the planning of the physical plant. Those with backgrounds in education and social work were able to contribute to the kibbutz committees responsible for those areas.

Grofit's economy for many years was based entirely on agriculture—primarily onions, melon, cow fodder, milk cows, and chickens. We also have two orchards of dates and mangoes. A few years ago we decided to broaden our economic base. While looking for a traditional industry, we went into the tourism business. We opened a small campground, and we believe it has strong potential to grow. And we take in laundry for the entire southern Arava region.

The fundamental challenge before us, however, is to expand the population of the kibbutz. Even one hundred members is not enough to ensure a thriving community. Our new recruits come from three major sources—the Israeli youth movement, American Habonim, and individuals who come our way. The last group includes young families from Israeli cities and immigrants in absorption centers.

The first source, the Israeli youth movement, was the original backbone of Grofit, but it has not sent people regularly in several years. North American Habonim, which recognized Grofit as one of its official settlement projects, has sent one small garin, Garin Harif, which arrived in 1985. We have hosted three Workshops, and several of those who attended Workshop here have returned to visit during their junior year abroad at Israeli universities. Grofit adopts them, subsidizes their transportation to the kibbutz, and becomes their second home in Israel. They often work here during their vacations, which is doubly welcome because of our chronic labor shortage.

When the Habonim members come, they find a kibbutz with a warm and open atmosphere. Grofit members make an effort to accept people, socialize with them, and make adjustments for newcomers.

Still, the past ten years have not been without difficulties. Of our entire garin, only nine people remain. Nine other American Habonim graduates joined us as individuals. Twenty members of our garin have returned to the United States.

In the early years, I don't think people knew what they were getting themselves into. The kibbutz did not understand how to absorb Americans—or indeed any "foreign" population with different language, background, and attitudes about how things should be done. There were conflicts then and there are still some conflicts now. But we have learned many lessons and have come to accept that people with different training and perspectives make the kibbutz a more interesting place to live.

We came to Israel with a commitment to make a difference. And we are making a difference in the development of our region. I learned that sense of personal commitment in Habonim. It would have never been enough for me to let others do what I think is the real work. When I step back and look at what we have done, I feel satisfied.

Habonim in the 1970s: American Issues to the Fore

At home in America, the 1970s were a riotous, chaotic time in the life of Habonim. The movement was still riding the crest of the energy generated in the 1960s. Indeed, the spirit of rebellion that began in the New York area in the middle of the last decade was now spreading throughout the country.

Aliyah played an important role. With the departure of the garinim to Gezer and Grofit, Habonim members were filled with a sense of accomplishment, with a feeling that "we"—the unruly young Labor Zionists of North America—were in the vanguard of building a new Israel.

During the summer of 1971, a group of *madrichim* at Machaneh Bonim renewed the attempt to convert Habonim from an educational movement to an explicitly political one. Their program was a one-page manifesto, drafted over drinks at Christie's, a luncheonette near camp in the Catskills village of Hunter. The "Christie Manifesto" was submitted to the movement's national convention at Camp Moshava in Maryland at the end of the summer.

The Christie Manifesto, composed by David Twersky and Sydney Nestel, was a virtual repetition of the Habonim revolt led by Max Langer in 1962. It called for the elimination of the younger age groups, making Habonim exclusively a high school and college-age movement. It also proposed restrictions on the role of the shaliach, who "should not have any decision making power." But there were innovations as well. Christie proposed that "all future ve'idot (national conventions) be open to all bonim and ma'apilim, i.e. all members of the movement." Langer's influence was still strong, but it had been tempered by the 1960s and the New Left philosophy of "participatory democracy."

Christie reflected the political mood of the movement as America entered the seventies. It was also, in part, a response to the growing alienation in Israel, felt strongly by American movement members, between the Labor party and the Zionist left—a product of mounting anxiety over the continued occupation of the territories.

"Habonim should clearly state that it has no ties with the Israeli Labor Party, or with any other political force in Israel," Christie read. It went on to urge that Habonim "work to create a healthy Jewish community in North America, which necessitates our functioning as a dynamic socialist-Zionist opposition to the status quo, i.e. Habonim works to drastically reform the American Jewish community."

The Moshava *ve'idah* referred the Christie Manifesto to the movement's national Merkaz, which in turn submitted it to a referendum of the movement's members. It was turned down. Education and political action were never to be an either/or proposition in North American Habonim, and they continued to coexist in the 1970s just as they had in decades before.

Behind the would-be revolutions, however, was a growing involvement in domestic North American issues that began in the days of civil rights and the Vietnam war, in the late 1950s and 1960s, and continued into the 1970s. In rapid succession the movement began adopting resolutions endorsing the lettuce and grape boycotts of the struggling United Farm Workers of America, and sent out educational material to its camps and chapters on such topics as nuclear weaponry, unionization, and women's rights. In 1976, Habonim even published a book, *Sisters in Exile,* a collection of articles on women in Jewish life from a feminist viewpoint.

The following items, which appeared as unsigned articles in movement periodicals during the 1970s, are typical of the irreverent activism pervading Habonim throughout the decade.

Rochester, 1973:
The Farmworkers and Officer Bozo

From a Movement Newsletter

At the A&P here, where just a few weeks ago common folk and busy shoppers mingled peaceably, the progressive forces of Habonim Labor Zionist Youth have made great strides in the battle against corrupt exploitation and bourgeois revisionism. Twenty of us joined together outside the supermarket to protest the sale of lettuce picked by non-union workers.

A private law enforcement official, known affectionately to our members as Bozo, sidled over to us.

"Oh, you commies out here making a ruckus again?" he asked us.

"No sir, Mr. Bozo," we replied. "We are picketing the supermarket on behalf of the United Farm Workers."

This Enemy of the Working Class did his best to persuade us to leave. But we linked arms and stood our ground. It was truly uplifting. As Officer Bozo got into his green Volkswagen, we continued to march.

We were also inspired by the comments of those passing by. "Why don't you idiots go back to Peking where you came from?" one intellectual old lady shouted, in a voice laced with revolutionary fervor. I thanked her for her input.

Later in the day, Officer Bozo returned and offered to relieve us of the burden of carrying our signs. We politely declined. He then offered to escort us from the site, violently if need be. And, indeed, when one of our members expressed his emotions in a passive, nonviolent finger motion, Officer Bozo almost committed an act of aggression.

Despite the danger, we will carry on the struggle from Washington, D.C., to Tel Aviv, from the White Plains of Gandeza (a Spanish Civil War song popular at Habonim camps in the 1960s) to the dining room of Kibbutz Degania (Aleph and Bet). Habonim unite! We have nothing to lose except our friends at A&P and Pepsi.

Ann Arbor, 1975: The IWW Strike
From a movement newsletter

Habonim members in Ann Arbor were part of a successful strike that led to the recognition of an Industrial Workers of the World local at a bookstore in Ann Arbor.

The strike began when three employees of the Charing Cross Book Store notified their employer that they wanted to join the IWW. The next day they were locked out of the store and told that it had been sold and was to be reopened under a different name. The employees decided to picket there and at Borders Book Store, a larger establishment owned by the same person.

At the same time, Frank Cedervall, an organizer for the IWW, gave a talk to the leadership of Habonim in Ann Arbor. Calling himself "the last of the old soapbox orators," Cedervall gave an impassioned speech. At its conclusion, three members of Habonim immediately joined the picket line. Over the next week, additional members of Habonim picketed the store, enough to dissuade a significant number of shoppers from entering.

With growing confidence, we vowed to return with twenty members that Tuesday. We copied the words to all the old union songs so we could sing as we walked. But when we arrived at the appointed hour, the picket signs had been taken down. To our delight, the strike had been settled. The employees had been rehired by the new bookstore and the IWW contract recognized.

The experience reminded us that dissent liberates the dissenter and action reinforces morality. Those lessons are too easy to be forgotten in the Me Generation.

New York, 1973: Habonim and the Gravediggers' Strike

Sandy Simon
New York 1989

Any time is a bad time to be digging in a cemetery, but digging at dusk just may be the worst. As the shadows stretch out, any noise becomes ominous. The two Habonim members standing in a pit in Queens tried to ignore their jitters. We had only three more feet to go, and then we could lie down, try the grave out for size and head home. We always lay down to try out our work for size—it was our way of showing the spooks we weren't afraid. Two shovels more. And then the ground kicked back. A foot protruded up from the earth—or, more precisely, a leg. Just a leg. A single, truncated leg.

It was the spring of 1973, and the contract between the New York metropolitan cemetery owners and Local 365 of the Cemetery Workers and Greens Attendants' Union had expired a few months earlier. Work stoppages aren't usually considered a viable option for cemetery workers; the footage on the evening news of anguished families standing around an unburied coffin does not engender public support for the workers' demands. This is especially true in New York, with its large Jewish population. In accordance with biblical injunction, traditional Jewish law dictates that burial must take place within twenty-four hours of death, or a day or two at the outside.

And so, the cemetery workers issued an ultimatum and waited for the owners to come to the negotiating table. Deadlines were replaced by more deadlines, but without the power of a strike, there was no pressure and thus no talks.

After a few months of deadlock, a strike was called. I don't remember whether the union actually voted to strike, or whether the walkout was simply ordered by the union's enduring president, Sam Cimaglia. I do remember the television news clips showing the last gravediggers' strike. And they showed members of Betar and the Jewish Defense League leading "strike teams" to the cemeteries. For a not-so-modest fee, they would strike a blow against what they called anti-Semitism by striking physical blows against the cemetery workers. After that, they would bury the coffins of the Jewish dead.

As a member of Habonim, I had been sensitized to the needs and rights of workers, including the right to strike; I had equally learned of the right of all people freely to follow their religious persuasions. As a teenager, I firmly believed there was a simple solution to every problem, no matter how intractable it seemed. As *merakez eizor,* New York regional director of Habonim Labor Zionist Youth, I decided to put my principles in action.

So I called up Sam Cimaglia. After a few moments of low level detente (I expressed my sympathy for his members' plight, and he expressed sympathy for those whose religious beliefs required speedy burial) I suggested a plan. Habonim would coordinate a team of volunteers to dig graves. If a family had a letter signed by a rabbi, stating that the burial was required by religious belief (and not mere convenience) then we would do the job. For our work, we would charge whatever the cemetery owners charged for digging the plot, and we would donate the money to a strike fund for the workers.

Sam expressed profuse enthusiasm for the idea, with one caveat. He said he would agree to let our volunteers dig the graves. His workers would even advise us. But he did not want to accept any money. The union would help us because it was the right thing to do, and not to make money.

At first, it was only Habonim members who showed up at our national office at Sixth Avenue and 16th Street, in the old Farband building. Three or four volunteers would receive the address of a cemetery, a letter from a rabbi and another letter, signed by Sam and myself, addressed to the strikers on the picket line and authorizing our volunteers to dig. At the graveyards, the workers respected the letters. Frequently they even gave the volunteers suggestions and encouragement.

The atmosphere in the field was like the construction days before summer camp, when staff would go up to get the campsite ready for the summer. Some chaverim made up songs, some played games, and some took the job very seriously. When the family began arriving at the gravesite, however, the joking ended. Our exercise in working the soil became all too real.

As the strike continued, there were more work assignments than volunteers, and we began taking taxis from job to job. We asked the families to contribute twenty-five dollars to cover the cab fare and the rental of our shovels. Sometimes we forgot to ask, and at other times families would insist on giving much more. No amount of explaining seemed to be enough to convince the mourners that we could not take money. Sometimes it was just too hard to argue with families in the middle of their bereavement. And so a separate bank account was opened for the small sums that exceeded our expenses. The plan was to use it for some charity, although I am embarrassed to admit I never followed through to find out what became of it.

As our energies began to flag, Habonim members took to the streets and subways to recruit more volunteers. Next to the signs of the subway preachers and prophets they posted fliers describing our activities and asking others to pitch in. The media were pursued, too, as a way of informing rabbis and the Jewish community at large about our project. Some news organizations were helpful in publicizing our work, which increased the number of cases referred to us and gained us a few more volunteers. Unfortunately, the real darlings of the media were Betar and the Jewish Defense League, who were screaming into the television cameras about the coldhearted cemetery workers. Vowing vengeance all the way, they offered their own services to Jewish families, charging hundreds of dollars per grave. As a teenager back then, I could never understand why the slimiest characters were the best media masters. I still can't.

On the other hand, I did begin to understand a lot during the strike about compassion. At the office of Local 365 in Queens, many of the union officials I met were workers who had been permanently injured on the job. The union still saw to their livelihood, even though they could no longer wield a shovel. I suppose I had assumed that cemetery workers would be callous and cold after living with so much grief on a daily basis. After all, I reasoned, they make their living from others' loss. And yet, their behavior showed that their jobs had made them more sensitive to the human condition, not less so.

We, who were so new to the experience of gravedigging, went through a great many strange, even eerie incidents during the strike. There were jokes, too, most of them too, well, grave to repeat out of context. As for the leg kicking out of the ground, we developed quite a few theories before we learned the truth. Had we dug in the wrong place? Was there some buried mystery? The cemetery owners, who were not the least cooperative with our efforts during the strike, refused us access to their records, so we had no way of knowing who was buried where. Much later, we learned that the owner of the plot we were digging on that forbidding dusk had had a leg amputated during World War II. The family had bought a plot and buried the leg, so the departed could some day rest "whole."

And in a strange way, the lives of these cemetery workers had a wholeness that touched all of us who were privileged to be "scabs"—albeit with union blessing—and to help them ride out their strike.

Not long ago, I heard a radio news report about the threat of another cemetery workers' strike. I yelped at the unmistakeable sound of Sam Cimaglia's voice. Out there in Queens, the hometown of Archie Bunker, their union family was still intact.

Communal Living in America: The Bayit

The urban collective has a long and honorable history in the Zionist youth movement, combining as it does many of the same virtues that distinguish the kibbutz itself. It allows its members to pool their incomes and share their lives in the intimate manner dreamed of by the early pioneers of kibbutz life. It gives would-be chalutzim a chance to test their aptitude for communal living and shared decision making. And it provides a valuable pool of leadership personnel for the local youth movement.

In reality, of course, the comparison with kibbutz is largely specious. A communal house near a college campus only brings together a group of students for a few years while they earn their degrees. The kibbutz asks a lifetime commitment from its members and seeks to form a building block in the construction of a new society.

Nonetheless, Habonim members have taken the *bayit*—the communal house—very seriously.

From the movement's early days, communal living was both a convenience and an ideological value to post-high school age members who were leading the movement and preparing to go on aliyah. Before the founding of the state, those planning to settle on a kibbutz in Palestine often went to the Hechalutz organization's training farms in New Jersey, Ontario, Minnesota, California, and elsewhere. At these hachshara farms they tried their hands at agriculture and got their first taste of group life. With the birth of the state, hachshara was replaced by trial periods on kibbutz itself, and the Hechalutz farms were closed, with the exception of the Hashomer Hatza'ir farm in Hightstown, New Jersey.

Urban communes, while less ambitious than the hachshara farms, hold a cherished place in the memories of Habonim members from the movement's very beginnings in the 1930s. One of the most storied was the *bet garin* established shortly after World War II in the Seagate section of Brooklyn by the members of Garin Aleph, which would eventually settle at Gesher Haziv. The Seagate bayit became the focus of the movement in the city, a way station for garin members preparing for aliyah, and—perhaps most important—a personnel resource for running the local and national movement. The garin left for Israel in 1948.

Beginning in the mid–1960s, several social changes came together to transform the bayit from an occasional convenience to a near permanent fixture in Habonim life: the rebirth of the garin after the hiatus of the fifties; the rise of near universal college attendance among Jews; and the youth rebellion, bringing with it the rising acceptance of young people leaving home and moving out.

In 1965, members of Garin Etgar rented a rambling house in the Rogers Park section of Chicago, which would become the nerve center of Chicago Habonim for nearly a decade. After the aliyah of Garin Etgar to Gesher Haziv, the bayit was taken over by Garin Maor, which shortly opened a bayit in Philadelphia as well. Then, in 1969, the short-lived Garin Omer opened a bayit in the Bedford-Stuyvesant section of Brooklyn.

It was not long afterward that the words "bayit" and "garin" were detached. By 1973, groups of Habonim members in college towns from Ann Arbor to Berkeley were moving into houses and apartments together, pooling their incomes and calling themselves a bayit with no relation to aliyah plans. Some of these houses took on group responsibility for leading the local movement; others made such a commitment strictly voluntary. Some were not even limited to Habonim members.

In fact, the word bayit had spread by 1973 far beyond the confines of Habonim. In Madison, Wisconsin, for example, a group of left wing Zionist students set up housekeeping together on a street called Langdon, where they declared themselves "Kibbutz Langdon." At Columbia University, a group of Jewish students—some of them neither left wing nor Zionist—took over an old fraternity house and declared themselves Bet Ephraim, with the blessings of the university housing office.

The bayit in Princeton, New Jersey was typical of the flourishing communal spirit of Habonim and its periphery in the 1970s.

The Princeton Bayit, 1976–77: Beyond Our Ken

Jill Benderly
Brooklyn 1988

What a motley crew we were: four Habonimnikim, two Orthodox Jews, and a poet. The seven of us, two women and five men, lived collectively in a house not far from Princeton University from 1976 to 1977.

At first glance, we were atypical of the Habonim collective houses that flourished in the 1960s and 1970s. The typical bayit brought together leaders of Habonim in a major city, who formed the core of a garin that was planning to settle together on kibbutz. In contrast, the Princeton bayit came together via Jewish life on campus, rather than through involvement in the youth movement. We set up house for one school year only, as five of us would graduate that June. While most of us spent time in Israel before or after college, we never considered group aliyah.

But our experiment succeeded in interweaving four strands of Habonim values: communal living, Jewish culture, youth leadership, and progressive politics.

Ideology learned at Habonim camp guided our communal structure. We ran our finances according to the principles of *kupah*—from each according to one's ability, to each according to one's need. The four Habonimniks, Sandy, Josh, Betsy and I, enforced this principle zealously. I remember a long meeting in which I insisted that the house pay for one member's medicated shampoo. To him, the shampoo was a personal luxury; to me it was his need. We decided kupah would cover contraceptives, too. Meetings relentlessly sought to apply socialist principles to our daily lives. We even made a rule banning the word "people" as in "People should empty the dishwasher," mandating instead that we criticize individuals by name.

In such a good Jewish household, social life centered on mealtimes. We all had to learn to cook kosher vegetarian food. Each of us prepared dinner once a week, with two cooks assigned to Friday night dinner.

I remember Shabbat dinner as a series of culinary and cultural adventures. Friends clamored for invitations to Friday night festivities. Excitement grew as the challah dough rose, and the cooks of the day concocted course after course. Every week, a theme—French, Indian, Chinese meals followed one another in dizzying succession. The gastronomical nadir? A soybean cook-off, to rid us of forbidden leavening before Passover.

Two people prepared a Friday night cultural presentation as well. Along with the traditional blessings came poetry and music to start the Shabbat meal. We sang rowdily, beating out the rhythm with our silverware— everything from the Grace after Meals to "Red Fly the Banners, Ho" ("One is for the working class, strong and united, ho!"). And one evening, Lewis the poet stunned us by playing the first few lines of Beethoven's Fifth by clinking his fork on perfectly tuned wine glasses.

From Yossi and Barry, our two Orthodox housemates, we learned holiday rituals. We ate in our backyard *sukkah,* and some of us even slept in it. Cheating a little on religious prohibitions, Josh and Sandy saved the *sukkah* from collapsing in a midnight storm. They patched it up quietly, and the next morning when Yossi said he thought he had heard hammering, Sandy replied, "It must have been a dream."

The bayit's basement and backyard were a haven for young people from the Habonim group in the town of Princeton. The local group, which began as an offshoot of Philadelphia Habonim, came into its own under our leadership. Now the kids had a place to hang out on the weekends. Besides weekly meetings run by Josh and Sandy, our basement housed rehearsals of the Habonim folk-dance troupe, and lively kumsitzim in which Sandy's mandolin led the local Habonim string band while we sang along. We once hosted a national Habonim conference for college-age chaverim to discuss urban communal living in Israel.

While the youth movement flourished in the basement, campus radicalism occupied our living room. Lewis and I and our comrades edited the *Princeton Forerunner,* a "wholly socialist" alternative newspaper, on the dinner table. The paper covered the unionization efforts of university workers, protests against Princeton's investments in companies doing business with South Africa, feminist critiques of sexism on campus, and activities of the Third World Center and the Student Political Organizing Committee. Lewis and I put steady energy into SPOC, which had its origins three years earlier in the Princeton Radical Jewish Union that Sandy helped start.

The bayit was the nerve center of many projects, but sometimes we just got on one another's nerves. How could someone study for tomorrow's exam over the din of pot-clanking, manifesto-writing, hora-rehearsing, and lovers' quarrels?

Yet the friendships held together. At our ten-year bayit reunion, we had a lot of catching up to do. Lewis helped initiate an ongoing group living project on Princeton campus. Now he writes legal briefs instead of poetry. Sandy and Josh both went on to become directors of Habonim Camp Galil, near Philadelphia. Josh and Betsy got married and are active in a chavurah and in Reform Democratic politics. Sandy and Barry still work too hard in science labs, but in their free time, Barry is a synagogue president and Sandy plays mandolin in a band. Yossi the doctor has three kids, and still bakes a famous cheesecake. I stuck with left wing journalism, and I still live in a collective house.

In our different ways, we all live by the values on which we built the bayit: community, leadership, creative Jewish ritual, and activism.

San Francisco, the 1970s: "I Feel as If I Pulled a Fast One"

Paul Blanc
San Francisco 1985

Most people cannot identify a precise event that changed the course of their life for the better. As a discrete phenomenon, unfortunately, disaster is more typical. Perhaps that is why I feel a little sheepish when I reflect on my involvement with Habonim in the late 1960s and 1970s. I feel as if I pulled a fast one, as if I got away with something. After all, who is allowed to have such unqualifiedly good memories in this day and age? But such are mine.

I was just shy of thirteen when I went to my first Habonim activity. I was taken by a family friend. Mike was older than my eldest brother, which made him unbelievably mature. He had a beard, I think, and he drove a car. Standard transmission. He must have been all of seventeen. And here I was, being escorted by the coolest person in the world to an event which had nothing to do with adults and wasn't like anything I had seen kids do on their own before.

My first activity was a *kumsitz,* a sing-along. It took place in a dark room with a candle burning in the center. A bunch of teenagers sat around in a circle singing folk songs—political folk songs, Jewish folk songs. All of a sudden I realized that there were other people outside of my own family who knew who The Weavers were. Habonim has always been associated in my mind with music and with voices in song.

Next I went on a hike. We rode in an open truck, singing again and then hiked an easy trail on a sunny afternoon. We stayed until after nightfall, long enough for a campfire. I also remember playing a game where flour in a shaped bowl had to be cut away until a match fell.

If I were pressed, I'd have to admit that I don't remember anything specifically having to do with Zionism in all these early images. And yet, in a way that is hard to identify, Israel permeated everything. Although it is a cliché, it was as if the medium was the message. The movement was some kind of deranged replica, passed down by oral history and held together with hope and chutzpah. It preserved a way of thinking and acting that had gone out of style thirty years or more before I showed up at my first kumsitz.

So I grew up to be a madrich and to go on Workshop. Yes, I still feel compelled, at times, to explain why I didn't make you-know-what. And I have a little confession: my closest friends are still those that I made in Habonim.

Garinim and Aliyah: Garin Tohu, the Late '70s

Almost immediately after the establishment of Gezer in 1974, the reborn kibbutz on the Tel Aviv-Jerusalem highway became the focus of attention of much of the movement in North America. Its sister kibbutz, Grofit in the Arava, attracted some dozens of volunteers and received a trickle of aliyah. But Gezer, in the center of the country, with its powerful core of well-known movement veterans and influential campus activists, received a constant stream of visitors.

Garin Gezer, after its aliyah, left behind a small cadre of members charged with organizing a second garin. They organized new rounds of regional conferences, sending hundreds of invitations to former kibbutz volunteers and Israel program graduates. The result was Garin Gezer Bet, which made aliyah in 1975 with some twenty members—two of them Habonim graduates. Garin Gezer Bet, in turn, left behind the seeds of Garin Gezer Gimel, which came to Gezer in 1976 with more than thirty members, none of whom had a Habonim background. All had been attracted through the garin's outreach efforts to the public.

Some movement veterans contemptuously dismissed the two follow-up groups as "mail-order garinim," but Garin Gezer Bet and Gimel left important marks on the kibbutz and on Israel. In the meanwhile, however, a new generation of garinim was forming within the movement itself.

Like Garin Gezer, Garin Tohu ("Unformed and Void") was born outside the formal Habonim framework, coalescing through the on-campus interactions of Habonim members and other Jewish student activists. Tohu began with a group active on the campus of the University of California at Berkeley in 1973. True to its name, it avoided making a decision on its target for more than two years. When it finally chose a place to settle, the choice was Gezer. But the discussions were lengthy and painful, as illustrated by the following selections from Garin Tohu's newsletter, *Behind the Green Line*.

Some Notes from Garin Tohu 1975

Pam Musickant
Madison, Wisconsin

. . . Are we being naive about the ability of kibbutz to fulfill us as a group? Will our pursuit of cultural and intellectual "grouphood," whether through Judaism or poetry, be enough to satisfy us, to influence the way we relate to each other and the group? It struck me recently that Judaism is the only ideal we have verbalized. I think that we may have taken too much for granted and have assumed that each of us holds common ideals and have projected them on to the garin.

We would like to create a more fulfilling cultural base. I do not see anything new or radical in this but I do see another implication. Is the concern that each of us feel toward pursuing our "careers" or "interests" due to something in the back of our minds that tells us that while the kibbutz is what we have chosen, it may lack something that we are unable to conceptualize at the moment?

Ken Bob
New York

. . . When dealing with questions of politics, culture, and Judaism, I think it will be easier for us to do what we want at Gezer. First, they are Americans and will better understand our craziness and second because the kibbutz is small and looking for a personality. I feel that we can help build that personality. Going to an Israeli kibbutz, even of comparable size, will not be the same. It will be five to ten years older, more settled in its ways, and less likely to accept our notions. Since it is personally important to me to have the freedom in setting up the religious, cultural, and political life on my kibbutz, I opt for Gezer.

Someone may ask if I want to live on an island of Americans in Israel all my life. My answer is no. I would like to attract like-minded Israelis, South Americans, Europeans, and others. The television and news articles on Gezer have attracted some Israeli volunteers. My idea is to set up a life-style and attract others to it rather than go to someone else's way of life and either change it or be marginal.

Bradley Burston
Berkeley, California

I want to raise an issue about which I feel the tugs and pangs of a whole crew of conflicting emotions. It is the question of serving in the military in Israel. There is something about an army that arouses in me the most contradictory of moods. I am at once enchanted and repelled, stirred and revolted. Something in the cadence of the drum or the color of certain flags inexorably draws me. I feel like a disembodied marionette. Until my stomach clamps and reminds me of what it is armies are in business to do, how they make what is called a living. At that moment I am stuck fast.

When I was growing up, I skirted the issue. I resolved that I would go into the U.S. Army—I never doubted I would—only after I became a medical doctor—another sure dream. I would be an officer and never have to worry about killing.

But Vietnam, a high draft number and a losing battle with premed courses in school changed the master plan. Though I avoided service in the U.S. Army, I realized that I was faced with serving as a grunt in the Israeli army.

I don't see the Israeli army as a distant Comitatus, salvaging the receding fringes of an inept empire. Rather, I see it forced to play the ill-fated lead in the central tragedy and irony of Israel. That is, in a state founded so that once and for all time, my people could live as equals in the world without fear of being killed merely for being ourselves, only one institution can keep them, on a day-to-day basis, from being killed by people unwilling to let them have a place to live. The Israeli army has made many terrible decisions, but the real crime they are accused of is the crime of self-defense.

Still, I am not prepared for what I have to do. In many ways, I remain the youngest child of that huge family in which I grew up. I had to ask the Four Questions at the Passover Seder until I was twenty-one. I find myself approaching army service with the same mute, institutionalized dread with which I faced the months preceding my Bar Mitzvah.

What is this thing that I can only understand in terms of uniforms and automatic weapons on crowded buses, which appears in my mind as a cross between a physical education class and Hebrew school? It has been described to me as a responsibility and a privilege. And it is. I will serve because I want to be an Israeli.

I don't imagine it will be pleasurable. But I am starting my life over, which is not the most pleasurable task itself. And this time, I am shouldering a greater responsibility for my own childbirth. I have a feeling that serving in the army may just be the spanking I need to get me to cry out, for the first time, in Hebrew.

Because of differing college graduation dates, Garin Tohu broke into two stages, Tohu Aleph and Tohu Bet. Garin Tohu Aleph made aliyah in 1977, with its final destination Kibbutz Gezer. First, though, it went for six months' hachshara at Kibbutz Tzora, a South African Habonim kibbutz outside Jerusalem that served as mentor kibbutz to Gezer.

While Garin Tohu Bet was in the United States preparing for aliyah, Gezer was approached by an American settlement group that had no connection whatever to Habonim. The group, based in Santa Cruz, California, called itself Garin Leviathan. It consisted of young Jews committed to some of the most avant-garde social ideals then current in American society. They were hoping to find at Gezer a home base to build a life around those values.

The members of Gezer were at first taken aback by the intensity of the vision of Garin Leviathan. While the discussions were going on, however, the Leviathan members at Santa Cruz linked up with the members of Garin Tohu Bet, an hour's drive north in Berkeley. The result was Garin Ami-ba ("My people comes"), which joined Gezer in 1978—again, after six months' hachshara at Tzora.

In a sense, the coming of Garin Ami-ba ended Gezer's founding period. The first five garinim to Gezer—Garin Gezer Aleph, Bet and Gimel, Garin Tohu and Ami-ba—were all of a piece, products of their time. They were built on a core of Habonim graduates, and were augmented by Jewish student activists and former kibbutz volunteers who were drawn to the idea of the new kibbutz. Habonim's leadership role in Jewish campus activism played no small part in the process.

By the end of the 1970s, the era of American campus ferment was over, and with it, the momentum of campus-based garinim dissipated. By now, however, the movement was producing a steady stream of internally generated garinim as in earlier decades. They began arriving in Israel in the early 1980s, first Garin Shalhevet to Gezer in 1983, then Garin L'Gezer in 1985, the same year that Garin Harif settled at Grofit. As the 1980s came to an end, American Habonim had come to regard Gezer and Grofit as well-established settlements—so well established that in 1988 a new garin, Gal Hadash ("New Wave") departed to start a new American Habonim settlement, Kibbutz Ravid, in the Galilee. Their effort lasted less than two years.

8

In the Likud Era

The Habonim-Dror Merger

For all its cherished independence in thought and action, Habonim always existed with a complex network of family and political associations. It had a "senior movement" in the American and Canadian Labor Zionist movements. It was part of a worldwide youth movement, Ichud Habonim, which in turn was linked to the kibbutz movement. Through the kibbutz movement it was affiliated with the Histadrut, Israel's federation of labor. And through its senior movements, it was indirectly connected to the Israel Labor Party.

Like the most up-to-date of modern families, Habonim's relatives rarely meddled in its daily affairs. The youth movement was free to adopt controversial foreign policy stands, as it did in the case of Vietnam, and even to reject the larger movement's settlement policies in the occupied territories.

Toward the end of the 1970s, though, a series of political earthquakes in Israel changed the landscape on which the North American youth movement built its independence.

Habonim's most immediate affiliation is to world Ichud Habonim and the kibbutz movement. It is from the kibbutz movement that Habonim receives its *shlichim,* and it is toward life on kibbutz that Habonim directs its young members, seeing communal settlement in Israel as the highest expression of the movement's ideals. Six kibbutzim in Israel—Kfar Blum, Ma'ayan Baruch, Gesher Haziv, Urim, Gezer, and Grofit—are living testimonies to Habonim's daily link with the kibbutz movement.

In the beginning, it was be recalled, "the kibbutz movement" in Habonim's life was Hakibbutz Hame'uchad, the first large federation of kibbutzim, created in the 1920s. After the bitter kibbutz movement schism of 1950–51, Habonim's kibbutzim—and hence Habonim—went wholeheartedly with the new grouping, Ichud Hakvutzot Vehakibbutzim. The older Me'uchad movement attempted to preserve its presence within American Jewry through the creation of Dror.

Habonim and Dror coexisted on the American scene, more or less amicably, for three decades. To the outside world it often seemed strange that there should be four separate kibbutz-oriented youth organizations (including the left-wing Hashomer Hatza'ir and the Orthodox B'nei Akiva), none of them more than a tiny outpost in capitalist America. Movement members, however, tended to be fiercely loyal to their own group and contemptuous of the others.

By the 1960s, the schisms began to seem more and more irrelevant even on the Israeli scene. The small Achdut Ha'avodah labor party that had split away from Mapai, taking the Me'uchad kibbutz movement with it, had long since lost any real raison d'être. In 1968 it merged back into Mapai, along with another splinter party called Rafi, to form one major labor party, known simply as the Israel Labor party.

And yet the kibbutz movements remained separate entities. For a full decade after the creation of the Israel Labor party, negotiations proceeded fruitlessly over a merger of Ichud and Me'uchad. Part of the difficulty was lingering bitterness over the split, twenty years earlier, that had rent so many farms, factories, communities, and even families into warring halves.

At the same time, much of the difficulty was truly ideological. The Ichud had evolved over the years into a liberal, antidogmatic movement. It gave its member-kibbutzim a great deal of leeway for experimentation, while the other kibbutz movements looked on disapprovingly. As a result, various Ichud kibbutzim had developed some individual habits that appeared to the more rigid Me'uchad movement as extreme deviations from kibbutz ideology. Many of those "deviations," it is worth noting, began in the kibbutzim of North American Habonim.

The most controversial of all Ichud innovations, for example, was *linah mishpachtit* or "family lodging," the practice of having children sleep in their parents' homes rather than in children's houses. Although it was taken for granted by the very first kibbutzniks of Degania, family lodging was eliminated in the early years of the kibbutz movement's evolution until it was raised as a principled demand, decades later, by the young Americans of Gezher Haziv. By the 1970s it had spread to a majority of Ichud kibbutzim, yet it was still virtually unknown in the Me'uchad.

There were other Ichud "deviations," too, that began as "American" quirks: maintenance of a synagogue on the kibbutz, for example, originally a concession to the personal needs of American kibbutzniks' parents who came to visit or retire on kibbutz. And then there was the Urim Experiment—sending the kibbutz's children to high school in a regional public high school, not an all-kibbutz school. This last was fiercely controversial even in the Ichud; in the Me'uchad, it would have been inconceivable.

Despite these differences in tradition and practice, overwhelming sentiment had built up in both movements by the mid–1970s that the reasons for separation had long since paled in comparison to the arguments for unity. The kibbutz movement as a whole, which in 1948 had been fully 10 percent of Israel's Jewish population with dreams of becoming the dominant way of life, was down to less than 3 percent and falling.

Hostility to the very idea of kibbutz was on the rise among many Israelis. The parties of the right, newly united into the Likud bloc, were growing rapidly in popularity and electoral strength. If and when they actually came to power in Israel, the kibbutz movement could be forced for the first time to face a government whose economic programs, tax structures, and agricultural and credit policies might become weapons with which to bludgeon "Israel's noblest experiment."

Then, in 1977, the unthinkable happened. Menachem Begin, the charismatic leader of the anti-labor Herut party, became prime minister.

The Begin "earthquake," as the 1977 election was dubbed in the media, had deep roots. For decades, the Labor party had ruled Israel with what many people, even labor sympathizers, saw as a paternalistic arrogance. Then, too, with its ideological and cultural roots in the Jewish pale of Eastern Europe, Labor's leadership and symbols were alien to a growing mass of the Israeli working population that originated in North Africa and the Middle East.

For much of the Sephardic community, Begin was, as they chanted at rallies and marches, "king of Israel." Although he was born in Poland, Begin's nationalistic, biblically spiced rhetoric appealed to Sephardic mistrust of the Arabs and deep attachment to Jewish tradition. And so, where Ben-Gurion had once consigned Begin to the outer fringes of Israeli politics (Ben-Gurion often said he would form a coalition government with "anyone but Herut and the Communists"), Begin's mounting popularity during the course of the 1960s turned him from pariah to Leader of the Opposition. In the end, a series of major and minor political scandals shook up the leadership of the Labor party in 1974 and 1975, and in 1977, Menachem Begin stepped into the prime minister's office.

Begin's march to power was accompanied by a noisy, venomous drumbeat of hostility toward the labor movement. And no single sector of the movement faced more venom than the kibbutz. Begin saw the kibbutz as a ruling elite that had humiliated him and his Revisionist followers for decades, through its leadership of powerful institutions such as Mapai and the Histadrut.

Hostility toward the kibbutz ran even deeper among many of Begin's followers. Tens of thousands of Sephardim retained bitter memories of their first years in Israel during the mass immigration of the 1950s, when they were housed in rude tin-hut and tent camps and sent out for menial day labor—working, in many cases, for the well-fed and well-clothed "lords" of the kibbutz. That they could have joined the kibbutz and shared its relative "affluence" made not a dent in their resentment. The immigrants could not trade their patriarchal family structures for the futuristic equality of kibbutz. Instead, they sat in their tent-camps, and later in poorly built development towns, and watched with envy.

When Begin took power in 1977, among the first acts of his new Likud government were a series of tax changes, agricultural subsidy cuts, and credit reforms aimed directly at the kibbutz movement.

* * *

Back in the North America, Habonim was undergoing a slow, almost imperceptible decline, even without Begin's help. From a post-1948 high of more than three thousand members on the eve of the Six-Day War, Habonim was down to about seventeen hundred members by the end of the 1970s.

In part, the movement was suffering from the overall decline of organized Zionism in the post-1948 era. For most Jews, Zionism had completed its primary task with the creation of the state. Its corollary task—motivating American Jews to uproot themselves physically and transplant to the Middle East—appeared more and more hopeless with each passing year as Jews successfully integrated and assimilated into North American life.

There was another process working against Habonim as well. The changing culture of urban America and the West was working to undermine every sort of organization based on collective participation. Four decades of television were eating away at Americans' ability to take action. The "idiot-box" was creating a youth—particularly in the urban middle class, where Jews were to be found—that expected quick stimulation with minimum effort. To be sure, television played a powerful role in mobilizing Americans to action in the civil rights and anti-Vietnam war movements. In the longer run, however, its impact was one of inertia. As the world flooded into Americans' living rooms with all its complicated and seemingly insoluble problems, the very idea of banding together to change society began to seem naive.

In any case, many American Jews were finding less and less reason to want to change society at all. American Jews were fully urbanized and college educated by 1975; within two generations they had risen from the ghetto to become by most statistics the most affluent ethnic or religious group in the United States. Habonim's revolutionary message to transform one's life seemed faintly ridiculous to most American Jews, and it was becoming difficult to make it heard at all.

Even the Habonim summer camp was becoming difficult to maintain. The Jews of North America were developing more refined tastes in recreation to go with their new position in life. Habonim was hard-pressed to compete with the wealth of camps that offered young people their choice of computers, tennis, and round-the-world cruises.

*   *   *

In 1975, Habonim and Dror began the slow process of merger. It would be a hesitant, painful process. The final merger came only in 1981 in the wake of the merger of the Ichud and Me'uchad kibbutz movements into a single United Kibbutz Movement.

At the outset, the movements looked for ways to cooperate in a limited way, to test their compatibility. Dror had bases in only two regions: in the New York area, and in Toronto and Ottawa in Eastern Canada. Since Habonim had been forced to close its camps in Ontario and Quebec over the past decade, and had little success redirecting its Montreal members to camp in New York, Canada seemed a natural place to start the experiment. In the summer of 1975, Dror's Camp Gesher in Ontario became a joint Habonim-

Dror project. Both movements' leaderships waited expectantly in New York for the results of the cooperative venture.

It went well—so well that merger was now placed on high priority. The next stage was the effective joining of the two movements' New York regions in the fall of 1977. At the time, Habonim was active in Manhattan, Brooklyn, Queens, two locations on Long Island, and in Rochester, New York, and Lakewood, New Jersey. Dror had groups in Queens and Manhattan.

According to an interim report submitted to Habonim's central committee in November by Dan Sreebny, New York regional education coordinator, the merger added "a few chaverim" to Habonim's groups—ten or twenty came to the regional seminar at Thanksgiving—and a Dror shaliach was now available to work on organizing new groups in Westchester, Connecticut, and New Jersey. The movement also gained a Manhattan office, Sreebny wrote, and "since our *moadon* [meeting hall] was torn down last year, this is helpful."

On the down side, "the Dror chaverim are afraid of losing their identity and existence. They are therefore opposed to losing the symbols of their movement—name, slogans etc. There is also the conflict of movement positions on the occupied territories."

In December, the merger was brought for a vote to Habonim's national convention, where the case for merger was presented by the mazkir Habonim, Yudie Fishman of Los Angeles.

The Case for Merger with Dror: A Mazkir's Report

Yudie Fishman
New York 1977

We are faced at this *ve'idah* with a need to clarify the movement's policy towards Dror: Should we merge with Dror, our sister youth movement; should we decide not to merge, or should we postpone any discussion?

The first point to be made is that there is no justification for two movements with a common ideology to exist in a situation where they are isolated from each other at best, and where they are in competition with each other at worst. The key point here is common ideology. We should attempt to unite the two Labor Zionist youth movements in this country. We must decide if there is enough drawing us together to make it worthwhile to overcome the difficulties involved in merger.

Both movements educate toward chalutzic aliyah in garinim. Both movements are committed to a vision of a socialist Israel, based on the Jewish labor movement. Both movements are affiliated with kibbutz movements. Our movement in Israel, Ichud Hakvutzot Vehakibbutzim, is currently involved in merger negotiations with the kibbutz movement of Dror, Hakibbutz Hame'uchad. There is no substantial difference in our respective analyses of kibbutz life. We can say that we have a consensus on these major areas of ideology.

Next, we must turn to the barriers to merger—those areas in which the two movements disagree or conflict. The first issue is that of autonomy. Habonim is affiliated with a kibbutz movement, but we are an autonomous body. We determine our policies through our own democratic institutions, by ourselves. We do not receive directives or orders from any party or movement in Israel or anywhere else. Dror, due to its difficulties in organizing in this country, has a much stronger relationship with its kibbutz movement. Hakibbutz Hame'uchad plays a central role in the directions that Dror takes. Again, as a result of difficulty in establishing a "native" leadership, Dror shlichim play a more direct role in the decision making process than do shlichim in Habonim. Though shlichim are just as important to Habonim as they are to Dror, their roles are different in the two movements.

The second group of issues that separate the two movements is under the heading of movement traditions and policies. This includes the area of programs, where Habonim emphasizes the Workshop, whereas Dror emphasizes its Summer in Israel program for tenth and eleventh graders. Songs, names of the *shchavot* (age-groups), emphasis on *tzofiut* (scoutcraft), and various terminologies—all these things are of a small nature, but very important to chaverim with a love for their movement and its traditions.

The last major area of disagreement is that Habonim does not support settlement in the occupied territories, and Dror does. The major *mifal* (settlement project) of Dror is Garin Yarden, which is planning to settle at Kibbutz El Rom on the Golan Heights. Behind the single issue of this particular garin lies the potential for other disagreements of a political nature.

In the areas of autonomy, decision making, the role of shlichim, traditions, the territories, and politics, the two movements have differences. To ignore these differences would be a serious error. However, we must attempt to overcome them, if we feel that to do so would benefit the movement. Being larger, adding four *kinim,* a new camp in Eastern Canada, new shlichim, new ideas, new faces, and new people are positive things that come with unity. Are they worth the effort of overcoming the difficulties and differences and perhaps compromising on some issues?

Merger is not an abstract concept; a merger is accomplished through negotiations based on policy. This ve'idah, if it chooses to proceed with the merger talks, must also adopt the conditions by which merger is acceptable. I feel that discussion of our conditions must focus on two issues that are central to us, and two issues where there is room for compromise. The first two issues are autonomy and decision making. We are autonomous, and we are youth leading youth. We cannot compromise on these issues. On issues of tradition, names of shchavot, and the like, we must be willing to compromise. Rituals and symbols are important, but not worth blowing the merger over. The issue of Garin Yarden is a controversial one, but perhaps we can overcome it. After all, it is a garin of Dror, and would not have to be a mifal of the united movement. Though we must not compromise our political convictions, we should be flexible enough to allow Garin Yarden some support.

Let us try to remain sensitive to the needs and fears of the chaverim in Dror. They do not want to be swallowed, with their movement lost and their identity submerged. We must proceed carefully and with understanding.

* * *

The 1977 ve'idah of Habonim approved the merger. Dror's national secretariat had approved it a month earlier. Now the two movements established joint working committees to examine the mechanics.

Over the next two years, elaborate plans were developed to pave the way for the final merger. Timetables were set, showing which Dror chapters would be required at which point to participate in Habonim's K.M. Bet leadership training program, who would go to Workshop and the like.

By the time the final merger was ready to be implemented in 1980, however, much of the discussion had become moot. Dror's winterized camp serving the New York area, Ein Harod at Ellenville in the southern Catskills, had to be closed down. So did Habonim's camp in the northern Catskills, Camp Tel Ari at Hunter, which housed the national leadership training camp, Machaneh Bonim.

The numerical decline of the Labor Zionist youth movement in North America was continuing, and the combined forces of two youth movements could not stop it.

New York, 1981–82: A Mazkir Remembers the Begin–Reagan Era

David Kornbluh
Kibbutz Gezer 1985

Habonim in the early 1980s was a lonely, lost place to be, both personally and politically. I know. In 1981 and 1982 I was mazkir, the secretary-general of the movement, and I had it in spades.

In many ways, I learned how little the movement's ideological education prepares one for the harsh facts of leadership and responsibility in the real world. On a larger plane, it was a daunting task to take the reins of the Labor

Zionist youth movement during the height of the Begin–Reagan era. As alone as I was in Habonim's national office, Habonim was even more alone in the Jewish community.

The process of becoming mazkir was almost banal—a result of the standard progression of movement membership. I had joined the movement as a child in Los Angeles because my parents were looking for a cheap summer camp. I went and was hooked. The experiences that most moved me, such as Shabbat at camp and the chance to discuss ideas with my peers, drew me in deeper. By age sixteen, I was *rosh ken* and in charge of the organization in Southern California. I attended Machaneh Bonim, went on Workshop, and served a summer as rosh at Camp Gilboa.

While I was in college, the mazkira and the central shaliach flew me from California to New York and asked me to finish college a half-year early and become mazkir. My parents didn't think much of it, until I managed to graduate with honors.

At first, the idea of being mazkir struck me primarily a personal challenge. It looked like a growing experience. Then, too, being mazkir seemed like an opportunity to understand Zionism from within. I was a member of a garin that planned to settle together at Kibbutz Gezer, and I wanted to understand what aliyah would mean. At the same time, I wanted to put in some full-time work for the movement after years of frustration at having to split my time between Habonim and school.

Once I decided to take the job, however, an agenda began to form in my mind. My specific goals were to put the national office in closer contact with the kinim and to increase the size of the movement. I believed we could double our membership. And I wanted to put more educational content in the activities in the city.

Second on my agenda was to reactivate the movement's older members: to get the college-age members involved in progressive Zionist activity on their campuses, and to regenerate the idea of group aliyah to kibbutz through the garin. Third, I wanted to help develop a progressive Zionist approach to an Israel under Likud rule.

My first day in the New York office, I felt lonely and lost. It seemed as though I was the only one who did not know what to do. I did not even understand what people were talking about half the time, what with all the initials they were throwing about—AZYF, WZO, KAD. I read some mail and tried to look busy. Not too long afterward, I got very busy indeed.

This was a time of confusion for the American Jewish community. Menachem Begin had been elected prime minister of Israel four years earlier. American Jews, it seemed, wanted to identify with Israel but found it difficult to relate to Begin.

At the same time, the Reagan-era mood of conservatism was gaining ground in the community. A minority spoke out against Reagan's social cuts, but the majority seemed satisfied. On the left, the antinuclear movement was at a high point. The movement against U.S. intervention in Central America was just beginning. The dominant trend among young people could be summed up in video games, computers, and Punk.

Habonim was peripheral to the anti-nuke and anti-intervention movements, although we were clearly a part of that community. Within the Jewish and Zionist community, however, we had a very high profile indeed. We were a positive, anti-Likud, pro-Israel alternative, sometimes the only one. The movement that I took over was holding its own with a membership of about seventeen hundred. When I left, it was a bit larger.

Two of my most immediate problems involved in-house Zionist politics. The World Zionist Organization was in the process of forming Telem, an umbrella "movement for Zionist fulfillment," and Habonim had been asked to join. Within our own movement, we were in the middle of negotiations over a merger with Dror, the youth movement of Hakibbutz Hame'uchad. Both affiliations went through without a hitch.

Far more significant was the growth of the Progressive Zionist Caucus. Through our college members, we succeeded in building a national network of campus groups that succeeded in presenting a serious anti-Begin presence.

In fact, we were one of the very few centers of real opposition to Begin in American Jewry during the early years of Likud rule. The Habonim office became the national address for oppositionist Zionism, and remained so after I left. In the process, we expanded the movement itself, and the idea of the *bayit,* of ma'apilim living together in off-campus communal apartments, came back in force.

I divided my time as mazkir between running the office, staying in touch with the local branches and representing the movement at different functions. I think my low point came one time after I visited five cities in four days and still felt out of touch. It made me feel that no matter what I did in New York, I could not have a real impact on the kinim.

Sometimes, the meaninglessness of it all was downright hilarious. Funniest of all, I think, was my meeting with Menachem Begin.

In the summer of 1982, right after the outbreak of war in Lebanon, Prime Minister Begin came to New York to drum up support. One Friday afternoon, I got a telephone message telling me I was invited to a meeting Saturday night at 10:30 p.m. at Begin's suite in the Waldorf Astoria Hotel. By the time I received the message, it was too late on Friday to check if it was a joke or for real. I couldn't understand why the meeting would be on Saturday, and so late.

I spent all day Saturday at the Clearwater Folk Festival up the Hudson River, sitting on the grass and listening to music. Driving home, my friends dropped me off at the Waldorf. I changed into my Habonim shirt and told them to wait ten minutes. If it was a joke, I would be right back.

So here I was, on my way to meet Begin. I walked into the Waldorf and asked for Prime Minister Begin's suite. I was told to go to the twenty-third floor. When I walked off the elevator, two guys who made Rosey Grier look small asked me who I was. I told them, and a little guy stepped out from behind them with a clipboard and a list of names. "Mr. Kornbluh, right this way," he said.

I entered a room, and found myself surrounded by the presidents of the national Zionist organizations. There were ten of them, I think. It dawned on me that I was there to represent The Youth. Everyone else had on a three-piece suit or the equivalent, so I was glad my blue Habonim shirt had just been cleaned. Nobody seemed to notice the grass stains on my pants.

Fifteen minutes later, we were ushered into Begin's room. He plunged right into things, telling us how all of Israel supports "Operation Peace for Galilee," and how Israel has the most humane army in the world. It was quite a display, this high class briefing of the American Zionist movement. The women from Hadassah were awestruck and could not stop saying, "Yes, yes, yes, we know, we know."

When the time came for questions, I raised my hand and said I thought American Jews would feel better if they believed "Operation Peace for Galilee" would lead to some kind of solution for the Arabs on the West Bank. I wasn't terribly articulate, but it didn't matter; even before I finished, Begin started screaming. "What is all this talk about a Palestinian state? We have no problem in Judea and Samaria!" And so on.

I did not get an answer to my question, but after the prime minister and I were finished, Rabbi Wolfe Kelman of the Conservative movement asked about protests in Israel against the war. Begin insisted it was only a handful of leftist agitators. Kelman said he was taken aback, since his son was a member of Kibbutz Gezer and had participated in what looked to him like mass rallies.

With that, the audience was over. People shook hands with Begin, and I took the subway home to Brooklyn. It was a thoroughly useless but entertaining evening.

By contrast, the high point of my term as mazkir was a *kinus ma'apilim,* a national conference of college-age members that took place in 1981 with two hundred fifty people attending from all over the country. Two new garinim were formed there, as well as a *misgeret aliyah* that planned to establish itself as a garin in the future. We in the office had been planning to break the tendency of each returning Workshop to create its own garin, and move towards the concept of larger garinim forming around a target date for aliyah. And we were successful. I also think that we broke old social barriers and opened up the ma'apilim to accepting new people.

When I finished my term as mazkir, I spent two months with my family preparing for aliyah. I was a little bit at a loss over what to do. My phone stopped ringing. And I felt tired.

Being mazkir meant being a role model and counselor to the entire movement. Always being "on," always being mazkir, was difficult, especially with my closest friends. It was hard to have any real peer-relationships. I felt I couldn't let my guard down enough to allow the people working with me to get close. My personal relationships were generally good but distant. That felt ironic, working in such an intimate movement.

And I honestly do not know if I personally made a difference. It seems the movement has cycles of its own. It rises and falls in response to events in history and society. I don't know how much one person can influence it. I like to think that I was a good role model and a decent leader, and I am proud that I did the best job I was capable of at the time. In general, I could not have given more.

"Underground" in America, 1985: Habonim–Dror as Covert Action

Elliot Appel
1985

It ain't easy being a college-age member of Habonim-Dror North America (H/DNA). When you were a kid there was no problem. You told your friends: "My camp is better than yours. Our counselors are better and what they do is good." To apathetic teachers and doting parents you said, "I go to a Jewish summer camp and sometimes to activities during the year."

In high school it was a little harder to explain away. But you managed. "It's a counselor training program." That was much easier than mentioning Zionism, socialism, or communal responsibility. You didn't tell your parents that you're doing what you're doing because you actually believe it all. Instead, you said you go for the friends and the good times (which may, indeed, be true).

You explained Workshop by saying that you really would enjoy taking some time off from school, and Workshop seems like a constructive and cheap (!) way of doing it.

But when you return from Workshop and become a ma'apil, it ain't so easy to explain what you are doing anymore. Most people go undercover.

Sure, you can be active on campus in leftist and Zionist groups; you can even be outspoken and find a lot of people who agree with you. But if you let them suspect that you had any help whatsoever in reaching certain opinions, they start to question how free-thinking an individual you are. When questioned, you stammer: "Well, it's this socialist, Zionist organization that's a lot of fun but really does meaningful stuff."

"Like what?"

"Well they . . . we . . . it has this utopian vision of Israel."

"A who?"

"You know, like, they want to make the world a better place and help be a light unto the nations and that kind of stuff."

". . . I see. Well, I've never heard of this Habo-thing before. Is it new?"

"No, it's about fifty years old."

"Well, how did it start?"

"By smuggling weapons into Palestine in the thirties and forties."

"How come I have never heard of it?"

"Well, it's pretty small and it's been going through a sort of an identity crisis for the last, say, forty-nine years."

". . . Uh-huh . . . I see. So why are you a part of this . . . uh . . . strange, starry-eyed, revolutionary something or other?"

"Because they're doing real stuff. And we help kids learn how to think."

"Huh!?"

"We talk about what we think is wrong about Israel, kibbutz, and homo sapiens in general and what we can do about it. And we have a good time with kids so they'll think about the same things and do it with more kids."

"So, it's a focusless, self-perpetuating, brainwashing operation, right?"

"Well, sort of. But it's not as bad as it sounds."

"I had thought you were a responsible, rational person. And here you tell me that it's all because you had fun as a kid with a lot of people who thought this way."

"Well, critical thinking does not have to be initiated through individual, independent revelation."

"Well, you sound pretty well convinced. I can set you up with another former friend who is now a Hare Krishna. You two should get along fine."

And that's a conversation with a critical, reasoning, open-minded person. Others will give you, "I really am not interested in political stuff," or "Ideology is ridiculous. Talk concrete stuff."

Try telling a professor about H/DNA. "Ah, youthful idealism. Someday, you'll see how the world is really set up. Meanwhile, have fun. But do try not to do anything bad to innocent children (like mine)."

Worst of all are your parents. Unless they are already "sympathetic" to the movement's ambiguous ideals, they will worry about losing their baby to the horror of aliyah. You tell them: "I do it to keep in touch with what is happening in Israel and to hold on to my Jewish identity. I also like working with kids." Or you say nothing and let them think it is just social, even though your friends are all over the place, and it costs a fortune to call (let alone see) them.

So what do you do? Run, nearly desperately, to greet your buddies in the movement at a convention where only those "in the know" are present. You meet like a pack of spies coming into the headquarters of the Mossad, the Israeli CIA, "somewhere in Israel." You let your guard down because everybody here knows the real you.

But you had better hide that facade that you left behind. Don't let anybody see what you're like out there, lest they judge you impious. Don't let on too much about your real life, lest someone ask you how you handle your internal schism.

What is idealism? Does it have a place in the eighties? Is what we are doing considered idealism? Are we doing what we want to be doing, or is all this a focusless, self-perpetuating brainwashing operation? Is all of our endless and fruitless soul-searching merely a subconscious attempt to reattain the good times at summer camp? The answer to these and less mundane questions coming up.

Tel Aviv, 1986: "I Believe in Our Hopes for the Future"

Gonen Haklay

Tel Aviv 1986

After serving for two years in the Israeli army, I have decided to come back to the States and work in the movement. I intend to be involved on the national level and live with my fellow garin members. Then I will join the first wave of Garin Gal Hadash.

Why am I doing this? Well, it was not an easy decision to make, and I certainly have my doubts. On the whole, however, I believe it is the right thing to do.

By way of explanation, I want to communicate some of what I have learned as an Israeli soldier. Not all of my experiences have been pleasant, yet I feel I have come to understand Israel from a new perspective. The beginning was extremely painful (and I do not mean that only in a figurative sense), but with time I learned to adjust. As I moved up in rank and experience, my day-to-day conditions improved, and this made my life easier.

Ironically, the most troubling part of my service took place just before I finished. During my last three months in the army, I was stationed in the West Bank. Had this been six months earlier, I would have been stationed in Lebanon. At present, some of the troops who were previously located on the northern front are being sent to Greater Israel "to maintain the public order." I spent most of my time doing patrols in Dahaishe.

Dahaishe is a refugee camp right next to Bethlehem. There are thirteen thousand people living there, in very crowded, unsanitary conditions. Many, although not all of the residents are very poor. Dahaishe became famous a couple of years ago, when Rabbi Moshe Levinger, the Hebron settlers' leader, rented a place there with his gang. From there, the settlers' movement Gush Emunim held daily demonstrations to protest the Arabs' throwing stones and Molotov cocktails at cars traveling along the main road south from Jerusalem to Hebron, Kiryat Arba, and Beersheba.

Levinger has moved back to Hebron, but he still comes back to Dahaishe from time to time. At Chanukah time, he lights a large menorah across the road from the camp—tact is not his strong point. I am sure this doesn't do much to change the hatred of the Dahaishe residents toward Israel, except perhaps to strengthen their resolve.

Every day for at least six hours, I would walk through this place. This gave me a lot of time to think, mostly about how Israeli policy in the West Bank practically invites rock throwing. Youth in this place have no other way to express their frustration; their chances to advance in life are small. Even with a college degree, teaching in an Arab town is about the best they will ever do. They cannot vote. They are represented only by a terrorist organization, the Palestine Liberation Organization, which is not doing much to improve their lives.

The burden lies, I feel—I know—on Israel. We need to create conditions in which Arab youth will have the freedom to speak out without tying themselves to the PLO. Unfortunately, this is precisely what we are not doing! Nobody, not Labor, not the Citizens Rights Movement, nobody. Nothing is being done to make these people come out, to allow them to take even a small measure of responsibility for their own lives. In other words, there is no real effort to encourage representatives of the Palestinians with whom we will be able to sit and talk. It is absurd that a government so active in the quest for negotiations should carry out policies so detrimental to the realization of its professed goals.

We are too easily taken in by steps which do not go far enough. Stopping the flow of money to West Bank settlements is a negative step. We foment hatred and its physical expression, violence, in the territories because we are afraid to take chances in the way we relate to the problems the area poses while it is in our hands.

Garin Gal Hadash must take an active, political stand on these and other issues. Our debates should not only focus on the struggle to build our own group. Of course, our lives on the kibbutz will be of great importance. But to ignore the urgent problems of the country and the people—which is something too many kibbutzim do—would be an incredible mistake.

Soon I will be leaving Israel. I will be leaving "home" not to get away from the many problems and challenges we face here, but because I believe in Habonim-Dror, in the Progressive Zionist Caucus and in all our hopes for the future. In the final analysis, it is up to people like ourselves to educate younger chaverim and help to ensure the success of kibbutz, Israel, and the Jewish people. This is the reason why I am coming back to the States.

The Movement Enters the Nineties:
"Something Is Happening Out There"

Simmy Ziv-el
Kibbutz Nir Eliyahu 1988

"One of the first things you should do when you get to the States is sell Camp Na'aleh."

With these inspiring words, the new central shaliach to Habonim-Dror North America—yours truly—was greeted in the Tel Aviv offices of World Habonim in September 1984 by outgoing shaliach Gary Ben-et. Just a few weeks later, I boarded a plane on my way to my first venture in real estate transactions—and in a foreign country, to boot.

The day after I arrived in New York, I went to the Habonim-Dror office and met a chaverah of the movement, Dodi Buxbaum, who, as I came to discover, came from a family with a long Habonim history.

"So, what are you going to be doing on shlichut?" she asked me.

"Well," I began, "for starters, I'm going to be selling some old camp called Na'aleh." A minute later I was thrashing about in a puddle of tears as Dodi cursed my unsentimental, South African callousness.

Based on what I had heard from movement graduates in Israel, I expected to become a veritable expert in real estate. The way it sounded, my task was to engage in a wholesale sell-off of Habonim camps, meeting halls, and offices. The so-called "classic *ken*" no longer existed, I was told, and no alternative framework had been found for regular weekly activities. The financial situation of the movement was disastrous. Things did not look hopeful, but at least, I consoled myself, it was clear where things were headed— or so it seemed.

After completing four years of shlichut, the picture I retained was a very different one.

It is true that the classic Habonim structure of members meeting in local *kinim,* under the educational guidance of their madrichim, exists in very few cities. Movement activity is limited largely to summer camping and a few weekend seminars and reunions through the school year. Even the camping is precarious. During my tenure we were forced to shut down Na'aleh and Gilboa, our camps serving New York and Los Angeles, the two largest Jewish centers in North America. Only five camps remain: Galil in Pennsylvania, Moshava in Maryland, Tavor in Michigan, Gesher in Ontario, and Miriam in British Columbia.

And yet, somehow, I learned that the state of Habonim-Dror North America cannot be described as a simple "downward spiral." During my four years in American, enrollment at Machaneh Bonim—now meeting at Camp Tavor—continued undiminished. The same was true of the Workshop;

in two of my four years the Workshop's numbers warranted sending two groups. Most significantly, a new garin was formed by the movement's older members, Garin Gal Hadash, which went on to found a new kibbutz in the Galilee. And new aliyah groups followed them.

In fact, one might say that the "no kinim, no madrichim," structureless model of Habonim-Dror organization has yielded remarkable results. Something is happening out there, even if it is not yet visually clear to the movement's leadership. What it is can only be guessed at this point.

In the end, it seems, Habonim remains as it has always been, a process of people touching other people. Once, that touching took place within a defined structure: kvutzot, kinim, camps, regions, madrichim, and chanichim. Today, the old structure no longer exists. Yet the people are obviously there, and they are finding other ways to continue touching the lives of their fellow movement members.

Yes, I eventually sold Na'aleh. But today, the symbolic significance of the transaction seems far less important to me—and, I might guess, to the Buxbaums and countless other movement families as well. Habonim's problem, like Israel's, is not the question of giving up land. The issue for us remains the people, the relationships between them, and their commitment to an idea.

Toward the Twenty-First Century

Melody Robens-Paradise and Sharon Roling
New York 1991

Habonim Dror approaches the twenty-first century in a fast-changing world, a changing Israel, a changing kibbutz movement, and a changing North American Jewish community. The current generation of Habonim-Dror has witnessed radical developments that have altered the very face of the world during the 1990s—the end of the Cold War, the fall of the Berlin Wall, the dissolution of the Soviet Union. We have also witnessed the closure of a Habonim kibbutz, only one year old.

As our world is pushed and pulled by the pressures of political realities, Israel faces pressures from a world that is alternately hostile and supportive and the continuing growing pains of a nation still struggling in its youth. The last decade has witnessed the outbreak of the Palestinian uprising in the territories, the intifada. It has witnessed the entrenchment of the hawkish Likud government and the politicization of the Israeli religious parties. The emergence of extremist right-wing parties such as Kach and Moledet has helped to legitimize the right-wing policies of the Likud. We have watched with horror as Scud missiles fell upon Tel Aviv. We have watched with joy as hundreds of thousands of Jews from the Soviet Union and Ethiopia have found freedom in Israel. We have seen Israel struggle economically, socially and politically under the weight of this immigration.

North American Jewry is also undergoing radical transformation. Young Jews face pressure to enter the rat race quickly and to find jobs that will guarantee them a lifestyle similar to that of their parents. For the first time in North American history, it appears the next generation will not live as comfortably as its parents. Increasing numbers of North American Jews are unaffiliated, and statistics suggest the rising rate of intermarriage will result in the decline of a community of non-Orthodox Jews in North America. Attitudes toward Israel are marked by a growing sense of distance, even disenchantment. Many Jews had a hard time supporting Israel while the intifada raged and Prime Minister Yitzhak Shamir danced around the peace table.

Habonim-Dror faces its own crises, beginning with the ongoing crisis of the kibbutz movement. The problems of kibbutz affect Habonim financially, politically and ideologically. They leave us with the prospect of losing our first line of Israeli support, losing most of our shlichim, losing much of our financing. Within the World Zionist Organization, too, our support is threatened. Control of youth and education programs has been given over to the newly created Joint Authority for Jewish Education, dominated by UJA-federation campaigns and controlled by mainstream Jewish educators. They control the traditional sources of funding for Zionist education; yet they show little sympathy for traditional Zionist youth movements. The voice of the youth movement, always a small one, is lost amid the great financial voices of the federations and the United Jewish Appeal. Yet they now control our fate.

The hardest ideological blow to Habonim-Dror, though, has been the failure of Kibbutz Ravid and Garin Gal Hadash. To understand the path on which Habonim-Dror is now embarked, it is necessary to understand our reaction to the members of Garin Gal Hadash who founded—and eventually left—Kibbutz Ravid.

The members of Gal Hadash believed the answer to the conservative challenges of the 1980s lay in the establishment of an ideal community where progressive Zionists could work to make Israel a better, more politically correct place. This ideal community in Israel would be free from fears of Jewish assimilation, of immersion in the North America rat race. It would seek to bridge gaps between Palestinians and Israelis, between the sexes, between social-political activism and apathy.

The movement initially followed Gal Hadash the way a parent might follow a child's development. In our eyes they were fulfilling the ultimate dream of Habonim-Dror, although it was not necessarily a dream most of us would have followed. There was immediate interest in Gal Hadash. At the same time, a feeling of skepticism arose.

As Gal Hadash grew and its members became more and more immersed in their own issues, the movement became distant and angry. Members felt ignored, abandoned by their madrichim and role models. The feelings at first were expressed only in private, but by the first (and last) year of Kibbutz Ravid's existence, a counter-Ravid group had grown up in the movement. Resentment grew as ma'apilim were left with a struggling, stagnant movement.

As the members of Gal Hadash began to leave Ravid and Israel, a new mood arose in the movement. Some of us laughed and said, "I told you so," but behind our grins we felt uncomfortable. As much as we resented Ravid, we wanted it to survive. We asked them to give their vision another try. But they could not. Shortly after Ravid's first birthday, in June 1990, Gal Hadash disbanded.

After some months of stagnation and apathy, a new generation of madrichim assumed leadership roles in the movement. This generation has accepted Ravid's failure and its implications, and has decided to take the future of the movement into its own hands through change and restructuring. We believe we have recognized and accepted the political and economic realities facing the movement in the changing world of the 1990s.

To most of the current generation of Habonim-Dror, Labor Zionism represents an outdated ideology of draining swamps and throwing up kibbutzim overnight. This ideology seems irrelevant to most members today. The values of Labor Zionism remain extremely important, but the term has lost its meaning. This became increasingly apparent during the brief period between the departure of Garin Gal Hadash and the emergence of new leadership. While we were licking our wounds, we stopped functioning as a youth movement.

Most of us now believe the Labor Zionism of the twentieth century is evolving into a progressive Zionism of the twenty-first century. The new generation of Habonim-Dror recognizes the needs of the individual as an essential element in the communal experience. The chalutz/chalutza of the twentieth century is now a progressive Jew who believes in social action; social responsibility; a just, secure and peaceful Israel; gender equality; cooperation; compromise and coexistence. We no longer need to build the state of Israel physically. It is already built. We now need to build the state of Israel spiritually and politically. Our contribution is to the larger society. Aliyah with these values is recognized and respected wherever the individual or group decides to go, whether in kibbutz or town.

Every generation of Habonim thought it might be the last. Every generation worked to bring the movement through the latest crisis. With the privilege of hindsight, we know that Habonim has pulled through crisis after crisis, and we believe that we will do the same. The difference today is that it is no longer enough merely to survive the crisis. We need to build a movement that is stronger than we found it, more self-sufficient, free of crisis. This is the only way a movement can function in the next century. We do not believe that we will be the last generation.

Part III

9
Habonim at Camp

Camping and the Youth Movement

More than any other institution in the life of the movement, summer camp epitomized the Habonim experience. Of course, the movement in the city had its charms: the Friday evening Oneg Shabbat, the Sunday afternoon meetings and discussions, the outings, the weekend seminars. Still, when most members think back upon their years in Habonim, it is camp they remember first.

This is natural, for the idea of summer camp was the most organic expression of Habonim education. If the aim of the movement was to build a new Jewish character and prepare youngsters for a life of pioneering, what better road to those ends than leaving the city for a month or more spent building an ideal—if temporary—community?

Although it began as an adjunct to the regular program of the Labor Zionist youth movement, camp quickly became its central locus. As a marketable commodity in American life, it was an effective tool to attract new members. And as the years progressed, there were many rueful parents who watched their children spend 99 percent of their time in tight-knit Habonim circles, and finally go off to Israel. Many parents have reflected on the irony: "I only sent them to that particular camp because it was the least expensive."

To many Habonim members, movement activities in the city were only a way to mark time between summers. For Habonim camp was a unique experience. Its aim was not to entertain the kids, nor to teach them sports skills, but to create an environment in which children could grow and learn to take responsibility for themselves, where they could develop ideals and face the test of living by them. Camp was time-bound but the issues campers faced there were timeless.

Through its camping program, Habonim has contributed mightily to the innovative educational techniques now common in American Jewish education. Simulations, role play, and life experience were routine at Habonim camp, long before they were generally adopted by the educational community at large. The summer educational program was limited only by the imaginations of the generally bright, witty, and bold *madrichim,* the counselors. Innovations, such as the Hebrew-speaking Camp Amal, the Machaneh Bonim national leadership camp or the K.M. Bet in Israel program, quickly became models for other programs of their type.

What distinguished Habonim camping and its other summer programs was that they were not ends but means: means to accelerate the larger personal growth process that Habonim sought to nurture and foster. Camp provided a space, far from parents, school, and other sources of adult authority, for preteens and teenagers suddenly maturing and discovering the world. And that was a heady experience indeed.

Accord, New York, 1933: The First Summer

Jacob Lemberger
New York 1957

Shortly before I left Poland for America, I attended a convention of a Zionist scouting organization with which I had been affiliated. It was held in the foothills of the Carpathian Mountains. It was there that I first saw what a camping experience can do to build the spirit, ideology, and leadership of a youth movement.

The lingering memory found its expression in America when I became a member of the central committee of the Young Poale Zion Alliance. In our discussions through the early 1930s, many of us were thinking in terms of making the Labor Zionist youth movement a youth movement in fact and spirit, rather than a mere replica of the senior Poale Zion party. As I joined in those discussions, I remembered that camp in Galicia, thought of the middle-class vacation camps then popular in New York and wondered: Why not a YPZA summer camp?

Other members of the YPZA national executive were like-minded. As for the senior movement, Berl Locker, then national secretary of the Poale Zion, accepted the idea enthusiastically. But most other leading members of the senior movement were skeptical, and some were even opposed. There were two main objections, one of which was a lack of funds.

The second objection was more difficult. The Labor Zionist movement, our senior chaverim noted, already had a children's summer camp in the Yiddishist-oriented Kindervelt, operated by our fraternal order Farband on the grounds of its Unser Camp resort in Highland Mills, New York. The YPZA, it was felt, should make use of Kindervelt in any way possible.

After much discussion, we decided to go ahead regardless, and in the summer of 1932 we made an experimental beginning at a separate site on the Unser Camp grounds. Sophie Udin, an educator and a founder of the

Pioneer Women organization, assumed the leadership. The summer went well, and yet, while all the participants gained in their knowledge of Labor Zionism and leadership techniques, it was generally felt that the real spirit of a *kvutza* or kibbutz in Eretz Israel—a place built by our own hands, where we worked, governed by its own members—was lacking.

The following winter and spring of 1932–33, therefore, strenuous efforts were made to obtain a camp site of our own. Finally, with the help of Goldie Meyerson (Meir), who was then Histadrut's *shlicha* to the Pioneer Women in New York, we obtained the use of a beautiful spot at Accord in the Catskills. Jacob Katzman, then national secretary of YPZA, directed our first Kvutza, but he had to leave in the middle of the summer to prepare for the forthcoming YPZA national convention. At his insistence and that of the national executive, I took over for the remaining period.

The campers were a most heterogeneous group. Among them were several of the best members of the YPZA from several communities, young people with organizational traditions, leadership abilities, and a fine Jewish background. At the same time, however, we also had some newcomers who could not even pronounce the name of the organization. One of the four tents consisted of ten boys from Orange, New Jersey, to most of whom camping and the Young Poale Zion were utterly alien. They came because the tuition was only seven dollars a week, and where could one get such a bargain, even during the depression?

Under the circumstances, it was very hard to improvise a program to keep the campers busy, to mold a cohesive group and to institute self-rule and discipline. To this day, I don't know how it happened, but we succeeded in instilling the proper spirit of cooperation and a form of self-government.

The first few weeks were the hardest. I had to conduct all the discussion groups and Shabbat programs, supervise all the camping activities, and assign work for the daily work crews. These work crews had the task of bringing some modicum of civilization to this wilderness, keeping the grounds clean, providing wood for the stove, carrying water from the well, and a multitude of other jobs, including kitchen duty. My first substantial help came with the arrival of Mr. Margolin, a Hebrew teacher, who immediately instituted a learning program in Hebrew, Jewish history, and the geography of Eretz Israel.

While we were struggling to create our community, suspicion of our efforts continued among the leadership of the senior Labor Zionist movement in New York. We won the movement over only gradually. Our first success was with the visit of Meyer Brown and Shmuel Siegel, two movement stalwarts who came to see their families and brought back good reports to the city about the goings on at Accord.

The tide was truly turned, however, after Golda Meir came to spend several days with us. Her discussions on chalutziut were an inspiration to the campers, but her report to the senior movement afterward was of even greater importance in winning attention—and approval—for Camp Kvutza.

The camp reached its true maturity when we instituted our forms of "self-government." Representatives to a camp council were elected by all the campers. The council took its task seriously. Work was assigned judiciously and without favoritism. Everyone, without exception, had to participate in kitchen duty, which was quite a chore under our primitive circumstances: there was not even a heater for hot water. Everyone had to help, too, to police the cleanliness of the grounds and tents, and share in whatever manual labor was required. The council proved its effectiveness by seeing to it that once a task was undertaken, a program mapped out, a decision arrived at, they were carried out in a responsible fashion. Once during that time, we even had the whole camp sit in judgment of a camper who broke discipline and left camp without permission to go to a dance in a nearby hotel.

The age range of the first season in Accord was probably older than at any subsequent season. There were quite a large proportion of chaverim who had completed their aliyah training and were awaiting entry certificates to Palestine. It would not be an exaggeration to say that more campers of this first group went to settle in Eretz Israel than from any group since. Many have made their mark in Israel as chalutzim and leaders in the labor movement.

The first Accord Kvutza was rich in adventures as well as ideology. There is a limit to the punishment that even a secondhand army tent can take from the elements, so it was not surprising when a tent was occasionally blown down. This was taken in stride.

But one stormy late afternoon, when the wind had reached hurricane strength and the rain was coming down in sheets, the camp found itself without a single tent standing, without even a place for the campers to sleep. If ever the spirit of Kvutza was manifest, it was during this emergency.

With a few exceptions, all the campers were transferred to a nearby hotel. By the time the exodus began, the brook had overflowed its banks and water covered the bridge. The taller and older chaverim had to carry the younger ones, and most of the chaverot, on their backs to the other side. The few who remained in camp tried as best they could to sleep on the tables in the dining room. Unfortunately, the roof leaked, and no matter which way one turned, one got wet. This did not diminish the spirits of those who stayed behind.

The morning after remains vivid in memory years later. The sky was overcast, our clothing was soaked, and we were all sleepy, wet, and cold to the marrow. We emerged from the dining room and began a snake dance to the tune of Chopin's *Funeral March*. As soon as the sun came out, the tents were put up again, and the cots and campers' possessions were put out to dry. All around us, good people urged us to use common sense and break camp. We ignored them and finished out our summer with renewed spirits.

That first season at Accord was the proving ground for the concept of a summer camp run by youth for youth. It pointed the way toward self-discipline and self-government, and it proved that a camp of this kind lends itself to serious study in the ideology, history, and problems of our movement, while giving the campers a practical demonstration of communal living.

Fundamental to our camp program was the idea that no member of the staff was paid or received any other special consideration, aside from the authority earned by good leadership. It was deeply gratifying when, months after the close of that first season, participants got together to evaluate their achievements and spoke of the experience with a yearning and nostalgia for summer months well spent.

Most of the campers attended the Young Poale Zion convention in Philadelphia, held immediately after the close of camp on Labor Day weekend 1933. It was mainly due to the influence of their united stand that the convention decided on a reorganization of the Young Poale Zion, introducing scoutcraft, reemphasizing Hebrew, and laying the groundwork for what later became Habonim.

Habonim Camping Over the Years: A Review

It all began in 1932, with fourteen *chaverim* in one tent at Highland Mills, New York, living and studying together for a month. The following year, the Young Poale Zion Alliance established its first camp at Accord in the Catskills, named *Kvutza* after the communal farms of the *chalutzim* in Eretz Isarel (now known more generally as kibbutzim).

Accord stands out in the memories of its old-timers for sheer physical beauty and rugged conditions. During that first summer, the fundamentals of Camp Kvutza were established: collective-democratic living, a full Jewish life, and self-labor.

Inspired by Accord, two more Kvutzot were opened in 1935, one near Montreal and another, Tel Hai in Michigan, serving Chicago and the Midwest. By 1939, Moshava in Maryland and Kinneret in Michigan were founded.

Close to fifteen hundred chaverim attended Habonim camps in 1940, and in preparation for the 1941 season, new camps were projected for Texas and Manitoba. The summer Kvutza had become Habonim's most powerful educational weapon. It had also become big business.

With the camps' expansion came a need for better planning and direction in their administrative aspects. As a result, the Cincinnati convention of Habonim in December 1940 called for the organization of a Habonim Kvutza Committee. The committee established a series of minimum requirements, set to work on the first Kvutza Manual, and set up a systematic program for selecting the volunteers to staff the camps.

This hardly meant that Kvutza was becoming standardized. In educational methodology, the camps ran the gamut from experiments in Lieberman's *Creative Camping* to semimilitary discipline. Only a few were on permanent sites; most of them were rented. Some were on-again, off-again affairs. For example, the Philadelphia chaverim managed to open a camp in 1939 on a site borrowed from the anarchist movement, but it lasted only a year, and the

Philadelphia movement did not have its own camp until Galil was acquired in the mid-1940s.

In 1943, Camp Avoda was operated for the first time at the Hechalutz training farm in Creamridge, New Jersey. Avoda was an experiment aimed at attracting nonaffiliated American Jewish youth to a summer of chalutziut and collective living. Its proximity to the Hechalutz collective farm was its main educational tool. Through the 1940s, a number of highly successful Camp Avoda seasons were conducted at the movement's farms, most with groups drawn from within the movement.

During the summer of 1945, one thousand six hundred youngsters attended eleven camps outside New York, Baltimore, Chicago, Detroit, Los Angeles, Dallas, Winnipeg, Toronto, Ottawa, Montreal, and at Creamridge. The following year, 1946, was perhaps the peak year of Habonim camping when more than two thousand campers attended Kvutza. By now, Galil was operating near Philadelphia. For a time, St. Louis had its Kvutza Tel Natan. New York bought a new campsite at Amenia, New York, which for several years was a work camp in the process of construction.

The first quarter-century of Habonim camping saw some significant experiments which left a lasting impact on Habonim and American Jewish education. Foremost among them was the national Hebrew camp, Amal. Its first season in 1948 opened at a rented site in Vermont, with twenty-six campers. Housed at Amenia in 1949 and Killingworth in 1950, the camp boasted fifty campers and gained the backing of bureaus of Jewish education in six cities, most of which sent scholarship students. Amal gained a reputation in its time as one of the foremost Hebrew-speaking camps in the country; Habonim was the only Zionist youth movement to sponsor a Hebrew-speaking camp. While Amal was discontinued after 1953, it set the precedent for intensive programs of Hebrew study at all Habonim camps.

Another important experiment was *Machaneh Madrichim*, a seminar focused on leadership training. The first national machaneh madrichim was held in the summer of 1940, training madrichim to lead the junior high school age group. The experiment faltered during the war years, but was renewed in the late 1940s, until it was replaced in the early 1950s with the universal adoption of *Kvutzat Madrichim Bet* ("K.M. Bet"), the counselors' training section at every Habonim camp. In addition, every year since 1948 has seen large seminars for high school and college-age members either at the end of the summer or during winter vacation.

The summer of 1950 saw another experiment that had long been under consideration, when Toronto conducted a "rambling camp." A number of chaverim made a long trip by truck, carrying full supplies and equipment and camping each night at previously selected sites.

New camps were acquired regularly through the 1950s, including a permanent New York campsite at Red Hook in 1953 and the Midwest site at Three Rivers, Michigan in 1956. In 1956, too, Vancouver Habonim acquired its own camp, Camp Miriam, on the site of the former Canadian Cooperative Federation on Gabriola Island.

One of the most enduring institutions of Habonim camping, introduced in the early 1950s, was the annual *Maccabiah* that brought together the camps on the east coast of the United States in August for a three-day jamboree of sports and culture. The campers competed in sports, scoutcraft, singing, and Zionist knowledge, and each camp mounted a full-scale musical play, frequently in Hebrew.

Seven Kvutzot were conducted in 1957, all on permanent sites: Camp Habonim, Red Hook, New York; Camp Kvutza Galil, Ottsville, Pennsylvania; Camp Moshava, Annapolis, Maryland; Midwest Camp Habonim, Three Rivers, Michigan; Camp Naame, Saugus, California; Camp Kvutza, St. Faustin, Quebec; and Camp Miriam in British Columbia.

The summer of 1960 was the first summer that Habonim camps were no longer called Kvutzot, but *machanot*. This was to conform with the Hebrew terminology of the newly formed Ichud Habonim, which joined World Habonim in the English-speaking countries with Ichud Hanoar Hachalutzi in French and Spanish-speaking lands.

The 1960s saw Habonim camping reach a peak and begin to decline. During the summer of 1962, New York Habonim acquired a second campsite at Hunter in the Catskills, named Tel Ari, which served the members from New Jersey and upstate New York. It also served, beginning in 1963, as the home of the first national summer-long leadership training camp, *Machaneh Bonim*.

At the same time it lost its New Jersey campers to Tel Ari, Camp Habonim in Red Hook gained its own Hebrew name, Na'aleh ("Let us go up"). Then, in 1964, the last English-named holdout, Midwest Camp Habonim, was given the Hebrew name Tavor, after a historic spot in the Galilee. Camp Naame, in the Southern California low desert, was sold at that time, to be replaced by Camp Gilboa at Big Bear Lake.

During the time that the New York region was served by two camps, the annual Red Hook-Galil-Moshava Maccabiah was split in two, with one jamboree for the two New York camps and another for the southerners. Starting in 1965, the high school age *bonim* at all four camps were withdrawn from Maccabiah and brought together in a Pennsylvania park (later at Tel Ari) for three memorable days of hiking and discussion, *Mifgash Bonim*, planned and led by the chaverim of Machaneh Bonim.

In 1967, the New Jersey and upstate New York chaverim were brought back to Na'aleh, giving Machaneh Bonim sole run of the Hunter mountainside of Tel Ari for most of the next ten years. The return of the Tel Ari campers to Na'aleh that year resulted in one of the largest single summers in Habonim camping history, with nearly two hundred fifty campers.

On the final day of Maccabiah in 1967, the younger campers from all three camps were joined at Na'aleh by the older hikers finishing their Mifgash Bonim. At the closing evening assembly, nearly a thousand Habonim campers were massed around a flaming fire sign and later gathered for an all night *kumsitz* sing-along, surely one of North American Habonim's most powerful moments.

It was during the sixties that Habonim camping in Eastern Canada entered a period of instability, a harbinger of later developments elsewhere.

Toronto Habonim, which had participated since the late forties in the Farband operated Camp Kvutza in Lowbanks, Ontario, finally acquired its own camp in 1964. However, Camp Amikam in Sprucedale lasted only three summers, and was forced to close for financial reasons after the 1966 season. The summer of 1965 was the last season for Camp Kvutza in St. Faustin, Quebec; after that, Montreal Habonim joined forces with Farband Camp Kindervelt in Prefontaine, which was renamed Camp Dan. In 1970 it, too, was closed.

In 1968, the mosquito-plagued Na'aleh campsite at Red Hook was closed and a newer, more modern site was acquired at nearby Elizaville. In the late 1970s Moshava, beset by the encroaching suburbs of Annapolis, was sold, and in the mid–1980s the camp was moved to an attractive new site northeast of Baltimore.

Finally, in 1975, Habonim in Eastern Canada joined with Dror in the joint operation of Camp Gesher at Cloyne, Ontario. It would prove to be the last new Habonim camp opened before the end of the 1980s. Shortly after that, the decline began: Tel Ari was closed in 1976 and Machaneh Bonim transferred, first to Galil, later to Tavor in the Midwest. In 1982, Gilboa in California was unable to open for lack of funds and leadership. In 1984, Na' aleh was forced to close.

Entering the nineties, then, Habonim was operating five camps: Moshava in Maryland, Galil in Pennsylvania, Tavor in Michigan, Gesher in Ontario, and Miriam in British Columbia.

Habonim Camping, Past and Future

Sidney Troy

Lakewood, New Jersey 1984

Summer camping began as a natural outgrowth of Habonim's year-round activities. The idea evolved that members who had been involved in the chapters in the city would continue to meet in a summer setting modeled after the kvutza or kibbutz in Israel. But as the movement grew and the nature of the Jewish community changed, the summer camp became the focal point of Habonim's activities and the strongest vehicle for bringing new members into the fold. Through the summer camp, we approached the general Jewish community, trying to entice parents to send their children to a Labor Zionist camp based on the principles of kibbutz living.

This change set the tone for the development of Habonim. After a summer at camp, the campers became the nuclei for our chapters in the city and the backbone of the winter activity. Camp became the key to recruiting new members and to the movement's growth. The Habonim Camping Association was established in the 1950s to provide central coordination for our efforts and to assist the camps flung across North America. The association helped to resolved management problems and staffing issues and to establish minimum educational goals and standards. It represented Habonim on the boards of national camping organizations and set up guidelines for insurance coverage on all the camps.

Habonim took its camping very seriously. One of its leaders, Danny Isaacman of Philadelphia, who later became president of Gratz College, the Hebrew teachers college in that city, wrote his doctoral dissertation on the role of summer camping in Jewish education. For years, the Jewish communities in Philadelphia, Baltimore, and elsewhere granted scholarships to Jewish students to attend Habonim camp. At times, Gratz College and similar institutions elsewhere even gave credit for Hebrew courses taught at Habonim camp.

Over the years, however, the nature of sleepaway camps changed, and Habonim, like other camp operations, was affected by those trends: family camping became more popular; dozens of summer programs in Israel were established; and fewer and fewer children attended sleepaway camps for the entire season.

In response, American camping began to fine-tune its offerings, often concentrating on a single theme or activity. Sports, weight reduction, computer, and foreign language camps and other special interest programs were set up.

No less important, the growing affluence of American Jews led to increasing expectations on the part of parents and campers alike, in terms of the level of sophistication they demanded of summer camp facilities. The rustic primitiveness that once was Habonim camp's charm became an economic liability. Unfortunately, there was little capital available to upgrade camp facilities.

These trends combined to create serious problems for Habonim camping in the late 1980s. Increasingly, Habonim found it difficult to attract campers in sufficient numbers to remain viable in today's market.

If Habonim camping is to survive, it must adapt to the rapid changes in American Jewish society. It would be tragic to lose the special thrust that Habonim camp gave to so many of its chaverim.

Memories of Habonim Camping

New Buffalo, Michigan, the 1940s: Getting One's Bearings

Mona Shapiro Schwab, 1985

When I was ten years old, my parents sent me to the Workmen's Circle camp for two weeks. My older sister, on the other hand, had gone to the Habonim camp. When I arrived home, my parents had heard that the Habonim camp was great fun, so they sent me there for the last week. It only met for four weeks in total.

When I arrived, I was assigned to a cabin. The younger children were in cabins; the older kids were in tents.

On that first night, for reasons I don't recall, I went to bed early. Perhaps I was tired or didn't feel well. Suddenly, there was a rainstorm. All the other campers were in the dining hall, and I was not missed. The rain woke me up. It was dark and thundering, and I was really frightened. I realized that I was the only one in the cabin. Rain was coming in through the screen even though the tarpaulin was pulled down.

Just as I was getting my bearings and trying to figure out what to do, I was rescued. It seems that my sister had forgotten that I had arrived at camp that night and had not mentioned it to anyone. She received some flak for that.

I was bundled up in a blanket and taken to where the rest of the campers were. I got a lot of attention and spent that night in the infirmary, well protected. The next day, I walked through the camp watching the older boys repairing the tents that had been damaged by the heavy rain.

I loved my week there, especially being on night watch. My group, the solelim, were assigned the 9:00 to 11:00 p.m. time slot. It was the practice to play tricks on whoever was on duty. That made the watch a lot more fun.

Everybody worked at camp. Some did latrine or kitchen duty. Others picked up around the camp. I believe that my kitchen duties primed me for future kitchen patrol with Pioneer Women and temple sisterhoods.

The following year, I returned to camp because I had loved it so much the year before. But because there were many more campers that year, the youngest kids were assigned to the hotel building. I didn't want to be there and promptly decided I was not going to have a good time and left. Dumb me. I didn't go back again until I was a teenager.

Lake Dallas, Texas, 1941: A Parent's Impression of Camp Bonim

Unsigned 1941

I was very much impressed to see the smooth running of our camp, where scores of boys and girls enjoyed a month of outdoor wholesome recreation in a truly Jewish spirit. The entire credit of this undertaking is due to the fine planning of the committee in charge, led by our Hebrew school principal, Mr. Yaakov Levin, who planned every detail and activity and work from the time the bugle was blown in the morning at 6:00 a.m. until taps at 9:00 p.m.

The camp was conducted in a pioneer Zionist spirit. Hebrew speaking was predominant. Although a good many of the campers were not pupils of the Hebrew School, they, too, caught the spirit and were at home in all the activities.

The Jewish dietary laws were strictly observed. It was particularly thrilling to witness the Sabbath Eve observance at camp. Special Sabbath cloths were used on the tables and each girl at the camp lit candles. A short Kabbalat Shabbat service was held, with song and prayer by the entire group, after which the blessing over the wine was recited. Each child received a glass of wine. An elaborate Sabbath meal was served after which the hall rang with Hebrew songs. On Sabbath morning, out in the open under a large tree, called the Tree of Knowledge, a short Sabbath morning service was held.

For a half-hour each morning and afternoon under the Tree of Knowledge, a discussion of Bible, history, and other Jewish subjects was held with a period of questions and answers by the campers.

One of the most outstanding cooperative efforts was the general commissary in which all the spending money of each camper was pooled and each one received what he needed during his stay in camp, which exemplified the spirit of one for all and all for one.

All in all, it was the finest undertaking of its kind and a great credit to Habonim Gordonia.

Red Hook, New York, Early 1950s: Learning About Group Process

Yaacov Baumgold
Jerusalem 1985

I began my career in Habonim with two days of intensive crying at the beginning of the 1953 camp season at Red Hook. I had been to summer camp many times before, but at Red Hook I didn't know a single soul. I was miserable for those first two days. But somebody pulled me through into the activity.

There was always something to do. I lost myself and became a part of what was going on. I thrived at Red Hook for many years. The whole year seemed to revolve about the summer, when we went to camp. The construction weekends and the camp committee meetings were bits of summer vitality that brightened the rest of the year. There was nothing, absolutely nothing, like the experience at camp—learning to use tools, to have responsibility, to do a job well. The contact with counselors, the shlichim, the educators, and the menahelim—each one made me richer. Slowly, the underlying message seeped into me. I was to learn about commitment and what it meant to believe—to believe that we are doing something important and to believe that we make a difference.

I shudder to think how I would have turned out without Habonim and camp. I can't separate out the effect it had on me as a psychotherapist. I know that I learned a lot about group process in Habonim. I remember it in the discussions on leadership training.

I learned skills, too, which I carried into my later life. After I was too old to be a camper, I was a counselor in training, then a madrich, and finally a merakez. That is when I got into technical and managerial matters exclusively. After a few years of being a business manager, I went to the wild west of Oklahoma to learn psychology. Then I came to Israel to put it all together.

Hunter, New York, 1963: The First Summer at Machaneh Bonim

Miriam Greenspan

We came, dumping our trunks and dufflebags into a prodigious pile, slipping out of our alien, tailored clothes into something more indigenous to the atmosphere. We came from all over North America, each with our own predetermined image of what Machaneh Bonim would be like. Some images were hazy, some sharp and precise.

We came with a wide range of backgrounds as well. Some of us spoke Hebrew fluently, some scarcely at all. Some had grown up in Habonim. For others, this was their first Habonim camp experience. Some were widely read in the literature of socialism, Zionism, and Jewish affairs. Others less so.

The summer reflected the deep chasm in the backgrounds of the forty-seven members of the first Machaneh Bonim, but ultimately we accomplished much of what we had set out to do.

Our first major task was to build the physical quarters of the camp we were prepared mentally to inhabit. We cleared woodland, built tent platforms, hoisted tents and established other vital necessities. Nobody will forget that week—the hours clearing land and the deafening screech of saws at work on the boards that became our floors.

It is hard to take something like Machaneh Bonim and to set it before oneself as if it were a morsel to be chewed, digested, and regurgitated. Some people were disappointed with the Hebrew and work programs. The educational program was, in general, well organized and successful. If we traveled in vague and general realms in the first section, they led logically and coherently to the problems of kibbutz and Zionism. The most successful endeavor, perhaps, was our group visits to other Zionist camps. No doubt our staff must have been a little anxious when a corps of our members returned singing the hymn of Betar, the right wing Zionist Revisionist youth movement. But the value and challenge of learning of other movements while defending our own was evident.

It would not be true to say we built a tightly knit society that summer. The basic gaps among us were too broad to be spanned in so short a time. The camp divided into an "old" members' wing and a "new" members' wing. But when the final day came, it was, at last, everybody's camp. It was everybody's tent being hauled down, everybody's tears at "deconstruction." Once more the trunks and dufflebags were piled high, but their owners were no longer strangers. They were, in a sense, a living entity.

The summer had brought disillusionment for some. But to most it brought a proud sense of fulfillment. I recall the words of the poet who wrote: "Though nothing can bring back the hour of the splendor in the grass . . . we will grieve not, rather find strength in what lies behind." To which I add, "and what lies ahead."

Cloyne, Ontario, 1975: The First Summer at Camp Gesher: A Shaliach's Report

Gil Slonim

Montreal 1975

For the last several years, after the closure first of Camp Kvutza and then of Camp Dan, we in Montreal Habonim felt the need for our own camp very strongly. This year, after working out an agreement with the Dror youth movement to share their camp in Ontario—Gesher—we took a large step toward filling that need. And, if our first summer at Gesher is any indication, the "shiduch" (match) between the two youth movements seems to have been a successful one.

A group of fourteen staff members and forty-five campers from Montreal, many of whom were brought up in Habonim, joined people from Dror in Ottawa and Toronto, and the two movements worked together and complemented each other to create a well-rounded and enjoyable program.

Much of the educational programming at Gesher took the form of special theme days and evening programs in which the entire camp participated. Just a few days after the campers arrived, they were divided into three groups—chasidim, Yemenites, and "black Jews"—for a "Jews Around the World Day" in which they had to dress and act according to the customs of their respective group. The day included a carnival, and closed with each group performing a wedding ceremony in one of the three traditions.

One program that is a traditional favorite at Gesher is *"Ha'apalah* Night." The illegal immigration to Palestine during the British mandate period was reenacted by the campers, who were awakened in the middle of the night and taken a couple of miles down the road from the camp. They then had to find their way back into camp, with the help of the "Haganah" and the "Palmach," always being careful to avoid the "British" who were stationed along the way.

Evening programs, especially those on Friday nights, were special events. The theme for a particular Friday night would be announced in advance, and each kvutza would decorate its cabin according to the theme. On Chasidic Night, for example, the program consisted of chasidic songs and dances, as well as readings and stories about chasidism. Each kvutza was responsible for preparing and presenting a different part of the program, so that most of the camp participated actively in some way. Other themes that were dealt with in a similar manner were kibbutz, which was presented through a skit and a debate, and "shalom"—an evening of songs, poems and readings on the theme of peace.

Two other evening programs deserve special attention. On Tisha B'Av, the entire camp marched down to the beach in a silent procession where they witnessed the "burning of the Temple"—a wooden frame that had been soaked in kerosene. Then everyone assembled in the Bet Tarbut, the activity hall, where the program dealt mainly with the Holocaust, again through a series of readings, poems, and songs. Many of the campers were so moved by the program that they decided to observe the tradition of fasting the following day.

The final Friday evening was *"Erev T'nuah"*—Movement Night. It was designed to remind the campers that movement activities do not end with the closing of camp. It began with the lighting of a firesign on the beach, with the mottos of Habonim and Dror lit up in flames. Then a skit was presented, showing the different stages a movement member goes through, from the initial shyness at his first movement meeting, through marriage to a girl from his kvutza, and aliyah to kibbutz. It was one of the most successful programs of the summer, and hopefully its effects will be seen when we see familiar faces from camp at our Habonim meetings in the city.

Of course, Gesher also had many of the activities of nonmovement camps—swimming, boating, sports, games, hiking, and scoutcraft. But even some of these activities had a different flavor at Gesher. One thing that stands out in my mind is a *sichah* (discussion) that we had while away on our canoe trip—sitting around the fire at our campsite, talking about the difference between Gesher and other camps, and the importance of trying to define and maintain a Jewish identity for nonobservant or secular Jews. The discussion went on for quite a while, and I think it would have gone on even longer had it not been for the mosquitos and the realization that we had a hard day of paddling and portaging ahead of us.

While one is working at a camp, the pressures and frustrations of day-to-day life make it hard to develop a perspective on how, in general, things are going. But looking back, I feel that our experience of the past summer was very positive and that Gesher has the potential to become an outstanding camp.

Hunter, New York, 1979:
Farewell to Tel Ari

Unsigned

March 28, 1979 marked the end of an era in Habonim. On that day, we bade a final farewell to a beloved and cherished site in upstate New York, Camp Tel Ari. Located in Hunter, New York, Tel Ari began in 1963 as the camp for New Jersey and Upstate Habonim. It was named for Ari Lashner, a leader of New York Habonim who made aliyah to Kibbutz Kfar Blum and fell in the hostilities that preceded Israel's independence.

It was also in 1963 that the movement opened its permanent leadership training camp, Machanah Bonim. Tel Ari was chosen as the site. Machaneh Bonim was established alongside the regular camp for younger members, occupying an area near a barn and an old campfire pit. After several years, New Jersey Habonim members began to attend Camp Na'aleh, across the Hudson River in Red Hook, New York. Tel Ari became the permanent home of Machaneh Bonim. And so it was, with one exception, until 1975.

The cabins at Tel Ari were warehouses of Habonim history and trivia. The walls were covered with the names of members who passed through those august buildings, recording their impressions and leaving words of fond advice for those who would follow. Many now live at Gesher Haziv, Grofit, Urim, Gezer, and Kfar Blum.

The members moved on, but Tel Ari still stood. The sign collection still stands by the cabin called "Gesher Haziv" at the top of the hill. The roof of the dining room is still adormed by the symbols of the thirteen summers at Tel Ari plus the *semel,* the symbol of national Habonim.

In 1976, it was no longer possible to open Tel Ari. Vandals had broken in during the winter; the electricity and water lines had been damaged. The longtime caretaker, Egbert Dibble, passed away. For three-and-a half years the camp was up for sale. Finally the sports field was sold, followed by the main camp itself.

On March 28, 1979, we said our farewells. We removed whatever we could of historical interest or practical utility. There was little left—just the site, speaking loudly to our memories. We could hear the presence of so many of us there.

As the sun poured over Hunter Mountain, we held a ceremony. A Habonim membership card was buried between the gazebo and the moadon. It is the last trace of Habonim at Tel Ari. May it remain there until the end of time.

The Habonim Camping Program

Kupah: The Common Fund

Abraham Cohen
New York 1943

One of the most radical features of Camp Kvutza is the elimination of "private capital." In keeping with the principle of collective living, the camps have always emphasized the concept of keeping all campers and staff on an equal basis with respect to money. This has not been achieved without some difficulty, and every year, each camp takes up anew the question of how to operate the common fund. The educational value of these discussions is obvious, involving as they do questions of equality, individual rights, group responsibility for the individual, means of curbing excessive demands, and the like.

The common fund generally functions as follows: all money in the possession of the campers and staff members is placed in a common fund administered by a committee. All requests for supplies such as stamps, stationery, toothbrushes, and combs are placed with the committee, which fills the orders as the finances permit. No accounts are kept of what the individual camper gives or gets. Where a request is considered to be out of line with the budget or unjustifiable for any other reason, the committee advises the camper accordingly, at the same time enabling him or her to defend the request, if he wishes to do so. The only exception to this general practice is made in situations where the camper deposits with the committee some money to be kept for his return home.

Experience has varied. As indicated, the common fund is not instituted without prior discussion and acceptance, frequently over the objections of a minority. Occasionally, difficulties arise, particularly with nonmembers of Habonim or with new campers. On the whole, however, it has been accepted and has worked out very satisfactorily. Where it includes the agreement to share among the entire camp all foods and candy sent to individual campers, the troublesome problems associated with these gifts, problems familiar to all camp directors, are virtually nonexistent. How well it has been accepted by the campers is illustrated in the anecdote about the child who, in a discussion as to whether or not there should be a common fund, asked: "If we don't have one, how will we be able to get stamps and batteries?"

The National Education Program

From the National Office, 1941

Kvutza is here again and a bigger season of Kvutza is ahead of us. Instead of the seven camps last year, there are nine opening this year, including two which are permanently owned by our movement. In these tragic days, the strengthening of our own position should prove some source of consolation.

This year, the Merkaz has made a special effort to put out more education material for camp than in former years. We know, of course, that the material is still incomplete and insufficient; more material is now in preparation and will be available very shortly.

Here is a skeleton for the program to be followed:

1. Why Camp Kvutza?

We are living in a period of great stress. World-shaking events are taking place all around us. The future of all that has been dear to us for a long time is at stake. There is no certainty as to what the morrow will bring. Under such circumstances, are we justified to continue with our work along well-beaten paths? Kvutza, as another institution, entails a tremendous expenditure of time, money, and effort. What justifies this expenditure? The continued strengthening of our own effort is our sole guarantee against inner breakdown.

2. What Does It Mean to Be a Jew Today?

The old world of relative liberalism seems to be on the decline. The position of the minority is more difficult from day to day. The Jew feels it not only in the classical lands of persecution, but even in free America. What is the future of minority groups in this country? Is there hope for a cultural pluralism here or will the American melting pot force us to be submerged in it?

3. European Jewry: The End of an Era

Whatever the outcome of the present war, it will be known in Jewish history as marking the end of an era; the long era of relative prosperity for Jews in Europe will have come to an end. Discussion of Jewish position in Central European countries before the war: What is their position under Nazi domination, under Soviet rule, and in "neutral countries"?

4. How Are We to Continue?

The way of effecting Jewish continuity rests squarely upon the shoulders of American Jewry. What role will Jewish tradition play in this process? What will Palestine mean for us? How are we to give expression to Jewish cultural values in our everyday life?

Special Days: Capitalist Day at Camp Kvutza Naame

Saugus, California 1960

According to what we have been taught concerning revolutions, the change of Habonim Camp Kvutza Naame to the Republic of Naamestan was certainly a letdown. No powerful middle class or persecuted masses rose up against their masters in bloody battle. Rather, at a perfectly normal flag raising ceremony, our shlicha Nibby announced that due to various complaints, a new form of government was being installed—a "democratic republic." Did this show the camp's remarkable ability to adapt? Or did it merely reflect Nibby's willingness to trade her position for the post of chief justice in the provisional government and our acting rosh Jerry's desire to become vice president?

Whatever the case, the changeover was accomplished peacefully. The new government's first act was to dole out one hundred dollars in scrip to each citizen and to serve breakfast gratis. Displaying its obvious inexperience, it offered high wages to civil servants. Meanwhile, citizens began to form corporations to bid at auction for public property.

In the true spirit of bureaucracy, the government made it compulsory for each corporation to present a list of its members, to buy renewable licenses to operate, and to buy licenses to bid at the auction. At the auction, the dining room, swimming pool, shade trees, and most of the bathrooms were sold at wildly inflated prices.

By this time, the money in circulation had been reduced considerably. But our misguided government, instead of increasing the value of the currency, left prices as they had been. By lunch, a disturbing proportion of the Republic's citizens were dependent on social security.

After a period of national recuperation, trials were held for people who had broken the law. The showcase was the trial of Bruce Fein, a counselor-in-training who was charged with spreading Communist propaganda and corrupting the youth of the state. He was found guilty and sentenced to six hours of hard labor.

Then the government brought a vital question to the assembled citizenry: Should the republic be allowed to continue to exist? The answer was an overwhelming "no." The republic went down in a blaze of glory as we danced around a fire fueled by Naamistan currency.

Chugim for Our Time: Latter-Day Interest Groups at Camp Kvutza Galil

Hank Kaplan
Portland, Oregon 1988

The weirdest things I ever did at camp were *chugim,* the special-interest groups that we programmed during the campers' daily schedules to allow for "enrichment" and broadening.

The *chug* was a wide-ranging category that allowed for the camper and *madrich* (counselor) alike to express their special interests. Traditionally, they included such essential summer camp fare as arts-and-crafts, choir, advanced swimming, and drama.

My own specialty was guerrilla tactics. Some readers will recall the heyday in the mid–70s of the (fictional) ICZTO, the Inter-Continental Zionist Terrorist Organization. Well, I ran the boot camp.

For two summers at Camp Galil, in Ottsville, Pennsylvania, I taught kids the essential arts of stalking, sneaking, tree climbing, sniping, and camouflage. Mud wallowing was basic; kidnapping techniques were advanced. I had spies who would eavesdrop for me on anybody, anywhere. I blindfolded two dozen kids and taught them to walk through the woods in the dark. There is something enthralling, I have found, about watching kids walk into trees.

I taught them ordinary scoutcraft skills for extraordinary purposes. There were knots for tying captives, nature appreciation for honing camouflage skills. Capture-the-flag games became chess matches. Once, I dramatized a lesson in human obliviousness by camouflaging a half-dozen kids as bushes— atop the recreation hall. Nobody noticed.

One night, when some madrichim from Moshava, in Maryland, came to raid Galil—a popular, ongoing form of intercamp rivalry—I woke up my guerrillas. We apprehended the raiders in short order.

Chug Shabbat, the special Saturday afternoon "quiet-time" programming, was reserved for shorter subjects that could be covered in one session. Hubcap stealing was a favorite, along with gefilte-fishing, spear fighting (using pillows as spears), and one that stands as a timeless classic: tree climbing with introductory Russian.

My own personal favorite was self-wrestling. At its peak, I had ten kids throwing themselves to the ground, flipping themselves over in full-nelson holds, and eventually pinning themselves or conceding outright. Once they got good enough, we would pair them up for tag-team matches.

Where did I pick this stuff up? Some of it was my own. Some of it, too, must date back to my own years as a camper at Na'aleh in New York in the early 1970s, where our madrichim first introduced such innovative chugim as basic tree climbing, *"Tochamish"* (introductory conversational gibberish), "dig-ditching" and the memorable "Quenchy-Benchy"—the art of making polite conversation on ordinary topics like the relative merits of different toothpaste brands. All this, I am sure, formed a basis for my own art.

Where I got the idea that I could teach true guerrilla tactics to an unruly rabble of feral fourteen year olds, I cannot guess. It did seem to be an effective vent for creative energy, and it appealed to their sense of insurrection. I like to think that part of the point of Habonim camp was creative expression for its own sake. I don't suppose the development of these particular, esoteric skills would have met with wide parental approval, but I know I have studied much more useless things in school.

A well-rounded chalutzic education should instill more than ideology. It should teach a little weirdness too, recalling an ageless slogan from Habonim's early days: "It's chalutzic to be schmutzic."

Lonely at the Top:
On Being *Rosh Machaneh*

David Kornbluh
Kibbutz Gezer 1985

One of the great ironies of Habonim for me is that, for all the leadership training programs we sponsored, the movement never really prepared us for the responsibilities of leadership. This probably hit home most strongly even before I became mazkir, during my summer as *rosh machaneh,* or camp director at Camp Gilboa. Those were probably the two most intense months of my life—more so than being mazkir, more so than living on kibbutz, certainly more than anything since.

The most difficult conflicts, and the ones I was least prepared for, involved the clash between movement ideals and friendships, on the one hand, and responsibility for a camp full of young children on the other. Two weeks into the camp season I had to fire one of my oldest friends, who had gotten involved with a camper. A few weeks later—just after my twenty-second birthday—I had to step into an insoluble feud between the business manager and the cook. The only solution I could find was to fire the cook, who was my best friend's mother. Shortly after that, the nurse, a woman in her thirties, came to my cabin one night and told me she was lonely. I told her to call a friend. I grew up fast that summer.

As rosh machaneh, I was forced to learn the fact that people lie about anything and everything. I never could figure out why people would tell me things that obviously were not true, and while I eventually decided that such things came with the job, it still doesn't make sense to me. But it made being mazkir easier.

The positive experiences of the summer were just as personal. My favorite time of day was teaching Hebrew to the ten year olds. They were always so excited to be with the rosh machaneh that they would come up to me all day long, reciting their Hebrew lessons.

One amel was always getting in trouble for taking two snacks every afternoon. His madrich complained to me. I explained that the boy came from a very large family and was at camp on a full scholarship. We decided to let him have the two snacks. He was the happiest child in camp.

These were the lasting experiences of leadership in Habonim: handling a strike by teenage girls who didn't want to go on a hike without bathrooms—and watching them come back three days later, filthy and feeling that they had accomplished something wonderful. Teaching a child to swim, and then discussing kibbutz an hour later. Gaining confidence in myself.

I used to spend my free periods sitting by a tree, out of sight, and watching. I discovered that there were many camps going on at once, many different worlds. What the campers took home was not necessarily what we had planned so thoroughly. What we provided was only the general atmosphere, the backdrop for the real camp experience, which the campers provided for themselves.

Part IV

10
Habonim on the Land

Letters from Kibbutz:
Three Snapshots, 1941, 1958, 1989

The Palestinian Way

Tuvya Kohn
Kvutzat Naame (Kfar Blum) 1941

The story of Naame is a good illustration of the "Palestinian Way"—a way forced on us by necessity and carried through by sheer obstinacy. The "Palestinian Way" means putting the cart before the horse; it means settling on land and then getting title to it, putting up buildings and then finding means of financing them, taking on commitments for work and then buying a tractor to fulfill the commitments. It means building a settlement in one of the worst malarial spots in the world.

The story of Naame had its beginnings in the struggle for Jewish labor that took place in the orange growing districts immediately after the 1936–39 disturbances. When our kibbutz settled in Binyamina, in the center of the country, to await our turn for permanent settlement, we knew we were facing a fight with the local Jewish farmers. The farmers of Binyamina had earned a bad reputation almost from the settlement's founding as far as the employment of Jewish labor was concerned. And so it was! In the course of one of our attempts to picket the groves against cheap unorganized labor, violence broke out. As a result, one of our boys was sentenced to exile in Metulla, far to the north, for a period of three months.

We entered into negotiations with a hotel owner in Metulla, which ended in our taking over the management of the hotel for a period of eight months. Here was another case of putting the cart before the horse. When we signed our contract, we had a shortage of skilled cooks and not one person experienced in hotel management. Months of unbearably hard work were in store for the fifteen people we sent to Metulla.

Metulla whetted our appetite for the Galilee, however. We decided to hang on in spite of everything. We did whatever work we found, and meanwhile we kept our eyes open for the prospect of renting land. Then came the opportunity to rent 125 acres near the Arab village of Naame. We jumped at it. We stood watch over the fields so that the water buffalo would not eat the sprouting grass.

With the spring came the time to harvest our hay. Our entire group of fellows and girls went down to Naame. For several weeks we worked from dawn to dusk, cutting, raking, baling, and loading the hay. Then we learned for the first time the meaning of malaria. One by one the workers felt weak in the knees and began to run a temperature. Quinine was taken at mealtimes like salt and pepper. At one time only one healthy fellow was left on the place. He had to be watchman at night and do the necessary work in the day.

Daily conditions were not easy. Members both ill and well were crowded together, eight and ten in a room. Our home was an old Arab house that harbored in its many nooks and crannies a wide variety of creeping things in addition to the ever-present mosquito. Hot and cold running water was not included in the lease. All our water was brought by donkey from the muddy Jordan, half an hour's walk from our camp. By the banks of the Jordan our girls did the laundry like the wives of our forefathers in biblical days. They performed to an attentive audience of Arab passersby.

The nearest doctor and dentist are at Kfar Giladi, two hours' ride on horseback. Filling a cavity means the loss of a day's work while riding on a wagon without springs, as all your internal organs change place with one another to their mutual discomfort and yours. Your sitting equipment becomes badly worn, your head, on the rebound, pounds down on your spinal column like a pile driver.

At night there is a much shorter way of communicating—signaling. During the British invasion of Syria, all signaling was banned. Then we were indeed cut off from the outside world. But now, signaling (Morse code transmitted with flashes of light) is a regular event every evening. Thus, when a patient is awaiting the result of a blood test to determine if he has malaria or not, he expects it to be signaled that evening. Signaling is used for everyday affairs as well. If a neighboring kibbutz wants us to lend them a tin of kerosene, they put their request in Morse code and flash it to us.

Now we are awaiting our first winter in Naame. What it will be like, no one can tell. For the hopes of final settlement—of beginning to build permanent buildings and work our fields systematically, being reunited with wives and children on our own land—for this, any inconvenience that we go through now seems a small price to pay.

Sacred Rituals in a Revolutionary Society

Eddie Parsons
Kfar Blum 1959

Recently, I read a news item about the engagement of the crown prince of Japan to a commoner. It seems that emissaries of the crown prince brought symbolical gifts to the bride. Other messengers came to the bride's parents to ask for her hand in marriage. In accordance with the prescribed custom, the parents refused on the ground that their family was not worthy. The messengers retired for a ceremonial five minutes, returned, and overcame the feigned reluctance of the parents. All of this was strongly reminiscent of certain rituals in our kibbutz society, which are in no way less formal in character. The following are a few examples:

The Throwing of the Key

In a kibbutz, a key doesn't only lock or unlock locks, it is a symbol of authority. So while there may be five or six women working in the children's clothes store, only the woman in charge has command of the keys. In the same way, five or six people may drive a specific motor vehicle, but only one of them has the key to the ignition. Duplicates are not handed out readily.

Now the people with these awesome burdens of responsibility are, from time to time, beset with problems for which they see no solution. Not infrequently, they succumb to despair and lose their tempers. At such moments they tend to blame their misfortunes on the farm manager, the *merakez meshek,* our chief executive officer.

At these times, conditions are ripe for the ritual of the "Throwing of the Key." The ceremony generally takes place in the work manager's office at about 8:30 a.m., when a maximum number of people are milling around to find out their work assignment for the following day. The aggrieved chaver makes his or her appearance with fire or tears in the eyes, depending on temperament. "Niumka," they address the farm manager, "this is the end. I cannot stand it anymore. I resign." At this point, the resignee tosses the keys to Niumka and stomps out in what only can be called a huff.

To the uninitiated, it may appear that the displeased functionary has resigned. But that is not the case. In the entire history of the kibbutz movement, nobody has ever resigned during the ritual "Throwing of the Keys." This symbolic display is merely the first gambit in a long, drawn out series of conferences designed to remedy a given situation. The farm manager will go to the comrade's house. They will have a long, heart-to-heart talk. They will refer the matter to the appropriate committee. Eventually, the bride will accept the proposal.

The Ritual of Refusing Office

The kibbutz has six elective offices. Each one of these requires a certain amount of administrative ability and initiative. And while each entails a goodly number of headaches, they come with enough perquisites—frequent visits to town, the right to take a few days off without accounting to anybody—to compensate adequately.

However, unlike America where people campaign for office, on the kibbutz the prospective officeholder is expected to resist his election with the utmost ferocity. If a person wants to be elected very much, he merely protests in the general assembly that he is utterly unqualified for the job. The general assembly will then elect him with a huge majority, if not unanimously.

But some members require additional ego-massaging. These people will appeal to the general assembly to reverse their decision the following week. The additional vote of confidence they will then receive is usually enough. Some true egotists, however, demand an extra two weeks of private cajoling as well.

Every now and again, a case will arise in which the candidate overstates his opposition and his refusal is taken at face value. Then the candidate faces the exacting task of resisting election while letting the public know that he can be had. On the other hand, those few who really do not want to serve can issue Shermanesque declarations that they will not serve, even if it means that they will have to leave the kibbutz. To date, nobody has left the kibbutz for that reason.

Donning the Slippers

Even in as healthy a society as kibbutz, people occasionally fall sick. A social problem develops during the convalescence period, a problem resolved through ritual means.

After the worst of the illness has passed, but before the chaver can return to work, he begins to take short strolls during the warm parts of the day. He goes to the dining room for meals and the store to pick up the small necessities of life. But it is not customary for members to wander about the kibbutz during work hours not dressed in work clothes. The convalescing comrade needs some insignia to let the general public know that what he is doing is legitimate. The sign is felt slippers. By wearing felt slippers instead of work shoes or sandals, the member announces that he is convalescing and his ambulations are socially sanctioned.

It seems that even the most revolutionary societies need the solace of sacred ritual.

"It Was Not an Easy Time"

Gonen Haklay
Kibbutz Ravid 1989

The aliyah of Garin Gal Hadash and our adoption of Kibbutz Ravid as a movement settlement project was meant as a rejuvenation. It may instead have been an aberration.

Four Years That Seemed Like One

As the 1980s advanced, Habonim-Dror found itself in a steady decline. Kinim were not functioning, camps closed while others struggled to stay open another year, and no longer were large garinim organizing and making aliyah to the Habonim kibbutzim, Gezer and Grofit.

Gal Hadash (literally, "New Wave") was founded in 1983, but it first became a serious group in 1984 when a number of members, mostly graduates of the Thirty-First and Thirty-Second Workshops, had a chance to spend a year together while studying in Israel. We agreed in principle, though no formal vote had been taken, on the idea of building a new kibbutz. Through Progressive Zionist Caucus groups in Tel Aviv, Jerusalem, and Haifa, we found there were other young people who shared our ideas.

At the start, the kibbutz movement did not take our group very seriously, but they were willing to help us search for a site. We began an extensive search, making weekend visits to sites from the Arava to the northern Galilee. Information was gathered and sent to our members in the United States, and in December 1985, when most members were back in America, Gal Hadash decided to make its home at Kibbutz Lavon.

Lavon, sitting on a mountain in the eastern Galilee above the town of Carmiel, was a small settlement without a permanent population, no permanent housing, no agriculture to speak of, and no industry of its own. Despite the drawbacks, we were taken with its beauty and the hope it seemed to offer that we could fulfill all of our goals as a group. We chose to ignore the place's many objective problems and concentrated our efforts on building toward the future, and on trying to sell that future to others.

And sell we did. Although Gal Hadash maintained a *bayit* in Tel Aviv from the beginning almost until the aliyah of our first stage in January 1988, the focus of the garin activity was in North America from the summer of 1985 on. With a base in the national office of Habonim-Dror, whose staff consisted almost entirely of Gal Hadash members for three years, the garin held national conferences about four times a year and grew from nine to thirty-five members. All of this growth occurred at a time when no other secular Zionist youth movement in North America was able to organize a garin.

What differentiated us, I believe, was our ideology—in concrete terms, our descriptions of the kind of society we wanted to build on our kibbutz. Our outreach focused on attracting people interested in our idea of a nonsexist, nondiscriminatory, progressive Jewish society. Many of our people were specifically interested in working on Arab–Jewish cooperation—which was, in fact, probably the main reason we chose to settle in the Galilee.

A second feature of our growth was our early realization that we were not going to find enough people associated with Habonim-Dror to start a kibbutz. The result of our aggressive outreach program was that more than half our members were not from the movement. Many had never heard of Habonim-Dror, and others joined us from other movements: Hashomer Hatza'ir, Young Judaea, and the Reform movement.

In early 1987, we discovered that most of the land Kibbutz Lavon sat on did not belong to the Jewish Agency, but was owned by Arabs in the area. When we questioned the kibbutz movement about it, we were told that the land would be expropriated if no other solution could be found. That February, less than a year before our aliyah, we informed the kibbutz movement that we refused to settle on expropriated land. In March of the same year, fifteen of us arrived in Israel for a whirlwind, one-week tour of potential new sites. Those seriously considered included Gezer; Tuval, a five-year-old kibbutz with South African and English Habonim members; Kadarim, seven years old, with Australian and New Zealand Habonim members; and Ravid.

Kibbutz Ravid, founded in 1981, had been disbanded due to severe social problems in 1986 and had not had permanent settlers since then. It did have lots of permanent housing for both singles and families, more agricultural land than many other young kibbutzim, an established cinder block factory, and one of the most beautiful views in the country from its hilltop overlooking the Kinneret. It seemed to us to be a more realistic place to live and fulfill our ideals.

Although the vote to move to Ravid was unanimous, the discussions were by no means easy. We eventually came to the conclusion that, although many of us had strong connections to Gezer and the people there, the non-Habonim members had no connection. Furthermore, they had linked their futures with Gal Hadash, the garin that was going to build a new kibbutz, so moving to Gezer meant the chance of losing all of them. In the end our desire to build our own society, from scratch, won out.

One Year That (Sometimes) Seemed Like Four

Reality proved to be different from what we imagined. During our first year on Ravid, most of our energy went toward establishing ourselves as a community. Living together with the North Americans of Gal Hadash was a group of Israelis, almost all of them still in the army. In a small community varying between thirty-five and sixty people, the struggle to overcome the many differences—cultural, ideological, language, age, and commitment-level—was immense. A good deal of time was spent trying to deal with the Israelis on a basis of equality, even though most of them were likely to leave after their army service. On a daily basis that effort was sometimes exhausting.

The first year saw us prove ourselves in many ways. We held the place together financially (no easy task in Israel today). We built a viable infrastructure, and the society functioned on a daily basis. The discussions we did not have, though, were the ones we had over and over before we arrived. We did not discuss in depth what kind of Jewish life we wanted as a community. We were not active in the community outside the kibbutz, because there was so much to do in the community inside our kibbutz

"The first year will be very bad" was something we were told many, many times before we came, something we said to ourselves many times. And yet, however well we may have understood it, when "very hard" turned from part of a sentence to part of your life, having understood it beforehand meant little or nothing. When I was asked how things were at Ravid, the most honest general answer I could give was, "interesting." Sometimes very good, sometimes not so good, but certainly not dull.

It was not an easy time to settle on kibbutz. The kibbutz movement was bankrupt, the political situation was very hard even on a small kibbutz in the Galilee, far from the West Bank. Kibbutz, as viewed by the rest of Israeli society, has been taken off its pedestal. All these factors contributed to a feeling of uncertainty.

*   *   *

The uncertainties ultimately proved to be Ravid's undoing. In June 1990, after less than two years on the land, the last Americans departed Ravid.

Gesher Haziv 36 Years Later

Nahum Goldwasser
Kibbutz Gesher Haziv 1985

On January 29, 1949, a headline appeared in one of the Israeli newspapers, reading: "American and Israeli Youth Found a Kibbutz in the Western Galilee." A few lines later, the story continued: "During the morning hours, Kibbutz Bet Ha'arava and a garin of American Habonim settled one of the most beautiful olive-covered hills in the Galilee."

Today, the hill is still covered with olive trees. And the quonset huts left behind by the British are still there as well. But other species of trees are there now, and the faded British cement prefabs today house temporary groups, including the American Habonim Workshop when it comes to Gesher Haziv. To the east, above the roofs of the turkey pens, you can see the broad strips of ripening wheat, cotton, and potatoes, green, brown, and yellow bordered by the yellow-green of avocado trees in full bloom.

The center of Kibbutz Gesher Haziv has moved to an adjacent hill. A rolling, well-kept lawn is surrounded by purple jacaranda, crimson ornamental plum, and silver-green olive trees. Two large, low, Mediterranean-style buildings sit among the trees—the dining room and the cultural center. On the perimeter are one- and two-story stucco homes, some with air-conditioning units and television antennas. On the horizon to the west, the Mediterranean sea shimmers.

Of course, the impression that this is nothing but a well-tended country club is belied by the loudspeakers clustered on the antenna shooting from the roof of the dining hall. Orders during times of emergency are broadcast through those speakers. And jutting from some of the lawns are utilitarian concrete structures, the entrances to underground airraid shelters. The Lebanese border is only four kilometers away, in easy range of the Katyusha rockets that occasionally come flying in.

In this community of five hundred residents are twenty-four members of Habonim's Garin Aleph. They have thirty-one children on the kibbutz and twenty grandchildren. Although we number only about 7 percent of the total population, the North Americans at Gesher Haziv constitute one of the largest concentrations of Americans on any kibbutz or moshav in Israel.

To the extent that any white-haired grandparent can be involved in a youth movement, Gesher Haziv is still very Habonim-oriented. A steady stream of our members have crossed the ocean to tend to and nurture Habonim. Thirteen of the first thirty-four Habonim workshops made their home here. Today, members of Gesher Haziv work alongside the children of early Workshoppers.

The relationship between the movement and the kibbutz has been mutually beneficial. A large part of the adult population comes from subsequent Habonim garinim—Gimel, Hei, Etgar, and various individuals who have chosen to make their home on that "beautiful hill covered with olive trees."

Garin Aleph brought a strong dose of American pluralism and pragmatism to kibbutz life, particularly in its attitude toward Jewish tradition and religious ritual. The welcoming of the Sabbath includes many traditional elements, such as the lighting of candles and reciting the blessing over the wine. Although for years a nontraditional blessing was used, these days a complete, traditional blessing is often sung. To the nonreligious ceremony developed in the kibbutz movement to celebrate the Bar and Bat Mitzvah, Gesher Haziv has added a Sabbath morning service in which the weekly Torah portion is read.

Our religious practice continues to evolve. High Holy Day services have been held at Gesher Haziv since the beginning. In keeping with our pluralistic approach, the services have been Orthodox, Conservative, and Reform, depending on who led them. Several years ago, when the Conservative movement in America was looking for a home to train its Israel-bound settlement groups, Gesher Haziv members agreed by a 75 percent majority to convert our kitchen to kashrut—although the Conservative movement chose another kibbutz in the end and our kitchen remained unchanged.

Pluralism is evident as well in Gesher Haziv's attitude toward politics. Though it is affiliated with the United Kibbutz Movement, which is identified with the Israel Labor Party, and the majority of its members vote Labor, the kibbutz will pay an individual's membership dues to any Zionist party the member chooses. Both Garin Aleph and the members from Bet Ha'arava have been extremely wary of allowing party politics to play a divisive influence on kibbutz life.

But perhaps Garin Aleph's greatest contribution was its determination to have its children sleep at home in defiance of accepted kibbutz movement policy at the time. From its first days in training at Kibbutz Ramat Yochanan, Garin Aleph insisted that its children would sleep and play in their parents' homes and not in children's houses. That decision was heresy to the kibbutz federation, and some movement leaders saw it endangering the very foundations of the kibbutz movement. Still, it was tolerated with a shrug of the shoulders, as if to say: "What can you expect from people raised on Coca Cola and hamburgers?"

Today, of course, more than half the settlements in the United Kibbutz Movement have their children sleeping at home, and the trend has now begun as well in Kibbutz Artzi of Hashomer Hatza'ir, in response to strong grass roots demand.

The achievements of Garin Aleph may seem modest. But we did help to establish a viable community on the Israeli landscape that has been a magnet to Habonim and other American settlers. Perhaps just as important, it has developed a nondogmatic, pluralistic life-style, something sadly in short supply in Israel today.

Urim Over the Decades

Shimon Kasdai
Kibbutz Urim 1985

In many ways, our reality at Urim has outstripped our dreams. Far from the dust hole that confronted the first Bulgarians and North Americans who settled this spot in the Negev in Israel's early days, Urim today is a beautiful, thriving, successful—even computerized—community. In some ways, we have been forced along the way to make compromises and "solve" problems by ignoring them and looking the other way. But the truth is, we have created a more just and egalitarian communal society in many ways.

After nearly forty years, Kibbutz Urim has population of more than six hundred people, including two hundred seventy members as well as children, resident parents, and temporary workers. More than eighty members are graduates of North American Habonim. Another thirty-plus are their sons and daughters who have chosen to live here as well. Some of them now have children of their own.

It was the formation in 1962 of Garin Daled that marked the renewal of organized settlement groups in American Habonim after a long hiatus. Garin Daled came to Urim in 1963. Two years later, Urim began to host the Habonim Workshop. Workshop graduates were instrumental in forming Garin Maor which came to Urim in 1969 and 1970, and Garin Negba, which came in 1972. Negba was the last Habonim settlement group to come to Urim, but individual settlers still find their way to us.

The American influence is pervasive at Urim, in some subtle and not so subtle ways. The last decision in which the American population had an overwhelming influence, while acting as a unit, was in the decision to have children sleep in their parents' apartments. That decision was made in the late 1950s. But even today English is spoken freely in the dining room, and we consume more ketchup than might be expected. And some have said that we take a moderate, easy-going approach to many facets of our day-to-day life. That moderation may be attributable to our background in the movement.

One Urim innovation that caused a nationwide controversy in the kibbutz movement at the time was our decision, in the late 1960s, to send our children to the regional comprehensive high school at Eshel Hanassi. We were the first kibbutz in Israel to send our children to school with nonkibbutz children. That effort at integration with our neighbors remains one of the pioneering steps in a movement that often seems to have lost touch with Israeli society. The step reflect a unified decision by the entire kibbutz, reflecting the North Americans' full integration into the community as well as their impact on it.

Urim's members include people who graduated from Habonim from the 1940s through the 1970s. Remarkably, the movement seems to have affected us all in similar ways: Habonim represented the major expression of our Judaism and of our social consciousness when we were in America.

But there are differences as well. The Garin Bet generation generally spoke Hebrew to their children. It was important for us to be "Israeli." The younger Americans often make it a point to speak English to their children, so they can acquire a second language naturally and so the children can communicate freely with their grandparents. Being Israeli is taken for granted by the younger generations of Americans.

Urim is on the threshold of a new era. The kibbutz veterans are in their fifties and sixties. New generations, who have witnessed our successes and our failures, our strengths and our weaknesses, hold the future of the community in their hands. But the communal memory of Urim has helped shape the personality, character, and approach to life of our children, and North American Habonim is an integral part of that memory.

A Visit to Gezer: Tattered Kibbutz Blues

J. J. Goldberg
New York 1990

Dusk had already settled over the Ayalon Valley on Israel's central plain, when the newcomers finally reached Kibbutz Gezer from the airport. A gaggle of veteran kibbutzniks, dusty in their blue work-clothes and battered high shoes, assembled on the lawn to greet New Yorkers Mitch Glenn and Nancy Abramson and their two children, bringing them cakes and flowers and helping them settle into the little apartment that will be their home for the next year.

"This is really a lifelong dream for us," said Mitch, a Manhattan computer specialist, to the earnest well-wishers surrounding him. "Between our jobs and all the work you do when you're not working—taking care of the kids, fixing up around the house—you never have time for each other, for friends, for any kind of community. We'd been thinking about all the different places around the world where we could spend a year together, and we finally decided it was time to try kibbutz."

As we spoke, Nancy, a Reconstructionist cantor by trade, tried to sort out their mounds of belongings and attend to the immediate needs of Molly, age eleven, and Ariel, age four. Tonight they are bedraggled, jet-lagged immigrants, but come tomorrow they will be new pioneers, the latest in a century-long stream of diaspora Jews who have recast their lives to join in the Jewish state's best-known social revolution, what Martin Buber once called "the experiment that has not yet failed."

Tonight's scene at Gezer is one that has been repeated thousands of times since Degania, the first kibbutz, was founded on the shore of Lake Tiberias in 1909. The same mix of mangled Hebrew and languages from home, the same confused stares met with warm smiles, the same dusty tile floors and metal cots. Degania was founded by young Russian-Jewish leftists fleeing the abortive 1905 Russian revolution; Gezer was founded by young American Jews on the heels of the 1960s.

There are a few differences, however. For one, most of the kibbutzniks gathered here this evening are not farmers. Ex-Montrealer Sheldon Shulman, age thirty-four, works in Jerusalem as an attorney with the Foreign Ministry; ex-New Yorker David Leichman, age forty, commutes to Tel Aviv, where he is director of the Society for the Preservation of Nature. Others work in the kibbutz's graphics studio and glue factory. For many, the tattered kibbutz blues they wear are just something to relax in after hours.

In any case, newcomers Mitch and Nancy are not really planning to join

Reprinted with permission from *The Forward*, July 27, 1990. Copyright © 1990, Forward Publishing Co. Inc.

Gezer. They will pay rent during their year here, and the kibbutz will pay them for each day they work rather than tour. It is an arrangement most kibbutzim would not have tolerated a decade ago, but times are a-changing in the kibbutz movement.

"It's a new era. We're just beginning to learn what it means and how to survive," says Leichman, who has championed innovative approaches at Gezer's weekly meetings.

Nancy and Mitch have joined dozens of people renting space at Kibbutz Gezer this summer. On any given evening, in addition to the kibbutz's seventy members and eighty children, the dining hall may be feeding the Israel Little League baseball camp (Gezer's Hambo Field is said to be the country's finest all-turf diamond); a group of American archaeology students digging at Tel Gezer, the ruins of the ancient walled city that loom over the cowshed and cotton fields; a traditional American Jewish youth summer tour, and a decidedly non-traditional collection of tourists, guests in Gezer's new low-priced "bed and breakfast" program, staying in modest apartments that were once occupied by kibbutz members.

Some members had opposed the stream of paying guests, fearing they would disrupt the intimacy of the kibbutz community. Some, too, are unhappy at what they consider rank capitalist profiteering. But the kibbutz figures to clear about fifty thousand dollars from tourism this summer, and in this new era, that is something with which kibbutzniks can no longer argue.

There was a time—about thirty five hundred years ago, according to the Bible—that the sun stood still for a long day-and-a-half over Ayalon, a couple of miles east of here, letting Joshua defeat his Canaanite enemies against steep odds. Today the enemy is debt, mountains of it, and time is not standing still.

It's about four years since the once proudly self-sufficient kibbutz movement discovered it was more than two billion dollars in debt—debt most of Israel's one hundred twenty thousand kibbutzniks knew nothing about. Since then, compounded interest has ballooned the burden to more than five billion dollars. There was even a period more than a year ago, during the tough, four-way debt negotiations involving the kibbutz movement, the banks, the government and the Jewish Agency, that some spoke of the end of the kibbutz.

This crisis, and the larger one of labor-owned industry, led Labor to insist in 1988 coalition negotiations with the Likud that party leader Shimon Peres become minister of finance, in the naked hope that he would—as Likud critics warned—"raid the Treasury" to save the kibbutzim.

But Peres turned out to be a tough negotiator. The final kibbutz deal—combining rescheduling, forgiveness and refinancing—has resulted in drastic belt-tightening throughout the kibbutz movement.

"One of the problems was that the banks wanted to shut down about a dozen of the worst-off kibbutzim, which the movement refused to accept," says former Californian Norm Frankel, Gezer's elected farm manager. "They paid a certain price for that, and some people are still complaining about the price. But the movement was real clear—you don't shut down a kibbutz because of finances."

Kibbutz debt is a mixture of loans to the central kibbutz movement and obligations of individual kibbutzim, which the movement has traditionally backed as a matter of socialist course. Much of the total came from over-expansion during the hyper-inflation of the early 1980s, when Israelis thought they could borrow forever and interest rates would never catch up with the wild growth.

"A lot of the debt is factories that were built during that period and never made a profit, leaving a kibbutz with a big plant that's not making money," says Muki Tsur, secretary-general of the United Kibbutz Movement. "Part of it is loans that wealthy kibbutzim undertook to finance expansion, which they're paying out over twenty years with no problem. There are also a few kibbutzim with a huge debt that they will never repay."

Another chunk of the debt—a hefty five hundred million dollars of the original nut—came from an investment deal between the United Kibbutz Movement and a mysterious financier named David Balas, who is now in jail. No one seems to know where the money went, but it's gone. The news of the massive speculative disaster, which broke in 1984–85, shook the con-fidence of kibbutz members throughout Israel.

"It's kind of a shock to think that you've worked in the dairy every day for fifteen years, just trying to make an honest living and build the country, and then one day you wake up to find out you'll be in debt for the rest of your life because of some idiot in Tel Aviv," said a recent Gezer departee, who asked not to be quoted by name.

Gezer was founded in 1974 by thirty-seven Americans from the Habonim Labor Zionist youth movement, and grew to one hundred four members by 1984. Today it is down to about seventy. But that is deceptive. Because of its central location near Tel Aviv and its international reputation as an American island in the Middle East, it has a steady flow of newcomers. This inflow partly masks an attrition rate even higher than the totals indicate; sixty people have left Gezer in the past four years, including all the original founders.

The reasons for the loss appear twofold. One is debt: Every kibbutznik in Israel has felt the tighter budgets, reduced amenities, pinched housing, less study and travel. As prospects for a better living decline, some leave. Other kibbutzim have fared even worse than Gezer.

But Gezer also has a unique problem. Its founders came here just out of college, with flags flying on a wave of 1960s-era enthusiasm. As the realities sank in—the grind of physical labor, the complexities of modern agribusi-ness, the harshness of Israeli life, reserve duty, homesickness—some gave up. More and more, those who stayed behind found themselves holding the fort, missing their friends and confronting a constant stream of new faces. And as they neared forty, each in turn wondered: Is this how I want to live my life?

A few have moved to older, more stable kibbutzim; a few more have moved to Israeli towns. Most have returned to America. Today, visiting veterans from the early days find precious few familiar faces at Gezer. Yet the kibbutz survives, even thrives by current movement standards.

"We're doing better than most of the other kibbutzim our age," says Frankel, the farm manager, who came here in 1978. "Our debt is only about ten million dollars, which is below average for younger kibbutzim. And we're actually breaking even on our running expenses."

Gezer will gross about six million dollars in sales this year, Frankel says, including one-point-five million from the glue; one million from its feed center, which sells fodder to area farmers; one million from its dairy, and the rest from eggs, cotton, wheat, grapes and graphics. The picture is somewhat unusual: Among kibbutzim nationwide agriculture now accounts for less than half of total income. Industry makes up more than fifty percent and tourism is rising.

What is not unusual, according to Muki Tsur and others, is the basic soundness of the kibbutz economy. Despite the debt crisis, industrial growth in the kibbutz movement was close to eight percent in 1988–89, when the country as a whole declined more than two percent. Kibbutzim were even further ahead of the rest of the country in overall growth and in exports.

"Gezer could actually start chipping away at our debt," says Frankel, "but as a young kibbutz we're tied to the Jewish Agency, and it's just not helping these days. Their budgets are more limited than ever—I guess because of all the Russian immigrants they've got on their hands—and it seems to me the bureaucracy has gotten worse."

Gezer has seen much worse days than those. In the past the kibbutz has actually broken up and reformed four or five times, depending on how you count. First founded in 1945 by a group of German Jewish youth, it was overrun in 1948 by the Jordanian Legion, which killed nineteen members and sent the surviving men to a POW camp near Iraq for eighteen months. After the war Gezer regrouped, but part of the spirit was buried in the military cemetery near the silo. When the German reparations agreement was signed in 1954 some members took the money and ran. In 1961 the kibbutz dissolved.

The kibbutz movement sent in various groups to farm here during the 1960s, but none stayed more than a year or two. In 1970, the land was given to a group of Americans from a 1960s-era Boston Jewish commune for their permanent home. It was them that the Habonim group intended to join in 1974, but in the midst of the planning in 1973, the Boston group dissolved. The founders of current Gezer inherited a ghost kibbutz.

"The kibbutz movement is part of a larger crisis," said Tsur in a recent conversation. "It's a crisis of the Israeli economy, but also of Israeli science, art and society in general. The common denominator is that there was an attempt by the Likud, beginning in 1977, to make Israel a center of 'liberal' finance. They didn't take into account the fact that this is a country that still demands a great degree of social solidarity. We need to emphasize production, not finance."

"Well, the system couldn't stand up to the experiment. The result was a situation that any orthodox Marxist would envy—the banks went bankrupt and have been effectively nationalized. And, of course, we had that five hundred percent inflation not too long ago."

"In the kibbutz movement," Tsur added, "there were those who say it happened to us because we weren't faithful to the original kibbutz vision—because we went into all kinds of industry and finance—and there are those who say we were too faithful and didn't adapt. So the debate is not economic but personal, spiritual, value-based."

Whatever the causes, he said, "there's a great risk of personal tension, of breakdown in our traditional social frameworks" as the crisis drags on.

No one knows kibbutz social frameworks better than Tsur, age fifty-two, a teacher, historian and philosopher who has written extensively on the inner life of the early kibbutzniks—their gossip, their daily habits, their doubts and their moral anguish. Born Shmuel Tsur in Jerusalem—Muki is his childhood nickname—he is one of the few public figures in Israel or anywhere who is best known as a fictional character. A popular series of Israeli children's books written in the early 1950s by his aunt, Yemima Czernowicz, featured a mischievous imp named Muki who was frankly based on the author's nephew.

Tsur, a member of Kibbutz Ein Gev on Lake Tiberias, was elected to head the kibbutz movement in May 1989. It was the first contested election in living memory. His three opponents were all cut from standard kibbutznik cloth—farm-and-factory doers with solid administrative records. Most observers said the movement's choice of the ethereal Tsur was a bold gamble, choosing soaring vision over stolidity.

"It was rather daring of the movement to elect me," Mr. Tsur acknowledges. "I'm a known personality, and they knew they were choosing a philosopher. But not to exaggerate—I also know how to run an office and manage a staff."

Riding out the crisis, however, will require not only good management, but wisdom, Tsur said. "It won't be easy to hold it together. So far wisdom has won out, but it's too early to say what will happen in the end."

Other Forms of Settlement

Habonim has always viewed itself as a kibbutz-oriented youth movement —affiliated to the kibbutz movement, pointing to kibbutz as the highest expression of its values, and sending to kibbutz the largest single segment of its Israel-bound graduates.

Throughout the movement's history, however, some of its graduates have chosen to make their lives in other types of Israeli agricultural settlements, the *moshav ovdim* and the *moshav shitufi*. The moshav ovdim (usually referred to simply as the moshav) is a cooperative smallholders' settlement in which each family farms its own plot. It is cooperative in its economics, in that major economic activities—marketing of produce, major purchasing, and the like—are carried out by the community.

The moshav shitufi is sometimes called a cross between the kibbutz and the moshav—it entails collective production and private consumption. The community maintains a single farm and other economic enterprises, which are worked by the group. The members do not receive collective goods and services based on community set priorities; each family is paid for its contributions, and spends its income as it chooses. Frequently, member-families are free to maintain their own private plots on the side, and to supplement their incomes.

The distinction between the moshav shitufi and the kibbutz has been blurred in recent times. In the late 1970s, nearly all of Israel's moshavim shitufi'im—seven of them—affiliated with the United Kibbutz Movement in order to participate in its centralized purchasing, marketing, financing, and other services. In the late 1980s, as the kibbutz movement overall began experiencing severe economic and social stresses, many of the member-kibbutzim actually began loosening their communal structures. In the process, it was widely remarked, they came more and more to resemble the moshav shitufi.

Groups of Habonim members have settled at two moshavim shitufi'im: Bet Herut in the early 1930s and Yodfat in the early 1970s, and at one moshav, Orot, in the early 1950s.

Moshav Shitufi: A Two-fold Dream

Carl Allentuck
Moshav Bet Herut 1985

Although Moshav Bet Herut was never an official settlement project of Habonim, for most purposes it can be considered a movement settlement. Of the sixty-three original families at Bet Herut, twenty-eight had belonged to Habonim or the Young Pale Zion, including a few from the South African movement. Of the older generation, a dozen or so were from Poale Zion in America. Clearly, the membership was overwhelmingly of American Labor Zionist backgrounds.

In the early days of Habonim, the educational program was centered completely on the kibbutz. An impressionable young member could easily get the impression that Palestine consisted of wilderness and a few kibbutzim populated by small bands of dedicated pioneers. The *shlichim,* our Israeli advisors, were almost all kibbutz members who looked upon it as their task to build settlement groups for kibbutz. I do not remember any other alternatives presented, certainly not the moshav, in which families farm individual plots and cooperate on economic matters. In the context of the pioneering ideology preached in those days, the moshav—even our own moshav shitufi variant, which farms collectively but divides the income to allow families their own full freedom of choice—was seen as a second-rate ideological compromise.

Bet Herut had been founded in 1931 by members of Poale Zion who understood that their settlement in Palestine could not be the same as those of younger people who were more able to overcome harsher and more primitive conditions. They felt they needed a secure economic base immediately.

Our community came to serve as a magnet for members of Habonim who, for whatever reasons, became disillusioned with kibbutz life. Several of our families have lived on other Habonim settlements such as Gesher Haziv, Ma'ayan Baruch, and Kfar Blum. The main influence the graduates of Habonim have brought are those values they grew up with in the movement— the belief that society should be fair; that people should not exploit each other; that people should help each other in times of need; that income should be equal or nearly equal for all; that each contribute according to his or her ability; that each is cared for in sickness and old age; that a decent standard of living from birth to death could be expected; that education and culture was important.

I think that we have realized those ideals. In its second and third generations, Bet Herut has maintained the idealistic spirit of its founding generation. The number of people leaving in disappointment can be counted on one hand. The management of the economy is almost entirely in the hands of our sons and daughters.

We had a lofty, twofold dream: to rebuild Israel and to build a just, egalitarian, free, fair, and humane society. As much as human beings can achieve aims like those, I think we have.

Moshav Ovdim: The Ability to Decide for Myself

Yonatan Edelson
Moshav Orot 1985

Orot, the *moshav ovdim* or "workers settlement" where we live, was founded in 1951 by a group of Jewish chicken farmers from New Jersey with the idea of absorbing new immigrants from all English-speaking countries.

In the early days, several members of Habonim who wanted to farm, some who had been living on kibbutzim and some in Israeli cities, joined the moshav. But as time passed, it became obvious that waiting for immigrants was an exercise in futility, and we opened the settlement up to all comers. Today, Orot is an amalgam of Jews from more than twenty countries. Yet the founders' spirit can still be felt.

The moshav has about fifty families working in every branch of agriculture—dairy, orchards, flowers, bees, and poultry, for example. Some people work outside the community to supplement their income as well. But we like to say that children is our finest crop. Today, some of our families have three generations living at home.

When I first moved to Israel in 1950, I had two ideas in mind. I wanted to be a farmer, and I wanted to make a contribution to the cultural life of Israel. As a member of Garin Bet, I went to kibbutz, where both those goals seemed possible to achieve. There I married and began a family.

But as time passed, I found that kibbutz was too crowded for me. I needed more space and the ability to decide for myself the priorities in my life.

A moshav—a farming settlement in which each family is more or less independent but works cooperatively with the others—seemed like the best alternative. The balance between farming, family, and art created a tension which has run through the whole fabric of our life. The concessions we had to make were of our own choosing.

Today I feel the circle closing. I am working the land: sculpting in clay; pruning trees; carving clay. The twin aspirations of my life have merged in a way I could not have imagined, yet inevitably connected to the Zionist dream of my youth.

The Urban Collective Experiment: Kvutzat Shaal B'Carmiel, 1968 to 1972

Gary Ben-et

Kibbutz Bet Ha'emek 1985

On the eve of Rosh Hashanah 1968, the eighteen adults and six children of Garin Shaal arrived in the development town of Carmel in Israel's western Galilee, determined to establish a permanent commune there.

The move to Carmel represented the culmination of an ideological struggle in Habonim. Movement members in the 1960s had begun to question the meaning of pioneering and the role of the kibbutz movement, which they saw as increasingly isolated in Israeli society. The members of Shaal felt that for the kibbutz movement to maintain and increase its influence in Israel, it must be directly involved in urban Israel. It must establish collective groups in Israeli towns.

The name of the garin reflected that belief. The word *Sha'al* means "footstep," but it was also chosen as an acronym for Garin *Shitufi Ironi Le-Carmiel*, the Urban Cooperative Garin to Carmiel.

Although the members of Shaal never called themselves a kibbutz—others would later use the word *irbutz*, a contraction of "kibbutz" and *ir*, the Hebrew word for city—we saw ourselves as an integral part of the kibbutz movement. After first organizing in 1964, we struggled for four years for official recognition from the kibbutz movement. Despite the support of World Habonim, we never received that recognition.

On arriving in Carmiel, the original Shaal group was given a neighborhood with sixteen apartments. One was quickly converted into a communal meeting room and another to a day-care center. The economic basis of our community was totally collective, but because we were organized around the family unit, our life-style more closely represented that of a *moshav shitufi* cooperative settlement than that of a kibbutz. For example, using a system of general allowances, we prepared and ate our meals in our own apartments, although Sabbath meals and holidays were conducted in the meeting room. And while it was our intention to establish a communal economic project, most of the members of Shaal worked outside the community and contributed their salaries to the collective treasury. This arrangement persisted because many members wanted to pursue specific professions, and because we could not find a suitable economic venture without the help of the kibbutz movement.

In addition to maintaining a close-knit society among ourselves, with all the traditional features of kibbutz democracy, we saw our main goal in Carmiel as political. We wanted to influence the course of life in Carmiel and the direction of the town's development. Shaal members were active in all aspects of the town's political, social, and cultural life, even though some members of Shaal worked as far away as Haifa. The group was very outwardly directed.

The kibbutz movement during this period was deeply engaged in the struggle over the question of children sleeping in their parents' homes, which was slowly spreading among kibbutzim despite opposition from their central organizations. The custom of families eating dinner in their apartments was just beginning to surface. And only one kibbutz in the entire movement had reached the stage of guaranteeing a college education for all its children. Indeed, in the days before high tech industry came to kibbutz, a college education was seen by some as potentially dangerous for kibbutz members. So it is not surprising that many leaders of the kibbutz movement viewed Shaal with serious reservations. In the 1980s, our story might have turned out differently.

As it turned out, in 1972 we formally dissolved and our members dispersed throughout Israel. Kvutzat Shaal in Carmiel never had more than thirty adult members. We failed, I believe, for the following reasons, among others.

In 1969, one out of every forty adults in Carmiel was a member of Shaal. In 1972, due to the rapid growth of the city and the stagnation of our group, only one out of every two hundred adults belonged to Shaal. Although we were joined by a small garin from South Africa, an expected second wave of Garin Shaal from America never materialized—due, in part, to the pressures of the war in Vietnam and the draft. Our small numbers meant our influence in Carmiel was limited. And finally, the internal pressures of a small group became overwhelming.

We never were able to establish a serious economic project. A collective enterprise would have helped to build the cohesion of the group as well as providing a more secure financial footing. In several periods, Shaal faced extreme financial crises. Survival itself was a challenge.

Finally, there were serious flaws in the way we initially conceived of Shaal. And, again, we never received any serious guidance from more experienced people in the kibbutz movement.

In the end, Kvutzat Shaal was but a fleeting four-year experiment that had some influence on the early development of one Galilee development town. More importantly, however, it was an experiment that almost succeeded. It may be that our experience will help another group, in another time, in another place to bring the idea to reality.

Kibbutz Life and the Ex-Kibbutznik

Tuvya Kohn

Jerusalem 1985

I left Kfar Blum thirty-five years ago. Plenty of time to forget. But I have not forgotten. The impact of ten years of kibbutz life seems permanent.

Like the American myth of rugged individualisms, the myth of kibbutz life—pioneering, initiative, opportunity—is inspiring and real. It affected real people's behavior in the real world. But for me the kibbutz was not a myth taught in school or passed along by my parents. I lived that myth from 1939 to 1949.

After I left the kibbutz, I lived for a while on a moshav. Later, I worked for Koor Industries, a conglomerate owned by the Histadrut, and I was an employee in the private sector. Since I retired, I have worked as a volunteer. I ask myself now, what did I learn on kibbutz?

On kibbutz I learned how to enjoy working hard. It is true that the kibbutz is home to some lazy people. And there are those who contribute so little they can only be seen as parasites on the community. And, in a way, the kibbutz encourages indolence by not penalizing it directly.

On the other hand, the responsible members of the kibbutz worked extremely hard without regard to direct compensation. I was surprised to find when I left kibbutz for the dog-eat-dog world of private enterprise, the proportion of idlers was no lower than on the kibbutz. In fact, many highly paid executives were lazy.

The proper way of life on kibbutz was internalized, rather than the result of external force. We would worry about crime if a high spirited member stole a watermelon for a party, but there was no violence and doors were never locked. Some people did not even bother getting married in those days. If a boy and girl decided to live together and have children, it was nobody's business but their own and the housing committee's. Sure, the kibbutz has had its fair share of scandal—but no more than its fair share. I have known members of Kfar Blum for forty-five years, and from their behavior nobody could tell they were "living in sin."

It seems to me that young people today cannot understand how they could possibly survive, much less be happy, without color television, air conditioning, and a private car. But the happiest period of my life was when we had no electricity, no running water, no refrigeration, no heating, and no sewage system. It is a unique feeling, when for the first time you can have water simply by turning a knob, when you can switch on a bulb and not worry that the wind will blow out your kerosene lamp, or when you can sit on a real toilet seat instead of having to make a mad dash through the rain to sit on a board over a hole in an outhouse.

On the kibbutz, I worked at several jobs, some for years, some for just a short period of time. I learned that pleasure can be found in any meaningful job at all levels. The smooth rhythmic movement of the scythe can be as sensual as dancing or sport. Strenuous physical activity produces the heady sensation of being young and strong. Night guard duty is an opportunity to be alone with the moon and the stars. Joy can even be found in routine, mechanical operations. Because of my kibbutz experience, work for me became a normal human function and not merely a way to earn a living. The only effect that retirement has had on me is that now I am free to choose my work.

I spent most of my working days in Kfar Blum in the fields, often alone. Every day I looked at Mount Hermon to the north, the Hills of Naphtali to the west and the Golan Heights to the east. I did not just observe the scenic beauty; I absorbed it. Sitting on a tractor, plowing a thin furrow foot by foot, I saw myself as a dot in the landscape. It was a deeply religious experience to realize how small a part of creation we are, yet how significant a part. In plowing the soil, I was communing with nature, and at the same time building a new world. And, I might add, no flag-waving chauvinist loves his country more than a man who works its soil and knows its topography.

I loved the kibbutz for its impracticality. Had the founders of the kibbutz movement been practical, they would have looked to easier ways to make a living. It was not practical to settle in the midst of malarial swamps. And why place a small settlement of thirty people in the midst of three large Arab villages? During the War of Independence, I despaired for our future. But the other members of our kibbutz were more serene. And they were right.

To this day, I am an incurable optimist because of that experience. My love of freedom borders on anarchy. I believe in freedom because I have seen it work. I have seen people work with dedication, not motivated by greed or fear. I have seen people learn to live together without worry about legal sanctions. I have learned that a free society is a possibility, though not a certainty.

Today, Kfar Blum for me is a living reminder of a myth I once lived. Many of the old myths have lost their potency. And perhaps in today's reality, the new myths are better. But I am no longer a young man, and I prefer the old myth that helped mold my life.

11
Habonim in Israeli Society

Founding the Association of Americans and Canadians in Israel

Moshe Goldberg
Hofit 1985

For the most part, Americans who left the kibbutz in the early years after independence had a hard time adjusting to Israeli life. The country simply was not ready for them. Most official immigration efforts were directed at absorbing the flood of new immigrants from the Arab countries.

Employment was hard to find and even those with a high level of technical skill often didn't speak Hebrew well enough to get along. On top of that, there was no suitable housing. While Habonim prepared its members emotionally and intellectually for a full Jewish life in a Jewish state, we were woefully unprepared to face the hard facts of economic and social life in Israel outside of the kibbutz. To make matters worse, many of us who left the kibbutz felt guilty—that we had betrayed our friends, that we had somehow failed.

I had come shortly after World War II, together with my wife Lillian, after working in the national office of Habonim and for several years before that as a field organizer. I had been an active member of Young Poale Zion Alliance even before Habonim was founded, and it was natural that we head straight for kibbutz. We settled at Kibbutz Kfar Blum. After about a year on the kibbutz, however, we decided to leave, and so, during the second cease fire of the War of Independence, we left for the city. I joined the Air Force, where I was put in charge of manpower. I eventually became a colonel.

But most of the Americans who came to Israel between 1949 and 1951 did not manage the transition to city life. The vast majority returned to the United States, despite the efforts of a small, underfunded department the Jewish Agency established to address the problems of newcomers from Western countries.

During the Sukkot holiday in the fall of 1951, a meeting took place at Kfar

Blum to discuss the problem. Herman Pomerenze, a Chicago Labor Zionist leader from the early years, took the lead; with him were David Breslau and Kieve Skidell, both former national secretaries of Habonim. They decided to call a national meeting of all immigrants from the United States and Canada. Advertisements were placed in newspapers announcing the meeting, which was to be held at the Tel Aviv offices of the newly formed World Habonim. Saadia Gelb of Kfar Blum was mazkir of World Habonim at the time, so cooperation was not difficult to obtain.

The response was electric. A standing-room-only crowd attended, and it was decided on the spot to establish the Association of Americans and Canadians in Israel. The organization was apolitical and included American *olim* of all viewpoints, but the Labor Zionist impact was profound. Included on the initial steering committee were David Breslau, Ralph Cohen of Bridgeport Habonim, Herman Pomerenze, and Sophie Udin, a founder of Pioneer Woman, who directed the first Camp Kvutza at Kindervelt-Highland Mills. I was appointed executive director.

The aim of the organization was to encourage aliyah from North America and to assist in the integration of those who came here, on a nonpolitical, nonpartisan basis. We wanted to be a central clearinghouse for information from all the institutions involved in immigration and to help shape and influence immigration policy.

We also hoped the organization would be able to revitalize the Zionist movement in America. The thinking was that the Zionist movement most dynamically expresses itself through aliyah, so as important as education, fund-raising, and other activities were, aliyah, even on a small scale, was as essential to the vitality of the American Zionist movement as it was to Israel.

We conceived of a three-pronged approach to aiding in the absorption process once a person arrived in Israel. We were prepared to offer direct, personal service and counseling to every newcomer from the United States and Canada. We planned to establish financial institutions that could be deployed by the organization in its integration efforts. And we worked with public and semipublic organizations to create a favorable climate for North America immigration.

AACI has emerged as an address for Americans and Canadians coming here and those here in need of assistance. It is important that newcomers have a place to turn where somebody would understand them and represent them competently. And while AACI may not have been able to smooth out the bumps in the absorption process, it has helped make those bumps easier to surmount.

Serving the Community

David Lieb
Jerusalem 1985

It might seem a natural carryover from movement life in America for former members of Habonim to be deeply involved in communal bodies and associations active in every aspect of Israeli life. But that is not so. The transition from work in support of Israeli institutions abroad, to working within them in Israel, is neither easy nor automatic. A person must first establish personal roots and priorities in Israel. Representing constituencies and interest groups in civic organizations can only come later.

And yet, despite the obstacles, former Habonim members have been involved at every level of the World Zionist Organization, the Jewish Agency, and the various elements of the World Labor Zionist Movement. They have been involved in the central bodies of the kibbutz movement and the Labor party. They have made a special contribution to education. A former mazkir Habonim, Moshe Kerem of Gesher Haziv, served as director of the kibbutz movement teachers' seminary, Oranim. Former Habonim members have directed experimental schools, schools for the deaf, programs to foster Arab–Jewish understanding among students. Former Habonim members have been active in research institutes of all types.

Former Habonim members provide social services at every level of Israeli society. We are active in the peace movement, the feminist movement, the civil rights movement. Many are involved in the establishment of Reform and Conservative synagogues in Israel.

And while we may never lose our distinctive American accent, it is another aspect of the baggage we bring with us which has proven to be more important—the ideal of serving the community, the readiness to spend time, energy, and thought to help each other. The movement has given us the conviction that the principles of justice, mutual aid, and tolerance can be realized through our own efforts.

Habonim in Israeli Academia

David Goldberg
Jerusalem 1985

In preparation for this volume, an informal study was conducted of Habonim graduates in Israel. The largest numbers, we learned, are in kibbutzim and moshavim. The second largest group is to be found in academic life.

Our initial source of information was the grapevine and the many personal contacts that still remain strong even after many years. Beginning with the names we acquired, we compiled a list of ex-Habonim working in academia today in Israel, knowing that we had not by any means included everybody. We sent a questionnaire to some sixty people, hoping to form a picture of the backgrounds of the individuals, where they are working, whether they were in similar or related academic fields before their aliyah, their initial experiences in this country, and finally, how if at all Habonim had influenced their choice of career and the way they dealt with their work.

The largest number of those currently engaged in academic pursuits came to Israel either before 1950 or after 1970. Interestingly, only three of the people we interviewed came during the 1960s, when America was experiencing the upheavals of the New Left: the hippies and the counterculture, the revolt on campus, the antiwar movement, and so on. All those trends, we knew, had their impact on Habonim during that era, as did the drug culture. That was also the period of denigration of an academic education as something that was, at best, irrelevant. These various influences, we believe, may well have contributed to the low number of American ex-Habonim who entered the academic world in Israel during that decade, or who had been in it before coming here.

Among those now in academic institutions in Israel, few had been in the same pursuit in America—although divergent pictures emerge when the periods are considered separately. Of the twenty-one individuals who came before 1970, only six had been in academe before their aliyah. Of the thirteen who arrived after 1970, ten moved from university in America to university in Israel.

Few who had been in nonacademic professions before aliyah went directly into university work immediately after coming here; some first joined kibbutzim, others worked as elementary or secondary school teachers. Two journalists, although now in academic life, have continued to write for the Jerusalem *Post*. A number had had professional government positions or had worked as teachers in America, and on the whole these entered directly into those or closely related fields in Israel. The professionals eventually began to teach their field of specialization in universities, whereas most of the teachers changed their fields after coming here.

* * *

One area of Israeli life where Habonim members might have been expected to leave their mark—but have not—is politics. The curious lacuna has not gone unnoticed. In the following article, a leading Israeli political scientist and journalist considers the reasons.

In Public Life in Israel

Yosef Goell

Jerusalem 1985

When I began to look for Habonim graduates in public life in Israel, I quickly discovered that there were almost none. Sure, there are and have been North American Habonim graduates in the leadership of their kibbutzim, on city and regional councils, and in mid-level political party positions, but no North American Habonim graduate has held an elective political position with enough visibility to be even fairly well known to the public.

The great exception, of course, and the one that virtually proves the rule, is Golda Meir, graduate of Poale Zion in Milwaukee before the Young Poale Zion was formally constituted as a youth movement. If one wished to be generous, you might throw in a graduate of Irish Habonim in the thirties, President Chaim Herzog. But that would be about it.

Perhaps Habonim has sent too few graduates to Israel—two thousand or so from North America over the years—to expect that a national leader should have emerged. In fact, North Americans overall number less than one hundred thousand in an Israeli Jewish population of about three-and-a-half million, or less than 3 percent. On the other hand, considering the deep involvements and commitments of so many Americans in their native society before they came to Israel, it seems curious indeed that so few have made a name in Israeli politics. One can almost count them on one's hand: Golda Meir; Moshe Arens, variously foreign and defense minister; Yehuda Ben-Meir, former Knesset member and deputy minister from the National Religious Party.

Interestingly, all three are products of the Zionist youth movements. Meir came to Israel under the influence of her teenage years in Poale Zion. Arens, who like Meir was born in Russia, first achieved a name for himself as a leader of American Betar. Ben-Meir was a leader of Chicago Bnei Akiva. It was the old boy network that brought them to prominence. If they were few, it was partly because so few came to Israel.

The numbers may also be in part a reflection of the quality of political life in Israel. From my training in political science, I know that anyone not possessing burning ambition and an inextinguishable drive for power should not get into power politics. In Israel, you can add a third requirement: a cast-iron conscience.

I know this from personal experience, too. In the early 1950s, I was the secretary of my partly American, partly native Israeli kibbutz. If so inclined, a person could use a position like that as a stepping stone into politics. I was not so inclined and was kicked out of office in 1951 because I refused to allocate a sufficient number of workdays for the election drive that year of the dominant labor party, Mapai. For the Israeli members of the kibbutz, denying the party's demand for "volunteers" was such a heinous sin, it overrode all other aspects of the job I was doing.

Later, I worked for a year as a coordinator of the youth movement in the northern part of the country. I had frequent contact with Abba Houshi, mayor of Haifa, and Yosef Almogi, the secretary of the Haifa Labor Council. Both were Mapai stalwarts as well, and despite Houshi's personal ability, both epitomized machine politics at its most nefarious. Almogi was busy at the time breaking an "unauthorized" seamen's strike. One of the tactics he used was denying the wildcatters medical benefits, which was easy since he controlled both the union organization and its health plan. I wanted no part of tactics like that.

I am not saying that Israeli politics is dirtier than politics in other countries. I don't believe that is true. But the cliquish, old boy club, "bolshevik" atmosphere of Israel's Eastern European-style politics has not appealed much to North American Habonim graduates, an atmosphere in which the party is the supreme arbiter of right and wrong, in which a political career requires decades of biting your tongue as you climb the greasy pole, clinging desperately to the coattails of the ringleader. Habonim graduates' idealistic—and individualistic—visions have been largely out of step with the reigning ethos in the country's political parties.

Moreover, Habonim graduates who opted out of politics found more suitable alternatives in the kibbutz, in the army, in the universities, and eventually even in the private sector. I think that in the long run, Israel has been the poorer for the off-putting nature of its politics. As a teacher, I have seen the best and the brightest students shy away from political careers for the past twenty-five years.

In the early days of Zionism, the best, it seems, plunged into politics. Now we seem to find our leaders from the ranks of the power-hungry only.

Bending Reality to a Dream: Working for Change in Israel

Ira Cohen
Jerusalem 1985

It could be that I live in Israel today because my parents were looking for an inexpensive Jewish summer camp twenty years ago. They found Habonim Camp Moshava, and I found *kupah,* constructive work, days of capitalism and revolution, and the endless discussions. We talked about man, meaning, God, peoplehood, justice, Judaism, sharing, equality, and Zionism. It made quite an impression on a thirteen-year-old boy who had never thought about anything more profound than why the Washington Senators always lost.

After a while, the Habonim message was too heavy. The bottom line, as I recall it, said that to be an authentic and fulfilled Jew you had to live not only in Israel, but on kibbutz as well. And not just any kibbutz: only a Habonim kibbutz would really do. By the time I was sixteen, I was no longer committed to that imperative, though I was still inspired by the values underlying it.

My feelings about being Jewish at the time could have been summed up, more in less, in serious involvement in United Synagogue Youth, a Jewish, though not religious, home, and the last name of Cohen. During the Six-Day War, though, it all came to a head. I realized that I could be part of the action in determining the destiny of the Jewish people. I could be an actor rather than a spectator.

I resolved to move to Israel. To be honest, I was motivated not only by the pull of Israel but the push of America. As a child of the sixties, I participated actively in civil rights, Biafra, Soviet Jewry, antipoverty activism, and, of course, the antiwar movement. The prevailing mood in America, as I saw it, was "love it or leave it." I was alienated from the American reality. Leaving it would not be so hard.

I first came to Israel in 1969, when I spent my junior year at the Hebrew University. Needless to say, the reality of Israel did not match the dream I had in mind. Despite a wonderful year, I was especially disturbed by many Israelis I met. They seemed conservative, conformist, and chauvinistic. Like others before me, I found that I liked Israel, it was just the Israelis that I could do without.

After graduation, I spent two years hitchhiking around the world. I spent Simchat Torah in Moscow one year and shared Purim with an Israeli building crew in Ethiopia. I also visited the Jewish communities in Prague, Budapest, Bucharest, and Cochin.

When I returned to the United States, a group of friends and I opened The Kosher Kitchen, the only kosher restaurant in the Washington area. We served more than just chicken soup. We offered Jewish entertainment, free adult education with topics ranging from Jewish feminism to Jewish funeral practices, a meals-on-wheels program for the elderly, and an afternoon drop-in center—all at no charge. We ran the restaurant collectively. You could say that we were antiprofit.

After three and a half years with The Kosher Kitchen, I moved to London to coordinate Project Areivim. Under the auspices of the World Union of Jewish Students, Project Areivim was an innovative program designed to recruit young Jewish activists from large Jewish communities and send them to small Jewish communities where their special skills were sorely needed. Our motto was the classic saying, "All of the people of Israel are responsible, one for the other."

It was working with Project Areivim that I first clashed with the official-dom of the World Zionist Organization. The newly formed Student Division of the WZO decided that it should be the center of all Jewish student organizing efforts in the world, and to that end it organized a putsch at the WUJS convention in Jerusalem in 1979. The WZO slate captured not only all the leadership positions but filled the positions on the projects with their own people as well. For a year, I tried to protect Project Areivim. But my days, and the project's, were numbered.

I moved to Israel shortly thereafter, and joined a group of new young immigrants determined to change the WZO into a positive tool for Jewish and Zionist revival. Though we were critical of its politics, we affiliated with the World Labor Zionist Movement. We called ourselves Labor Zionist Renewal and pledged to fight for the visions of social justice that inspired the Second Aliyah, and ourselves. We wanted to influence the direction of the Jewish Agency and the WZO. We wanted to establish an alternative vehicle for those not satisfied with politics as usual.

Labor Zionist Renewal was short-lived. Many of our members went on to form the nucleus of the young adults section of the World Labor Zionist Movement. Through our efforts, in part, we blocked the election of Herut's Ariel Sharon to head the aliyah department of the Jewish Agency, following his resignation as minister of defense in the wake of the 1982 Lebanon War.

In another direction, I joined with other graduates of Habonim to form Kadima, the English-speaking section of the Labor party. We concluded that if Israeli society is to fundamentally change, the political parties must be the vehicle for that change. Ironically, except for voting, most Israelis are completely uninvolved and terribly cynical about political parties. They see party functionaries as having abandoned their principles in the short-term pursuit of power for its own sake. The parties seem like closed clubs.

In its few years in action, Kadima has grown in numbers and influence. If we were a branch instead of a section, we would be the most active in the party. Dozens of Kadima members have been active in recent campaigns. We have attracted up to eight hundred people to our rallies, and we meet regularly with members of the Parliament and party leaders and even West Bank Arab activists. Real power still eludes us, but our voice in party forums is growing.

Perhaps the most important contribution we can make to Israeli politics is the values we bring with us: volunteerism, tolerance, respect for others, a tradition of democratic behavior, equality for women and minorities, good citizenship, and religious pluralism. Each of those seems to be in short supply.

I came and stayed in Israel to help create a relatively new society. I have embarked on a remarkable adventure in what I think is the most dynamic, intense, and interesting country in the twentieth century. I feel living here gives my life a special meaning even when I do nothing more than buy a loaf of bread at the grocery. I emotionally point out to friends that my children's identity cards have Jerusalem as their birthplace. It is the small things, singing songs at Lag B'Omer campfires, seeing children in costume for the week before Purim, visiting kibbutz veterans living and working by their values, the peace in Jerusalem on the afternoon of Yom Kippur, that remind me what I am doing here and enable me to put up with the bureaucracy, the political situation, and the monthly paycheck.

And Habonim? Habonim gave me the dream and the desire to bend the reality I find to that dream.

Religious Pluralism in Israel

Hillel Shuval
Jerusalem 1985

Although Habonim is a secular movement, it has never subscribed to the extreme antireligious attitudes of other movements on the left such as Hashomer Hatza'ir. We believed in a continuity in Jewish culture and heritage, and emphasized the revitalization of the basic moral and ethical precepts of Jewish tradition.

In Israel, to our sorrow, we have found a society that is in many ways hostile to the premise that Jewish heritage lies on a continuum. All too often, Israeli life is divided into stagnant, mutually hostile realms of "religious," meaning rigidly Orthodox, and "secular"—often synonymous with antireligious, in reaction to the rigidity of the Orthodox establishment.

The forces fighting to bring out the best in each aspect of Jewish life in Israel—the secular and the religious—have not yet gained the strength to set the agenda for Israeli society. But among those forces, such as they are, American immigrants have been in the forefront. And Habonim graduates have been among the leaders.

When I joined Habonim in 1943, I brought many of these ideals with me from a deeply committed Jewish and Zionist home. I grew up in a home where the richness and warmth of Jewish tradition and ceremony were nurtured, though stripped of theological baggage. My father, Yehuda Shuval, was an active Zionist leader and a rabbi trained at the Jewish Theological Seminary. He became an early disciple of Mordecai M. Kaplan, the founder of the Reconstructionist movement. It was my dream to establish a home in Israel with an atmosphere like my father's home.

I graduated from university in the spring of 1948 and immediately volunteered to serve in Israel's struggle for independence, first in covert activities in the United States and then, in August 1948, with the Israel Defense Force. After the war, I devoted most of my efforts to building my professional career, at the Ministry of Health and later at the Hebrew University. But like many American immigrants, I chafed at the Orthodox establishment's complete domination of religious life. I felt that the religious political parties were continually expanding their control over people's personal lives, stifling religious freedom in the process. I was very disappointed that the Labor party habitually deferred to the Orthodox in these matters.

After I got married and had children, I began to search for a form of identification with Jewish traditions above and beyond simply living in Israel. I was also looking for a symbolic way to challenge the Orthodox rabbinate's vise on religious life, to demonstrate my belief in religious pluralism.

In 1958, my wife Judith and I were among a small group of Jerusalemites who formed a congregation called Association for the Renaissance of Religious Life in Israel. The group included a number of Jews from Reform congregations in Europe and America and led to the founding of the first Reform synagogue in Israel, Congregation Har El.

Other members of Habonim were among the founders of Congregation Mevakshei Derech ("Seekers of a Path"), an innovative, non-Orthodox synagogue in Jerusalem. Still others are in the leadership of Conservative and Reform congregations all over the country, and still others have been in the forefront of the recently formed Movement for Humanistic Secular Judaism, which is looking for a secular approach to Jewish identification and continuity.

As the years passed, I felt the need to find effective political paths to protect civil liberties and religious pluralism in Israel. I joined the Democratic Movement for Change, founded by the late Professor Yigael Yadin in 1977. When the DMC split apart before the 1981 elections, I went with Shinui, the party founded by Professor Amnon Rubinstein.

Outside the world of party politics, I have been deeply involved in Peace Now. More recently, I was named to the executive of Hemdat, the Committee for Freedom of Science, Religion and Culture. Headed by former Supreme Court Justice Haim Cohen, the committee represents a coalition of non-Orthodox religious groups, together with professionals in fields such as archaeology and pathology, who joined together to lobby against the Orthodox-inspired and right-wing led erosion of civil liberties that threatens us all. Together we work to promote religious and cultural pluralism in Israel.

Achieving political and social change in Israel, I have found, is a difficult and frustrating process. But it is more frustrating to sit on the sidelines and not even try.

A Conversation among Social Workers

Rose Breslau
Jerusalem 1985

A few mornings ago, I had coffee with a friend in a café on a side street of the Ben-Yehuda pedestrian mall in downtown Jerusalem. It was one of those pleasant days with just a hint of a hot wind in the air that brings

Jerusalemites out in all their multicolored glory. The crowd appears to be restless, searching, constantly moving.

My companion and I enjoy many different types of people. But today we reflect on what we were like in our youth movement days and what the movement meant to us. We remember the closeness and influence of our circle of people. We can still feel the intensity of the warm and caring atmosphere, the sense of belonging, of being a part of something important and extraordinary. We wonder if we could have found a way to introduce the essential nature of the movement to a larger group of people.

We have talked in this fashion many times. I remember that my companion had come to the movement as a young adult. I came as a ten-year-old child, through my brother David, who had encouraged me to join the short-lived but vibrant Gordonia. My images of Gordonia feel vivid but remain elusive in my mind's eye. I remember the tension and excitement of the "older" people who first gathered to initiate Gordonia groups in our hometown, Camden, New Jersey. Within a few weeks, there were many children dancing, singing, and running around. I was elected secretary of my age group. Suddenly, I was in a different corner, on a different street.

When I was eleven, I received a diary for my birthday. Gordonia, my group, my circle of friends filled many pages. And so it was: from Gordonia to the union with Habonim in 1938, my intense participation in all activities; on staff at Camp Kinneret near Detroit, director of the camps near Montreal, Winnipeg, Toronto, New York and Philadelphia. I was director of the Philadelphia chapter and the New York region, editor of several magazines and anthologies, national camp coordinator, editor of educational materials, involved in all aspects of defense and immigration work. It was a time to stand up and be counted.

In December 1947, together with a small group from Hashomer Hatza'ir, I left from New York, bound for Eretz Israel. I carried an identity card that classified me as a nurse; my American passport was stamped with a "special" visa. We rose early the day we were scheduled to arrive in Palestine. Dawn was breaking over the Haifa skyline. As I walked down the gangplank in Haifa port, the first thing that caught my eye was a British tank manned by British soldiers pointing their guns into the port. The newness was strange, fascinating, disturbing, and impressive, yet somehow familiar as well.

After wandering through the land of Israel for a while, I decided to train as a social worker. I worked in a Jerusalem slums project and with tuberculosis patients from all corners of Israeli life, including Bedouins and village Arabs. It was a heady, intoxicating experience, and it motivated me to seek advanced training. I returned to the United States, where I completed my master's degree in social work, specializing in group and community work. On returning to Israel, I worked in Bar-Ilan University's School of Social Work, as student field-work instructor in community work, group work, and case work. Here again, my assignment brought me in contact with every aspect of Israeli life—there were native Israeli students from all backgrounds, Israeli Arab students, and Jewish immigrants.

Choosing the challenging road has always been a part of a youth movement with an ideologically oriented philosophy, and it seems to me that I can trace the roads that lead back to Camden, New Jersey. Habonim values mesh with those underlying effective social work—accepting differences, caring for the individual, working with the group, training leadership. They are here, in front of us, surrounding us.

Over the years, my companion and I have talked to many former members of the movement now in the "helping" professions. We have found that for many, the intense intellectual and emotional experience in Habonim was the incubator of a sense of responsibility for the people around us. Perhaps the consensus was expressed by a person currently working with retarded children, who said, "I can honestly say that much of what I did and do with my life and the kind of person I am is a direct result of the warmth, the friendship, the creativity, the intellectual and emotional excitement, I experienced in the movement."

I like to think that one of the many things which I received and then gave in Habonim is the sense of being, not possessing or obtaining, but being as a process that grows and flourishes with each experience.

In a Development Town

Sarah Poster-Levin
Ashdod 1985

Not many Habonim graduates are to be found living in development towns and the small cities of Israel, but some of us live here nonetheless. My own Ashdod is no longer considered a development town in terms of size or economic development. But in attitude and aspirations, the people in the neighborhoods of Ashdod are closer to those in Ma'alot than, say, Tel Aviv.

The best part of living in a small town is the sense of belonging. Of course that sense is taken for granted on the kibbutz and the moshav, but in urban Israel as well as elsewhere in the world, people live anonymously in their neighborhoods and even their apartment buildings. There is no anonymous living in Ashdod. Indeed, some Americans who tried living here complained about the "neighborly intervention." They took it as busybodiness.

Having grown up in Chicago, I have often wondered what life was like in the small cities of the Midwest. I think life in Ashdod must be similar. You know not only your neighbors but most of the people on the street as well. You are on a first-name basis with the people who provide your basic services and work or own the stores at which you shop. There is a comfortable feeling of familiarity.

Some years ago, I was scheduled to go on a six-week mission abroad at a time when my husband was to be on reserve duty. My daughters were still very young at the time. Shortly before I left, a delegation of my neighbors descended upon us. I was astonished to find that they had organized my children's lunch and after school schedules and were prepared to see to it that there would be no obstacle to my departure. "After all," one said, "what are neighbors for?"

My children have grown up in the homes of friends and neighbors who come from almost every country that Jews come from. I am embarrassed to say that I have made the poorest contribution to the gastronomic education of my children. What do you do when you are required to bring an example of food from your country of origin to a party at school? We had to settle for chocolate chip cookies. We claimed they had a mystical influence on the healthy physical development of American children.

In Ashdod, ethnic background is important in every aspect of life. To a large degree, it governs social relationships and political activities. Since we live among large primary immigrant groups, it is the norm for people to maintain their own language and traditions. Being American is like being *pareve*. It is not like being Moroccan or Romanian. We have no strong tradition to maintain, nor are we surrounded by a large American community. So we have been able to assimilate those elements of the cultures around us which we find appealing. We enjoy Persian, Indian, and Ethiopian music and are quite expert at Moroccan and Georgian dances. My children, who are now in the army, are amazed that many of their new friends know nothing about the customs of Jews different from themselves.

I did not consciously set out on a career in politics, but today I am secretary of the working women's organization Na'amat, an elected political position. I have served a term on the city council, and I am a member of the central committee of the Labor party. I have found that in small towns, the door to political participation is open to those who are willing to work and not just give advice.

We came to Israel not only to be here physically but to contribute to society. And I believe that Israel ultimately will be judged by the quality of society we build. To a large degree, it will be the success of development towns, the creation of a democratic life-style among people whose roots lie in nondemocratic countries, and the development of intimate relationships that allow people of diverse backgrounds to understand and respect each other which will be the measure of the success of Israel. Conversely, the failure to build a high quality of life in these towns will be devastating to the Zionist enterprise.

I believe that the mainstream of Israeli life can be found in Ashdod and Dimona, Arad and Hatzor, Ma'alot and Yavneh. In those towns, the dreams we had in Habonim, the dreams of a very special society must be realized as well.

An Accidental Career in Academia

Louis Guttman
Jerusalem 1985

Like many members of Young Poale Zion, I never actually joined Habonim. I was too old by the time the movement was formed. But more or less by chance I was active in its formative days. The leadership of YPZ in Minneapolis, first Moshe Cohen, then Saadia Gelb, and then my brother Nahum, moved to New York, assumed the leadership of YPZ and created Habonim.

I became involved one summer when Moshe Cohen's father fell ill. Moshe, who was national secretary of YPZ at the time, returned to Minneapolis to take his place in the family grocery store. I used to go to the store to help him write educational material for the new Habonim movement.

When the YPZ branch in Minneapolis became Habonim, I was asked to organize it on a volunteer basis. I was in college at the time. Saadia Gelb also asked me to be on staff at Camp Kvutza in Accord during the summer of 1937. It was the first time I ever went to summer camp. I was faced with a crisis right away. When it came to constructing the site, I had no idea how to go about it. So I just gave the order, "Put up the tents," and the kids did it very well. They were all very experienced.

I thought that the summer in the country would be a good opportunity to learn about nature so I went on every nature walk conducted by Joey Criden. But every time Joey would point something out, one particular camper would correct him. Both Joey and I learned a great deal about flora and fauna that summer.

With my experience at Accord behind me, I was asked to be on the staff of Camp Tel Hai the next summer and the following year was sent to Green River, Ontario, to head the camp there. I found myself teaching everything from the geography of Palestine to singing. I can't sing.

In 1939, I received my college diploma and took over the local Habonim movement. Aharon Remez, the Israeli shaliach, taught scouting, which was a crucial part of the educational program. Knowing that he would not be there for long, and that I would not be there much longer either, I was anxious to find a replacement. I asked Skinny Bassis, who was in the Boy Scouts and not in Habonim. He agreed, and became so involved that he married a Duluth Habonim girl and wound up at Moshav Bet Herut.

I received a predoctoral research fellowship, which I spent at the University of Chicago. I lived in a swank dorm and looked after the movement at the same time. At one time, I remember, a visiting shaliach, Yosef Israeli, came and spoke to us about Palestine's urgent need for farmers. He opposed higher education, arguing that agricultural training was the most important type of education. And here I was, an academician, running the movement. In the end, events would change his mind. But that gets ahead of our story.

I was teaching at Cornell University when World War II broke out. I was called to Washington to serve as a consultant to the secretary of war. I studied morale problems in the U.S. Army. I spent the war years commuting between Washington and the Cornell campus. In 1943, I married Ruth.

After the war, Ruth and I decided we wanted to go to Palestine. My hope was to be sent on a research grant, in order to solve the problem of admission to the country, which was severely restricted by the British mandatory authorities. Fortunately, I won a postdoctoral fellowship to study social change in Palestine. I was given what I think was the first temporary worker's visa issued to a Jew. The fellowship was later extended for an additional year.

Once in Palestine, I approached the Haganah in Jerusalem with the idea of studying its morale problems in the city. Nobody understood what I was talking about, but I managed to establish a volunteer unit under the aegis of the local Haganah leadership. I proposed for our first project to study the underground radio, to try to determine what people wanted to hear.

When the War of Independence broke out, the volunteer unit became a formal part of the army. I was given the rank of major and conducted morale studies in all the uniformed branches of the armed services. During the siege of Jerusalem, morale was very high. No problems there. But I did establish a clinical counseling service for the fighters, which eventually became a permanent part of Hadassah Hospital.

During the first truce in 1948, Ruth and I attended a Genetics Congress in Sweden. When we returned, I learned that the head of the Education Division of the General Staff had discovered our Jerusalem research unit, the only such unit in the country. He ordered it to be disbanded. I vowed that this would not come to pass. I knew that my old friend Yosef Israeli, the shaliach who disapproved of higher education, was now serving as director-general of the Ministry of Defense. I arranged a meeting with him at his offices in Tel Aviv.

My driver and I left Jerusalem on the Burma Road, the winding, precarious goat track carved out of the Jerusalem hills by the American Colonel David "Mickey" Marcus, to bypass the Arab blockade on the main Jerusalem highway. When I finally arrived at defense headquarters in Tel Aviv, the door to Yosef's office was closed. I waited a long time before I knocked. When I did, he answered and scolded me for being late. Then he told me to wash my face as dust from the Burma Road was all over it.

After I explained my problem, Yosef introduced me to Isser Harel, head of the secret security services. He was sympathetic and took me to Ya'akov Dori, the chief of staff. Dori decided that from then on, the research unit would be attached directly to the General Staff and not to the Education Division. We were moved to Jaffa and I became the first chief psychologist of the Israel Defense Force. Eventually our unit was demobilized and assigned to the prime minister's office. The unit was now given the name Israel Institute for Applied Social Research. And it might have never come to pass without the aid of a man who said he was opposed to higher education.

12

In the American Jewish Community

The Movement as Leadership Training Ground

Yonaton Shultz

Los Angeles 1988

During a typical workweek at the Jewish Federation-Council building in Los Angeles, I naturally run into any number of active leaders in Southern California's organized Jewish community. One week not long ago, I decided to keep track of the Habonim graduates I met. They included the executive director of the Jewish Vocational Service, the head of one of the area's largest Jewish nursery schools, two Hebrew school directors, a senior consultant to the Bureau of Jewish Education, and the L.A. Federation representative in Jerusalem.

There may have been more—I didn't stop to frisk passersby. Many of the ones I met are acquainted with each other, but some are not. Most did not grow up in the same city.

What they all shared was a background growing up in Habonim, and a deep current involvement in the Jewish community, whether in lay or professional capacities.

Together with many of my friends from Habonim days, I have often pondered the impact that our movement experience has had on our lives. And while I struggle with the *content* of that experience—the values of the Labor Zionist ideology, much of which still seems valid and important—my thoughts keep coming back to the *vehicles* of movement education, and most of all to the experience of learning to live and function in a group of friends, to the Habonim peer-group framework. To *chevrah*.

Even today, most of my own social life is still based around the *chevrah* of people I grew up with in Habonim. Our ties have endured because we spent our important adolescence together. What can compete with eight or ten summers of living together, or with that Workshop year away from home for the first time?

In Habonim, we came to know people so deeply that other friendships have sometimes paled by comparison. Friendships from school seemed superficial: How could sitting side-by-side in a classroom compare with the experience of sitting around the campfire and schmoozing late at night, or preparing educational programs we were sure would change the world, or slogging through a patch of bananas together on a hot morning in the Galilee?

The depth of human relations nurtured through the movement experience hit me with full force only about a decade ago, when my wife Janet became sick. Shortly after the diagnosis, we became involved in a support group for cancer patients and their families. Many of the participants spoke of friends who had abandoned them once cancer was diagnosed. We were shocked. Nothing of the sort had happened to us. Our chaverim from Habonim were always there for us. They gave us more than "how are you?"—they showed a willingness to get involved, to share the horror we were going through, to accept us even with cancer. If anything, some of our friendships became stronger. Our chevrah seemed to feel that they needed to make contact, even if we had grown apart over the years. Word of our trouble seemed to spread through a network of Habonim people, and they converged.

When we heard from our fellow members in the family therapy group how cancer could lead to a loss of friendships, we were first shocked, then incredulous—and only then did we come to learn how Habonim continued to affect our lives.

Our movement experience is more than lifelong friendships, however. The values we were exposed to were ones we adopted and firmly believed in. Few words came up in our discussions more frequently than "commitment." The word meant to us the need to believe in something outside ourselves: to accept ideals, identify with them, and act on them.

The core of our beliefs was the classic Labor Zionist concept of *hagshama atzmit,* or self-fulfillment, which never meant that we must fulfill our own whims, as the sixties youth culture had it, but rather that *we ourselves were responsible for fulfilling our beliefs.* We learned that we were accountable, and could not simply fall into life's easy paths. Some of us took this thought to the conclusion offered by the movement, and settled on kibbutz. Others did not, and those who think about it usually suppose that these are the "Habonim dropouts," the ones who did not follow through on "self-fulfillment."

But a look at the Jewish community around North America shows how untrue this is. At nearly every level of leadership in the organized Jewish community one finds large numbers—phenomenal numbers, considering the movement's tiny size—of former Habonim members. Acting on the beliefs learned in Habonim, we have moved into careers in education and the rabbinate, in Jewish community work, labor organizing, and even politics. Scratch the surface of any sizable Jewish community in the United States and Canada and you will find our graduates acting out their movement ideals in adult roles.

Even in these careers, we often find that our approach is different from that of our colleagues. At times we sow confusion because of our unique vision. Our expectations of ourselves and of others are different from those of the typical American Jew. Our insistence on fairness in programs and equality in the workplace can be disruptive, even vaguely suspicious to our fellow workers. And yet we do insist—on fairness, on equality, on applying in practice the Labor Zionist idea of democracy in Jewish life. We have carried into the daily life of organized Jewry the ideals that we absorbed and discussed in the youth movement. The world of the executive washroom, of insider-trading, and looking out for "Number One," is totally alien to our movement approach.

One of the key vehicles through which we grappled our way to fleshing out the idea of equality was the summer camp principle of *kupah*. Beginning with the requirement that ten-year-olds share their candy—and decide its distribution democratically—we graduated to the idea that every movement related expense had to be shared. Whether it was a regional seminar with one price for all participants that covered everyone's transportation costs, or a shared college apartment that pooled everyone's resources and covered everyone's needs, the movement taught us to take for granted a concept that is still alien in America: from each according to his ability, to each according to his need. For us, this was no longer radical social theory, it was common decency.

My mother likes to recall an incident that occurred during my first summer at Habonim camp, where she was the camp nurse. It was her custom, after taking a sick child to the doctor in town, to stop off for a chocolate malt. One day, she took me to the doctor, and on the way back we stopped at the malt shop. Looking up at her, a ten-year-old child three weeks into his first summer at camp, I told her I couldn't accept the malt. "It's not *kupah*," I said, or so she recalls. The message of Habonim, it seems, had come through loud and clear, even to a new camper with an incipient addiction to chocolate malts.

Of course there were times when we got carried away with our ideas. I'll never forget the summer of 1960 at Camp Naame in Saugus, when the staff decided it was not in the spirit of kupah to keep extra food around for snacks after the kids were put to bed. Unfortunately, we were staying up late to plan the next day's activities, and we were hungry. In the end, we voted to allow ourselves coffee and tea—to stay awake—and bread with mustard and relish. This seemed fair, since bread was readily available to any camper who was hungry. Why the mustard and relish, I'll never know, other than the fact that no sane person would ever think of that combination. It must have struck us as the only ideologically acceptable mix that nobody in his right mind could argue with.

It was equality we were struggling with, constantly, and our leaders were no more equal than anyone else. In fact, being a madrich did not confer extra privileges. To the contrary, leadership only added responsibility for the fulfillment of equality and fairness. It meant denying ourselves extra food privileges at meals. More painfully, it meant that we ate last in the dining room. And late at night, it meant mustard sandwiches.

Of course, it was never far from our minds that all these value struggles gained their meaning from their role in preparing us to deal with the most important task conferred on Jewish youth in two thousand years—establishing and building up the Jewish state. We were the first generation in two millennia that had the privilege of planning the Jewish people's future in its own state—the first with the freedom to argue about what kind of Jewish society we wanted. That knowledge, the daily consciousness of our mission in Jewish history, informed and underlay all our discussions of Zionism, commitment, kupah—and mustard sandwiches.

That vision of Jewish life set the tone for our involvement in Jewish communal life. Movement concepts of commitment and equality required that every chaver get involved personally. It was never enough to see a problem and complain. The movement demanded that we get off the sidelines and join the fray.

Today, around the country, that means running government programs to distribute surplus food, leading national and local Soviet Jewry organizations, heading a nursery school. It means working at low pay as a union organizer, editing journals and newspapers, serving the Jewish community's governing institutions as both leaders and gadflies, and creating new systems to strengthen the democracy and Jewishness of American Jewish life.

In training us for leadership and then demanding that we serve, the movement handed us a powerful tool. For me, after serving as a madrich for six or seven years, student teaching was a breeze. My supervising teacher never understood why I was not the least bit intimidated by the high school seniors in the Government class assigned to me. But after working with a kvutza of fourteen-year-olds, my first year as a madrich—at age fifteen—high school seniors were a cinch. Planning lessons for a twelfth-grade Government class was not much different from a movement *sichah*. And explaining Congress and the presidency was certainly easier than transmitting Borochov to a group of restless madrich-trainees on a sunny Sunday afternoon.

For those hundreds of Habonim graduates working in the Jewish community today, our movement experience trained us well. In the movement we learned about involving and motivating. We learned group work techniques as part of daily life in the movement. We learned how to get across an idea, how to argue logically and accept a democratic defeat. We learned how to work with others to plan an activity and implement an idea. We knew the meaning of teamwork long before the Japanese brought it back to U.S. manufacturing. We learned how to take a stand, how to support ideas with action, and how to find common ground—through compromise with trusted allies—in order to advance a larger goal.

The Movement as "Guilt-Producing Parent"

Martin and Ethel Taft
Los Angeles 1988

In 1951, Habonim brought us together. By 1956, we were married and living in a suburb of Los Angeles, far from the kind of life we had envisioned when we met. Our intense involvement with Habonim was a thing of the past.

Of the past, and yet not so. Consider some highlights from our life since then:

The Bamidbar Branch of the Poale Zion-Labor Zionist Organization of America created a cultural oasis in an otherwise non-Jewish wasteland in the far suburbs of Los Angeles. Its development was the result of the efforts we put forth together with various Jewish chicken farmers and other like spirits who somehow had wandered into the desert east of the city.

The Torah Day School of Alhambra, California, though it lasted only three years, represented a prodigious effort to bring intensive, quality Jewish education to the San Gabriel Valley from 1961 to 1964.

The alienation and frustrations engendered by our participation in the local temple accelerated our identification and involvement in the Los Angeles chapters of Poale Zion and the American Habonim Association, a group of "Habonim alumni" formed in the 1960s that later merged into the Labor Zionist Alliance. From the outset we were and are still viewed as part of the *yungvarg,* the Young Turks of the movement. Increasingly over the years, we both have assumed various leadership roles in all areas of what has become the Labor Zionist Alliance, including the presidency of the Los Angeles City Committee.

In his professional life, Marty has been a mechanical engineer and university professor. In 1968 he founded a corporation called Socio-Economic Systems, a firm dedicated to solving problems of systems in which people problems are more important than those of machinery. When environmental legislation was passed in California, Marty founded and was president of the first branch of the Association of Environmental Professionals.

Ettie, trained as a social worker, quickly found a place for herself in service to the Jewish community. As she moved up through the ranks from case worker into management, she became increasingly involved in the development of a local association of professionals in Jewish community service. Parallel to that, on a continental level, she was drawn into the work of the Conference of Jewish Communal Service, eventually serving as its president from 1986 to 1988. As associate executive director of the Jewish Family Service of Los Angeles, Ettie was in the forefront of developing innovative programs to serve such diverse populations as refugees and the homeless.

In recent years, Marty's skills as a consultant to governmental and nonprofit agencies have been enlisted in a variety of volunteer activities within the Jewish Federation-Council of Los Angeles. He serves on the federation's board of directors, and has been involved in the work of various committees. Most recently, as the federation began to allocate some resources to the promotion of aliyah, Marty helped to develop an information management system for the Aliyah Demonstration Project, as the federation program is known. He also heads the aliyah project's employment committee. Ettie, for her part, was instrumental in the development of creative counseling services to potential *olim,* adding her own vital dimension to the project.

One might well expect that the foregoing range of activities would be deeply stimulating and satisfying, as indeed they are. Yet we both still feel a gnawing feeling that something vital is missing. Our experiences in Habonim during our adolescence undoubtedly influenced our adult lives. What were these influences?

Initiative: If it needs doing, do it. Obstacles are merely challenges to one's ingenuity and perseverance. Never let others do for you what you can do for yourself.

Individuality: Be yourself. Take a position and be willing to defend it. Plan carefully and implement your ideas. Do all of this within the framework of a cooperative life-style.

Interdependence: Group decision making by consensus with respect for individual feelings.

Concern for the survival of the Jewish people: Labor Zionism and secular Judaism provided the ideological framework that would ensure continuity.

Self-fulfillment *(hagshama atzmit):* The focus of most of the activities of Habonim and the highest ideal was to achieve "nirvana" by going on aliyah to a kibbutz. Anything less than that was seen as seriously compromising one's ideals and forsaking the movement.

All the above was powerful stuff, and tended to attract young people who were inclined to be intellectual, introspective, and sensitive to the human condition. Though all were impacted by the teachings of Habonim, most did not take it to its final step, namely aliyah to a kibbutz. There were those who stayed behind and played out their disappointment in not fulfilling the goal of aliyah by pursuing passivity vis-à-vis the Jewish people.

Others who remained in North America became Jewish community activists to varying degrees and in a variety of professional and voluntary arenas. For some, the path they followed also included continued interest and support of Habonim and the assumption of leadership roles in the Labor Zionist movement.

Earlier, the observation was made that in spite of the intensity of our involvement in Jewish and Zionist endeavors, there still remained the disquieting feeling that we had yet to meet the ultimate test. Habonim, the guilt-producing parent, had done its work well. Today, even as we plan our aliyah, we recognize that we owe that parent a debt of gratitude for the rich and challenging life we continue to traverse together.

Part V

13

Retrospective Views of the Habonim Experience

Of Jubilees and Jewels: Habonim Across the Decades

Daniel Mann

Washington 1985

The year 1985 marked the fiftieth anniversary of the North American founding of Habonim, the pioneering Labor Zionist youth movement. Of all anniversaries in Jewish life, the fiftieth holds the greatest symbolic import: in Hebrew it is called *yovel,* from which comes the English word "jubilee." As the book of Leviticus reminds us, the fiftieth-year jubilee is the time to "proclaim liberty throughout the land."

Nineteen thirty-five—the year North American Habonim was born—was hardly a vintage year for proclaiming liberty. That was the year Italy invaded Ethiopia and the Nazis promulgated the Nuremberg Laws. In the United States, despite the initial success of Roosevelt's New Deal, it was still a time of depression and isolationism. It was a different world, remote from the one we know today.

The world in 1935 was still innocent of the German reentry to the Rhineland, the Spanish Civil War, Stalin's purges, the annexation of Austria, Kristallnacht, Munich, Pearl Harbor. In Palestine in 1935, the unforeseeable future still shrouded the 1936 Arab uprising, the 1937 partition proposal of the Peel Commission, and the 1939 White Paper.

In American and world Jewish life the mid-1930s saw the establishment of both the Jewish Labor Committee and the World Jewish Congress (as well as the *Jewish Frontier*), and we were still several long years away from the birth of the United Jewish Appeal.

Fifty years may be just one percent in the long sweep of Jewish history, but how remote and far away 1935 now seems! So many forces and events have convulsed the world since then that the intervening years are often

334 Builders and Dreamers

described in metaphors drawn from the upheavals of nature: a half-century of human earthquakes and volcanic eruptions, of sea changes in Jewish life and rivers of blood and tears, and also of new stars shining in the heavens; fifty years of Zionist revolution stretching from the desperate, early days of Youth Aliyah, through the massive rescue of displaced and oppressed persons, to the reawakening of Soviet Jewry and the current redemption of the Jews of Ethiopia—that same Ethiopia that Mussolini invaded a long half-century ago.

What can this half-century mean to the young Habonim member of today? It is now two decades since the Six-Day War, which means that a Habonim member, even a leader or graduate in his or her early twenties, has no personal recollection even of that traumatic, historic watershed, and barely remembers the Yom Kippur War, Arafat at the United Nations, the Zionism/Racism resolution, or the Jackson-Vanik Amendment.

That is what makes the founding of Habonim so startling, for what comes through the record of those days is something remarkably modern and current. It grew out of a Labor Zionist movement that was committed to concepts and life-styles transplanted from Eastern Europe, or adapted from pioneering Palestine—Yiddish, socialism, secularism, labor. Yet in creating Habonim, that movement declared its understanding of the fact that *America was different*—that the young American Jew, though still in the first or second immigrant generation, was already a different breed from his or her European counterparts. Labor Zionist leaders perceived a land unprecedented in Jewish history because of its unique and mutually reinforcing system of constitutional liberties, pluralism, open frontiers, and middle-class values. They came to terms with a nation which preferred pragmatic idealism to political ideologies, and a generation of young Jews communicating in what was (at least then) a very non-Jewish language, American English.

(It should be noted that Canada, an integral part of North American Habonim, was usually "one generation behind" and always contributed its own flavor, but in a larger sense what is being said here about the United States pertains to Canada as well.)

The burning issue in 1935 at the founding convention of Habonim, and at the Poale Zion central committee, was something called "autonomy": restructuring the organizational relationships between the adult Labor Zionist movement and its own youth organization. But the real question was autonomy for what purpose? And the answer was more education and less indoctrination, more Hebrew and also more English, and—above all—more emphasis on *chalutzic aliyah,* or pioneering immigration to the land of Israel. The change of emphasis was not 180 degrees, but the shifting priorities of American Labor Zionist youth activities were significant enough to warrant the establishment of a new, "autonomous" youth movement called Habonim.

Listen to a voice from those days:

Many of us were born in the United States. Some came to the country as young children. Our schooling, our style of life, our thoughts were molded by the country we lived in. We loved this country with its sense of human dignity and freedom, its pioneers, and its absorption of the downtrodden and poverty-stricken millions of human beings who flocked to its shores. We were overwhelmed by its vastness, its mountains and plains, its lakes, rivers, and oceans. There were before us the grandeur of the West, the charm of the South, the beauty of the Appalachians, the awe of Niagara, the breadth of the Hudson. We were conscious of the stirrings of new forces in American literature, art and music. The life of America was our life: the jazz, the night club in Harlem, the new forms of the dance, the new theater, the politics of the country, the stirrings of the vast labor masses—all this was part and parcel of our day-by-day living. . . .

Zionist, Poale Zionist, consciousness grew out of this strange soil, and at times against the wishes of the parents who were aghast at their children's "peculiarities." Why dream of the liberation of the Jews? How about other peoples enslaved by cruel despotic governments? Why far away Eretz Yisrael? There was a working class to be helped in the United States. There were problems to be solved here: tender children working beyond their strength, exploited by those intent on profits; there was a large mass of workers with no job security. Why Eretz Yisrael? There are two million Jews in New York City alone. Much must be done for them, to hold them to some kind of Judaism, to teach their children about their glorious heritage. Why not work here at home?

With a few minor changes of wording and emphasis, those paragraphs might have been written today. But in fact they were written by Sophie Udin in 1957 for *Adventures in Pioneering,* the book about Habonim camping edited by David Breslau, and the period they described was the early 1930s, over fifty years ago.

Or consider some instructions given to a group of *shlichim* (Israeli emissaries) coming to the United States to do educational work with Habonim:

You are going forth, not only to bring *chalutzim* to Israel. You must remember that our lives in the Homeland are pieces in the mosaic of experiment, of cultures, of experience and longings. Try to bring out that which is distinctive in American Jewish youth; and together with them, you will build the framework for a pioneering Jewish youth.

Could not those instructions be given to *shlichim* coming to America today? But in fact those were the words of Berl Katzenelson, the mentor of the labor movement in prestate Palestine, to the first major delegation of *shlichim* going to America in 1939, as recalled by Yosef Israeli in *Arise and Build* (also edited by the indefatigable David Breslau).

So we celebrate a very contemporary event this year in noting the founding of Habonim in 1935. To summarize what has been accomplished in the ensuing years one could concentrate on the movement's institutional achievements: Camp Kvutza, which actually predates Habonim; the Youth Workshop in Israel, itself approaching thirty-five years; perhaps the publications and other projects and activities. But the quintessential Habonim experience was—and still is—very personal.

* * *

The establishment of Habonim in 1935 and its activity since then constituted a kind of civil disobedience within Labor Zionism, with inevitable friction between the youth and the "seniors." The friction continued even when *we* became the seniors, started acting like a Habonim PTA, and then institutionalized our relationship as Habonim "alumni." Yet the linkage was really symbiotic and sympathetic, as evidenced by all those "seniors" in Poale Zion and Farband who were and are part of Habonim history. Most notable is the strong connection of women, leaders of Pioneer Women in particular and Labor Zionist women in general, whose role in the development of Habonim was not that of stereotypical Jewish mothers but rather of supportive, caring partners.

What marked Habonim's relationship to society, though, was not so much civil disobedience as constructive activism, whether in the heady days of its founding and the related mergers with Young Poale Zion and Gordonia in the 1930s or in the central role played by Habonim in the "illegal" immigration of the 1940s. And some of the more recent chapters are equally significant. In 1958 Habonim was the only Jewish youth organization to participate in the "Youth March for Integrated Schools" in Washington, only a few years after the historic Supreme Court decision. In the late sixties and early seventies Habonim played a leading, at time dominant role in the coalition of Jewish youth and students demanding more Jewishness in the institutions of American Jewish life, and agitating for more democracy and more decisiveness in the Zionist movement.

The inevitable reaction to this kind of recital is: Where are the graduates today? First and foremost, they are in Israel—some two thousand of them, in *kibbutzim, moshavim,* cities, in every field of endeavor, trying to live the "normal Jewish lives" that Zionism promised while contributing to the development of a unique nation and society. One of their most noteworthy achievements has been in the area of Israel–diaspora relations, from the founding of the Association of Americans and Canadians in Israel in the 1950s to the establishment of the American high school program at Kfar Blum in the 1960s and the more recent linkages of the kibbutz movement with so many of the major movements in North American and world Jewish life.

And what of those Habonim graduates who did not (yet) get to Israel?

What many of us recall from our Habonim experience is that it was characterized, indeed pervaded, by a high degree of individualism and pluralism. Unlike almost all of the other so-called *chalutz* movements, that special genre of Jewish youth organization dedicated to persuading and preparing its members to live as pioneers in the *kibbutzim* of Israel, North American Habonim refused to move its members toward that goal through arbitrary demands, collective discipline, or ideological dogmatism. Thus it was possible for Habonim to produce an *aliyah* high in both quantity and quality without alienating those of its graduates still living in the diaspora.

This, however, does not mean that we who stayed behind are totally comfortable where we are. The fundamental Zionist idea encapsulated in the first line of the 1968 Jerusalem Program—"the unity of the Jewish people

and the centrality of Israel in Jewish life"—is something we not only understand in our heads but feel in our hearts and our bones. The remarkable
result of our having experienced ideological direction while expressing our
individual predilections through Habonim is a level of participation in Jewish
life far beyond what might have been expected from a movement whose
membership never exceeded four thousand, even at its peak in the late 1940s.

The record of the North American Jewish community over fifty years
reveals significant cadres of Habonim graduates among its volunteer and
professional leaders, its rabbis and its educators, its writers and its editors—
none of them completely at ease in the diaspora but for that very reason
contributing creatively to its continuity. The Labor Zionist organizations—
Pioneer Women and the Labor Zionist Alliance—have been the most visible
beneficiaries. But Habonim graduates are truly everywhere in the front
ranks of North American Jewish life, in such numbers as to suggest an elite
academy for grooming of Jewish leadership—which would not be far from
the truth.

There is one more set of values which we got out of Habonim that is
especially timely. It is our more serious variation on all those one-liners
about "never having to say 'I'm sorry.'" For ultimately what we learned in
Habonim was *Labor Zionism*. Today a Labor Zionist is someone who never
feels the need to apologize for or equivocate about being totally committed
to strengthening Israel and the Jewish people while at the same time being
equally and totally committed to building a better America and a better
world—and who sees those commitments as compatible, complementary,
and mutually reinforcing. How to reconcile those values with the personal
sense of unease mentioned earlier is a relentless challenge, but it is a tribute
to Habonim that so many graduates are able to cope with these disparate
truths in ways that are both publicly constructive and personally gratifying.

* * *

Anniversaries are often spoken of in jeweler's terms: silver, golden, diamond. On this fiftieth-year jubilee, let it be said that *Habonim itself is the
jewel:* the most meaningful instrumentality of North American Labor Zionism in the fullfilment of the cardinal Zionist imperatives of education and
aliyah; the most significant contribution by North American Labor Zionism
to Israel; and the most effective guarantor of our own future as a Labor
Zionist movement in North America.

For fifty years we have been blessed by our personal involvement in and
with Habonim, as members, leaders, graduates, parents, spouses, support-
ers, advisors, and friends—sometimes all of the above. May we be doubly
blessed as we renew and enhance those roles in the years to come.

For Israel Has Not Been Forsaken

Yair Pischi
Kibbutz Yifat 1985

Ten years have passed since I finished my service as shaliach to Habonim in Los Angeles, and it still requires no effort to recall the pictures in my mind's eyes. I can still see Gilboa, the Habonim summer camp in Idyllwild, California. Sabbath is approaching and all the campers, after fooling around for the entire week, have gathered in the "Shabbat Valley," scrubbed and groomed, wearing their Sabbath clothes. They clasp their hands behind their backs and gaze skyward while the sun sets below the treetops. They sing the Bialik hymn welcoming the Sabbath Queen.

I shall never forget the talk I had with the driver of the yellow bus that took the children to a winter weekend at Camp Gilboa. He stayed with us there and watched the rehearsals for the Neshef, the elaborate yearly pageant for which Los Angeles Habonim was famous. He watched us practice the songs and dances and play games between the rehearsals. In short, he saw the Habonim spirit. He told me, "In all my life, I have never seen such happy children." I truly think that camp drew these children closer to Israel, no less than the school, synagogue, or home.

Before I started my *shlichut,* I apprehensively asked my predecessor to tell me about American youth. He tried to comfort me, saying, "They are crazy but nice." And that is how they were. They were full of ideas and creativity. For every subject—Tisha B'Av, Soviet Jewry, everything—they found an educational way to present it to the younger members. For example, in the camp dining room they designated a Hebrew table. Those who dared to eat at that table could speak only Hebrew, even if they were just asking for seconds.

I fondly remember a *rosh machaneh* (camp director) who once had a discussion with the staff before the camp season began. He asked, "What type of program should we prepare—education or amusement? Choose between the two."

I was astounded by the very question. They, however, jumped right on it and an intense argument broke out. In the end, he said that he thought the program, however educational it might be, had to be so enjoyable that the children would want to come back again and again. With this spirit we could build the movement.

I would stand moved every time camp ended, watching the farewell hugs and the tears—tears that made Zionism more than speeches and trumpets, tears that made Zionism a personal experience and contact. The stories, songs, and dances did their work. When camp ended and we had to dismantle the animal farm, the children refused to let the calf and chickens they had fed all summer be slaughtered for meat. I had to return them alive.

I remember the first time I watched a Workshop leave for Israel. The Yom Kippur War was over but there was still firing along the Syrian border. The Workshop would be at Kibbutz Ma'ayan Baruch in the northeast Galilee, close to the line of fire. I traveled with the group to the airport and watched the parents sending their children off. It reminded me of how it is when soldiers join the army.

Before I came to America, I had met a few young Americans on my own kibbutz, Yifat. They were volunteers or students in the ulpan Hebrew work-study program. They were never with their parents, always alone. And now, here I was in America, meeting their parents. Suddenly, it was hard for me to tell young people to come to Israel, knowing the first thing they would have to do is join the army. But not to tell them would be impossible.

"You have come to break up the family," an old Jew told me once, when I visited him in his penthouse. I knew he had a point. So I had to be sure, truly sure, that bringing these young people to Israel was really necessary.

On the other hand, at the bar mitzvah ceremony of one of the members, the sexton at the synagogue said to me: "I think the distribution is fair. The Israelis give the blood and we give the money." I asked him if he would be willing to switch roles for a year or two.

Sometimes I would wonder: if the parents of Habonim members were so frightened that their children might move to Israel, why would they drive their children across town, time after time, so they could take part in an activity? Maybe, deep down, they wanted a representative in the Promised Land, they wanted part of a dream they didn't realize themselves.

One year, wandering around Los Angeles during the Succot holiday, I saw a succah. Since no one was there and I have never lacked chutzpah, I walked in. I saw a New Year's card from Israel. Handwritten on it were the words, "Let our sons return to their homeland." It was a heart-rending cry, full of longing to return home.

I remember a Jewish doctor who came to me during the difficult days of the Yom Kippur War. He asked that I send his son to Israel, even though the boy was only sixteen years old. He wanted his son to feel the link.

But you must believe and continue to believe. One Habonim madrich told me, "I am already very tired of organizing groups. I don't feel like leading any longer. But if you ask me. . . ." And I did ask him, because to do nothing is to be an American. To be Jewish, you must care.

"I don't know which I am, an American or an Israeli," one Habonim member told me. "But first of all, I am a Jew." Two black girls once stopped a well suntanned member of Habonim and asked her if she was white or Mexican. She answered that she was Jewish. "That's worse still," they replied.

I met many Jews in America who were proud of their Jewishness. One told me that he always wore his Star of David on the outside, and did not hide it under his shirt. A Jewish horse-breeder named his fastest horse "Vaz-zatah." One woman taught her parrot to say, "Give me a kiss," in Hebrew. A Jewish doctor never forgot to send New Year's wishes from Tal, his dog.

I once showed slides to an elderly group of Labor Zionists. They had come to America at the same time my parents went to Palestine. Whenever they could, they sent money to Israel or financed Habonim projects. One old chavera told me: "My family in Israel wants me to give *them* the money. But I contribute it to the country. That is more important."

Even in big, rich America there are financial problems for Zionist youth movements. We did not have our own meeting hall for evening activities. We had access to rooms in the Labor Zionist community center, but not our own space. The Labor Zionist movement had a large Yiddish library, but no permanent meeting center for Habonim. So we often met on Friday evenings in the apartment where some of the *ma'apilim* lived together.

As it happened, the ma'apilim had a Jewish neighbor upstairs who loved his quiet and peace. When the members began to sing, he would call the police. In the middle of the Habonim Sabbath festivities, a policeman would come, look around, and see that it was not what he had expected. He would leave, only to return a half-hour later, apologize and listen for a while. In this way, the upstairs neighbor fought for his rest, and the policeman learned to hum several Jewish songs.

"I remember thee, Zion." Ten years have passed and each day I go to the mailbox to take out the newspaper and letters and climb the hill back to my home. Sometimes, among the letters is an invitation to attend the wedding of a former Habonim member who is now making a new home on a kibbutz in the Negev or the Galilee. They invite us to share in their joy. It is a kind of joy beyond description, a proof to all those doubters and mockers, that, after all, it was worth the effort. Jewry still has some strength.

Growing Up in a Labor Zionist Home, the 1940s

Dvora Berkenblit Hartzook
Jerusalem 1985

I was born into Labor Zionism. My parents, Feigele and Yisrael Berkenblit, were dedicated Labor Zionist idealists from the moment they stepped on American soil as Russian immigrants in 1914. In 1925, my mother went to Palestine, where she worked in the Free Nursery in Jerusalem with Rachel Yanait Ben-Zvi, the revered pioneer-authoress and wife of Israel's second president. Only illness forced her back to America.

It was not easy being born into Labor Zionism. My mother was away for months at a time as national field organizer for Pioneer Women. My father, an agent for the Metropolitan Life Insurance Company, spent several nights a week at meetings of the executive board of the Farband-Jewish National Workers Alliance or at our local Labor Zionist center. My parents were always attending meetings, celebrations, and conventions, and as children my brother Yehiel and I were always taken along. People were always staying at our house in Crown Heights as well. More than once I had to give up my bed to a dear comrade from Philadelphia or wherever.

We spent our summers at Unser Camp and Kindervelt, the Farband summer camps in Highland Mills, New York. These retreats—one for adults, one for children—were the center of the entire movement from the 1920s to the 1960s. Abba Eban, Golda Meir, Louis Segal, Hayim Greenberg, and many other leading lights of Zionist labor passed through.

My earliest recollections of Habonim take me back to Utica Avenue in Brooklyn, where the Crown Heights chapter was founded. My father had helped establish a Labor Zionist center in an abandoned Chinese restaurant. He spent day and night renovating the place. In the afternoons I studied Hebrew and Yiddish there. Habonim meetings were held every Friday night. Artie Gorenstein was our leader. David Breslau and Murray Weingarten, from the national office, visited regularly. Saadia Gelb was the movement's spiritual leader.

When the Crown Heights branch began to lose members, I joined the Flatbush group and was reunited with many of the friends I had made at Kindervelt. In addition to the discussions, the singing, and the dancing, we collected money for the Jewish National Fund and were activists in every way possible. I remember the thrill I felt as stood in front of the entrance to the IRT subway soliciting funds for the JNF with my collection box getting heavier and heavier with nickels and dimes.

Perhaps my most unforgettable summer was at Habonim Camp Kvutza at Killingworth, Connecticut, in 1945. I was fifteen. There I met Matya Korastoff Shuval, who later became my dearest friend in Israel. Rose and Dave Breslau, Artie Gorenstein, and Murray Weingarten were all there. We lived in tents, tried to speak only Hebrew, and stood watch at night. The menu consisted of radishes, peanut butter, and radishes.

When I was eighteen, I began to travel on the IRT subway between Brooklyn and Manhattan to my new job with the National Committee for Labor Israel. Its offices were one floor above those of the Labor Zionist Organization of America. After a full day at work, I would volunteer my services there, sending out mailings and organizing rallies. The great rally at Madison Square Garden, where David Ben-Gurion and Stephen S. Wise spoke, is still etched in my memory.

My younger brother Yehiel was the first member of our family to reach Israel. He left with Garin Bet in 1950. He trained at Kibbutz Ramat Yochanan and was a member of Kibbutz Hamadia for five years. When he left kibbutz he went to Tel Aviv, where he married a sabra and raised three sabra children and two sabra dogs. For three decades he has served as chief bursar at El Al airlines.

When I made aliyah with my parents the following year, the entire Labor

Zionist movement bid us farewell at a special gathering in the Grand Ball-room of the old Capitol Hotel in Manhattan. For many of the fifteen hundred people who attended, it was a way to identify themselves with Labor Zionist ideals. We were a family fulfilling the movement's highest goal: settling in Israel.

In 1952 I married Abraham Hartzook, and the following year we moved to Yavne, near Rehovot. My husband is a research agronomist working for the Volcani Institute for Agricultural Research. In 1979, we were in Zambia, where he conducted research on behalf of the Food and Agricultural Organi-zation of the United Nations. It was not the first time we had been sent abroad. In the early 1960s, we lived in Tanganyika, where Abraham also conducted research.

Professionally, I have taught English for the past thirty years. I did not pursue university studies until I was a mother of three small children. I have taught English to children and adults of all ages.

For me, Labor Zionism means being deeply rooted in Israel, where my children and my grandchildren live. It is the quiet self-dignity of being proud Jews in a Jewish homeland, leading a wholesome and creative life and re-building a strong Israel.

I Never Left Habonim

Pinchas Rimon

Kibbutz Kfar Blum 1985

I never left Habonim. What I have been doing all my life and am still doing today reflect my youth background. Many Habonim alumni can make this same statement, though they live in other countries, are of different generations, and engage in diverse professions. When alumni meet, they may express a variety of opinions on current issues, but will find there is little disagreement about the basics. The tenets of Habonim, never learned as a catechism, are part of a larger philosophy expressed in daily activities and by examples of shlichim and movement leaders. The principles are meant to be lived by.

For fifty years, Habonim has emphasized the unity of the Jewish people and the centrality of Israel in Jewish life. It has expressed a nondoctrinaire, pluralistic approach to Judaism, a commitment to morality, social justice, and democracy, a devotion to Jewish education and Jewish continuity. Most important, Habonim has always demanded direct personal participation to achieve goals and abjures mere talk and empty phrases.

It is no surprise, then, that our Habonim people in Israel, beginning with the earliest olim, volunteered for the Palmach, worked in Aliyah Bet, and served in youth movements as shlichim. In the kibbutz movement, they led in the fight to "liberalize" child rearing: the move to have children sleep at home with their parents. Both in and out of the kibbutz, they have attempted to find a common meeting ground for traditional and secular Judaism. Preserving the link between Jews in Israel and in America is an important Habonim precept. In consonance with that principle, our alumni have been founders and officers of organizations and programs serving as a bridge between Israel and America, such as the Association of Americans and Canadians in Israel.

Education is probably the most widespread Habonim pursuit in Israel. There are more educators and teachers—ranging from the nursery to the university—among us than all other professionals. In America, too, we are strongly represented in the Jewish schools, in the rabbinate, and among Jewish communal workers. In a very real sense, these people have never left Habonim.

When I peruse a camp roster or a Workshop list, I often nod my head in recognition and conclude that there are "Habonim names" that go on for decades. It is apparent that Habonim institutions, such as camp and Workshop, are not only supported by former members of Habonim, but are also largely populated by their offspring. The Habonim tradition has been preserved through the generations, and parents and grandparents vicariously experience Habonim all over again.

My own experience has probably been of longer duration than that of most, but it has not been atypical. My formal departure from the movement occurred with my mobilization in World War II, but the interval between my return to the United States from military service and my departure for Palestine was marked by work on behalf of the Haganah and Aliyah Bet. That work continued even as I studied at the Technion in Haifa. Not long after settling in Kfar Blum, I was invited by the newly founded World Habonim to edit the new world movement publication. Shortly afterward, my regular work in the kibbutz machine shop was interrupted for only a couple of months when I was asked to help with a Youth Aliyah group on the kibbutz. There were further interruptions in work when I taught part-time at the Habonim Institute and in the First Workshop in Kfar Blum. I seemed to be drawn willy-nilly to educational work. The direct Habonim connection grew even stronger when I became madrich of the Third Workshop and a year and a half later, central shaliach to Habonim in North America.

When finally I became a physics teacher in the regional high school in Kfar Blum, there was no longer an obvious Habonim link. But no one so deeply involved with young people and education over so long a period could content himself with mere formal teaching. Both inside the classroom and out, the Habonim experience played its part.

Sixteen years ago, I became more directly associated with Habonim as director of the Kfar Blum American Tenth Grade Program. The Tenth Grade Program—through which almost five hundred youngsters have passed— exemplifies the continuity of Habonim, not only because the Habonim outlook is basic to the program, but because so many participants are drawn from a Habonim base. Even in the very first year, the program attracted youngsters from Habonim or appealed to parents who had once been Habonim themselves. How surprising it was to encounter a newly enrolled student whose mother had been a camper in a camp I had directed thirty years earlier. But during these many years there have been others who were members of the Habonim family, including the children of ex-Workshoppers. The Habonim generations spread out in concentric waves and I seem to have come full circle, to work once again with North American Jewish teenagers, much as I did three and four decades ago.

It is remarkable to find such continuity and devotion as one finds in the Habonim tradition over a period of fifty years. Parents have maintained that tradition and frequently have managed to transmit it to their children. The virtue of those who have grown up in Habonim is that they are blessed with a deep-rooted, pristine, naive youth-movement Zionism. In these turbulent times, they succeed in adhering to a philosophy that serves as a counterbalance to the forces which are sundering and polarizing the Jewish people and encouraging the growth of extremism in the state of Israel.

Growing Up in a Labor Zionist Home, the 1980s

Charlotte Levy
Detroit 1985

I have often described Habonim as my third parent. This statement is as much a reflection of the home where I grew up as of my movement experience. My family had a profound effect on my educational and intellectual development. So did the movement. Each complemented the other.

Perhaps the most significant result of the Labor Zionist orientation I found at home and in the movement is a commitment to the realization of goals. The visions my brothers and sisters and I cultivated as Zionists regarding Israel and the diaspora were not detached models of an unattainable reality. Zionism was not merely a nationalist movement but a social ideal. We are committed to the implementation of that ideal.

For me, the ideal, and the values associated with that ideal, were manifested in a range of the most mundane forms—dinner-time discussions-turned-arguments, regular attendance at movement activities, particularly those held at our house instead of a meeting center, and a reputation/association with the infamous Levy clan that has followed me the world over. I am proud of that.

There are those who claim that the advocates of our ideological school of thought live in a ghetto of sorts. I claim that by virtue of our ideological convictions themselves, that could not be the case. But my contact with the nonmovement Jewish population underscores the extraordinary nature of the education I received in the movement and my home. The content of Jewish life in many American families is not of the caliber experienced by my generation. My experience both in the home and in the movement grows increasingly rare. In the lives of many of the children I lead in the movement today, Habonim-Dror is the sole source for a positive Israel-oriented experience.

Like a Walking Dream

Hank Kaplan
Portland, Oregon 1988

I grew up in the movement in the early 1970s. That was a time when self-questioning was a fad. Idealism was almost a competition: more-radical-than-thou was chic. Self-realization was what life (not just Zionism) was all about. In the movement, we were taught to equate the notion of personal fulfillment with the doctrine of self-realization for the Jewish people through building a democratic socialist homeland and all the rest of it.

Thinking about those times, it's tempting to eulogize our adolescence, but I'm not sure I'm ready yet to pronounce that person dead. Even with the passage of so much time and so many changes, I confess it's not hard to tell that I'm a product of the movement.

What are the wages of a misspent adolescence squandered on kibbutz-hopping and ideological hair-splitting? While I was struggling with the sacrifices of *kupah* at camp, my brother was out chasing girls; while I was spending my summers inculcating impressionable young minds with the virtues of socialist Zionism, my school friends were making money for wheels and college tuition.

Among Jewish youth, Habonim has interrupted more educations than teenage pregnancy, caused more lost wages than a recession. Some of us embraced the ideology with earnest fanaticism; others took to counterculture as a credo, or found in Zionism a convenient pretext for hormonal expression. The movement was supposed to educate us toward chalutzic aliyah, but looking around at a random cross-section of my old *chevrah*, an impartial observer might conclude that Habonim camps are yuppie basic training schools.

I've heard people say they later felt betrayed by the movement. Some who went to Israel were disappointed. They were led down a garden path of manifest destiny, anointed in an historic role as part of the machinery of social change, handed a rough sketch of the next social order, and sent in search of the palette that would turn the blueprint into a living utopia. And nothing happened. Or at least, nothing worth staying there for.

As for me, though, I somehow always felt I got more from Habonim than I gave. Humor and friendship are not the ends of socialist Zionism; they aren't even mentioned on the Blue Card (I wonder if it's still blue?). For so many of us, the *process* of our indoctrination made a more lasting impression than its content.

Idealism is easy to outgrow. But it's also a seductive habit for those who can still manage it. I think most of my old *chevrah* are more cynical, more jaded—and yet more idealistic than your standard, run-of-the-mill, garden-variety American Jew. If cynical idealism sounds contradictory, maybe it's explained by the fact that so many of my chevrah suffer from internal moral angst.

I've been to Israel twice since I supposedly outgrew the movement. I follow Israeli politics and read the *Jerusalem Post*. I have no intention of living there, but I'm still a half-assed Middle East junkie. The last time I went was three years ago. At the time, my colleagues wondered why an experienced, practicing attorney would take a year out of his career to go traveling and then spend five months of that sabbatical wallowing in mud and herbicides in a Middle Eastern cotton field.

Maybe it still touches my soul. Through all the alienation of work, the routine hassles of mortgage payments and parking spaces, the stockpiling of professional contacts, wardrobes, software, insurance policies, and gardening tools, there is still a piece of me that remembers a vision and a joy that lingers just beneath the psyche of so many with whom I've shared *kupah*.

When I see someone I know, whom I haven't thought of in years, when I hear a few words of idle gossip about people I have lost track of, when I see the eyes of an old chaver with whom I no longer have much to share, something old still passes between us that feels like a musty draft, but clouds the eyes like a walking dream.

"To Go Against the Stream"

William Goldfarb
Tel Aviv 1985

Long before the word "movement" was used by civil rights activists, it was used by Zionist youth. And it implied that this was not a mere social organization with superficial ties and clubbiness, but a body of people with serious ideals and with a very serious commitment to those ideals.

Putting the matter in a rather simple way, there are, in general, three possible approaches to the structure of a movement. A movement can be bland, *parve,* with a credo which is easy to accept; it asks merely for annual dues. Or it can be an elitist group—ideological, dogmatic, doctrinaire, highly-disciplined, perhaps collectivist. Or it can be neither the one nor the other.

The third course, that of being neither bland and minimalist on the one hand, nor strict and doctrinaire on the other, is the most difficult. It is the course of being neither a radical nor a conservative, but a liberal. It is the course of being neither a capitalist nor a communist, but a socialist. And, historically, these middle-of-the-road positions have always been suspect from both sides and have always had difficulty sustaining themselves.

A movement which seeks to reject both the bland and the doctrinaire seeks instead to attain freedom of action within a framework of discipline, and freedom of thought within a framework of ideology. This was the course which Habonim took, and takes, and this is its strength and its weakness.

A movement such as Habonim, educating toward this course of action and philosophy, must take a position, define that position and assert it with vigor, but, constantly, in the very act of asserting its position, the movement must recognize that there are other positions and that not every one in the movement need follow the party line. Indeed, there is no party line. For example, Habonim from the beginning stressed the centrality of aliyah, thus aligning itself with Zionist activism, and did so long before it came into vogue. It stressed aliyah both as the highest national need of the Jewish people and as the highest aspiration of the individual. It denominated aliyah as "self-realization." This is a serious and demanding ideal. One fulfils it not by speeches, not by meetings, not by resolutions, but by moving to Israel and living a Labor Zionist life.

But Habonim, from its inception, refused to say that aliyah, while it was the highest and the best, was the *only* way. The movement really does believe—clichéd and truistic as it may sound—in the Jewish people, in all of its manifestations, in all of its vocations, and in all of its locations.

In the time of the struggle for the state of Israel, the struggle against the British and against Arab terror, Habonim identified itself with those political forces in Zionism that stressed the need for physical resistance as a form of defense, the need for arms, training, attack when necessary, the use of force when necessary. But it quite profoundly and bitterly rejected the concept that only the use of force, only the use of terror, could be "the way."

In Israel from the very beginning, Habonim accorded the highest priority to agricultural settlement (because it believed that only if the land were worked by Jews would this be a Jewish land) and within the Jewish settlements, to the Labor movement settlements; and, within labor settlement, Habonim said: "the kibbutz is the highest form." But it never said "only the Labor settlement," and it never said "only the kibbutz." And the Habonim person who went on aliyah and did not go to a kibbutz or to a moshav, or having gone, did not stay, was not a failure, was not a traitor, was not a betrayer of the doctrine—because there was no doctrine. He had sought another way.

In short, this Habonim had a profile, a personality, which could be seen as a weakness because it was flexible, because it was not rigid, because it was multi-faceted. But in this free and permissive framework, Habonim also found its strength, because it was able to attract and mold people who could think independently, and who could react to situations on the basis of their individuality.

We used to stress, in a somewhat distorted English rendering, the phrase of Berl Katznelson, one of the ideologists and thinkers of the Labor Zionist movement, that we believe in "the right to be confused."

And yet the movement made demands. It did not advocate or practice the bland, superficial type of social action which characterized many of the organizations to which Jewish youth belonged in the days when Habonim was being formed. Nor did it accept a way of life based on polemics or logic-chopping. It said, and says, to its members: "If you believe, act—because the belief and the action are inseparable. Without some measure of action, the belief itself is not meaningful."

This is the hardest course for any movement to take. It is harder to educate people to go on aliyah, it is harder to educate at all—if you say in advance "this is *a* way; there are others." But there is also a great dividend to be derived from this type of education—a dividend in intellectual honesty, in breadth of character, and in breadth of outlook.

Habonim produced people, who, having the right to be confused, were not confused, and who, having the right to choose, chose. And, in so choosing, members of Habonim were very active in the middle and late forties in the activities surrounding so-called illegal immigration (Aliyah Bet) to Israel, which preceded the establishment of the state; in the manning of ships, the organization of American crews to transport the survivors of Hitler to Israel, sometimes via Cyprus.

And its people did go on aliyah. Many of them did go to kibbutzim and moshavim, and many are visible in the cities.

Habonim was, and is, first and last, a *youth* movement. Children leading children, and frequently acting like children. They lacked *savoir-faire. Haboneh,* the magazine for the younger people, traditionally came out with its Purim issue just before Pesach and its Pesach issue just before Shavuot. And they lacked money sense, and their organization invariably botched administrative details.

But they dared to do things. They fought with the Jewish Agency. They wrote open letters to the members of the Histadrut Executive in Israel. It was done with humility and sensitivity, with intelligence and guts and with an informing sense of responsibility.

Habonim knew how to go against the stream, not because it felt it was desirable to go against the stream, but because its objective lay upstream. Over fifty years ago, these young people, with no professional background and with a great deal of nerve, organized a camp, and then another camp and another camp and a network of camps, with a new idea in their camping. Camping which would be fun and pleasure, but with an earnest sense of purpose, physical labor, self-government and learning.

And nearly thirty-five years ago they decided that the time had come to try to take some of their leadership cadres, when they finished high school, and have them spend a year in Israel, in the most meaningful kind of experience they could find for them, in a "workshop" which would combine a variety of purposes.

This is not even to speak of the large number of people in the U.S. and Canada who, by virtue of their exposure to this Habonim movement, were motivated to embark upon Jewish studies, in some cases to learn their first Hebrew words. It introduced to Jewish tradition many children who came from homes in which Jewish tradition was not observed. There were children in Habonim to whom the Sabbath evening program was their first contact with Shabbat and to whom the observance of Tisha B'Av in a Habonim camp was the first contact with the full tragic force of Jewish history.

The movement gave many young people a sense of identification with Judaism, and with the Jewish people, and with Israel—that no other force or combination of forces could hope to do. In short, Habonim provided young people who came into its orbit with meaningful activity and direction, with a deep commitment, with a sense of purpose and a sense of excitement. And all this was in striking contrast with the vast majority of their contemporaries.

Habonim has always been a small movement, and some of the adjectives I have used may sound a bit flowery for a small movement. I suppose that it will never be a large one. But its importance has been out of all proportion to its size.

It is a self-motivating movement with positive ideals and a sense of striving to fulfil them. It never quite fulfils them, but, then, that is the nature of ideals.

"It Is Not Given to Us to Foresee the Future"

Muki Tsur

Kibbutz Ein Gev 1985

My *shlichut* with Habonim and student groups from 1969 to 1972 happened at a very specific time for North American Jewish youth.

The people that I met, the things that impressed me, and shaped my views on many issues, appear in retrospect to be very time-bound and specific to the era. Much has happened since then both in North America and in Israeli society; it is hard for me to understand all that has changed since then, and where North America's Jewish community is heading. Still, it is clear that those years of the late sixties and early seventies were a very special time, leaving in their wake changed values and a good deal of nostalgia. They also left a residue of despair and the seeds of a return to establishment values.

The period had a great cultural influence on the future, but I cannot judge to what extent. What was clear to me then, and still seems an important starting point for the work of a shaliach today, is the tremendous influence of America's political and social culture on the existence, cultural forms, and feelings of hardship of the American Jewish community.

Chaim Arlosoroff, the brilliant Zionist diplomat of the 1920s and 1930s, tried during his own brief American shlichut to analyze American sociology as the mold in which a still unformed American Jewry would be shaped. He may have been the first to define the terrible conflict facing the shaliach: the conflict between the need, on the one hand, to work with an organized Jewish community that lives the Jewish past and is prepared to defend it— to work with the community in order to influence its future—and the knowledge, on the other hand, that this very past is perpetually losing its hold on the present.

What I did not know in 1969, what I still do not know today, is how much potential for growth is inherent in the American Jewish community. It is clear to me that Israel and its centrality will continue to have a decisive influence on the ways of thought and criteria for Jewish–Zionist work. The live encounter with an Israeli society, as it wrestles with questions of economy, politics, daily culture, and forms of consumption as a Hebrew–Jewish society, will inevitably be vital in the formation of tools for work in the North American Jewish community. Yet it is clear that many changes will take place that will affect the ability of Israeli society consciously to live up to its mission in Jewish life.

We Israelis who have come as shlichim and are still going out as shlichim need to prepare ourselves for the changes that will affect us personally. We go out to meet the Jewish community abroad, but we also come face to face with ourselves. We return with many questions. I returned a Zionist, with much criticism but also self-criticism and expectations from myself, my community, and the society in which I live.

Many of the young people I worked with actually made aliyah and struggled to redefine themselves. Many of them returned to North America, and others never arrived. The ability to emigrate is different from the ability to put down new roots.

I know, admire, and love many who have succeeded in their dual task. In my opinion, if there are authentic Jews in our time, these are the ones. At the same time, I respect the decision of those who did not come and those who returned. I hope their experience and their pain will contribute to a continuous building or at least prevent erosion, both here and there.

As a native of Israel, I never experienced the answering of the divine command, *Lech lecha,* by which our father Abraham was commanded to leave his native land. Therefore I stood enthralled to see a handful of young people prepared to hear this call and transform it into a point of departure for the responsible rebuilding of the Jewish people and its culture. I believe in the partnership between American Jews and Israel only if we recognize its complexity and the price that is demanded. We are not called to "use" America's Jews, nor to pack their bags for them. We will remain skeptical about the Jewish community's capacity for creative growth, but we will also honor all those who, despite our doubts, manage to build an educational network, welfare services, and living ties with Israel.

I am sure that the Jewish community and its leadership can cooperate and flourish by meeting criticism and skepticism, no less than it cooperates with those Israelis who see the diaspora solely from the point of view of public relations and political and economic support.

In the past few years, America has received a problematic supplement in Jewish terms, in the form of a community of Israeli emigres, or *yordim,* and a community of Soviet Jewish dropouts, or *noshrim*. This painful phenomenon is partly the result of difficult developments in Israel's economy and society.

Israeli society is always struck from two sides because of its dual nature, as an attempt to normalize the Jewish people on the one hand, and on the other, as an experiment in creating a new purpose, a culture and a demand for a meaningful life. As a normal society, there is a push towards emigration to achieve a higher standard of living, and as a society striving toward meaning, it is incessantly given to disappointments as it fails to live up the daunting moral-cultural demands it makes on itself. Today's shaliach lives this tension with daily intensity. And the Zionist effort has continually been accompanied by a chorus of gloating from those who hoped for its failure.

Today's situation seems problematic in contrast with the period when I was a shaliach. The early 1970s were a period that seemed to discover Israel in all its strengths and America with all the shocks that were then passing through it. Yet in many respects, we who were shlichim at that time misunderstood the era we were living through. We viewed events in the Jewish community with a certain excess of drama, failing to foresee that we were involved with an idealism that was a passing fashion, with a crumbling charisma that would lead to an admiration of authority, with criticism that would turn to renewed fear.

If we were mistaken then, I suggest that we should not look at today's picture as a permanent one, either. It is not given to us to foresee the future.

"A Civilizing Effect"

Moshe Kerem

Kibbutz Gesher Haziv 1985

Around the time of the fiftieth anniversary celebrations of American Habonim, I was presented with what was for me a moving gift—a copy of a letter sent in 1947 to David Ben-Gurion on American Habonim stationery, signed by Artie Gorenstein (Aryeh Goren), Murray Weingarten (Moshe Kerem), and David Breslau. It was found by a former member of Habonim who was going through the Ben-Gurion archives.

The letter begins with the following sentence: "The principal obstacle in the way of large scale Habonim expansion is the lack of adequate financial resources." This is followed by three closely typed pages about what we could do "if we had the money." My first reaction upon reading the letter, after close to forty years—Dave Breslau was sitting in my room at Gesher Haziv when I read it—was to burst out laughing. *Plus ca change, plus c'est la meme chose.* Every chutzpadik twenty-year-old mazkir Habonim, both before and since, has probably written a similar letter.

In its heyday in the late 1940s, Habonim had close to four thousand members. For years after, we kept saying that we had "three thousand," but we always managed somehow to evade the question of "who's counting?" To be sure, Habonim had a profound impact on its members regardless of numbers. It touched their lives and for many was the major factor that shaped them.

The question of Habonim's impact on the community around us is a more complicated one. We certainly did make a contribution to Jewish youth activity in America in a variety of areas: in Jewish summer camping, in the Workshop—one of the first attempts to bring young people to Israel for a year, in catalyzing Zionist student activity during certain key periods, in the quality of some of our educational publications, our organizing of the Kibbutz Aliya Desk, and more. But other groups, once having incorporated elements of the Habonim camping philosophy, have gone on to build much more extensive and successful systems. Other groups, once they got started, brought far greater numbers of young people to Israel in a variety of work-study programs. The Kibbutz Aliya Desk sent thousands of young people to Israel, but never succeeded in inducing more than a few hundred to settle on our settlements. Finally, Habonim itself never really got off the ground in terms of numbers. Why?

Was it really because we did not have the money? As a matter of fact, there were times when we did have considerable sums of money. In the late 1960s, for example, the Jewish Agency and the Israeli government launched "the American Plan," a program designed to channel huge financial and human resources into Zionist education on the North American scene, undertaken largely as a result of Habonim initiative. I recall a Habonim delegation in which I participated, being invited by Prime Minister Levi Eshkol to a cabinet meeting at which the program was discussed. For the next four or five years or more, the Jewish Agency financed no fewer than twenty shlichim to Habonim alone, helped buy and maintain ten summer camps, contributed to the purchase of a number of small centers around the country, in some cases jointly with the Labor Zionist movement, in other cases on our own.

It would seem that one reason, perhaps, for our failure to achieve a breakthrough was our ambiguous relationship with adults. We distrusted them. By definition, almost, "they" couldn't be "real Zionists." They must be hypocrites! We talked contemptuously about the Yiddish-speaking "senior movement" that didn't "really understand" the American Jewish community —even though many of them were themselves born and bred in America. It even reached the point where many of us, once we had determined *not* to make aliyah, would not be caught dead joining "them."

In a chalutzic youth movement, where personal example should be the key educational tool, we were against professional youth workers. We viewed our organizational sloppiness—and our wasting of money—as an integral part of the process of our self-realization, which the people paying for must swallow as a condition of their support. Shlichim were an acceptable form of adult help, since they represented self-realization and were not a threat, although we had our problems with many of them as well. And the poor, harassed adults who did support us with a lot of idealistic effort actually accepted this "ideology" of ours, perhaps because of their own hangups about aliyah. They swallowed our frustrating organizational sloppiness and irresponsibility, our self-centeredness (we did not really want any more members in our garinim—there were always some members whom some shaliach had foisted upon us, whom we could not wait to get rid of), and the built-in crises caused by successive generations of leadership "taking off" just after they had more or less learned how to run things. We actually convinced the "seniors" that this was the essence of Habonim, that changing it would kill the goose that lays the golden eggs.

And maybe it was part of the movement's essence. The truth may be, therefore, that the numbers we reached were the optimum numbers we could have reached in this type of movement. A breakthrough past this number would have entailed professionalism, continuity, with shlichim alongside but not instead of professional organization. So, for the type of movement we were—we actually were an organizational success!

This, of course, is an oversimplification. In fact, there were objective constraints on the movement's success. Despite our complexes, Habonim was an integral part of the Labor Zionist movement—to the point where a very significant portion of our members were the actual biological children of Labor Zionists. And yet the American Labor Zionist movement itself, while it had an impressive historic impact on the American Jewish community, was also an organizational bust (with the notable exception of Pioneer Women-

Na'amat). As a movement, it was part of that emotion-laden, idealistic hot-house, the Yiddish-speaking secular world that was chronicled so nostalgi-cally by writers such as Irving Howe, a world whose ongoing impact on American Jewry became increasingly that of an Isaac Bashevis Singer in English translation. It was a world that did not fit in either with UJA-federation secularism on the one hand or *balebatish* synagoguery on the other. The sociological evolution of American Jewry just did not include us, or aliyah for that matter, as a large-scale phenomenon.

So, we opted for quality.

Gesher Haziv was founded by Garin Aleph of Habonim, together with the Mapai-oriented faction of Bet Ha'arava, a kibbutz that had fallen to the Jordanians during the War of Independence. The organization of aliyah through garinim rather than as individuals, or small ad hoc groups of individ-uals, was more than just a better way of trying to ensure successful aliyah (a way, incidentally, which has long since proven its value). An essential part of the garin idea was to facilitate the specific contribution Habonim aliyah could make—as an extension of that "quality" which we felt we represented. We talked of a Habonim "project," a settlement that would be uniquely Habonim and would influence the movement "back home," that would build the movement by serving as a role model, by assuming a group responsibility for the movement's continuity, and last but certainly not least, by making a unique contribution to Israel itself.

Looking back at it with the realistic eyes of experience, it is difficult to match our actual accomplishments to our youthful aspirations. First and foremost, of course, we established and built a kibbutz, with all the great amounts of energy, work, and emotional investment that this process de-manded and with all the frustrations, disappointments, and profound satis-factions that accompanied it. As part of this process, the principal contribution of the kibbutz has been perhaps to enrich the lives of its mem-bers—certainly of those who have remained, but also of those who did not.

And what of a specifically American Habonim contribution to the kibbutz phenomenon? An American Habonim ambience which characterized Gesher Haziv? That is harder to define, and must be considered a matter for subjective opinion. Together with other Habonim settlements, we at Gesher Haziv did become an organizational address for the movement. We sent shlichim of our own and became a factor in choosing other shlichim. We became one of the principal homes of the Workshop. We fought for budgets. We explained the American movement to the Israelis, and they were in need of such explanation. The kibbutz movement developed as the institution that in effect assumed responsibility for the ongoing existence of Habonim and we were the mediating agent between the two.

It was a process that had its ups and downs, and there were periods when one or another of the settlements blew hot or cold, but in the long run, it has been a commitment of amazing strength and longevity. People who made aliyah forty years ago or more, people who are now grandparents, still feel directly involved. We kibbutznikim, for example, unlike many of the Habonim people in the Israeli cities, grew away from the Association of Americans and Canadians in Israel after our early period of involvement. Not so in matters connected with Habonim. The Habonim activists could always count on a Pavlovian reaction in a place like Gesher Haziv when they sounded the bell.

In the course of writing these thoughts, I happened to discuss the issue with a leading member of the newer, Israeli-born kibbutz generation. Had we Americans made any unique contribution to the kibbutz movement, I asked him? He thought for a moment, and then smiled.

"You had a civilizing effect," he said. "The shlichim who came back were somehow changed by you. Your perspectives were somehow broader, less provincial, more tolerant. You introduced us to a lot of ideas and a lot of people whom we otherwise would not have gotten involved with."

The compliment—if it was meant as such, and I have never figured that out—had some truth to it. The breakthrough, for example, of Ichud Hakvutzot Vehakibbutzim and later the United Kibbutz Movement in forging relations with the Reform and Conservative movements in America—and now in Israel—has resulted in the establishment so far of three kibbutzim by these movements. Perhaps equally important, it contributed to the development of a broad, positive, pluralistic approach to the question of Jewish tradition and identity in the kibbutz movement as a whole. None of it would have taken place without the direct initiative and ongoing mediation of the Habonim people.

The truth may be, however, that we never really "made it" in many areas in which we aspired to do so. None of us, for example, ever really made it here politically, although a number of us tried. We would seem to have had three strikes against us. In the first place, we gravitated toward the intellectual and the ideological, rather than toward the politico-technocratic *bitzuistim,* the pragmatists who have dominated labor movement politics in recent generations.

In the second place, we were from North America and lacked the political base either of the Eastern European establishment or, for that matter, of the native-born Israelis. And in the third place (which may be the first place), it seems we were just not tough enough, hard-fisted enough, to play that Israeli game successfully. We were products of Habonim. One prominent Israeli figure once remarked to one of the Habonim people that in order to play the Israeli brand of politics, one must break through the *"machsom ha-busha"*—the "shame barrier"—to deal nastily with people, including your friends. When I asked him if I had heard him correctly, he went even further and added that "those Americans who were capable of that probably never joined Habonim."

Pluralism as a state of mind has not been a salient feature of Israeli culture. This includes the labor movement and certainly the kibbutz movement. In this respect, we at Gesher Haziv have often felt that we were slightly suspect. We were the thin edge of the wedge of that "Americanization" which could undermine the system. This was not only a question, in the early years, of the clothes we wore, the foods we liked, the music we enjoyed (for "America" has since conquered these areas). It was a question of a lack of reverence for "principle" as understood by the Israelis. An outstanding example of our irreverence was the case of *lina mishpachtit,* or the lodging of kibbutz children in their parents' homes rather than in children's houses. Gesher Haziv was the first kibbutz, aside from two or three historical curiosities, which dared to change the system. It was our switch that gave legitimacy to what has since become a flood of change, turning the change into the norm. There are still some dyed-in-the-wool ideologues around who will never forgive us for it.

Success is, among other things, a function also of single-mindedness. It is not easy to maintain the balance between pluralism, which is perforce somewhat laissez-faire, and the single-mindedness needed to build a kibbutz which, though it is in the right place ideologically, may be in the wrong place geographically, and which has to weather the vicissitudes of outrageous fortune. Gesher Haziv's easygoing pluralism, for example, may have resulted in our accepting more than our fair share of "kooks" over the years. It may have resulted in allowing people too much latitude in matters such as private sources of income. Such a large concentration of former Americans in one kibbutz has made it difficult to create as Hebrew-speaking, Hebrew-reading, Hebrew-rooted an environment as I, for one, would have wished. Our concern for the individual may have infringed on economic success.

On the other hand, the "kooks" made life more interesting. Allowing individuals more latitude is an improvement on the less tolerant and consequently sometimes intolerable kibbutz of yesteryear. And the more positive attitude towards Jewish tradition, rooted in Habonim, which has resulted for example in the Gesher Haziv version of bar and bat mitzvah, is paradoxically a Jewish counterweight to the relative lack of Hebrew-rootedness.

If youth is not just chronology but also a state of mind, then Habonim's kibbutz component, certainly at Gesher Haziv, is still part of the youth movement.

". . . and a Preface to the Future"—An Address by the President of Israel

On the 50th Anniversary of North American Habonim

Chaim Herzog
Jerusalem 1985

Congratulating Habonim at the half-century mark of its existence, I speak as president of the state of Israel and in the name of the state, but I speak also as one who fifty years ago was one of the first *bonim* in Ireland.

Thinking of you, remembering all that you represent, I find myself over-whelmed by mixed feelings—appreciation, frustration, hope. Appreciation is evoked by the splendid achievements of the movement, a movement of *chalutzim* who are truly *bonim*—builders. Through labor and settlement on the soil, through devotion to culture and to the quality of life, you have been responding fully to the great challenge posed to this generation—the challenge of the rise of Israel, the realization of the dreams of generations and the vision of the Prophets.

With all that, frustration, too, is evoked. For your movement, so splendid in quality, is much smaller in quantity than any of us would wish. I do not mean to diminish the enormous importance of your accomplishments, but only to lament with you the disproportion between the size of North Ameri-can Jewry and the number of pioneers it has sent to Israel. If a movement like Habonim could have come nearer to exploiting the potential of United States and Canadian Jewry, how different the life of Israel would be, how much richer and more advanced! The course of Jewish history here and over the seas would have been profoundly affected.

Actually, Habonim represents the select minority; it reminds us of what might have been if American Jewry responded fully to the great Zionist challenge. Yet I for one continue to hope. My hope stems from belief in the Eternity of Israel and the Rock of Israel. I do believe that despite the drastic results of assimilation, many young American Jews will yet come to Israel to settle and to build. Here Habonim can be the spearhead, the leader in a mighty process.

There is, after all, a basis to build upon. The political and economic aid of North American Jewry to Israel is of the most vital importance. It has been so for years, and now in a time of economic crisis will, we hope, be expressed in direct aid to Israel's technological and industrial development. Yet even now we must not neglect aliyah, the true essence of Zionism, and we must concern ourselves with strengthening Jewish education and linking young people to Zionism and Israel.

That this is far from impossible I have felt during my visits to North America. In my speeches to Jewish forums I have constantly brought up the question of aliyah, and have been more than a little surprised by the positive reaction. I am convinced that if we struggle with all our might for the soul of young people in the diaspora, they will respond. And this encoun-ter with Habonim reminds me forcibly of what such aliyah can mean for Israel.

Habonim's role is not finished. May its fiftieth anniversary be recorded in history as the preface to great chapters still to be written.

Glossary

In attempting to pronounce the Hebrew and Yiddish words found in this book, use the following rules of thumb:

Ch is pronounced as the gutteral sound in *Chanukah* or "Bach."
A is always pronounced as in "father."
E is always pronounced as in "bet."
I is always pronounced like the vowel sound in "beet" (not "bit").
O is always pronounced as in "post."
U is always pronounced as in "put."

Achdut Ha'avodah. Labor Unity. A Palestinian Labor Zionist party formed by the 1919 merger of *Poale Zion* and Berl Katznelson's "nonparty" group. Merged with *Hapo'el Hatza'ir* in 1929 to form *Mapai. Also:* An Israeli party identified with *Hakibbutz Hame'uchad,* formed after an ideological schism in Mapai 1946, rejoined Mapai to form the Israel Labor Party 1968.

Aleh Uvneh. "Arise and Build." The slogan of Habonim.

Aliyah. *Lit.* ascent. The act of moving to Israel. *Also:* In Israel, the act of settling on the land.

Aliyah Bet. "Aliyah B," the "illegal" immigration brought through British blockade to Palestine before 1948.

Amel. (fem. Amela, pl. amelim, amelot). *Lit.* toiler. Post-1960: A member of the youngest age group in Habonim, age 10–12.

Avodah. Labor, work.

Bayit. (pl. batim). *Lit.* a house. A communal house where Habonim members live, often in preparation for aliyah. *Also:* at camp, the main building on the campgrounds. *Beit:* house of—.

Betar. A right-wing, militantly nationalistic Zionist youth movement identified with the Zionist Revisionist philosophy of Vladimir Ze'ev Jabotinsky and Menachem Begin.

B'nei Akiva. "The Sons of (Rabbi) Akiva." A Labor Zionist youth movement identified with the Orthodox religious *Hakibbutz Hadati* federation and *Hapo'el Hamizrachi* religious Labor Zionist party.

Boneh. (fem. bonah, pl. bonim, bonot). *Lit.* builder. A member of the high-school age group in Habonim.

Chalutz. (fem. chalutza, pl. chalutzim, chalutzot). A pioneer. Habonim-usage adjective form: *Chalutzic.*

Chalutziut. The act or spirit of pioneering.

Chanich. (fem. chanicha, pl. chanichim, chanichot). *Lit.* a pupil. In Habonim, any younger movement member.

Chaver. (fem. chavera), pl. chaverim, chaverot). Comrade, member, friend.

Chever Hakvutzot. The League of Kvutzot. A federation of non-Marxist, "intimate" kibbutzim, pre-1951. Closely identified with the agrarian ideals of Labor Zionist philosopher A. D. Gordon.

Chevrah. (pl. chevrot). *Lit.* a society. The special quality of intimate comradeship sought among youth movement members. *Also:* Any group of Habonim members particularly drawn together by shared experience and emotional bonds.

Chevre. "folks," "gang." From the Yiddish pronunciation of chevrah.

Chevrei. Members of ——, as in *chevrei garin* (members of a garin).

Chinuch. Education.

Choter. (fem. choteret, pl. chotrim, chotrot). *Lit.* striver. Post-1960: A member of the junior high school age group in Habonim.

Dror. *Lit.* liberty. A Labor Zionist youth movement active in North America 1947–81, identified with *Hakibbutz Hame'uchad* and the *Tnuah Le'achdut Ha'avodah.* Merged with Habonim to form Habonim-Dror.

Eretz Israel or **Yisrael.** The Land of Israel, or Palestine.

Farband. Yiddish for "alliance." Particularly, the Jewish National Workers Alliance, a Labor Zionist fraternal order, 1912–71, which merged with *Poale Zion* (formerly Labor Zionist Organization) and the American Habonim Association (formerly Habonim Alumni) to form the *Labor Zionist Alliance.*

Garin. (pl. garinim). *Lit.* a seed, nucleus. A settlement group whose members make aliyah together, usually to kibbutz.

Gordonia. A Labor Zionist youth movement identified with the agrarian ideals of A. D. Gordon and the *Chever Hakvutzot* federation. Founded in North America 1925, merged with Habonim 1938.

Habonim. *Lit.* the builders.

Hachshara. *Lit.* training. A training farm, one of several operated in the United States and Canada, usually by the *Hechalutz* organization, to prepare future kibbutz settlers in agriculture and group living. Farms existed near Anoka, Minnesota (1932–34); Creamridge, New Jersey (1936–51); Smithville, Ontario (1946–51); and Colton, California (1948–51). A separate farm was operated in Hightstown, New Jersey (1934–74) by the Hashomer Hatza'ir youth movement. *Also:* Today, a period of time spent by a *garin* on an established kibbutz before going to settle a new one.

Haganah. *Lit.* defense. The main underground military force operated by the Jewish community in pre-1948 Israel.

Hagshama. Fulfillment. In Zionist jargon, the fulfillment of the highest goal of Zionism, settling in Israel. For the chalutzic youth movement, complete "fulfillment" means settling on a kibbutz.

Hagshama atzmit. Self-fulfillment. Originally referred to the *chalutz* movement's expectation that members would take personal responsibility for the fulfillment of Zionism's aims and mission. Some early Zionist writers, including the kibbutz movement mentor A. D. Gordon, suggested that the act of settling on the soil of Israel actually offered "self-fulfillment" in the sense of fulfilling one's own *personal* potential as well. This became the accepted meaning of *hagshama* in *chalutz* Zionist youth movement parlance.

Hakibbutz Hame'uchad. The United Kibbutz. Federation of Israeli kibbutzim with which Habonim was identified, 1935–51.

Hakibbutz Ha'artzi. The National Kibbutz. Federation of Israeli kibbutzim identified with the left-wing *Hashomer Hatza'ir* youth movement and the *Mapam* party.

Hashomer Hatza'ir. The Young Guard. A socialist Zionist youth movement identified with *Hakibbutz Ha'artzi* federation and the *Mapam* party. Considered to the left of Habonim, with which it engaged in usually friendly rivalry and frequent cooperation.

Hechalutz. "The Pioneer." An organization to encourage youth Jews to settle on the land in Israel, founded 1905, refounded in 1915. In its final form, beginning in 1932, it trained future kibbutz settlers and assisted their emigration to Israel, and was directed jointly by the Labor Zionist youth movements (variously, Habonim, Hashomer Hatza'ir, Gordonia, Dror, B'nei Akiva).

Herut. *Lit.* freedom. A right-wing Israeli political party formed in 1948 by the followers of the Zionist Revisionist movement and led for many years by Menachem Begin. Joined with the Israel Liberal Party to form the *Likud,* 1973.

Histadrut. *Lit.* organization. Israel's central labor federation, founded in 1920. Full name: Histadrut Haklalit shel Ha-ovdim Be'eretz Israel (General Organization of Workers in the Land of Israel).

Ichud Hakvutzot Vehakibbutzim. The Union of Kvutzot (small communes) and Kibbutzim. Federation of Israeli kibbutzim to which Habonim was affiliated, 1951–78. Merged with *Hakibbutz Hame'uchad* in 1978 to form the *United Kibbutz Movement.*

Iton. (pl. itonim). *Lit.* newspaper. A movement newsletter.

Ken. (pl. kinim). *Lit.* a nest. Post-1960: a city chapter of Habonim.

Kibbutz. *Lit.* gathering. An Israeli communal settlement.

Kibbutz Me'uchad. See *Hakibbutz Hame'uchad.*

Kinus. *Lit.* a conference. A regional or divisional Habonim meeting (of a garin, for example), more formal than a seminar but less so than the *ve'idah* (national convention).

Kupah. *Lit.* a cashbox. A communal fund where Habonim members pool their money, as at camp or in a garin. More generally, the spirit of collective sharing inculcated by Habonim. *Also,* in colloquial camp usage: candies and treats paid for by the kupah.

Kvutza. (pl. kvutzot). *Lit.* a group. In early Zionist usage: a small, "intimate" kibbutz. In Habonim: The smallest organizational unit, made up of a group of five to ten members of the same age led by a *madrich. Also,* pre-1960: A Habonim summer camp.

Likud. *Lit.* consolidation. An Israeli political party. See *Herut.*

Ma'apil. (fem. ma'apila, pl. ma'apilim, ma'apilot). *Lit.* "one who dares." In common Israeli usage, a pre-1948 "illegal" immigrant. In Habonim, post-1960: A member of the oldest age group (18 and over).

Machaneh. (pl. machanot). *Lit.* a camp. Pre-1960: A city chapter of Habonim. Post-1960: a summer camp.

Machaneh Bonim. Habonim's national leadership-training camp, 1963–present.

Madrich. (fem. madricha, pl. madrichim, madrichot). *Lit.* counselor, guide. Post-1960: a Habonim group leader.

Mapai. Acronym of the Eretz Israel Workers' party, the main Labor Zionist party in Israel 1929–68.

Mazkir. (fem. mazkira). *Lit.* secretary. The national secretary of Habonim. Following the European sense of secretary-general, the post combines the senses of professional director and elected chairperson. *Also,* the secretary of any other group or institution.

Mazkirut. secretariat. Especially, the national secretariat of the movement—the national office staff, serving as the movement's day-to-day governing body.

Menahel. (fem. menahelet, pl. menahelim, menahelot). *Lit.* manager or director. Pre-1960: A Habonim group leader.

Merakez. (pl. merakzim). *Lit.* coordinator. An appointed organizer of a movement institution. Especially, an organizer of a local ken, designated by the national office, as distinguished from the elected Rosh Ken. *Not to be confused with:*

Merkaz. *Lit.* center. The Central Committee of national Habonim.

Misgeret. *Lit.* a framework. A group organized to consider the possibility of forming a garin.

Mishlachat. *Lit.* delegation. A group of *shlichim.*

Moshav. (pl. moshavim). *Lit.* seat. A cooperative smallholders' farming village. Also called **Moshav Ovdim.** Some American Habonim graduates settled at *Moshav Orot* in 1951.

Moshav Shitufi. A moshav with some attributes of a kibbutz—typically, collectivized production and individualized consumption. Some American Habonim graduates settled at *Moshav Bet Herut,* founded in 1931. Others in the 1970s joined *Moshav Yodfat.*

Na'amat. Hebrew acronym for the Organization of Women Workers and Volunteers in Israel. In the diaspora, the Labor Zionist women's organization (formerly Pioneer Women).

Noar. Youth. Pre-1960: The oldest age group in Habonim (eighteen and over) (renamed ma'apilim, 1960).

Oleh. (fem. olah, pl. olim, olot). *Lit.* ascender. One who moves to Israel ("makes aliyah").

Palmach. Acronym for *Plugot Machatz,* "assault units." The elite, full-time strike force of the largely volunteer *Haganah.* It was for the most part based in and led by the kibbutz movement, especially the kibbutzim of *Hakibbutz Hame'uchad.*

Pegisha. Meeting. Especially, certain national gatherings of Habonim members, as in 1934 and 1939, for reevaluation of goals.

Poale Zion. The Workers of Zion. Socialist Zionist political party, founded 1898 in Europe. In Israel, merged into *Mapai* in 1929. In North America, retained the name until formation of *Labor Zionist Alliance, 1971.*

Rosh. *Lit.* head. The top officer in any movement institution: Rosh Machaneh (camp director—pre-1960 Rosh Kvutza); Rosh Ken (chapter chair).

Shaliach. (fem. shlicha, pl. shlichim, shlichot). An emissary, especially an Israeli representative sent by the World Zionist Organization or Histadrut to a diaspora community for a two- to three-year term of youth work.

Shlichut. *Lit.* mission. The job of a shaliach. Also, the shaliach's term of office.

Sichah. *Lit.* conversation. A small group discussion session, the basic vehicle for ideological education in Habonim. *Also:* In kibbutzim, the weekly members' meeting.

Solel. (fem. solelet, pl. solelim, solelot). *Lit.* paver. Pre-1960: a member of the youngest age group of Habonim, age 10–12 (renamed *amel*).

T'nuah. (pl. t'nuot). A movement.

T'nuah Le'achdut Ha'avodah. The Movement for Labor Unity. The full name for the second *Achdut Ha'avodah* party, 1946–68 (see above).

T'nuah Me'uchedet. United Movement. An Israeli youth movement, formed in the wake of the kibbutz movement split of 1951, became the Israeli affiliate of World (later *Ichud*) Habonim.

Tzofeh. (fem. tzofah, pl. tzofim, tzofot). *Lit.* scout. Pre-1960: A member of the junior high school age group in Habonim (renamed *choter*). *Also:* (in some places after 1960) a member of an intermediate age group between chotrim and bonim.

Tzofiut. Scouting.

Ve'idah. Convention. The biennial national convention of Habonim.

Yishuv. *Lit.* settlement. The Jewish community in the Land of Israel, especially before 1948.

Zeire Zion. The Young of Zion. Labor Zionist party, close to the agrarian ideals of A. D. Gordon. Formed in North America 1920, merged with *Poale Zion* in 1931.